Soviet Composers
and the Development of Soviet Music

Soviet Composers
and the
Development
of Soviet Music

BY

STANLEY D. KREBS

*Associate Professor of Music
at the University of California
Santa Barbara*

W. W. NORTON & COMPANY, INC. · NEW YORK

FIRST PUBLISHED IN 1970

© *George Allen and Unwin Ltd 1970*
U.S. SBN 393 02140 8

PRINTED IN GREAT BRITAIN

To Muriel
my wife and fellow traveller

ACKNOWLEDGEMENTS

꒰ꔛ꒱

I deeply appreciate the help of my teachers, Messrs Demar Irvine, George McKay, John Verrall, Donald Treadgold, and Miss Kathleen Munro, in guiding me along a precarious path which has impinged on all their disciplines at the University of Washington.

I have used extensively the collections at the Library of Congress. I am particularly grateful to Messrs Sergius Yakobson and William Lichtenwanger of the Slavic and Music Divisions, respectively.

The Ford Foundation and the Inter-University Committee on Travel Grants have afforded the considerable amount of research time and travel. This book reflects their help, but not, necessarily, their views.

I owe Iurii Shaporin and many other Soviet friends a debt I cannot repay. I should like to name you all—may this book contribute to your creative lives.

PREFACE

Originally, the primary, and as much as possible, the exclusive source for the development of this discussion was to have been the music of Soviet composers. Freshly, even unexpectedly, armed with the tool of language, the author strode blithely into the field—one generally ignored by Western musical scholars. The few, tendentious Western considerations and the fifty-year accumulation of contradictory, propaganda-laden, dogmatically romanticized Soviet sources reinforced the notion that the music itself, and that alone, should occupy the author's shelves and work-table. Shortly after work was begun, it became clear that significant progress was being made only in the area of unanswered questions. It was equally clear that no Western study of Soviet music could be based on notes and scores alone. This realization, accompanied by the first probes into Russian-Soviet history and ideology in search of answers, set up reverberations, not all of whose demands have been met even now, a number of years later. A new start, which included several steps backward, has resulted in the form of the present paper.

This dissertation is divided into four parts. The first of these attempts, briefly, to provide the historical, ideological, political, geographical, and semantic framework for the fact of Soviet music itself. In some measure, the intent of Part One is to relieve the later parts of this burden. Parts Two, Three, and Four consider Soviet composers of, respectively, the old, middle, and younger generations. The matter of birthdate has been only coincidental in the determination of these groups. Matters of periods of training, location at critical times, and period of creative activity have seemed more important. Thus Prokofieff (born 1891) is included in Part Two (the older generation); Shaporin (born 1889), in Part Three.

There are well over 1,500 listed Soviet composers. A large number of these have received publicity of celebrity proportions, both in and outside of the Soviet Union—far too many to include in a study of this size, even if their musical merit suggested inclusion. The problem of selection for consideration here has been met by using various critical, and some arbitrary, yardsticks. The author is prepared to justify the inclusion of a given composer, or, perhaps even more importantly, the exclusion of another. The problem of ethnic distribution of composers selected has also posed a problem. The rather disproportionately high percentage of republican composers to whom chapters are devoted reflects the author's conclusion that the concentration of meaningful creative activity lies, or will lie, along the Soviet periphery rather than at the centre. Furthermore, it seemed essential to cover in some detail the history, development, and manipulation of creative music in one of the minority republics, by way of example. Georgia, with a solid, pre-Soviet cultural accomplishment on the one hand, and a relatively high degree of contemporary ethnic integrity on the other, was chosen.

The system of transliteration of the Russian language used is based on that of the Library of Congress, with certain modifications and omissions for readability. The system, with the nearest English pronunciation equivalents, where needed, follows:

Russ.	*Engl.*	Pronunciation	*Russ.*	*Engl.*	Pronunciation
А,а	A,a	f*a*	Е,е	E,e	yeh (e) or yo (ë)
Б,б	B,b		Ж,ж	Zh, zh	
В,в	V,v		З,з	Z,z	
Г,г	G,g	(hard)	И,и	I,i	m*i*[1]
Д,д	D,d		Й,й	I,i	po*i*[2]
К,к	K,k		Х,х	Kh,kh	(Scottish) lo*ch*
Л,л	L,l		Ц,ц	Ts,ts	
М,м	M,m		Ч,ч	Ch,ch	
Н,н	N,n		Ш,ш	Sh, sh	
О,о	O,o		Щ,щ	Shch,shch (i.e.) plu*sh ch*urch
П,п	P,p		ъ	Shch	
Р,р	R,r		ы	Y,y	famil*y* (approx)
С,с	S,s		ь	'	palatalizes preceding consonant
Т,т	T,t		Э,э	E,e	
У,у	U,u	m*oo*	Ю,ю	Iu,iu	
Ф,ф	F,f		Я,я	Ia,ia	

In cases of established Western usage, the transliteration system is abandoned. Thus: 'Tschaikovsky', and not 'Chaikovsky'. The foregoing provides the reader with all that is needed. Spoken or sung Russian requires more explanation. Russian consonant sounds may be soft or hard (palatalized or unpalatalized). For practical purposes, this is

---

[1] The Russian ending, '. . . ий' is transliterated as '. . . ii', except in last names where it appears as ' . . . y'. The ending '. . .ый' appears as '. . . yi'. Thus: 'sovetskii', but 'Miaskovsky'; and 'muzykal'nyi'.

[2] The character, 'й' is dependent and modifies the sound of the vowel it invariably follows. Thus, '. . . ойсй' is similar in sound, though not so emphatic, as the '. . . oy' in '*boy*' or the '. . . oi' in '*poi*'.

governed by subsequent vowels, the 'soft' set, я,е,и,ё,ю (ia,e,i,e,iu), and the mute Ьа; and the 'hard' set, a,э,ы,о,у (a,e,y,o,u). Since the 'a-ia', 'u-iu' and 'y-i' pairs, as well as the 'o', are already indicated by the transliteration used, one need consider only the 'э-е' (e-yeh) pair and the ё (yo). Since the Russian 'э' occurs infrequently, the reader may, with 95 percent accuracy, consider the transliterated 'e' always as 'yeh': 'delo' (d*yeh*lo), Vasilenko (Vasil*yeh*nko). The reader will err when encountering the Russian 'ё': 'med' (myod) and 'Petr' (Pyotr); and hard 'э' 'ekran' and 'Eshpai'. The incidence of error will be seven percent or less, an insignificant concession to readability. The consonants 'ts' and 'ch' are considered as always palatalized, and 'zh', 'kh', 'sh', and 'shch' are unpalatalizable—if pronounced correctly, no attention need be given the following vowel.

For those who wish to go still further: all ultimate, voiced consonants, or pairs of such consonants, lose their voicing. Thus: 'beg' (bye*kh*) and Prokofieff (Prokofyeh*f*). Only the vowel or vowels of the accented syllable, as in English, receive full sound value. The greater the distance, in syllables, from the accent, the greater the modification. This may be illustrated by using the phonetic symbol 'ə': khorosho (khə-ra-shó); Khachaturian (Khə-chə-tur-ián). Literal pronunciation of all vowels is characteristic only for foreigners and Siberian provincials, so one is doubly scorned. In singing, vowel handling is somewhat modified, depending on the pace of the words. The author has experimented with, and used in concert, a simple system of transliteration with successful results.

Finally, and seeking not to complain, but, rather, to assist further research in this field, the author is tempted to linger feelingly on the problems of accessibility of Soviet sources. To put it briefly, the scholar, armed with musical analytical knowledge, languages, all the history, the politics, the ideology, and the philosophy he can cram into his brain on short notice, still falls short of conquering all obstacles in his path of research. For he encounters suspicion, stubbornness, *nevozmozhnosti*, capriciousness, closed doors, disappearing persons, forbidden areas, and enough civil red tape to border in colour every page of 10,000 copies of this discussion. It has been observed that the ideal scholar properly to investigate Soviet music must be an impossible combination of trained, experienced musician and trained, experienced historian or political scientist. A career of successful diplomatic service would help, too.

CONTENTS

꙾꙾꙾

INTRODUCTION

In the early years of the twentieth century the styles and means of music began to multiply and spread out from their nineteenth-century stem like the ribs on a Japanese fan. By 1917 the development had already reached a proportion that would ensure the period a name from the musicologists. An important role in the ferment of development had been played by Russian composers and writers on music. The history of Russia's active participation in the development of Western music was not yet 100 years old, yet the growth of many of the ribs of that twentieth-century fan was associated with names like Scriabin, Stravinsky, Theremin, Schillinger, A. N. Rimsky-Korsakov, and Rachmaninov. After 1917, in what had become the Soviet Union, this momentum continued, but in an ever increasing environment of isolation. By 1932, it became clear, and officially observed and sanctioned, that Soviet Russian music was diverging, and had already diverged, from that of the rest of the West, travelling along a single rib of the fan. All the usual, nourishing lines of communication between Russia and the West were disrupted. For them were substituted momentary flashes of current news of music, composers, and ideology. Both East and West unaccountably grew to accept such 'peephole' sensationalism as valid, scholarly material. Simply writing about Soviet music made a person an expert, whatever his bias, ignorance, or level of scholarship. Conclusions were reached for their own sake. Thus, one eminent Western musicologist and publicist, named frequently to Soviet studies panels because of his pre-revolutionary Russian background, has twice appeared in print with the startling and pathetic conclusion that Soviet music reached a high level of stable maturity in 1932–3. In truth, however, the West's ignorance of Soviet music is matched only by the Soviet Union's of the West's.

The Soviet musical establishment, urged and economically, if not ideologically, planned by the government and Communist party, is vast. The state sponsored Union of Soviet Composers lists some 1,600 members. There are, in the Soviet Union, fifty opera and ballet theatres with substantial seasons. Soviet publishing houses publish more musical items than those of any other country in the world—over 2,000 items in 1961. The establishment includes, for its own support, an impressive, professional, musical education system: in 1958 there were over 1,200 seven-year music preparatory schools, some 150 music high schools (*uchilischcha*), and twenty-three conservatories. All these work together under central authority, meeting musical needs at all levels, feeding into one another, and producing, yearly, a pre-established quota of finished, professional musicians. In 1963, the Moscow Conservatory alone graduated 133 professionals, of whom thirty-four were composers. For the non-professional music lover, there is a government administered, network of housed, professionally led, amateur organizations. In 1957 there were 300,000 amateur circles registered in the Soviet Union, of which 96,000 were musical circles.

But it is not alone the size of the Soviet musical apparatus that demands attention. What is being produced musically in this huge, isolated, creative hothouse? Soviet music theoretically meets Soviet needs. What are the needs? Soviet music is supposed to be rooted exclusively in the traditions of the Russian musical past. What are those traditions? The stage Soviet music has reached, in the middle of this century, has not been achieved haphazardly. What have been the shaping forces? No other country in the world, including the other communist countries, presents the seemingly monolithic aspect that the Soviet Union does musically. What are the unifying elements of that monolith, if, indeed, it is one?

Finally, and hopefully, a study of this sort may lead to the shedding of light on the entire problem of governmental, or Party, control. The Soviet Union is a highly controlled nation—frankly so, proudly so. The nature, quality, authority, and dynamics of control are problems that have always concerned Slavic scholars. The means of music require a grip of unique shape. By investigating this grip, the matter of Soviet controls is seen in a new aspect, and their understanding may be closer.

In 100 years, these questions may be asked only in the footnotes of music history books; although other alternatives deserve consideration. But, for the present, we live in the presence of a tremendous and influential nation whose musical product and activity is immense. Similar Soviet activity in the other arts, and certainly in politics, science, history, and other fields, has been well and continuously covered in the West. But, by and large, scholars have chosen to ignore or dismiss the musical activity, except on the most superficial level. The reasoning seems to be that the Soviet musical product is rooted and fixed, out-moded, and, hence, of no value.

This is not the case. For upwards of 200 million people, Soviet music has a basic validity. Moreover, Soviet music is one of the ribs of the contemporary musical fan. Only one. But it is a part of the whole.

PART ONE

Soviet Russian Cultural Ideology and Music

CHAPTER I

꙾꙾꙾

Before October

The early twentieth century was a period of social, artistic, and political ferment in Russia, a legacy both domestic and foreign. This was nowhere more apparent than in St Petersburg, the most European city of a 'westernizing' Russia. External events, particularly the humiliating outcome of the Russo-Japanese war, added pressure to the often aimless social stirrings which Petersburg shared with Europe. The end of the war in the Far East was followed by revolutionary outbreaks in the years 1905–6. Participation of musicians, imagined or real, in revolutionary activity led to a number of resignations or expulsions from the St Petersburg Conservatory. Among the victims were Rimsky-Korsakov, Glazunov, and Mikhail Gnessin, the latter at the time a student. Composer-contrapuntist Taneev, in addition to contributing to the relief of the suffering lower classes during the revolutionary period, is reported on Soviet authority to have aided the small Bolshevik party with regular dues.[1]

Various cultural and musical currents clashed and coincided in St Petersburg of the early twentieth century. The conservatory in these years brought together the aspirations of the Rubinsteins and the direction and momentum of the 'Mighty Five', with a member of the latter, Rimsky-Korsakov, serving as director (until 1905) and professor of orchestration and composition until his death in 1908. Glazunov and Liadov continued the conservatory tradition, the former remaining its director until 1928. The spirit of the Beliaev circle[2] resided by then at the

[1] *Istoriia russkoi sovetskoi muzyki* (History of Soviet Russian Music), 4 volumes (Moscow; Muzgiz, 1956, vol. I, p. 8).
[2] Mitrofan Petrovich Beliaev, 1836–1904, a musical patron of the arts who encouraged young musicians, supplied funds for publishing music, supported concerts and instrumental groups, was called the 'Russian Esterhazy'. The Beliaev Circle was the name given that loose agglomeration of musicians who gathered in his home on 'Beliaev Fridays'. These included Glazunov, Liadov, Rimsky-Korsakov and, later Kryzhanovsky, N. Cherepnin, Zolotarev and others. Rimsky-Korsakov was the 'spiritual' leader.

conservatory, most of the 'members', indeed, being students of Rimsky-Korsakov. The Russian Musical Society, founded by Rubinstein, and from whose embryonic teaching activity the St Petersburg and other conservatories grew, continued its activity until the eve of the 1917 revolution. Its identity with the conservatory remained, and together the two formed the bulwark of St Petersburg musical traditionalism.

But nineteenth-century liberalism was equally characteristic of St Petersburg. The 'Evenings of Contemporary Music' were organized in 1901 and enjoyed the casual direction of Ivan Kryzhanovsky, Viacheslav Karatygin, and others. A sibling group was the 'Mir iskusstva' (World of art), an organization formed in the late nineties around the journal of that name, and which rebelled against both the academic tradition in painting and the tendentious movements to replace it. The *Mir* group strongly advocated Western contact, seeing in it the only hope for the sick, realistic nationalism they saw in their own Russian painting. As the trend and organization grew it reached into other artistic areas and, finally, powered by the fantastic drive of Sergei Diaghilev, changed its monoideological façade. Diaghilev's *Mir* was a strong bridge between the West, especially Paris, and Russia, especially St Petersburg, with cultural traffic flowing both ways. Although he had been a strong advocate of the earlier stand of the *Mir* group, Diagilev's main criteria for exporting and displaying Russian art in the first decade of the twentieth century was simply that it pass as Russian.

The *Mir* group and that group centred around the 'Evenings of Contemporary Music' practically coincided in the music area. These organizations were propelled by their timeliness and by the participation in their activities of almost all St Petersburg artists. The *ECM* sponsored concerts by contemporary European and Russian composers, an activity so popular and fast spreading that they sponsored themselves out of a job by 1912. The spirit of the *ECM*, however, continued in the outlook and performance of its participants for some time. The subsequent cutting off of contact with similar European organizations and thinking finally slowed and stopped the spirit of the *ECM*, but not until long after 1917.

Soviet historiography insists on rigid categorization. The phenomenon of a Trotsky, for instance, must become a well delineated symbol, and historical facts are interpreted, arranged, supplemented, and suppressed so that the symbol has precisely the value it should, and so that it fits precisely the pigeonhole supplied for it in the contemporary cote. The various trends in immediate pre-revolutionary Russian culture (and post-revolutionary, for that matter) have shared this treatment. Certain men and organizations become the heroes of the surge to Soviet power (Rimsky-Korsakov, Glazunov, and the St Petersburg Conservatory), and others become the villains of reaction and counter-revolution (Kryzhanovsky, the 'Evenings of Contemporary Music'). One must be wary of these categorizations: they are not for the scholar, including, lately, the Soviet scholar, but are for the immediate pragmatic aims of building communism.

With all their conflicts and contradictions, with all the fury and passion they generated, the new and old traditions formed the heterogeneous whole of musical St Petersburg. Intercourse between the new and the old, between the traditional and innovatory was enthusiastic and extensive as one would expect in a cosmopolitan city. The strains and tensions characteristic of the nineteenth century were largely resolved. The Stasov-Serov polemic was old-fashioned. The Balakirev circle no longer existed as an element bitterly opposing the conservatory.

Prokofieff and Miaskovsky were studying (until 1909 and 1911 respectively) with Liadov at the conservatory and having their music performed by the *ECM* group. Much of the musical activity centred on Diaghilev and his growing ballet, or on his imitators. Stravinsky, Prokofieff, Gnessin, and others worked with Diaghilev, the first two following him abroad. As Russian music continued to move abroad, so did the music of contemporary Europe flood the capital of Russia. The music of Mahler, Schoenberg, Ravel and Richard Strauss was regularly heard. Debussy and Reger conducted their own compositions on excursions to the Russian capital. The political and cultural leaders of Russia present and Russia future moved freely among St Petersburg, Paris, Berlin and Capri. St Petersburg Russia was as thoroughly within the Western European orbit as Peter the Great had ever dreamed.

Russian literature of the early twentieth century has been well covered by Western research and publication: certainly so in comparison to music. Categories of authors have long since become standard in speaking of Russian prose and poetry of that period: symbolists, acmeists, futurists, realists, naturalists, etc. Even if, indeed, such categories existed in literature, the student must be wary of them in music. The misguided attempt of Nicholas Slonimsky to categorize Russian composers (as well as their Western colleagues) resulted not only in a separate category for each composer, but frequently in a separate category for each of several works by the same composer. That Iurii Shaporin was a close friend of Aleksandr Blok[1] in no way makes of Shaporin a musical symbolist. Prokofieff is not a futurist by

[1] Aleksandr Blok, 1880–1921, a poet identified with the turn-of-the-century Russian symbolists.

virtue of his long friendship and artistic kinship to Mayakovsky.[1] Nor should one be led astray by the Soviet inclination to categorize the past, its events and personalities. One can safely say on the basis of known works that some St Petersburg composers were more, or less, traditionally oriented than others; more, or less, willing to try something new. Equally dangerous and misleading is the inclination to oppose St Petersburg and Moscow on improper grounds. Bernard Stevens in a highly inaccurate article has reiterated the quaint notion that the traditional roles of the two cities were reversed in music: St Petersburg was now the camp of the musical slavophiles, Moscow that of the westernizers.[2, 3] This is a naive rehash of the old Stasov-Serov feud which took place on St Peterburg ground at a far earlier period. Both St Petersburg and Moscow musical society were well aware of the West, but for Moscow it was the West of traditional German romanticism. Taneev, who was the inheritor of the Tschaikovsky mantle at the Moscow Conservatory, sought for creative answers even in the Renaissance period, whose culture Russia had not shared.

The solitary phenomenon of Scriabin defined by negative image the western outlook of Moscow. Paul Miliukov cannot avoid invoking Brahms when considering turn-of-the-century Moscow music (nor Wagner for St Petersburg).[4] Taneev, Rachmaninov, and Medtner are, indeed, considered eclectic in the central European tradition by many, but to deny the national character of the work of these composers, or their St Petersburg contemporaries, is incorrect and misleading.

Scriabin, his pupil Vladimir Rebikov (1866–1920) and, until his early death, Scriabin's son, formed an element of the Moscow musical scene which was unique, and which for many years had only a negative influence on Soviet music. To call Scriabin typical of the Moscow musical scene is also a popular fallacy. What teaching he did do at the Moscow Conservatory as in piano, not composition.

Maxim Gorky said that the period from 1907 to 1917 was the most

---

[1] Vladimir Mayakovksy, 1894–1930, a poet identified with the futurist movement. Mayakovsky was a revolutionary from his early years and wanted desperately to see the success of Bolshevism. Disillusioned, he committed suicide. He left, however, a large legacy of pro-Bolshevik poetry of high quality, written during his years of enthusiasm. His work has been the inspiration for many Soviet composers, the most recent of whom, Grigorii Sviridov, was awarded the Lenin Prize (1960) for his *Cantata on Lenin*.

[2] Bernard Stevens, 'The Soviet Union', *European Music in the Twentieth Century*, edited by Howard Hartog (New York: Praeger, 1957), p. 204.

[3] See page 26 for a discussion of the Moscow-St Petersburg relationship.

[4] Paul Miliukov, *Outlines of Russian Culture* (Philadelphia: University of Pennsylvania Press, 1942), vol. III, p. 129.

shameful and ungifted decade in the history of the (Russian) intelligentsia.[1] He saw it as a reaction, after the 1905 events, on the part of much of the intelligentsia against the ideas of revolution. The view handily supports the contemporary Soviet one. This gross enlargement and distortion of a grain of truth obscures a fundamental element of the Russian 'Silver Age' in the arts: Russian artists and intellectuals were breaking free from the bonds of politico-social polarity. Painting, literature, and music were now increasingly accepted on their own merits. Politics was not being discarded; it was being reined in, abreast of other cultural elements. This development was accelerated by, but not born in, the revolution of 1905. Moreover, it reflected once again the spread of the cultural base in the image and ideology of the great Russian creative artists of the nineteenth century. For these artists rarely thought of serving ideology through their art, in spite of present Soviet claims. That service was, historically, the concern of the second echelon.

The politico-social balance during these years was among three elements: an autocratic, strongly traditional, but increasingly feeble government; an exiled or underground, but smouldering, complex of revolutionary parties, or fragments of such parties; and, finally, an unconcerned intelligentsia, turning now to more theoretical pursuits, and with an ever more appreciative eye to the West. It was this unstable balance that was brought to chaos by a fourth element, World War I, and it was from the chaos that an expertly organized minority party wrenched the power.

[1] Quoted by Andrei Zhdanov in a report on the journals *Zvezda* and *Leningrad*, published by OGIZ, 1946, pp. 11–12.

CHAPTER 2

꒔꒔꒔

Axes of Development

Certain characteristics of Soviet music history must be defined at the outset of this paper. Those considered here are what the author chooses to call the Moscow-Leningrad shift, the relationship of the periphery to the centre, and the general problem of Russian semantics in regard to music.

LENINGRAD TO MOSCOW

The gradual shift of the Russian cultural centre from Leningrad to Moscow will lead the author to use the terms 'Leningrad period' and 'Moscow period'. Since this shift is closely followed in the rest of the paper, only the principal manifestations and reasons are indicated here.

Russian literature documents the philosophical and psychological 'pull' of Moscow.[1] In the nineteenth and early twentieth centuries, the tradition of Moscow as the great, beating heart of Russia was inherent in the thinking of the so-called slavophiles, just as St Petersburg was the darling of the Westernizers. If the distinction between the cities can be accepted, and, since a chauvinistic nationalism developed during the Soviet years in Russian music (see below), then the emergence of Moscow to musical prominence is a not unnatural development. On a sheerly practical plane, the demands of the revolution and subsequent civil war indicated that the seat of active government be removed from exposed Petrograd to Moscow. This, indeed, was given as the immediate reason for the return of the capital to Moscow after an absence of 200 years.

The eve of the revolution found the Moscow school weakly represented by Vasilenko and Ippolitov-Ivanov. Taneev and Scriabin had died two years earlier. The latent elements of both the traditional and the *avant-garde* were in Petrograd. In Petrograd in 1917 were Glazunov, Prokofieff, Miaskovsky, Asaf'ev, A. V. Aleksandrov, Shaporin, Gnessin,

---

[1] See, for instance, Anton Chekhov's *The Cherry Orchard*.

and many others. Of those named all but Glazunov subsequently removed to Moscow. Glazunov chose to go abroad. Shostakovich moved to Moscow in 1943, Dunaevsky permanently in 1944, Sviridov in 1958. Moscow conductors Samosud, Gauk, and Kondrashin are ex-Leningradites, as are pianist Sofronitsky and 'cellist Daniel Shafran. Another indication of the shift is the status of the conservatories, reversed after the revolution. Without joining the controversies of the nineteenth century here, it is generally conceded that by 1914 (or 1917) the Petrograd Conservatory was by far the more progressive and productive school. By 1945 the old St Petersburg traditions had been transplanted wholesale to Moscow. Shostakovich, Miaskovsky, Shaporin and Gnessin taught composition in the Moscow Conservatory. The St Petersburg violin tradition, identified with the name of Leopold Auer, became Moscow's by administrative device whereby top teachers and top talent were, and are, channelled to the conservatory in the latter city. By now the supremacy of the Moscow Conservatory is officially recognized by its being designated as the single conservatory with the responsibility for supplying musical cadre for the entire Soviet Union. Other conservatories, including that in Leningrad, serve geographically limited areas.[1]

THE CENTRE AND THE PERIPHERY

The remarkable development of musical culture in the peripheral republics, a source of great pride to contemporary Soviet musicologists, is actually a phenomenon with well-defined pre-revolutionary beginnings. Contemporary Soviet writing indeed emphasizes the 'beneficial and fatherly' role played by Russia, of any era, in the development of music on the non-Russian periphery. Thus 'the foremost Latvian social figures of the period [of development of cultural life in Latvia, 1850–70] were closely tied with the progressive Russian community',[2] whereas, the facts indicate the development of professional musical culture through schooling on the German pattern, Central European culture, and the fine tradition of Lutheran singing. Similarly, 'the annexation of Armenia to Russia in the beginning of the nineteenth century [and the] beneficial influence of the advanced Russian culture developed the Armenian progressive literature and art', and 'all accomplishments [in Armenia] in the areas of economics, culture and art are a result of the

[1] A controlled, reverse flow, from Moscow to Leningrad, has been evident since the mid-thirties, staffing the Leningrad Conservatory with Muscovites.
[2] N. Groenfeld and Ia. Vitolin, *Latviiskaia SSR* (in the series, 'Musical culture of the union republics', p. 14.

victory of Soviet power and the control of the Communist party',[1] whereas, there was a highly developed Armenian culture, including a sophisticated church and folk music, which lasts to this day, and which was apparently on a high level in the fifth and sixth centuries, a time when the Slavs strung loosely along the river banks to the north had only primitive concepts of government, culture, or theology.

That there was cultural and political intercourse between these countries is geographically obvious and is a matter of historical fact. But it is equally obvious that the destinies and ideologies of Armenia, Georgia, Latvia, etc., did not become identical with Russia's until Tsarist or Communist imperialism made it so. In the less developed countries, such as Uzbekistan, Tadzhikistan, Kazakhstan, and even Azerbaidzhan, the argument of Russian predominance is at least numerically sound since the Russian population in those countries is greater than the native population. The Eastern Ukraine has had close ties with Great Russia, but the Western Ukraine and Byelorussia have at times been more closely identified with the Germans and Poles, although steps have been taken in the last thirty years to eradicate any ethnic evidence of such influence.

In Central Asia, following the pre-revolutionary pattern, a musical culture has been carefully and systematically developed. The pattern is largely that of rigid nineteenth-century Russo-Western forms on which an idealized stock of scales, modes and, less frequently, rhythms of the indigenous music is superimposed. Materially the development has proceded apace, with conservatories and symphony orchestras in the capital cities of the Middle Eastern republics, and large cadres of musicians, represented by their membership in the various organizations provided. Composers of Tadzhik, Kazakh, Uzbek, and Azerbaidzhanian descent now abound. Their music sounds like that of any Soviet composer using oriental 'modes' in the manner of Rimsky-Korsakov and his disciples.

Any musical bond between the centre and a given peripheral republic tends to recapitulate the political-ideological bond. In the Baltic states masses of Russian 'settlers' have taken the place of Latvians, Lithuanians, or Estonians deported to the East. Russians hold key party and government posts.[2] Traditional Roman Catholic (Lithuania) or Lutheran (Estonia, Latvia) religion has been under pressure to yield to Russian

---

[1] M. Agaian, *Armianskaia SSR* (in the series 'Musical culture of the union republics', pp. 3, 4).

[2] Thomas Fitzsimmons, Peter Malof and John C. Fiske, *USSR: Its People, Its Society, Its Culture* (New Haven, Hraf Press, 1960, Seventh volume in the series 'Survey on world cultures'), p. 454.

Orthodoxy.[1] Similarly, music schools, as well as other schools, have adopted Russian formats. Russian supervisors are imported to conduct graduate examinations at the conservatories. Russian names appear in increasing numbers on conservatory staffs and theatre directorates. Baltic musical folklore is manipulated to emphasize the pro-Russian, or, at least, to nullify the impressive heritage of the anti-Russian. In Central Asia the indigenous groups are often now ethnic minorities since colonization from the Russian centre has established Russians in numerical superiority. Lip service is given to limited nationalism and certain national characteristics are even encouraged. Russians occupy positions of authority, although a façade of indigenous autonomy is preserved. Folk music, through special attention to the *ashug* (native folk bard), is controlled in content. Thus, the *ashug's* repertoire, if he is to be successful, contains epics on Stalin, collective farming, and the like. Composed music (like architecture and literature) is basically Russian in form with folk embellishment.

The development of music at and towards the centre has been remarkable not so much for its growth from small beginnings (the pre-revolutionary 'beginnings', if anything, are more impressive than the present), but for the striking phenomenon of organization and classification leading, at times, to a dogmatic semantic situation, wherein the vocabulary limitations and organization defines and restricts the activity as much as the musical activity affects the vocabulary and organizing. Special research problems involving Soviet Russian vocabulary will be discussed later. Those active in musical matters are organized legally by profession (unions); by establishment (orchestra, faculty, or factory 'clubs'); within the governmental apparatus (usually through an institution or union which is subordinate to either the Ministry of Culture or the Ministry of Education, or both); and by the party, whether the individual is a member or not (at various levels: there is a corresponding party organization for every governmental, union, establishment, institutional, etc., organ). Moreover a musician graduating from a conservatory (i.e. entering the economy) has qualifying and limiting entries on his diploma (for example: 'Qualified to teach theoretical subjects up to tenth grade level', or '. . . soprano, may play subordinate roles in provincial opera or teach singing in grades one to eight') which are legally binding for at least three years. Artists have 'ability' ratings which aid in the hiring process. Thus a recent advertisement reads, 'the Perm Area Philharmonic announces auditions for the following positions: (1) Baritone, first or higher category, (2) Solo-violinist, first or

---

[1] Fitzsimmons *et al.*, p. 141.

higher category, (3) Violinist, first or second category, (4) Lecturer-musicologist, first or higher category . . .'. Equally important, though not so binding, are the official classifications to which mature artists may aspire. These are the honours ranging from 'Honoured Artist (or Art Worker) of the X Soviet Socialist Republic' up to 'People's Artist of the Union of Soviet Socialist Republics', with about a half-dozen steps in between. Moreover, there are various Stalin Prizes, Lenin Prizes, labour prizes, orders, medals, and the like which have a recognized order of worth. In addition, the Soviet musician shares with his fellow citizens the general legal classifications as to race or nationality (Latvian, Russian, Jew, Armenian, etc.), class (worker, farmer, intellectual) and class background (parents' class). These classifications are extremely important in the Soviet mode of life, and the citizen carries heavy documentation concerning them, in addition to the mandatory internal passport. A Soviet citizen likes to know where he stands.

MUSICAL SEMANTICS

War, revolution, civil war, collectivization, regimentation, purges, early internationalism, subsequent nationalism, the demands of a rigid, yet shifting ideology, and the contradictions implied by the foregoing, have wrought some significant changes in the Russian language. On the one hand, in translation, it becomes pompous:

'Thus the language of Bolshevism became saturated with words and phrases which convey the image of grandeur, perfection, holiness and eternity . . . such (words) as grandiose (velichaishii), life-giving (zhivotvoriashchii), invincible (nepobedimyi), the most perfect (naibolee sovershennyi), limitless (bezgranichnyi), legendary (bogatyrskii), holy (sviatoi), miraculous, immortal and eternal'.[1]

Moreover the shift of word meanings from abstract to concrete notions is greatly accelerated. Thus one author notes:

'Communist rule has affected language . . . the regime makes an effort to give specific "scientific" meanings to various abstractions. Thus words...formerly equivalent to English..."democracy", "progressive", "cosmopolitan", or "cultural" have been stretched or squeezed into special molds, often far removed from non-communist usage'.[2]

The author also mentions the '. . . proliferation of abbreviated names for officials and institutions . . .' which become proper names. Thus the

---

[1] Dinko Tomasic, *The Impact of Russian Culture on Soviet Communism*. (The Free Press; Glencoe, Illinois, 1953), p. 212.
[2] Fitzsimmons, *USSR*, p. 497.

Zamestitel' direktora politicheskoi chasti gosudarstvennogo muzykal'nogo izdatel'stva (vice-director for the political division of the state music publishers) becomes the *Zamdirektor politichasti muzgiza*. Perhaps with such titles such abbreviations become necessary.

The militant nature of early communism and the current exhortative mode of propaganda and control also saturate the musical vocabulary. Thus we have the *muzykal'nyi front* (musical front), or *muzfront*, and 'musical shockworkers (or) shocktroops'. Further, Fitzsimmons characterizes the language of 'suggestion' from the top: 'The authoritarian nature of the regime [has given] such expressions as "it is suggested" . . . or "it is proposed", . . . imperative force.'

The regime has tended strongly towards the conservative in the arts from the first. Berdiaev says of the first leader: 'In philosophy and art and spiritual culture, Lenin was a very old-fashioned person; he had the tastes and sympathies of the people of the sixties of the last [nineteenth] century; he combined revolution in the social sphere with reaction in the spiritual'.[1] This is natural, since the period Berdiaev mentions may be considered as the golden age of Russian music. Moreover, it must be remembered that virtually the whole of the history of Russian music before the revolution was contained well within the nineteenth century. The abstractions of the nineteenth-century vocabulary are carried in their profusion into the present, but the word-relics are reassigned concrete meanings. Translated literally into English, run-of-the-mill Soviet writing on music seems highly embellished, thick, ponderous and pompous, and indeterminate in meaning,[2] but it is none of these to the Soviet reader. On the contrary, the meaning is all too clear.

The notions of 'modernism' and 'cosmopolitanism' have rigidly defined (in this case, negative) meanings which make it difficult to think or talk about the abstract notions represented by these words. The word 'classical', through various manipulations, has come to mean almost precisely 'romantic national' in music, so a broad basis for misunderstanding is laid down. Moreover, words tend to fall into value groupings and tend to fuse in meaning. Just as slight political deviation in the thirties became semantically identified with a vast 'bad' vocabulary (anti-revolutionary, wrecker, enemy of the people), so a

[1] Nicolas Berdiaev, *The Origin of Russian Communism* (London: Bles, 1937), p. 116.

[2] The manual for *Muzgiz* Russian-English translators reads, in part: 'English is terse, brief and crisp. In translating one must bear in mind, for every Russian word, a set of synonyms in a scale of diminishing intensity. Choose from the bottom of the scale.' Fitzsimmons (*op. cit.*) points out, for instance, that such phrases as 'imperialist war mongers', for all the impact it has, may be translated as 'western governments'.

musician experimenting with serial writing is classified, and *cannot help thinking of himself*, as 'decadent', 'formalist', 'modernist', and 'anti-people'. The terms have a strong synonym relationship.

Before one leaps to the conclusion that change, then, is characteristic of the Russian language, one should consider the vast changes in all Western languages during the twentieth century. Russian exhibits, paradoxically, a 'changelessness' in form, in that little or no vocabulary has been dropped since the nineteenth century. It is not so much the insignificant new words (abbreviations, etc.), but the dogmatic persistence of the old, with ever more concrete meanings.

CHAPTER 3

꒜꒜

Music and Politicians
Lunacharsky and Others

A deeply misunderstood, highly characteristic, and extremely important role is played in the development of Soviet music by the Communist party and the government. The highest ranks of government and Party were and are concerned with the arts. The character of this interest (which only later became interference, and ultimately control) was first established by a small group of highly individualistic men.

In July of 1917, between the two revolutions of that year, a splinter group of Marxist intellectuals led by Leon Trotsky decided to enter the Bolshovik party. They were accepted at the sixth Party congress in late July. It was a small group, highly educated, talented and capable and they had considered themselves until now political 'in-betweens' (*mezhraiontsy*). They 'substantially raised the intellectual level of the Party leadership'.[1] In addition to Trotsky, who was to loom nearly as large as Lenin in the early years, this group included Mikhail Pokrovsky who, as the leading theoretician on Marxist history and organizer of Marxist-trained professorial cadres at the greatest universities until his death and subsequent denunciation in the mid-thirties, had a large influence on cultural and intellectual life; and Anatole Lunacharsky who was to become the first Commissar of Education and Enlightenment, an office which controlled the cultural life and destiny of the country. Of the three, Trotsky had the most political and social weight, Pokrovsky was the most active organizer in education, including cultural education, and Lunacharsky was most concerned with the arts themselves. Trotsky and Pokrovsky are handled negatively under the current demands of Soviet historiography. Lunacharsky, by default, is

---

[1] Georg von Rauch, *A History of Soviet Russia* (New York: Praeger, 1957), p. 46.

2

credited with many of the still acceptable ideas of the three, as is Lenin himself.

Trotsky considered the problems facing the artist and revolutionary leader alike: What was to be the attitude towards the cultural super-structure of the recent bourgeois past? Was the 'new' art to assume a soldier's role in battling for a new stage in history; or was it to reflect and record that struggle? Was there, indeed, to be a 'new' art? Concerning the first of these questions, part of the cultural superstructure, the government, had already been replaced. A broad slice of cultural opinion insisted that the rest, too, must go. This was the stand of a segment of the Proletarian Culture (Proletkul't) group. They answered the question about the role of the new art. It was, indeed, to be on the front lines, sacrificing any other value to that of immediate socio-political expediency. Trotsky, however, rejected these notions. Such a stand now would commit the future to standards which only reflected a narrow segment of the post-revolutionary present.[1] The period of the dictatorship of the proletariat is transient and 'there can be no question of the creation of a new culture, that is, of construction on a large historic scale during the period of dictatorship'.[2] One must here bear in mind that Trotsky and his comrades never dreamed that the period of dictator-ship would not end relatively soon. He continues:

'The cultural reconstruction which will begin when the need of the iron clutch of a dictatorship . . . will have disappeared will *not* have a class character. This seems to lead to the conclusion that there is no proletarian culture and that there never will be any, and in fact there is no reason to regret this'.[3]

Trotsky and Lunacharsky agreed that the cultural superstructure changed slowly, building on the past. The proletariat, as a class, would merge into classless communism before they had a chance at building a class art.[4]

Trotsky, too, defined the relationship of party and culture.[5] The State, politics, language, culture and the Party itself were in that area viewed as ephemeral by Trotsky and other political thinkers of the early Soviet Union. These were the ingredients of the superstructure which would 'wither away' as all economic classes, including the

---

[1] Leon Trotsky, *Literature and Revolution* (New York: Russell and Russell, 1957, translated from the Russian *Literatura i revoliutsiia* which was written in 1923).

[2] Trotsky, *Literature and Revolution*, pp. 185–6.

[3] Trotsky, *Literature and Revolution*, p. 190.

[4] For an amplification of Lunacharsky's theories of class and art see below, p. 37.

[5] Trotsky, *Literature and Revolution*, pp. 218 ff.

proletariat, blended into one, stateless world commune. But for the post-revolutionary exigencies, Trotsky saw the Party acting on three stages. On one it leads, on the second it co-operates, and on the third it adjusts and orients itself. The Party may lead art only indirectly by preparing the socio-economic base. Otherwise it encourages or adjusts. 'Art must make its own way', Trotsky insisted, 'and by its own means. The Marxian methods are not the same as the artistic. The Party leads the proletariat but not the historical processes of history.'[1] Yet, although Trotsky and the Party encouraged the divers activity of the many artistic groups and circles, he felt the Party must still be revolutionarily vigilant, not hesitant 'to destroy any tendency in art . . . which threatens the revolution . . . or [which] arouses the internal forces of revolution, . . . proletariat, peasantry and intelligentsia, to a hostile opposition to one another'.[2] That was emphatically the domain of the Party. The problem was, and remains, where to draw the line on the wrong side of which art threatens the revolution. The line has been variously, even capriciously, drawn. As Edmund Wilson points out,[3] Trotsky himself was not consistent in the matter.

In considering Trotsky further, it is important to bear in mind that, beginning about 1925, his influence began to fade fast. In January of that year he was dismissed as Commissar of War, in October of 1926 he was dismissed from the *politburo*, in October 1927 from the central committee, and in November of the same year was expelled from the Party. He was then exiled to Alma-Ata, and in January of 1929 was expelled from the territory of the USSR.

Anatole Lunacharsky's (1875–1933) touch was unmistakable in the cultural development of the first twelve years of Soviet Russia. His influence was felt not only through his office, but through his personal activity as well. He spoke and wrote on cultural subjects and has many articles on music to his credit. He agitated at all class levels. He encouraged all sorts of search on the part of the artist, and to him goes the credit for salvaging much of the material artistic legacy of Old Russia from the brutality of the revolution and civil war.

Lunacharsky entered revolutionary activity early, joining the Social Democratic party in 1893. This activity prohibited his formal schooling in Russia so he removed to Zurich, studying philosophy and esthetics at the University and attending lectures by Russian Marxists Plekhanov,[4]

---

[1] Trotsky, *Literature and Revolution*, p. 218.
[2] Trotsky, *Literature and Revolution*, p. 219.
[3] Edmund Wilson, *The Triple Thinkers* (New York: Oxford, 1948), 270 pp.
[4] George V. Plekhanov (1859–1918), an ex-populist who shifted his attention and revolutionary dreams from the peasants to the proletariat in *Socialism and*

Axelrod,[1] and Zasulich[2] on philosophy and Marxism. He returned to Russia and the inevitable arrests and imprisonments, and by 1904 he was working with Lenin on the editorial board of *Vpered* ('Forward'), having adhered to the Bolshevik faction after the Bolshevik-Menshevik split in the Social Democratic party in 1903. During the submergence of the revolutionary parties caused by the reaction to the 1905 revolt, and due to a certain disillusionment shared by most revolutionaries, Lunacharsky attempted a theoretical synthesis of Marxism and some elements of idealist philosophy and religion—an attempt promptly damned by Lenin. Lunacharsky's partner in the theorizing was A. A. Bodganov,[3] another old Bolshevik who was to become the ideological leader of the Proletkul't, discussed below.

In 1906, due to Tsarist repression measures, Lunacharsky took the course of many revolutionaries and went abroad. His writing activity increased and was concerned mainly with esthetics, religious history, and philosophy. Although still a Marxist, he shared a certain political limbo, from Lenin's point of view, with Maxim Gorky and A. Bogdanov. That the three mentioned still occupied separate categories in Lenin's mind was indicated in Lenin's letter *to* Gorky suggesting that it would be well to separate 'Lunacharsky from Bogdanov on the matter of esthetics'.[4] By 1912 Lunacharsky was again appearing in the Bolshevik press. He returned to Russia after the February revolution in 1917 and participated in activities of revolutionary organizations. By this time he was close to Trotsky's position and this meant close, again, to the position of Lenin, since the latter had conceded enough to Trotsky to cause him to abandon his hopes of reuniting Menshevik and Bolshevik. The events before, during, and after the July uprisings brought the elements together. Both Trotsky and Lunacharsky were arrested in the uprising's aftermath, but were released again to aid the Kerensky provisional government in its action against the so-called Kornilov

---

the *Political Struggle* (1883). This was the first Russian Marxist work, and though no Russian Marxist party was even nominally established until 1898, he can be considered the father of Russian Marxism. He adhered to the Menshevik faction in 1903.

[1] Paul Axelrod (1850–1928), an early associate of Plekhanov's who also broke with Lenin and joined the Mensheviks.

[2] Vera Zasulich (1849–1919), associated with Plekhanov and Axelrod in the Black Repartition (Chernyi Peredel') splinter of the populists. Although a Marxist, it was in a letter to her that Marx himself recognized the traditional Russian peasant commune as a means whereby Russia could move directly to communism (or socialism) without the intervening period necessary for building capitalism. This became the argument of the rival Social Revolutionary party.

[3] Pseudonym of Aleksandr Aleksandrovich Malinovsky, 1873–1928.

[4] Lenin, *Sochinenie* (Works), vol. 35, p. 58.

revolt. The abortive attempt by Kornilov apparently to stabilize the government, resulted in failure for himself, the loss of prestige of the Kerensky government, and the freeing and arming of the Bolsheviks.

On October 25th/November 7th [1] the revolution began. The next day Lenin named his government. Lunacharsky was appointed Commissar of Education and shared the responsibility with Nadezhda Krupskaia, Lenin's wife, of administering the Party policy in the cultural area.

Lunacharsky was a multifaceted man. He had the typically Western outlook of the early Rusian revolutionary,[2] and musically, his ideas of greatness centred on Beethoven. His view of Tschaikovsky is entirely unacceptable in Soviet Russia today:

'New times must bring with them new songs, and Tschaikovsky in our time sounds sometimes effeminate, as though a bit flabby, too "countryish", too "salonish", too perfumed'.[3]

Although Lunacharsky was actually suggesting a wide palette, and although he goes on to name Tschaikovsky as still appropriate for the day (1928), such a statement would cause hysterical rage in present-day Soviet musicological circles.

Lunacharsky's esthetic views, which were at least timely, and which did much to define the liberal framework of early Soviet art, are equally unacceptable now. They are, in fact, difficult to understand in the present-day Soviet context. Briefly, Lunacharsky states that in a given social structure a given class can assume any one of four positions:

1. It may rule, comfortably in power with a broad future ahead. Artistically form envelops and contains content; technical mastery controls any problems posed for the artist. This situation yields realistic art, *classical* art.

2. The class may be declining, the present uncertain, the future dark. Technique suddenly becomes inadequate to face the demands of content. Touch with reality is lost and a *pessimistic romanticism* of desperation is yielded.

3. The class may be in the ascent, by Marxian definition 'revolutionary'. Again content overwhelms mastery, but now by its very

---

[1] Soon after the revolution a calendar reform brought Russian dating in line with Western dating, at a cost of thirteen days. Where confusion might exist both old style and new style dates will be given in this manner. Otherwise dates will be given in new style for the rest of this paper.

[2] Nicolas Berdiaev, in *The Origin of Russian Communism*, says that Bolshevism was the supreme expression of Westernization in Russia.

[3] Anatole Lunacharsky, 'Chaikovsky i sovremennost', *V mire muzyki* ('Tschaikovsky and the present', *In the World of Music*, Moscow: Sovetskii kompozitor, 1958), p. 362.

newness. There is a scramble for technique. The artistic framework is
rent and a clear, *vital romanticism* is the result.

4. The class may be completely subjugated with no aspirations to
power. The artistic yield, if any, is one of *religio-mystic romanticism*.

Types one and four coincide, as do types two and three. That is, both
the main romantic types occur simultaneously. Thus Wagner, starting
as a romantic of type three (under the influence of Nietzsche, the rise of
the 'revolutionary' bourgeoisie) became later a romantic of type two
(influenced by Schopenhauer, identified with the descending aristo-
cracy). It is significant that no value judgment is implied in Lunacharsky's categories.

Whatever the validity of this view, Lunacharsky presided over
Soviet art when he felt that types two and three were historically
inevitable. Since the logic of his esthetic categories shared the logic, if
not the letter, of Marxism, and since Marxist logic was inevitable, then
a liberal view, encouraging a dialectical development should be adopted.

Lunacharsky fought one manifestation throughout his years in his
post: the perversion and destruction of the classical tradition. Juri
Jelagin says of Lunacharsky that he was tactful and humane,[1] that he
gave everyone the fullest opportunity for creative work in all the fields
of art and gave his support to every serious, artistic undertaking.
'Because of him', states Jelagin, 'Russian art succeeded in weathering
the terrible years of revolution and civil war.'[2] Perversion of the classical
tradition remains today, but in an altogether different form. In Lunacharsky's time it was uncontrolled, and almost uncontrollable. Legally
the 'upper' class was the proletariat, the workers and some peasants.
Actually that class was relatively inarticulate, and the few who found
voice were badly educated and, perhaps, afflicted with an incoherent
feeling of revenge. It was the sacred task of the Party to assure opportunity for these classes, and that meant education.

Under Michael Pokrovsky, Lunacharsky's deputy Commissar of
Education, a sped-up system of education was adopted in the regular
schools. These were referred to as 'workers faculties' (*rabochii fakul'tet*,
or *rabfak*; the author will use the abbreviation). Under the *rabfak*, which
affected all levels of schooling, applicants classified 'bourgeois', or whose
parents were so classified, were not regularly admitted to educational
institutions; applicants with certified proletarian or peasant background
were given preference. Von Rauch says, 'The result . . . was a rapid

[1] Juri Jelagin, *Taming of the Arts* (New York: Dutton and Co., 1951),
translated by Nicholas Wreden.
[2] Juri Jelagin, *Taming of the Arts*, p. 64.

decline of the general intellectual level, attributable to the lack of a systematic curriculum and shallowness of thinking.'[1]

Michael N. Pokrovsky (1860–1932) was the image of the Marxist historian until his death and subsequent denunciation by Kirov, Zhdanov and Stalin in 1934. His view of Russian history coincided exactly with Marx's five classic economic stages. All historic events were interpreted in the rigid terms of economical determinism. Past rulers, famous men, and even traditions of Russia were given a blanket condemnation. Although, as Rostow points out,[2] the first five-year plan was an 'insult' to Pokrovsky's precepts, since it was *personally* and not *economically* determined, he was able to compromise handsomely, redefining historical truth as that which was of immediate propaganda value. In this case, that meant furthering the five-year plan and its accompanying collectivization. The seeds of Pokrovsky's denunciation and of the violent switch in Soviet historiography in about 1934 are contained in this contradiction.

Pokrovsky's theories had a firm effect on music, especially in the conservatories. The chaos at the conservatories in the early years is now minimized and attributed to the activity of the Prokoll or later Proletkul't. Actually it is difficult to avoid the conclusion that responsibility can be traced along Party and government lines. The severest crisis at the Moscow Conservatory will be discussed later. For the moment it will be observed that functions of grading, admittance, graduation, and curriculum were either abolished or placed in the hands of the student-proletariat, under the direction of the 'Red Professors'. This was Pokrovsky's battle organization, and its nucleus was found in the organization of Pokrovsky's fellow historians. The 'Red Professors' group including not only historians, reached a peak of 800 members by 1930[3] and included a number of the staff of the Moscow Conservatory. One of the leaders at the conservatory was, surprisingly, Alexander Kastal'-sky.

The unacceptable fruit of the educational system prodded the Party into some corrective action,[4] but, in the main, a thread of academic integrity was maintained through the necessity of using members of the 'bourgeoisie' to fill the gaping academic holes; by the occasional resistance, even horror, of Lunacharsky and the more responsible segments of

---

[1] Von Rauch, *A History of Soviet Russia*, p. 144.
[2] W. W. Rostow, *The dynamics of Soviet society* (New York: Mentor, 1954), p. 121.
[3] Rostow, *The dynamics of Soviet society*, p. 120.
[4] Von Rauch, *History*, p. 140.

the established artists; and certainly by the impact of the approaching New Economic Policy.

Another victim of the New Economic Policy, discussed below, was the Proletarian Cultural-Educational Organization of 'Proletkul't'. This widespread, important organization was originally the brainchild of Lunacharsky (contrary to present Soviet claims) and A. Bogdanov, whose real name was Alexander Alekseevich Malinovsky. Bogdanov (1873–1928) was one of the pre-revolutionary group of Russian communists who gathered for a time on Capri. He left the Party in World War I but was on hand with Lunacharsky to play an important role after the revolution. He and Lunacharsky organized the first conferences of the so-called proletarian art groups. Bogdanov sought to obliterate the distinction between the two socio-economical groups that had prevailed in the feudal and capitalistic eras: organizers and executors. The realms of intellectual and physical endeavour were to coincide. The first aim, then, of the Proletkul't was to train artists from members of the proletariat, and in 1920 there were said to be about 80,000 persons studying in *Proletkul't* studios.[1]

The Proletkul't was held free of party influence at the insistence of Bogdanov, Trotsky,[2] and Lunacharsky, who felt that art was not the domain of the Party. Bogdanov, moreover, insisted that the *Proletkul't* be organized as a third, progressive front, independent of and unaccountable to the other two: Party and government. What organization there was was loose, large, and contained divers creative elements.[3] Among the extremists were those who sought to deny the past, or to mangle it; and it was in their collective image that subsequent Soviet doctrine cast that of the entire *Proletkul't* movement. Although he continued to direct much cultural activity after the government had blocked formal organization of the movement,[4] Bogdanov was eventually labelled 'Menshevik', 'Trotskyite', 'bourgeois', and 'anti-people'.[5]

---

[1] Vyacheslav Zavalishin, *Early Soviet Writers* (New York: Praeger, 1958), p. 144.

[2] Trotsky, however, had little use for the literary output of many of the *Proletkul't* writers, and had little patience with Bogdanov's semi-mystic view of art as an independent force. See Zavalishin, p. 150.

[3] Among the early writers was Konstantin Tsiol'kovsky (1857–1935) who dabbled in stories approaching science fiction and who is generally credited with being the inspirer of the now discredited 'Cosmists' and 'Planetarists'. Tsiol'kovsky, also an inventor and scientist, is credited, at present, as being the father of Russian rocketry.

[4] Gleb Struve, *Soviet Russian Literature, 1917–50* (Norman: University of Oklahoma Press, 1951), p. 24.

[5] *IRSM*, I, 16.

Well known authors and composers[1] were, however, identified with the *Proletkul't*. These are now excused as 'having carried on significant work in spite of (Proletkul't's) harmful influence'.[2] Lunacharsky's leading role in the *Proletkul't* is largely disregarded, and he is portrayed now as a consistent ideological enemy of his good friend, Bogdanov. The Proletkul't was to re-emerge, in many of its aspects, with the later appearance of the Russian Association of Proletarian Musicians (RAPM), but for the moment, this first phase of early Soviet cultural background was engulfed by political and economic events The *Proletkul't* influence on established musicians had been small. More than all the theory, and more than all the 'cultural movements', what the government actually did, and how the composers reacted, is significant.

[1] Including Kastal'sky, V. Kalinnikov, Krylov, Vasiliev-Buglai, Briusov and others.
[2] *IRSM*, I, 20.

CHAPTER 4

꠹ꠗꠗ

Music and Revolution
1917-1932

The pandemonium of revolutionary events of and after 1917 was regarded variously by Russian composers. Although contemporary Soviet musicology, for its own reasons, insists that Russian musicians met the October (Bolshevik) revolution with great rejoicing,[1] there is ample evidence in earlier Soviet writing that the majority of the Russian intelligentsia, including the musicians, did not accept the October revolution at all. Indeed, it would have been difficult, since overt Bolshevik principles were not clear, and on the eve of the revolution, for tactical reasons, they were closely identified with those of the Socialist Revolutionary party. Where the 'power' would lay after the dust had cleared was by no means certain. Alexander Blok, writing in the twenties, after solidification of Soviet power, muses on the question of why the Russian intelligentsia, *especially the musicians,* did not accept the revolution.[2] Lunacharsky discusses the problem further in an early Soviet music journal.[3] Music and revolution, he says, are basically closely related. From this he reasons that the intelligentsia may not have accepted the October revolution because the Russian intelligentsia is basically amusical.

Lunacharsky's philosophy may bear discussing elsewhere. For the present, however, one can accept what Blok and Lunacharsky assume as a matter of fact: winning the intelligentsia over to the new order was a problem still not completely understood in 1926. The first years of the Soviet Union were painful ones. Out of the chaos brought by war, revolution, and (within months) civil war, the various trends of revolutionary thought sought their own ends. Most musicians, in retrospect,

[1] *IRSM*, I, 21.
[2] Alexander Blok, 'The Intelligentsia and Revolution'.
[3] Lunacharsky, 'The great sisters', *Muzyka i Revoliutsiia*, I (January 1926), p. 14.

were able to identify themselves with some revolutionary movement—
at least on demand. In reality they shared with the bulk of the intelligentsia an apolitical view. This was the real political heritage from the
years after 1905: None of the revolutionary parties[1] had won their
battle for the imagination of the intelligentsia.[2] Far from being fervent
factionists, the musicians found themselves flotsam on the waves of
revolutionary fury. Many were at least geographically identified with the
White forces surrounding the Red centre.[3] The intellectuals and composers of what are now the constituent republics of the USSR enthusiastically supported their own countries' nationalistic and independent
aims. Most of the peripheral countries, indeed, proclaimed their independence of the central Russian state.[4] All but Finland eventually
became part of the Soviet Union. Georgia maintained an independent
Menshevik government until February 1921, and the Baltic States were
annexed only in 1940.

Aleksandr Glazunov was still director of the Petrograd Conservatory,
a post he was to occupy until the eve of his departure for Paris in 1929.
He wrote very little during his twelve years in post-revolutionary
Russia.[5] Ippolitov-Ivanov, who was to continue as director of the
Moscow Conservatory until 1922, was silent. By 1917 Gliere was
director of the Kiev Conservatory and was to continue until his return
to Moscow in 1920. In Kiev, and later in Moscow, he worked
on his opera 'Shakh-Semen', and within ten years produced three

[1] The most significant: The two branches of the Russian Social Democratic
party, Bolshevik and Menshevik; the Socialist Revolutionary party; and, with
reservations, the Constitutional Democrats (Kadets).

[2] Exceptionally, some insignificant musicians and composers were actually
revolutionaries. Ivan Palantai (1886–1926) had a record of deportations and
arrests for revolutionary activity going back to 1906, and was already a Party
member in 1917, a rare if not singular phenomenon. His revolutionary activity
is complicated for present-day Soviet purposes, since he sandwiched his
revolutionary forays in between periods of equally intense religious activity.
Karl Rautio (1899–   ) was a revolutionary worker in an infertile field, remov-
ing to the Soviet Union from the United States in disgust in 1922. Vasilii
Smekalin (1901–40) was a Red Partisan. Peter Triodin (1887–1950) also bore a
record of arrests and deportations into October 1917.

[3] Aksiuk, Gnessin, Bagrinovsky, Bak, Batiuk-Bogachev, Verevka, Gadzhibekov, Zolotarev, Kamensky, Lutsky, Tiulin, and many others.

[4] Finland on December 6/19, 1917; the Ukraine in January 1918; Estonia,
February 24, 1918; Belorussia, March 25, 1918; Georgia, May 26, 1918;
Armenia, May 28, 1918; Azerbaidzhan, May 28, 1918.

[5] During the period 1917–29 Glazunov wrote his symphonic picture 'Karelian
Legend' (1918), 2nd piano concerto (finished in 1917), two songs on Petrarch
poems for voice and orchestra (1928–9), sixth quarter (1921), four preludes and
fugues for piano (1918–23), and two poem-improvisations for piano (1917–18).

ballets, 'Cleopatra', 'Krasnyi Mak' (The Red Poppy), and 'Komedianty'. These early ballets, especially 'Krasnyi Mak', were to have a forceful impact on subsequent Soviet ballet. Gliere also dipped into the new social well and produced such works as 'Comintern Holiday' (1924) and 'March of the Red Army' (1924) for band.

Sergei Vasilenko continued to teach orchestration and composition at the Moscow conservatory. He also continued his work as a concert entrepreneur in the Diaghilev tradition for some time after the revolution—as long as the last of the concert halls was not nationalized. He was chiefly active in the ballet genre in the early years, producing 'Noia' (1923), 'Joseph the Beautiful' (1925), and 'Lola' (1925–6). A third 'producer' of ballets was Boris Asaf'ev, also an active musicologist, who had a great influence on Soviet musical thinking and vocabulary. Asaf'ev put together three of his twenty-six ballets during the early Soviet years: 'Solvejg' (based on Grieg, 1918), Carmagnola', (1918), and 'The Flames of Paris' (1929). Miaskovsky was working on his Fourth Symphony in 1917, and was to finish eight more before the reorganization of the arts in the early thirties. Iurii Shaporin, with most of the others, was active in the *avant garde* musical circles of Petrograd-Leningrad. He was later to become president of the Leningrad branch of the Association of Contemporary Musicians. A slow, careful worker, Shaporin's chief musical contributions over the first fourteen years were an opera, 'Paulina Goebel' (1925), his only symphony (1928-32), and a number of art songs. Active in this generation were: Vasil'ev-Buglai (1888–1956, 'mass' music); Alexander Gedike (1877–1957, an opera 'Virinea', the Third Symphony, chamber music); Maximilian Steinberg (1883–1946), who was active at the Leningrad Conservatory, and whose students range from Shaporin to Shostakovich and beyond; Vasilii Zolotarev (1873–, opera and vocal forms); Alexander Kastal'sky (1856–1926), at or near the centre of many an ideological storm, opera, folk music); Alexander Aleksandrov (1883–1946) and Anatolii Novikov (1896–), the last two noted for their work in laying the foundations for 'mass' music, recognized as a new, separate genre in contemporary Soviet musical thinking.

Operatic performers Nezhdanova and Chaliapin continued their activity for some time under the Bolsheviks, the former subsequently dominating the vocal school at the Moscow Conservatory, the latter leaving the country in 1922. Serge Koussevitzky continued his conducting activities until his exodus in 1920. Among the critics and musicologists at work were Igor Glebov (pseudonym of the aforementioned Boris Asaf'ev), Paskhalov, Listopadov, Ivanov-Boretsky, Catoire, Braudo, Preobrazhensky, and many others, some of whose names are buried deeply under the burden of rearranging the past to support the present. Music scholars and their work will be discussed elsewhere.

Soviet historiography tends to interpret the past so as to support the present. Such names as George Konius (1862-1933, a composer who worked out one of the basic systems of abstract musical composition), Vasilii Kalafati (1869-1942, a gifted student of Rimsky-Korsakov who in turn was the teacher of Bogatyrev, Kushnarev, Gadzhibekov, Stravinsky, and Yudin, and by whom many foreign students were drawn to Petersburg-Leningrad), and Victor Kalinnokov (1870-1927, composer and teacher) were prominent enough in early post-revolutionary Russia to warrant a fleeting fame abroad. They, too, are buried in that portion of the past which does not serve the present.

The Western image of Russian music after Rimsky-Korsakov and before the emergence of the generation of Shostakovich is associated with the names Sabaneev, Medtner, Gretchaninov, Loure, Liapunov, Prokofieff, Stravinsky, Rachmaninov, and Cherepnin. None of these are mentioned above. All but Stravinsky and Rachmaninov (who left before 1917) left Russia after the revolution and before 1923. Of them only Prokofieff returned. Their leaving the country represents the last great dissemination of Russian music abroad, and no consideration of Russian music is complete without considering them. The Soviet attitude toward these men varies radically (Stravinsky is the 'Trotsky-image' in music (1957). Rachmaninov, on the other hand, could be considered the 'Plekhanov image'), and that attitude matters not the least. Only in so far as they have a definite impact on the subsequent destiny of Soviet music will they be considered here (Prokofieff, who returned, or Stravinsky, against whom the reaction has shaped part of the musical vocabulary). In the early years they continued to correspond from abroad, and their activities were faithfully reported in the music journals of the twenties, but officially they were dismissed as 'White Guard bandits'.[1] Officialdom had not the teeth to make the ideological bite it subsequently did.

Composers and other artists welcomed one apparent advantage of the revolutions of 1917: the release from the 'double censorship' of the left and right. On the one had was the official censorship of the government, on the other, that of the 'social' critics and writers starting with Belinsky. From the latter source there was always the pressure for art to serve the cause of social reform. Ernest Simmons[2] notes that 1917 brought freedom and creative *élan*. There were 'excitement, contending

---

[1] Andrey Olkhovsky, *Music under the Soviets* (New York: Praeger, 1955), p. 191.
[2] Ernest J. Simmons, *Russian fiction and Soviet ideology.*

movements, strident manifestos, blatant nonsense, brilliant theorizing. Art produced . . . reflected the determination to preserve (the artists') individual values in a world of revolt.'[1]

At first all non-Bolshevik newspapers and publishing were temporarily suspended.[2] but with the resumption of the cultural press, artists re-articulated their desires of February for an art free from politics. Lunacharsky approached the Union of Art Workers in mid-November with an idea of forming a State Council of the Arts and received a negative disinterested answer.[3]

The Marxist-Leninist view on culture and art, with which Lunacharsky's development on page 37 coincides, was that they formed a part of the superstructure of whatever historical social mode prevailed. The implication, as noted above, was that the superstructure changed automatically with the change of the material basis of society. Although this concept was later shattered completely by Stalin, it meant now that the State's sole leverage on the arts was through manipulation of the social mode. Present day Soviet music scholarship often refers to Lenin's famous remark in a conversation with Clara Tsetkin[4]:

'Art belongs to the people. It must spread out with its deep roots into the very thick of the vast labouring masses. It must be understood by these masses—loved by them. It must create and develop artists from among them.'

The generalities expressed are used today as reason for the direct influence of the Party on art, and it is altogether possible that Lenin, opportunist that he was, had also arrived at this position. But as Simmons points out,[5] Marxism had little to do with it; rather the Communist party realized that art, properly handled, was powerful propaganda.

The obligation of the new Russian government was to ensure the proper social mode: communism.[6] This meant turning the means of production over to the proletariat or, during the period of the dictatorship of the proletariat, nationalizing the means of production. Nationalization proceeded apace: banks in December 1917, the merchant marine in January 1918, grain dealers in February, mines in May, oil in June,[7]

---

[1] Simmons, *Russian Fiction*, introduction.
[2] Von Rauch, *History*, p. 63.   [3] Olkhovsky, *Music . . .*, p. 43.
[4] Vladimir Lenin, *Lenin on culture and art* (Moscow: Izogiz, 1938), p. 299.
[5] Simmons, *Russian fiction . . .*, Introduction.
[6] The classical modes, according to Marx, are primitive communism, slaveholding, feudalism, capitalism, socialism. Another set, apparently equally valid since Marx did not exhibit consistency in his names: Asiatic, slavery, feudalism, capitalism, and socialism (communism).
[7] Von Rauch, *History*, p. 125.

and the first two conservatories of music (Moscow and Petrograd) on July 12, 1918.[1] The principal theatres had begun a process of nationalization as early as December 1917. The Bolshoi and MKhAT (Stanislavsky) in Moscow and the Marinsky in Petrograd were State property by January 1918. Music stores, warehouses, and publishing houses were nationalized on July 18, 1917. Thus the great Russian publishing house of Jurgenson became what is now Muzgiz,[2] occupying today the same premises and using practically the same equipment. The two strongest vocal institutions in the country, the Petrograd vocal capella and the Moscow synodal school choir, were nationalized soon after the conservatories. All these schools and institutions were officially under the musical section of Lunacharsky's People's Commissariat for Education. The abbreviation *Narkompros* will be used hereinafter. Under *Narkompros* the first State Orchestras were founded.[3] This and other feathers in the cap of *Narkompros* in the early years usually represented the assumption of responsibility for an already existing organization. Some artistic unions were organized, not to direct cultural policy, but to give the artist a legal channel to authority. The unions were characterized by immense freedom of activity granted them by once-bitten-twice-shy Lunacharsky.

The year 1921 saw the end of the civil war and a nearly ruined country. Industry and farming had to be rehabilitated. Trade was nonexistent. Strikes were mounted spontaneously to protest the meagre rations doled out by the Bolsheviks. On March 1, 1921, the sailors at Kronstadt started what might have led to a third revolution. They found much sympathy among the people, but were ruthlessly suppressed. Von Rauch[4] gives these as the reasons for the State's inaugurating the New Economic Policy (NEP). Treadgold[5] emphasizes the political aim of conciliating the peasantry which threatened the dictatorship of the proletariat. By a partial return to the economics of capitalism, a medicinal dose, Lenin hoped to save something from the ruins of war and confusion of the Bolshevik agricultural policy. He also saw it as a means to separate the 'bourgeois' from the 'proletariat' among the peasants,[6]

---

[1] 'Decree concerning the Moscow and Petrograd conservatories' *Pravda*, Moscow, July 12, 1918. Signed by V. Ulianov (Lenin).

[2] See p. 30 for a word on abbreviations.

[3] The first was in Petrograd. The Petrograd orchestra simply assumed the name 'State Philharmonic Orchestra'. *IRSM*, I, 28.

[4] Von Rauch, *History*, pp. 124–128.

[5] Treadgold, *Twentieth Century Russia*, pp. 196 ff.

[6] There is no help from Marx here. He recognizes the peasantry only fleetingly in the Manifesto as 'potential *petite bourgeoisie*' and dismisses peasant life as 'an idiocy'. Lenin's afterthoughts about the peasantry were demanded by Russia's being overwhelmingly agricultural.

thereby setting up a classical dialectical conflict, to be resolved, of course, with the ascendancy of the proletarian peasant.

Limited private enterprise was allowed, and trading was encouraged partly by opening the borders to foreign interests. The latter was much to the liking of musicians and artists who had kept contact with the West surprisingly alive during the period of war communism.[1] The post-revolutionary intelligentsia was still oriented to the West. The period of NEP, free at least from armed conflict, was a period of much cultural exchange, new ideas and creative production. Art was given an apparent *laissez-faire* by Lenin himself in an appearance at the tenth Party congress in March of 1921:

'The cultural problem cannot be settled as swiftly as political and military problems. One must understand that the conditions for movement ahead are now lacking. (One may) conquer politically in . . . several weeks . . . in war in several months, but to be victorious culturally in such a period is impossible . . . (one needs) a longer period to adjust, to reappraise one's work, displaying greater persistence, insistence and systematic character.'[2]

Whatever portent may be in these words was ignored by most artists; the implication of freedom, however transitory, was seized upon.

Lunacharsky emerged more than ever as the bell-wether of the arts during NEP (1921–7). Cultural ties with Germany were particularly close, a phenomenon recapitulating the hopeful, to the Soviets, political situation. In mid-1922 Lunacharsky was able to make a statement during a spoken tribute to Glazunov:

I am very happy to note that the Germans, *who are now without question the most sensitively cultured of peoples* [underlining mine, SDK], have taken note of Glazunov's service . . . [awarding him] the rank of Member of the Berlin Academy'.[3]

Such an opinion and attitude toward Germany and the Germans would be unthinkable in Soviet music writing from the thirties to the present.

---

[1] 'War communism' is a generally accepted term among historians to refer to the period in Russia from 1917 to 1921.

[2] Lenin, *Sochineniia* (Works), XXXIII, 55. Note that these are the same ideas as Trotsky's (see p. 33).

[3] Anatole Lunacharsky, 'On the fortieth anniversary of A. K. Glazunov's creative activity', *V mire muzyki* (Moscow: Sovetskii Kompozitor, 1958), footnote on p. 105. The article was originally published in 1922 in the October 31st issue of the newspaper *Izvestiia*, and was a stenographic report of a speech given by Lunacharsky at the Moscow Conservatory on October 29th. The footnote was added the following year.

This was the period of the growth of well-defined cultural organizations. Most important of these, one embracing perhaps 90 per cent of the practising musicians and composers was the Association of Contemporary Musicians (ACM). The functions of the ACM closely resembled, although on a much broader base, those of the pre-revolutionary 'Evenings of Contemporary Music'. The aims of the ACM were simply explained in the statement of purposes printed in their first official journal *Towards New Shores*,[1] 'to stay abreast of current events in music'. That they did so may be seen by a partial list of contributors throughout the one year of publication. In addition to domestic Russians Goldenweiser (Moscow), Bogatyrev (Kharkov), and Glebov-Asaf'ev (Petrograd), there were countrymen abroad (Sabaneev in France, Saminsky in New York) and other foreign contributors (Haba writing on quarter-tones, Milhaud writing on polytonality and atonality, and Paul Pisk writing on musical events in Vienna, particularly those surrounding his teacher of composition, Schoenberg). Although no particular journal was noted for its long life, ACM published almost continuously during the NEP years.

At the same time, an organization with altogether different aims took shape, based largely in Moscow. This was the Russian Association of Proletarian Musicians (RAPM), the musical analogy of the far larger Russian Association of Proletarian Writers (RAPP). The proletarian group was effectively curbed by the ACM and remained a small, noisy, but unimportant group of second-rate composers for as long as the government did not intervene. The RAPM sought a new music: its ideas were in some ways close to those of the now defunct Proletkul't; although the former had not a shred of the progressive flavour of the latter. The wish of the RAPM was to ignore the contemporary West and to select traditions from among the simplest of Russia's past. The group was deeply fundamentalist and reactionary.

NEP ended in 1927. Lenin was dead, Stalin vigorously ascendant. Certain ACM elements had become identified with the unpleasant by-products of NEP—petty bourgeois mentality and cultural obeisance to Western technique and culture. These elements cast doubt on the whole of the progressive Association of Contemporary Musicians. Moreover, the Western contact, vital to both NEP and the ACM, was interrupted. The ACM died with NEP, a demise hastened by the Party. The Party gave official sanction to the RAPM, a fact now denied. The change was one of form only. Most of the ACM members now joined the RAPM, and, by

[1] *K Novym Beregam* was issued throughout 1923 by *Gosizdat Muzsektor*. The publishing address was that of the old Jurgenson company. The printing was 2,000.

force of numbers, they effectively changed the nature of that organization. A struggle continued between the progressive 'contemporaries' and the reactionary 'proletarians'; the unequal struggle continues only because of the implied Party support of the latter. Far more demanding of the attention of all was the collectivization of the countryside—the economic ingredient which supplanted NEP in 1928. This was a time of trouble, agony, and death in the Soviet Union. It has been aptly labelled the 'Second Revolution'. It was accompanied by industrial planning and development, the whole combined as the first of the famous five-year plans. It is curious that this first, severe action of a government now firmly in power, had little immediate effect on musicians. One must assume that music control lags: it has ever since.

CHAPTER 5

Music and Reaction, 1932-

The promulgation of the creative canons of 1932–6 was the third revolution: this one in the Arts. This was a cultural revolution of reaction, isolation, and chauvinism. In retrospect, it seems as important as the first, 1917 revolution and the second, collectivization, revolution of 1928. Just as 1917 was the dominating socio-political fact for the older generation of Soviet composers, so was 1932, and its aftermath, for the middle generation. 1932 came in like a lamb. Composers, young and old, gleefully parted with the RAPM. The newly formed, State organization, the Union of Soviet Composers (USC), was welcomed by all. This organization became, and has remained, the only professional organization for Soviet composers and musicologists. It is an appendage to the Ministry of Culture. That ministry and the Union publish jointly *Sovetskaia Muzyka*. Until 1957, and except for brief periods, this was the Soviet Union's sole musical journal. The USC operates in various areas. It is the official channel for communication between the leadership and creative musicians—a channel apparently in need of frequent Party dredging. Its various buildings serve as meeting rooms and permanent residences for many members and their families. In the same area, it maintains rest and recreation centres, arranges vacations there, or elsewhere, and maintains the health services for its members. In turn, the member is responsible to the USC for his whereabouts and status, or change of status, as indicated in the documents he carries. As a musical forum, the Union is divided into sections which govern the various musical genres. These hear and judge new works and arrange for their publication and performance, if warranted. The composer has the moral obligation of submitting his work for USC approval. Although this obligation is often ignored, the habitual violator may be criticized by his fellows and, ultimately, in the press. The Union keeps dossiers on its members, providing copies to other organizations, such as conservatories, where they may be employed. The USC also functions as 'employer' in a special

sense. The Soviet boast of no unemployment is an export euphemism
for laws that require that each citizen must contribute through labour to
the economy. The USC 'employs' some members at no salary, freeing
them from the work obligation, and providing time for composition.
When, in the opinion of the appropriate board, an individuals' period
of free time should end, then the USC may secure his employment
elsewhere. Thus the USC is at the centre of and dominates the lives of its
members. The implications were not recognized in 1932.

The accompanying isolation from the West, the intensifying nationalism, and the burgeoning cult of Stalin were, at first, misunderstood. The
beginning of political terror should have clarified things, but it took the
musical lesson of 1936 to point out that the destiny of the Arts and of
artists was very much a part of the destiny of the State and Party. Some
of the latter's functionaries were even then enjoying Soviet due process
in the famous Moscow Trials when, in 1935, Stalin went to two
operas. The first of these was *Tikhii Don* (The Quiet Don) by Ivan
Dzerzhinsky. A conversation among Dzerzhinsky, Stalin, and Molotov,
which took place during an interval, was widely reported in the Soviet
press. Stalin found the opera an excellent one. Here, for the first time,
and in Stalin's words, official definition of Gorky's term 'socialist
realism' was given for music. The writers and artists of the Soviet
Union had heard many words about socialist realism since Gorky's
exhortations in 1933. *Tikhii Don* was an example of socialist realism in
music. How far beyond the rather pallid accomplishment of *Tikhii Don*
could this definition stretch? Dzerzhinsky was known in the musical
world as a fairly talented hack. It was also well known that Dmitrii
Shostakovich had helped Dzerzhinsky solve some of the petty musical
problems *Tikhii Don* posed. Was this, then, the prelude to fresh
advertisement of Shostakovich abroad—the advertisement of a strictly
Soviet product? Was there, now, to be a 'Shostakovich school' of
Russian-Soviet composition? These questions were seriously posed
during the interval before Stalin's next night at the opera. In December
1935 Stalin attended a Moscow performance of Shostakovich's highly
successful *Lady Macbeth of Mtsensk*. Reporters, reflecting on the curious
matter of *Lady Macbeth*, have supposed a number of reasons for Stalin's
reaction. He disliked the dissonance, and the leadership box at the time
was over the brass section of the orchestra pit. However, *Lady Macbeth*
was not all that dissonant; there are many effective, lyrical passages. It
has been suggested that the libretto dealt ineffectively with social
problems. It is true that the libretto is psychologically complex, and
that the 'masses' are rather squalidly portrayed. Yet, the story is a
merciless exposure of pre-socialist, petty-bourgeois, Russian morality.

Actually, arch-puritan Stalin was grossly offended by the sexuality of the work and, musically, by the rape scene, whose brilliantly realistic orchestral accompaniment led one Western writer to coin the word 'pornophony'. The words used then to condemn *Lady Macbeth*— 'animalistic realism', 'naturalism', 'animalism'—are words now well established in the Soviet critic's lexicon for referring to excessive display of the erotic. On this basis, a mountain of evidence was formed. The attack was not so severe as it was broad. The entire Soviet press opened with a broadside that stunned the musical world. The question of *Lady Macbeth* was discussed in factories and on collective farms, in Party meetings, and endlessly in the usc. From these and other sources, letters of gratitude came to the leader—and these were duly published. Shostakovich's own expression of gratitude was the Fifth Symphony, subtitled, 'a composer's answer to just criticism'. A comparison of the Stalinist critique of *Lady Macbeth* with that of *Tikhii Don* provided the Soviet composer with his boundaries, for the ensuing discussions ranged far and wide. The Party and usc machinery, set up four years earlier, had been given its first run, one which demonstrated to all its function. All the bases of musical ideology that prevail today had been laid by 1937. The theorizing since, including the far more brutal party condemnation of 1948, has failed to indicate any new departure. Basic then, and basic now, are the interrelated creative elements of nationalism, Party glorification and service, exclusive creative and critical recognition of the Russian nineteenth century, denial of Western influence and isolation from the West, methodical eclecticism, concentration on programme genres, high propaganda content, humourlessness, and simplicity of idiom geared to the widest audience of the moment. It is necessary to repeat that this *status quo* was achieved in the ideology of music, not, necessarily, in the practice of music. If such had been the case, the mists of ennui would have made research unbearable.

A rash of conforming operas appeared in the wake of the *Lady Macbeth* affair—the work of the opportunistic group of middle generation composers. These included Khrennikov's *V Bur'iu* (In the Storm) and Kabalevsky's *Colas Breugnon*. Elsewhere, new Soviet musical works tended to the style of newspaper accounts of, or, at best, editorial comment on, the great (i.e. Stalinist) successes of the Soviet Union. Bridges, polar flights, dams, overfulfilled work norms, and shock workers all became the musical meat of socialist realism. Stalin himself became the most sung, living man in history. Odes, poems, songs, symphonies, oratorios, and cantatas all sounded his glory. And, in the hinterlands, vast numbers of folk songs on Stalin were 'discovered'. Two important documents of the time, the new Soviet Constitution and

Stalin's historical treatise, *A Short Course in the History of the Communist Party*, were of primary importance to composers. The 'Stalin' Constitution was honoured in the works of many composers. The *Short Course*, though not sung as much, became an historiographical guide to a re-evaluated history and to the glorification of Stalin. Through reading its pages it became clear that Stalin's role in the destiny of the Soviet state, and even in the pre-revolutionary Party, was far greater than had been imagined. Stalin, it seems, had been Lenin's rock, and the former had protected the latter from the false and treasonous Trotsky, Bukharin, Kamenev, Zinoviev, and others. Stalin, not Trotsky, had led the Bolshevik armies to victory. Stalin, not Bukharin, had been the most brilliant of Bolshevik theorists. Stalin and Lenin were the two great eagles of the revolution, and so it was in song and symphony. That these claims were false is, and was, so well known and documented that it requires no further substantiation here.

The now refurbished past, Russian and Western, was portrayed, musically, to the glory of the Soviet present. At the same time, the older generation of Soviet composers, and some members of the middle generation, paused. Periods of creative silence became typical now for composers as well as writers. This environment became the postgraduate school for the middle generation of Soviet composers. Its lessons were learned well, but acted upon variously. The school was new, and not subtle, but its curriculum was well established before the war temporarily closed its doors.

The Germans, in 1941, invaded an unhappy country. When it became clear that the initial Nazi success was due in part to the willingness of the citizens of many of the overrun areas to welcome Hitler's troops, the Soviet government immediately relaxed the terror and many of the political, ethnic, social, and cultural controls. Again, this was misunderstood. For Soviet music and musicians, these were the facts of the Second World War: First was the lessening of creative controls; second, a re-opening to the West, providing musicians from both the Soviet Union and the West with their first prolonged contact since before 1929; and third, the official concern for and massive relocation of the important musical cadres and institutions.

The period of war liberality saw some of the Soviet composers' finest work. Much of Shostakovich's and Miaskovsky's best chamber music was written. Gliere's voice and 'cello concertos did much to revive interest in that form. Many works temporarily withheld during the late thirties, notably Prokofieff's, now received their hearings. Experimentation, nourished by Western contact, flowered anew. The names of Shostakovich and Prokofieff were heard again in the West, and to them were added those of Kabelevsky, Khachaturian, and Shaporin. An interesting phenomenon, already noticeable in the thirties, became traditionally entrenched during the war: Soviet music always has its best foreign reception in the Western hemisphere, especially in the United States. The reception of the continental press and public was, and is, noticeably cooler than that in America. This foreign reception, especially in America, is hotly sought by Soviet composers as the one sure way to success at home. Unfortunately, the development of this point here would demand digressions leading far beyond the scope of the present paper. It is more to the point that these two facts of the battle, liberalism and the refreshing Western contact, are ignored or even denied in contemporary Soviet writing.

Certainly not ignored was the birth of Soviet patriotism. This became intense among Soviet musicians, the more so as the Red Army began to generate the momentum that carried it, finally, to Berlin and beyond. The patriotic symphony is best exemplified by Shostakovich's *Seventh*, with its many imitations. The heroic cantatas and oratorios (and here we see the rebirth of a form) were based on the content and success of Shaporin's *Na Pole Kulikovym* and *Skazanie o bitve za russkuiu zemliu.* Many musicians participated actively in the battle. Others visited the front for material in the manner of reporters. For the first time an appreciation of the vastness and potential integrity of the nation was gained by the Russian people, at least at the centre. The discontent or defection, imaginary or real, of some of the ethnic minorities was dealt with with a minimum of publicity. Only after the war were questions asked about the disappearance of certain ethnic groups from their traditional homelands.

A certain geographical understanding of the Soviet Union was gained by musicians during the war. It became the policy of the government to move important individuals and institutions from danger areas. The case of the Leningrad evacuation is typical. Tashkent became the new, musical Leningrad. The entire staff and student body of the conservatory and many composers and musicologists renewed their activity there. The Maly opera theatre, composers Dzerzhinsky, Chulaki, Solov'ev-Sedoi, and others went to Orenburg. The Leningrad Philharmonic, the Pushkin Theatre, and the Children's Theatre were removed to Novosibirsk, as were the composers Chicherin, Shcherbachev, Sviridov, and others. The Kirov (Marinsky) Theatre and the composers Popov and Hodge-Einatov went to Perm. Shostakovich went to the Moscow evacuation centre, Kuibyshev, whence he subsequently returned to Moscow. This concern of a seriously beleaguered Party and government for the musical cadres of the nation may well be evidence of the Party-State-artist relationship as important as the evidence of control, punishment, and reward. The one is far clearer in relationship to the other. The massive State care of the musical establishment was the second half of the promise of 1932—the first half had been realized in 1936.

The balance of the musical and creative factors of war was so firmly set by 1945 that the Soviet creative body accepted this as the long sought coming-of-age of Soviet art. It was, in fact, a five-year interim, of no lasting value, in those policies and directions established in 1932–6. Music and the Arts became matters of cold war fact. In 1946, certain Leningrad writers, notably the satirist Zoschenko and poetess Akhmatova, and a Leningrad literary journal, drew the frowning attention of the Party leadership. Andrei Zhdanov, a highly placed Party central committee member, and Stalin's heir apparent, revived the vocabulary of the mid-thirties in condemning the offenders. In the next two years, the citadels of Russian-Soviet literature, history and philosophy were stormed and sacked by the Party, and by Zhdanov, in the name of Stalin. Linguistics, and specialists therein, received special attention, for now Stalin emerged as an expert in this field with articles on linguistics. There was a gradual redefinition of the notion of the superstructure of society, a structure of which both music and linguistics were a part. Under full communism, language differences and the uneven distribution of creative talent were to have withered away, along with the State and the rest of the superstructure. But it now appeared that this 'withering away' would take the form of absorption into the mighty body of Russian thought and culture. The universal language, to replace those historically weaker ones which would disappear in the withering process, must logically be Russian, the great language of history and of Bolshevism. Creativity would be a gift shared equally by all and would function with the materials of the greatest of traditional and national Arts—the Russian. Pending the realization of full communism, the job for the present, the Party's job, was to define, guide, and protect these traditions for the future.

If the implications were not immediately clear to musicians, they became so in 1948. In a series of meetings with Soviet composers, climaxing but not ending in the first All-Union Congress of Soviet Composers, Andrei Zhdanov carefully documented the Party case against Soviet composers. The opening wedge was the unsatisfactory opera *Velikaia Druzhba* (The Great Friendship) by Vano Muradeli. But the third-rate Muradeli was swiftly left behind in favour of larger targets: the brunt of the attack was borne by the composers Prokofieff, Shostakovich, Miaskovsky, Shebalin, and Popov, and the musicologists

Asaf'ev, Livanova, and Gruber. Khachaturian and Kabalevsky were included as afterthoughts. Few composers escaped castigation. In the peripheral republics similar sessions were subsequently held, and Karaev, Balanchivadze, Arutiunian and many others were swept up in the net. Gliere and Vasilenko were mildly handled, and Shaporin seems to have escaped altogether. The bell-wether, Tikhon Khrennikov, gained immensely, of course. As suggested above, there was nothing new in the 1948 musical line but the scope. This was a return to the bases of 1936. Now these were amplified. Genre by genre, composer by composer, almost work by work, Soviet composers were told what was wrong, why it had gone wrong, and what the measures for correction should be. The words 'cosmopolitanism', 'formalism', 'popular enemy', and 'anti-revolutionary' were skilfully blended into an anti-Western syndrome. This term-group was further defined by association with incorrect choice of subject matter and non-traditional idiomatic usage. Thus, those who were influenced by Hindemith, Bartok, Honegger and, horror of horrors, Schoenberg, were imitating the music bought by foreign capitalists to enslave the working class.

Throughout the Union, scores of composers' meetings discussed the matter for many months. That such diverse groups, in such diverse locations, should arrive at identical answers, is a tribute to the functioning of the Party apparatus. The Party network is a principal agent of news and information dissemination within the Soviet Union. Long, explanatory letters are now sent out regularly to the various levels of Party organizations. In addition to political exhortation, these contain straight news, news background, and editorial comment. This provides Party members with a far greater understanding of what is going on than the average citizen. It fills the vast gaps left by the Soviet press, and, perhaps most importantly, it sharply distinguishes and elevates the Party member among the citizenry. The Party member is the oracle to be consulted. In recent years, by this means, Party members have had immediate knowledge of such secrets as Khrushchev's de-Stalinization speech of 1956, the confidential matters discussed by Richard Nixon and Khrushchev in 1959, and, if one accepts these communications as perfectly valid, the fact that in early 1959, a Russian rocket, destined for the Pacific, got out of control and overflew the Pacific, the North American continent and landed in the Atlantic, just short of the European mainland. This unique and highly effective means of rapid, authoritative communication, unaccountably neglected in Western studies, was used sparingly in Stalin's time. It was used, however, in the implementation of the 1948 musical controls. Zhdanov, and the Party central committee, sent letters, with bearers, to the local Party organizations. The bearers presented the letters and briefed the cells on all the pertinent details. After considerable study and analysis of the local musical situation, the local organization prepared its case, assembled the local musicians, and held court.

The pattern and substance of attack elsewhere were, thus, firmly established at the centre; and so were the pattern and substance of response. The behaviour of the Soviet composers in the face of Zhdanov's attack was the second act of the drama that shocked the rest of the musical world. The principals' response in 1948 recapitulated the response of the defendants at the Moscow purge trials of 1936 and 1938: full confession, abject and humiliating apology, expressions of gratitude to Stalin for his interest, and a plea for the mercy of the State. It is not safe to assume that this response was forced out of personal fear of the moment alone. There is ample evidence in Russian as well as Soviet history to indicate that the composers did, indeed, feel guilty, that they were, indeed, brimming over with gratitude, and that they felt quite comfortable in the stern grip of the Party and State control. The language and procedure involved throughout the cultural purge, received with such curiosity in the West, was familiar to those who remembered the Moscow trials, and familiar to those acquainted with nineteenth-century Russian literature. The prematurely abrupt confession, etc., of Dmitrii Kabalevsky established the pattern for the moment, but Kabalevsky was drawing instinctively on tradition.

Although particularly detailed and disproportionately publicized in the West, the musico-political events of 1948 were but one element of one stage in a fierce crescendo of terror, extending from 1946 to Stalin's death in 1953. Actually, from the vantage of 1962, it can be seen as a crescendo, starting at least by 1932, and only briefly relieved by the war. The immediate effects took the form of punishment for certain composers—punishment mild by Soviet standards: Shostakovich stopped teaching. Prokofieff apparently retired to the countryside. Asaf'ev died in January 1949, Miaskovsky in August 1950. There is no particular reason to believe they died from any but natural causes. Shebalin, who suffered most, was removed from his post as director of the conservatory, and was suspended from the faculty for three years. Similar shifting took place in the lower echelons and on the periphery. Much of this served to restaff the Union of Soviet Composers. At its head now stood Tikhon Khrennikov, everybody's villain.

The long range effects, on the other hand, took the form of punishment for the listener. The composers, apparently willing to follow the lead of the Party, were unable, successfully, to make peace with their muse. A lasting testament to their plight is the little volume, *Puti razvitiia sovetskoi muzyki,*[1] put together from the logic of Zhdanov and the central committee. This grim bible lists all past musical crimes and criminals in the first few chapters. The rest of the book is a composer's guide for each musical genre. There is no substantial record of any Soviet composer's failing to try to conform. For some, including Shostakovich, it meant a retreat into such things as music for motion pictures and the abandonment of symphonies. For some, it meant revision of tainted works. The Soviet oratorio-cantata genre was given a big shot in the arm. Chamber music all but disappeared. The mass song flourished. But the musical product of 1948-53 was obviously that of confusion, if not fear. As the terror mounted, the composers' struggle to conform became hysterical. There is little reason, then, to wonder at the stunning effect upon the nation, when, in March 1953, the Kremlin announced that the *Vozhd'* was dead. Stalin's hatchet man, Zhdanov, had long preceded him, dying in 1948, in suspicious circumstances.

For the younger generation of Soviet composers, the fact of 1948-53 was the dominant one. The next period, 1953 to the present, is too dangerously close for scholarly accuracy. Yet changes have occurred, and others have been claimed, which demand documentation and analysis. The fundamental questions are, have things changed, and, if so, how much, and in what ways? The spectre of Stalin is gone. He has been re-evaluated, recast, and reburied. With him, the personal condemnation of composers, although not the ideological bases, of 1948 has been stricken from history by the Central Committee.

The disappearance of terror seems real. The machinery of terror has been modified in Soviet law. The *need* for terror does not exist, but one must give ear to those who hold that there is never a need for political terror, that terror is its own *raison d'être.*

The apparent relaxation of control is not real. The fact that moments of Party intervention in the Arts in the past ten years have seemed comparatively mild, proves only that the source of control has shifted. Expunged of its personalities, the volume *Puti razvitiia sovetskoi muzyki* is as valid today as in 1948. The new source of musical control lies administratively in the hands of the USC, and ideologically and practically in the embrace of a conditioned public and conditioned musicians. The Party, as a governor of control, can, and does, augment, point-up, and re-direct at times. The sparing use of Party power is the chief indicator that, finally, a certain creative musical equilibrium has been achieved in Soviet music, as of about 1957. The elements of that equilibrium, though, are perishable. They are founded in the self-sufficiency of a

---

[1] Aleksandr Shaverdian, *Puti razvitiia sovetskoi muzyki* (Paths of development of Soviet music), Moscow, 1948.

nation, apparently successful, apparently comfortable, apparently superior. Musically the West is absent, or selectively present. The frequent, stereotyped, boredom-filled visits of Western composers' delegations to the Soviet Union and Soviet delegations to the West are ineffective, distastefully official substitutes for real, cultural intercourse. Moreover, an attitude toward the West, compounded of fear, resentment, scorn, respect, and interest, has crystallized. The Soviet press provides true, but highly selective, Western facts to support these, just as the Western press does with Soviet facts. Turning with relief from the West, the Soviet composer finds, within his own country, the things he needs and seeks: the machinery of music education, of a composer's life, of a composer's success are provided by the state. Severely insular, the Soviet composer does not admit the validity of experimentation, even as in Poland, or of a double style, one for the mass audience and one for the circle of sophisticates, as with Eisler in East Germany. But the memories of the middle generation of Soviet composers reach back to less static times. They, then, are one source of imbalance. Whether the Soviet Union continues its internal progress and remains successful, or whether it should falter and burst asunder, more contact with the West is inevitable—again a threat to the contemporary *status quo*. Perhaps the fundamental overbalance comes, or will come, from within. It has been said that the most dangerous moment for a totalitarian government is when it begins to reform itself. The last three years have seen certain attempts at liberalization and correction of past wrongs from within the Soviet musical establishment. On one hand this has resulted in the 1962 performance of Shostakovich's *Lady Macbeth of Mtsensk*, the first in twenty-five years; and in the first performance and publication of Shostakovich's *Fourth Symphony*, withdrawn by the composer in 1936. It has resulted in the 1962 tour of the Soviet Union by Igor Stravinsky, a man who as recently as 1957 had been called the most objectionable cosmopolitan of them all. On the other hand, it has recently resulted in a hasty intrusion by the Party and its leader, Khrushchev, into musical and other cultural affairs. The Party has intruded with a poorly prepared case, an altogether unusual situation which suggests emergency.

The danger signals are out, and the burden is on the young composers. The disappointment of the Soviet musical establishment in that generation is widespread and well known, and this cannot but be reflected outside the nation. Centrifugal forces, as before in Russia's past, have flung hope to the periphery. Baltic and Transcaucasian composers are eclipsing the Russian. The future of Soviet music seems to lie with these musical arch-Cossacks.

PART TWO

The Older Generation of Soviet Composers

Introduction

In 1882, at the age of twenty-three, Mikhail Mikhailovich Ippolitov-Ivanov finished the course in composition under Rimsky-Korsakov at the St Petersburg Conservatory. After working and travelling, especially in Georgia, this friend of Balakirev, Borodin, and Tschaikovsky moved to Moscow in 1893, teaching composition at the Moscow Conservatory. In 1894 he accepted nineteen-year-old Reinhold Moritsevich Gliere as a student, and in 1901, Sergei Vasilenko, a mature, educated man of twenty-eight, was also accepted into his class. In 1902 Gliere was given an assignment to coach an eleven-year-old musical prodigy, Sergei Sergeevich Prokofieff, at the estate, Sontsovka, where the boy's father was estate manager. A year later Taneev, Gliere's old counterpoint teacher passed a would-be composer over to his former student. This was Nikolai Iakovlevich Miaskovsky, at the time assigned to Moscow with an army sapper battalion. In 1906 Gliere's erstwhile pupils, Prokofieff and Miaskovsky met again under the same composition teacher. They had entered Liadov's class at the St Petersburg Conservatory and became fast friends with a third Liadov pupil, Boris Vladimirovich Asafiev.

In that year, 1906, Ippolitov-Ivanov was 47, Vasilenko was 34, Gliere 31, Miaskovsky 25, Asafiev 22, and Prokofieff was 15. These men, despite the disparity of age, despite the various student-teacher relationships among them, together formed the pre-revolutionary nucleus of Soviet music. These were the men who stayed in or returned to the Soviet Union. These are the core of the 'older generation', those who bridged the gap, creatively, between Tsarist and Communist Russia. They lived relatively long lives: Ippolitov-Ivanov died in 1935 at the age of 76, Asafiev in 1949 at 65, Miaskovsky in 1950 at 69, Prokofieff in 1953 at 64, Vasilenko in 1956 at 84 and Gliere in 1956 at 81. Their musical academic heritage is that of Rimsky-Korsakov, either directly or through his students. Though some eventually moved to Moscow, their creative outlook was that of St Petersburg. They were not slavophiles, nor were they westernizers. They were certainly not as fiercely nationalistic and contemptuous of the West as present Soviet (and some Western) writers hold. They were European composers, proud, to be sure, of their national heritage and the enormous potential their country promised. But they were also enthusiastic about the West and just as proud of being considered a legitimate part of its culture.

To these names one may add those of Vasilii Pavlovich Kalafati (1869–1942, pupil of Rimsky-Korsakov) and Maksimiliam Ossevich Shteinberg (1883–1946, pupil of Rimsky-Korsakov, Liadov, and Glazunov) who were not in the tight group mentioned above, but who have much, including the St Petersburg Conservatory background, in common with the six cited. Aside from these eight composers and teachers, their students and their students' students, there have been and are no composers of significance in the Soviet Union. Considering that some of the eight were in the relationship of pupil to the others, the list of composers may be shortened to three names: Kalafati, Shteinberg, and Ippolitov-Ivanov.[1]

[1] The importance of Taneev is, of course, not to be denied. Taneev, however, was not a teacher of composition as such. He taught counterpoint (and only until 1906 when he resigned from the Moscow Conservatory) to Gliere (an Ippolitov-Ivanov pupil), Goldenweiser (Rimsky-Korsakov), and was undoubtedly some influence on his colleagues Vasilenko, Catoire, Iarovsky and others.

CHAPTER 6

જ⁊જ

Ippolitov-Ivanov

Mikhail Ippolitov-Ivanov was born November 19, 1859,[1] in Gatchina near St Petersburg. His father was a master mechanic, thereby providing the composer with a certifiably proletarian background which stood him in good stead much later. His musical inclinations were discovered early and he began his musical studies in St Petersburg at the Free Music School. From 1872 to 1875 he was also a member of classes for young singers at the huge St Isaac's cathedral. Thereafter he immediately entered the conservatory, finishing the course in instrumentation in 1879. The same year he joined the revived Balakirev circle and began working for a diploma in composition under Rimsky-Korsakov at the conservatory. Ippolitov-Ivanov's musical potential and energy were impressive, and this was not lost upon such established figures as Balakirev, Stasov, and, especially, Rimsky-Korsakov. Upon graduating in 1882 he was the prototype for disciples of the 'Mighty Five'. The overture *Iar-Kmel*, first performed in 1883, was a typical outpouring, being a vaguely colouristic work based on two Russian folk themes. His development and achievements were such that towards the end of 1882, at the age of twenty-three, he was hired and assigned by the Imperial Russian Music Society (IRMS) to Tiflis (Tbilisi) to organize the IRMS activities there. He assumed his post the following summer and played an extra-curricular but not inconsiderable part in

---

[1] Ippolitov-Ivanov was born and educated at a time when he was to become a composer of the 'Silver Age' in Russian Art. Thus, though he is included here as a member of the Soviet transition generation, he was also a member of the second generation, after the 'Mighty Five'. In this latter group his colleagues, not included in this dissertation, were Liadov (1855–1914), Liapunov (1859–1924), Arensky (1861–1906), Taneev (1856–1915), Gretchaninov (1864–1956), Glazunov (1856–1936), Kalafati (1869–1942), and Kastalsky (1856–1926). Whatever the worth of their music, these composers have suffered the consequences of performance saturation in the early part of this century. They, and their generation of Russian composers, are of little interest to the present-day music historian. Even Soviet music scholars tend to ignore them.

Georgian native music development of the late nineteenth century. His duties were many and varied, and he approached them all with the expected vigour. He conducted symphony concerts and helped establish and taught in a music *tekhnikum* (now *uchilishche*). Soon he was a regular conductor of the Tiflis opera, and his own first opera, *Ruth*, had its première there in 1887 under the composer's direction.

Tiflis was far from a city of cultural illiterates in Ippolitov-Ivanov's time. Scenically, and in climate, Georgia is one of the most attractive areas in Eurasia, if not in the world, and cultured, well-to-do Russians and other Europeans had long established it as a resort area for extended vacations. The Italian musical tradition was strong and dominated. The exile of many of the principals in the 1825 Decembrists' uprising to the Caucusus had boosted at least the Russo-European intellectual level of Georgia. The Georgians themselves, for the most part ignored culturally by their European visitors, were a people with a vast and ancient culture, and within a decade or two of Ippolitov-Ivanov's first sojourn the thoroughly Georgian names of Paliashvili, Balanchivadze, and Arakishvili were to dominate the musical scene.

Ippolitov-Ivanov's mission for the IRMS was strictly a European one. The IRMS operated there largely to cater to the Russo-European crowds and to operate schools of music at a profit, musical or monetary. The established private schools of music, as well as the *uchilishche* where Ippolitov-Ivanov was director, had an insignificant number of Georgian students.[1] But Ippolitov-Ivanov was too much a disciple of the 'Mighty Five' to leave the rich store of Georgian church and folk music untouched. Western and Russian appreciation of native Georgian music had been largely confined to the musical bond between the Georgian and Russian Orthodox churches. The exceptional 'westernized' Georgian typically ignored his own culture for that of Petersburg or Moscow. Typical among Georgian musicians is the case of Kharlampi Savaneli (1845–90), the first Georgian with thorough musical training in the North. On his return to Tiflis he organized a music school (1874) whose staff was later augmented by two Moscow-trained fellow-countrymen, A. Mizandari and E. Alikhanov. The school was thoroughly European in curricula, was embraced by the IRMS in 1876, and, in 1882, Savaneli was replaced by Ippolitov-Ivanov. Ippolitov-Ivanov did what Savaneli would not have considered pertinent. He made occasional forays into the mountains to record and study the music of the people. The impulse of those like Ippolitov-Ivanov in the nineteenth century was not to

---

[1] A. Tsulukidze, *Gruzinskaia Muzykal'naia Kul'tura* (Georgian Musical Culture, Moscow: Muzgiz, 1957), p. 100.

'enrich' the people by feeding their own music back to them in standard European formats as is the practice today. Rather, Ippolitov-Ivanov, and later his friend and pupil Gliere in neighbouring Azerbaidzhan, sought colour and new expressive devices. Ippolitov-Ivanov was to use what he found, and to report on it, only after his return to Moscow. His most significant works during the Tiflis period were the operas *Ruth* and *Azra*. The latter was first performed in Tiflis in 1890.

As the IRMS representative and organizer in Tiflis, Ippolitov-Ivanov met many leading Russian cultural figures. Among his acquaintances were the author Ostrovsky, Anton Rubinstein, and Safonov. Perhaps his most valuable contact, though one briefer than contemporary Soviet musicologists imply, was with Tschaikovsky. The latter came to Tiflis to conduct concerts and to be present when his operas were mounted. It was, perhaps, partly due to the acquaintanceship of Safonov and Tschaikovsky that Ippolitov-Ivanov was eventually called to the Moscow Conservatory, although Safonov later left in anger,[1] and Tschaikovsky had long since severed his pedagogical connection with that institution.

In 1889 Ippolitov-Ivanov displayed his conducting talents to Muscovites in an IRMS concert, and, in 1893, the year of Tschaikovsky's death, he accepted a position at the Moscow Conservatory as opera director and teacher of composition. Among his pupils during the four years of his tenure were Gliere, Vasilenko, Goldenweiser, Igumnov, and Nikolaev. From 1906 to 1922 he was the Conservatory's director,[2] holding the position throughout the 1917 political changes.[3]

In 1895 Ippolitiv-Ivanov also assumed the directorship of the Russian

[1] Safanov resigned in 1905, see below.
[2] The 1905 uprisings were partly the cause of a change in the Moscow Conservatory directorship (Ippolitov-Ivanov replacing Safonov), just as they were in the directorship of the St Petersburg Conservatory (Glazunov replacing Rimsky-Korsakov). But the removal of Rimsky-Korsakov and the resigning of Safonov were differently grounded and exhibit, as well as anything, the bewildering double censorship from both left and right to which Russian artists were subject. In St Petersburg, Rimsky-Korsakov first encountered the right and fought it by supporting his pupils' privilege to protest to whomever would listen. He was removed from his post, whereupon Glazunov and Liadov resigned in protest. In Moscow, Taneev resigned, but in protest against his one-time friend Safonov's *suppression* of the students' voice. In the post-1905 reforms, which included granting autonomy to the conservatories, Glazunov assumed the St Petersburg directorship with Rimsky-Korsakov continuing as professor of composition. Safonov, under pressure from the 'left', had repaired in disgust to New York, leaving the conservatory for which he had done so much. Both the St Petersburg and Moscow Conservatories were closed for a while. The Moscow Conservatory re-opened with Ippolitov-Ivanov as director.
[3] His title was changed to 'rector' in 1917.

Choral Society,[1] until 1901, and directed the Moscow University amateur orchestra, an excellent group which has its present-day counterpart at Moscow State University. In 1898 he directed operas for Mamontov[2] until the philanthropist's withdrawal from opera. He continued his opera directing elsewhere thereafter.

During his first years in Moscow, Ippolitov-Ivanov realized his Caucasian research. Starting in 1894 he wrote the *Caucasian Sketches*, *Iveriia*, and *Armenian Rhapsody*. This was also the beginning of his intense activity in religious music. The Moscow choruses and his own religious nature moved him, and he is chiefly remembered and performed today (outside of Soviet Russia) in the church.

In 1922 his duties as conservatory rector were dropped, but he continued his former teaching duties. In 1924 and 1925 Narkompros,[3] whose musical division had assumed the functions, personnel and offices of the IRMS, dispatched him again to Tbilisi to reorganize the conservatory.[4] Upon his return he directed at the Bolshoi Theatre, alternating between this post and his conservatory teaching duties until his death, in Moscow, on January 28, 1935.

The importance of Ippolitov-Ivanov is only incidentally musical. He was creatively a traditionalist—a near arch-conservative. This very fact was important at the beginning of his career when the IRMS sought such a man, rather than the 'rebels' who abounded, for the Tiflis post. Ippolitov-Ivanov sought only to exert himself in the immediate environment. Where music was he went. Where music was needed, he supplied it. The intense conservatism of the post-revolutionary Soviet government suited him as much as the conservatism of the IRMS. He was impatient with innovation when it disturbed the course of things, but accepted it without comment when it seemed to appear in due course. There was, to him, nothing rebellious about conducting Rimsky-Korsakov's operas for Mamontov and Zimin, although these operas

[1] This Choral Society was a choral union existing from 1878 to 1915 with which some illustrious names were connected as directors: Albrecht (the founder), Arensky, Ippolitov-Ivanov, Vasilenko, and Safonov (after his return from abroad). The Society included a choral and conducting school.

[2] Savva Ivanovich Mamontov, 1841-1918, was a rich, qualified dillettante who subsidized and directed a private opera company. This company, the Moskovskaia Chastnaia Russkaia Opera, performed, according to Feodor Chaliapin, many Russian operas including those of Rimsky-Korsakov which the Imperial Opera would not or could not stage in the 1890s.

[3] See Chapter 4, p. 47.

[4] The *uchilishche* which Ippolitov-Ivanov had headed before had been redesignated a conservatory by the independent, Menshevik Georgian government in 1917.

were sneered at in the Imperial theatres. There were an orchestra, singers, and a score: Ippolitov-Ivanov needed nothing more.

Ippolitov-Ivanov was a stranger to controversy. The artistic manifestos, as well as the political ones, of the twenties and thirties were of little interest to him. As a composer, he wrote when music was needed with a disregard of extra-musical circumstances. When a jubilee march was called for, he wrote one, caring little that it was a 'Voroshilov March'. One suspects he didn't know who Voroshilov was.

Finally, Ippolitov-Ivanov's activity on the geographical periphery of what was to become the Soviet Union, especially in Georgia and the Caucausus, was significant. His work there serves as a teaching model to the present day. One can only wonder why he is given so little credit in official histories.

These items far outweigh, for purposes of this report, the significance of Ippolitov-Ivanov as a composer.

CHAPTER 7

꯹꯹꯹

Reinhold Gliere

Reinhold Moritsevich (Maurice) Gliere's musical life extended from deep within Tsarist times to within a few years of the present. He wrote three symphonies, four concertos, four quartets, and a number of vocal works. Otherwise, he was drawn to the stage: He wrote the incidental music to seven plays, five operas, and six ballets. Gliere's early career as a Soviet composer cast him in the role, with Boris Asafiev, of a creator of Soviet ballet. His subsequent career found him laying the foundations for Soviet concertos. His teaching career, at Kiev and Moscow, was long and influential, beginning with Miaskovsky and Prokofieff and including Aleksandrov, Davidenko, Knipper, Litinsky, Liatoshinsky, Mosolov, Rakov, Revutsky, and Aram Khachaturian. He was a capable and busy conductor and was one of the most highly honoured composers in the Soviet Union.

Gliere was surrounded by music from his birth, in Kiev, on January 11, 1875. His father was a successful instrument maker, specializing in work on wind instruments. The senior Gliere played French horn, trumpet, flute, clarinet, and other instruments with varying degrees of ability, and the entire family seems to have absorbed the father's gift. Gliere began studying violin at an early age with A. Weinberg, and soon his prodigious development gained him a place in the evenings of chamber music in his own or Weinberg's home. In spite of the musical atmosphere, or perhaps because of it, Gliere's parents were not enthusiastic about their children's following musical careers. They knew well the shortcomings of a musical vocation for a Jew in the Ukraine.[1] The senior Gliere wanted his son to be a doctor or engineer, but class and race restrictions militated against him there, too. At the age of ten, young Gliere entered the Kiev gymnasium. By 1890 he had made his first tentative efforts at composition and was preparing, under K. A. Bout, to enter the Kiev musical *uchilische* in violin. Studying concurrently in the gymnasium and *uchilishche*, he successfully took and passed

[1] The Gliere family was of Belgian Jewish extraction.

courses in theory and composition (with Rimsky-Korsakov student E. A. Ryb), in piano, and especially in violin. His achievement in the latter was great although his instructors, starting with Weinberg and O. Shevchik, changed consistently. Everything indicated that he should continue in Moscow.

In 1894 he entered the Moscow Conservatory as a violin student under Grzhimali. He indulged his interest in composition from the first, however, studying harmony with Arensky[1] and Konius,[2] polyphony with Taneev, and composition with Ippolitov-Ivanov. Gliere himself felt that Taneev played the central role in forming his creative outlook,[3] but his music does not reveal this. Gliere, however, later fastened on Taneev as a model for teaching. He often used a Taneev device in teaching counterpoint: four parts, the *cantus firmus* in whole notes, one voice in second, one in third, and one in ligature species. Gliere graduated in 1900 with the gold medal in composition, the conservatory's highest award. By this time he had already completed an opera (Earth and Heaven), his first quartet, an octet and his first symphony.

By the end of his stay in Moscow Gliere had become one of many musicians of the day who passed frequently between St Petersburg and Moscow. Thus, while still based in the latter city, teaching harmony and analysis at the five-year-old Gnessin school, he became an enthusiastic member of the revived Beliaev circle in St Petersburg. Two students were referred to him by Taneev in 1900. Both were ineligible for entrance to the conservatory, Miaskovsky because of his army obligations and Prokofieff because of his youth. Gliere, well acquainted with the music and musicians of both Moscow and St Petersburg, was instrumental in influencing Prokofieff ultimately to enter the conservatory in the northern capital.

Just as intercourse between the two principal Russian cities was common in the early years of this century, so was that between Russia and capitals of the West. In 1905 Gliere left for Berlin for further study. He was well referred and well received in Berlin; his second symphony was premièred there in 1907. Also in 1907 Gliere began an intensive study of conducting under Oskar Fried. Upon his return to Russia he

---

[1] Anton Stepanovich Arensky (1861–1906) was a composer, pianist, and director. In 1895 he became director of the Court a cappella Choir in St Petersburg. His romantic texts on harmony and analysis are still used occasionally.

[2] Georgii Eduardovich Konius (1862–1933) was a composer and teacher of theory who delved into the abstract theory of musical creativity as separate from technique.

[3] Igor Bel'za in *Kontserty Gliera* (Gliere's Concertos, Moscow-Leningrad, Muzgiz), p. 4.

embarked on a short-lived conducting career. His training, his talents, and especially his conducting gave him at the time the aspect of the 'big' Russian musician: the aspect of the *deiateli* like Ippolitov-Ivanov, Koussevitsky, Safonov and others. However, his financial backing, unlike those mentioned, was not up to sustaining the image. It may just as well have been his style of conducting, which has been described as 'not flamboyant in the respected manner of the time, but placid and thorough'.[1]

In 1913 the Kiev music *uchilishche* was upgraded by the Imperial Russian Music Society to a conservatory, and Gliere joined the staff. The creative atmosphere at the time, according to Vladimir Dukelsky, was heavily that of Scriabin. Scriabin's son, Julian, was also a pupil of Gliere's.[2] In 1914 Gliere became director of the conservatory and continued in that post until he left for Moscow in 1920. He was instrumental, therefore, not only in establishing the new conservatory, but in implementing its transition from an IRMS to a Soviet institution. Gliere's return to Kiev may be considered as symbolic of his extreme traditonalist turn about this time. According to Sezhensky,[3] 'Gliere was one of the first big composers responding to the call of Soviet power and assuming his stand in the ranks of builders of Soviet musical culture'.[4] Actually, and again this must be emphasized in connection with most of the older generation of composers, Gliere was apolitical, but expedient and conservative in the cause of music. He had little part in the various

[1] For this and certain other information about Gliere the author is indebted to Vladimir Dukelsky (Vernon Duke), a onetime student of Gliere's at the Kiev Conservatory and now a resident of Santa Monica, California.

[2] The Scriabin family had moved to Kiev after the composer's death. Young Julian died in the spring of 1918, apparently from a stroke suffered upon entering the water of the Don River. Vladimir Dukelsky says that in the temporary absence of the mother, Nicolas Slonimsky took charge of the week-long search for the body.

[3] K. Sezhensky, *R. M. Gliere* (Moscow: Mozgiz, 1940), n., p. 12.

[4] Ukrainian sympathies were strongly for independence. During the summer of 1919, when the Bolsheviks were holding the Ukraine, partisan activity against them was widely based. Vladimir Dukelsky tells of the interruption of a counterpoint class by a Cheka representative and two music commissars who required of the assemblage a Soviet opera within two weeks. The Bolsheviks were subsequently driven out and the Ukrainian Soviet Republic was proclaimed. Poland asserted military claims and under General Pilsudsky entered Kiev on May 7, 1920, but had to retreat, having succeeded only in uniting anti-Polish feeling. A military stalemate led to an armistice (October 12, 1920), and an end to the fighting (March 18, 1921), leaving Poland in possession of those areas historically Polish but ethnically partly Ukrainian and Byelorussian. Gliere's move to Moscow was made in 1920, when Bolshevik power in the Kiev area was, in spite of guerilla activity, a reality.

musico-political groups of the early Soviet Union. Since all these foundered, it has made of him, in retrospect, a hero today. However, at the time, he was criticized for his lack of interest and lack of political direction. For present day purposes his peripheral association with the Proletkul't[1] is ignored.

In 1920 Gliere became a professor of composition at the Moscow Conservatory, continuing in that post until the outbreak of the Second World War. His pupils, as mentioned earlier, were many. His creative attention had turned to the stage as late as 1917; until then he had but one opera (Earth and Heaven, 1900) and one ballet-pantomime (Crisis, 1912) to his credit. Of the three ballets written during the twenties: *Komedianty*, written in 1922 but not performed until 1930 after extensive revision, *Cleopatra*, 1925, and the *Red Poppy*, 1926–7; it was the latter which was to be hailed as the foundation of Soviet opera.[2] The story involves revolutionary activity in China. Musically it is a Rimsky-Korsakov-Glazunov combination of glittering orchestral colour and the Russian notion of oriental tunes.

In 1923 Gliere was invited by arrangement between Narkompros Moscow and Narkompros Azerbaidzhan to the latter republic to help in the 'Soviet' development of that country. This was the year that Ippolitov-Ivanov was invited under similar auspices and with identical aims to return to Georgia. It is difficult to see why Azerbaidzhan needed Gliere musically. Although the development of 'europeanized' music was not as great as in Georgia, there were sufficient strong musicians with European training in Baku.[3] Moreover, Gliere, with an almost total ignorance of Arabo-Turkic-Caucasian art could not expect to add to the extensive, Western based ethnomusicological research of the remarkable Gadzhibekov. It must have been difficult for Gadzhibekov, himself an opera composer, to say of Gliere's *Shakh-Senem*, 'it is the basis of the strong beginning of new Azerbaidzhanian operatic culture'. *Shakh-Senem* had subsequently to be purged of its Persianisms, a process which nearly made a new opera out of it, since Azerbaidzhanian folk music, contrary to Soviet theory, is largely Persian based. Contemporary Russian musicology has established the category, 'Russian music *about* the East' (author's underlining) into which *Shakh-Senem* is now placed. Moreover, the question of the musical logic of sending Gliere to

[1] Narkompros, which was essentially the old IRMS, was involved with folk music through association with the Proletkul't.

[2] *Cleopatra* also left its mark. It was the first ballet to incorporate exotic dances whose appeal is akin to that of a mild *Folies Bergère* presentation. The element has become standard in Soviet ballet.

[3] See the section on Uzeir Gadzhibekov, p. 132.

3*

Azerbaidzhan, as well as of the significance of *Shakh-Senem* is solved with this reasoning:

"The creation and mounting of *Shakh-Senem* strengthened Soviet operatic art and levelled a severe blow at the bourgeois nationalism which was trying to separate Azerbaidzhanian culture from Russian (and which) asserted the impossibility-in-principle of the enrichment of Azerbaidzhanian music with the experience of the Russian musical classics.'[1]

Gliere's mission, like that of many an established Russian musician, was a diplomatic one. Although *Shakh-Senem* contains some fine music, what Gliere helped establish was not the Azerbaidzhanian school of opera, but, rather, the tradition of Great Russian cultural hegemony over the Azerbaidzhanian minority. Gliere stayed in Azerbaidzhan through 1923 and 1924, and returned in 1929 for an extended stay. There is little evidence of a musical legacy, however. Gadzhibekov and other Azerbaidzhanians were fairly impervious to the influence of the facile Northerner and managed to Westernize their culture and pervert their folk tradition without his help.

When all independent cultural organizations were disbanded in 1932 and the Party and State assumed the organizational obligations of Soviet artists, Gliere correctly perceived the basically conservative thinking involved, and it naturally attracted him:

'The decision of the Central Committee (of the Party), thanks to its clarity and accuracy, is not only an organizational beginning, but also an artistic one in that (po skol'ku) it gives courage to Soviet artists to go ahead, firmly resolving the problems standing before Soviet art'.[2]

In 1937 Gliere became the head of the Moscow Union of Soviet Composers. From 1938 to 1948 he presided over the organizational bureau of the nationwide USC.

Gliere moved away from opera and ballet in the thirties, but not from the stage and screen. His activity during this period was in the dramatic theatres, where he wrote incidental music to seven plays, and in films. The mantle of composer of Soviet ballet passed to Alexander Krein and Sergei Prokofieff, the latter recently returned for good from a long sojourn in the West. Gliere's attention also turned to more 'social' music. During this period he wrote the *Festival Overture* to commemorate the twentieth anniversary of the revolution in 1937; *Fergana Holiday*, dedicated to the construction, then in progress, of the Stalin Fergana canal (using Uzbek and Tadzhik themes); the *Friendship of*

---

[1] *IRSM*, I, 166.   [2] *Musical Almanac* for 1932.

Peoples Overture, celebrating the fifth anniversary of the Stalin Constitution; and the *Heroic March of the Buriat-Mongol Autonomous Republic*.

With the advent of the war Gliere's teaching was interrupted and was never to continue. In common with many Soviet composers, his music took an even more nationalistic turn, but the change was not so marked in Gliere as in other, younger composers. Gliere, from his firmly conservative, nationalistic position became a leader in the move to an established style. Had he been a greater talent, a more articulate and stronger leader, the events of 1948 might not have happened. Under the Soviet system of rewards and punishments for artistic activity, Gliere was one of the most honoured of Soviet composers. He became a Peoples Artist of the Azerbaidzhan SSR in 1934, of the RSFSR in 1936, of the Uzbek SSR in 1937 and, finally, of the Soviet Union in 1938. He was awarded the Order of the Red Banner of Labour in 1937 and the Order of Honour in 1938. These years (1934-8), it must be remembered, were those of the Moscow trials and of condemnation for other artists such as Meyerhold and Shostakovich. Later, Gliere was to receive three Orders of Lenin (1945, 1950, 1955—these are usually birthday honours) and three first-degree Stalin Prizes (1946—Concerto for Voice and Orchestra, 1948—Fourth String Quartet, and 1950—*The Bronze Horseman*, a ballet).

Internal political strife in the South and East found Gliere on the musical front lines again with the drama *Giul'sara* (1936), based on Tadzhik folk collections, and some minor works on Buriat Mongol themes. To his many honours were added those of the republics mentioned.

During the period from 1939 through 1951 Gliere wrote four concertos which have had a considerable impact on Soviet music. These were for harp (opus 74, 1939), soprano voice (opus 82, 1942-3), 'cello (opus 87, 1947) and French horn (opus 91, 1951). The work for French horn and orchestra is the least significant, musically. The 'cello concerto, although it too is uninteresting and seems to indicate declining powers, was a milestone of a significant sort: this is not only the first Soviet 'cello concerto, but the first Russian 'cello concerto. The only example of anything approaching this genre in the history of Russian music is the Tschaikovsky Variations on a Rococo Theme.[1] Moreover, the work's dedication, to Mstislav Rostropovich, marks the beginning of a Soviet phenomenon that could well be the envy of Western composers. Rostropovich's thirst for new music is insatiable. There is hardly a Soviet composer of any stature, young or old, who has not been approached by the 'cellist. Gliere was the first. The many others have found that

[1] Igor Bel'za, *Kontserty Gliera*, p. 38.

responding to Rostropovich's request invariably means performance and often publication. By 1960 there was a tremendous body of 'cello literature under the collective Soviet belt, including an impressive number of concertos; and this is largely due to the demand of Rostropovich. He has, in the process, run afoul of some of the world's worst 'cello music, including perhaps the Gliere score, but that is easily forgotten. One need only consider the Shostakovich concerto[1] which Rostropovich inspired and which seemed to bring the composer far away from the banalities of his Eleventh and Twelfth Symphonies. The Gliere harp concerto was also unusual in its choice of instrument, and also was a refreshing exercise in orchestral economy. Whereas the 'cello concerto used an augmented orchestra, the harp work is supported by an orchestra of near chamber size. The former is the most monumental of the four concertos, the latter, the most intimate. In all the concertos the last movement is simple, dance-like and in 'brave' style. This pattern has become, with the inevitable exception of Shostakovich, the norm for Soviet composers.

In many other ways this quartet of concertos has formed the basis of the Soviet school of concerto writing. The second, for voice and orchestra, is the most widely known and performed, and, in itself, has become a concise reference on how to write a Soviet concerto. The choice of solo instrument is also unique in this concerto. That departure, the only one, is also the single facet of the work not duplicated since.[2] The first of two movements is an Andante based on two simple, contrasting, but rhythmically related themes. A muted, octave string passage in restless rhythm (Example 1) yields shortly to the first theme in the solo voice (Example 2 quotes the entire theme with some indication of accompanying colour). A counterpoint (characterized in Example 3) is mounted by the flutes and clarinets. The motion ends with the second theme already heard in the clarinet and horns, joined shortly by the soprano voice (Example 4). The material and its use so far epitomizes, for Gliere and most Soviet composers, the classical 'Russian', traditional sound, i.e. with characteristics of Eastern folk songs and instruments. The Western view, on the other hand, would simply place the foregoing material in the romantic category. Either view is right, depending on the direction of the glance. Further, the rhythmic fragment characteristic of both themes (♩♩♩) is developed briefly and with no strain on the intellect. The formal recapitulation contains further development in the form of virtuoso variations on the main theme in the solo voice

[1] See p. 202.

[2] The work was first performed in 1943 by the soprano Nadezhda Kozantseva.

and clarinet. The second theme returns briefly, properly in the tonic, and the opening material reappears to close the movement as quietly as it had begun.

The second and final movement is a gesture in the direction of rondo form. It is, in the main, a concert waltz with three principal themes. The first is declamatory (Example 5a), the second more lyrical with a touch of chromaticism (Example 5b), and the third is a waltz in the compelling, kinesthetic sense of a ball (Example 5c). Beyond that there is little more to say. Waltzes one and two are each presented twice, ABA, and waltz three departs to the mediant key. In the latter tonality, two fragments, the first (Example 6a) unrelated, assume prominence. The second fragment (Example 6b) is built on an introductory statement and accompanies the aimless, artless, coloratura vocal line. The tonality reverts to the dominant (C major), and waltz one returns in full orchestral voice. The coda is a variant of waltz three (Example 7), in staccato syncopes, which leads into a pyrotechnic, 11-measure cadence.

While withholding final judgment, one can recognize that the work may be disappointing as a concerto. The classic opposition and juxtaposition are ignored for coloratura display, broken only by tutti orchestral passages during which the soprano apparently regains wind. Developmental possibilities are largely ignored. The form accomplishes little since no problems are posed, statements are laconic, the accompaniment never goes beyond pianistic figurations. Yet, this combination of factors is almost essential to the safe but successful dramaturgy of presentation. Here, in the Western view, drama has displaced form: in the Soviet view, drama *is* form. It is this element, mainly, that lends the work its importance in Soviet composition. The implied 'orientalism' is notable, too, as a stereotype, and so is the unrestrained and unashamed use of an accompaniment which is essentially an orchestrated piano part.

Gliere's return to opera and ballet after a ten-year break, reaffirmed his position as a Soviet composer for the stage. Working as co-author with Talib Sadykov, Gliere's student at the conservatory Uzbek Studio, and a *nai* virtuoso, he wrote two operas: *Leili and Medzhnun* and a beefed-up, Russified version of *Giul'sara* for the operatic stage. In 1942–3 he wrote the opera *Rashel'*, based on de Maupassant's *Mademoiselle Fifi*. He returned to the ballet genre with *The Bronze Horseman*[1] (1948–9) and *Taras Bul'ba* (1951–2). His last ballet was

---

[1] The mounted statue of Peter the Great on the banks of the Neva in Leningrad, i.e. the 'Bronze Horseman', is used extensively in Soviet as well as Russian Art as a symbol of the city, of enlightened Tsardom, and of Russia herself. The nickname is from Pushkin's poem.

Gliere. *Concerto for voice and orchestra*

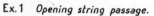

Ex.1   *Opening string passage.*

Ex.2   *First theme.*

Ex.3

Ex.4 *Second theme.*

Ex.5   *2nd movement themes.*

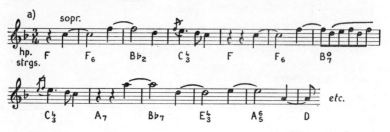

Ex. 6 *Unrelated fragments.*

a)

etc.

b)

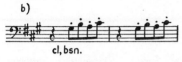

cl, bsn.

Ex. 7 *Variant, waltz three.*

sopr.

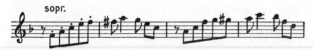

Daughter of Castille (1955) after Lope de Vega. But, in all these, Gliere seemed to be running on momentum. His *Leili and Medzhnun* was a poor third or fourth among the other settings of the old tale.[1] *The Bronze Horseman* was safe stage and was given performances. It is simple fare, and, in a greatly shortened version, still appears on the less demanding provincial stage. Gliere visited the Middle-East again and was given the welcome of an old friend. But the students to whom he returned had gone far beyond him.

Gliere was scarcely mentioned in the 1948 blanket condemnation of prominent composers. His health was not good in the last few years, and his teaching activity had long since ended, although he occasionally appeared for a conservatory master class. Although he continued working until the end of his life, his output in the last years was, for him, relatively small. Much of the time from 1948 on was spent at the Moscow Union of Soviet Composers' rest and recreation resort at Ivanovo. There the 'older' generation tended to gather. He saw a great deal of his two first students, Miaskovsky and Prokofieff, before their deaths in 1950 and 1953, respectively. Only Goldenweiser and Shaporin of Gliere's chronological generation were still alive when he died, in Moscow, on June 23, 1956.

[1] See pp. 313, 314.

CHAPTER 8

Sergei Vasilenko

Although of Ukrainian ancestry, Sergei Nikiforovich Vasilenko
was born in Moscow, on March 30, 1872 and remained closely
identified with that city throughout his life. The life was long:
he died at nearly 84 in 1956. His identification with Moscow and his
extended sojourn there at the Moscow Conservatory lend him an
importance far greater than his creative powers would suggest. He was
a doctrinaire composer, even in his continuous essays at 'modernism'.
He taught, and was a respected teacher, at the conservatory. He was
only mildly controversial, never enough to become embroiled politically, and he was highly honoured by the State. Vasilenko's career is
closely parallel to those of Ippolitov-Ivanov, Asaf'ev, and most of all,
Gliere. He shared with the latter a long life,[1] each was of the conservative 'Moscow' persuasion, both were interested in ethnomusicology as a
creative source. Of the two, Vasilenko was the more sophisticated,
Gliere, perhaps, the more talented.

Vasilenko's father was a teacher in a Moscow gymnasium, thus the
family fit into the lower echelons of the intelligentsia and the middle
class. Vasilenko's own training was typical of his class: gymnasium and
law school. Although he was attracted early to music, there was no
suggestion, at first, of its being a career for a middle-class Muscovite.
Nevertheless, by the time of his graduation from Moscow University's
juridical faculty in 1896, Vasilenko had already written some music,
notably the incidental music to a staging of Euripides *Alceste*.[2] By the
time of his graduation he was already involved at the Moscow Conservatory. He was an apt student and finished with the gold medal in composition under Ippolitov-Ivanov.[3] He had studied counterpoint with
Taneev, and he also graduated as an accomplished pianist. In that area,

---

[1] Gliere was Vasilenko's junior by two years. They died within four months of
one another in 1956.
[2] S. Vasilenko, *Stranitsy vospominanii* (Moscow: Muzgiz, 1948), p. 10.
[3] Gliere had graduated the year previously, 1900, also with the gold medal.

as well as in conducting, he was a pupil of Safanov's. In his memoirs, after the predictable doffing of the hat to Ippolitov-Ivanov and Taneev, Vasilenko gives much of the space to his relationship with Safonov.

Vasilenko remained in Moscow. He conducted in private opera companies, and by 1906 he was again with the Moscow Conservatory as teacher of orchestration.[1] In 1907 he became a Professor of orchestration and composition, at the early age of thirty-one. Thus his early professional career fell during the disturbing years after 1905. It is said of him during this time:

'In the years of political and social reaction resulting from the defeat of the 1905 revolution, Vasilenko fell under the influence of modish, modernistic tendencies which separated him for a long time from the realistic direction . . . Exoticism, impressionistic refinement, devilishness (chertovshchina) and symbolism . . . appeared, especially in such works as "The Garden of Death" (on Oscar Wilde, 1908), "Maori Songs" (1913), The "Exotic Suite" (1916) . . . "Child of the Son" (1929), and "Noah" (1932).[2]

Thus Vasilenko can fairly be said to have shared the curiosity of most Russian musicians during the period of experimentation starting around the turn of the century. But the experimentation was mild. He leaned strongly to Debussy and impressionism but seemingly never understood or accepted the atonal implications thereof. His harmonic vagaries are actually strongly rooted in tonality. Nor did the organic form and motivic development enter his style. He substituted drama for form and extended melody for motive.

In 1907 and continuing until 1917 he directed series of 'Open Historical Concerts' (Obshchedostupnye Istoricheskie Kontserty). These were the continuation of a tradition begun by Anton Rubinstein in the 1880s and were the forerunner of such 'innovations' in subsequent Soviet times. Vasilenko was active with his orchestra in 'factories and clubs, and even arranged music for the small groups demanded'.[3] Very little of his pre-revolutionary music is remembered. The most significant would be his first quartet (1899), his graduate work 'Legend of the City of Kitezh' and the 'Still Lake Svetoiar' (1900), 'The Whirlwind' and 'The Widow' (both for voice and orchestra, 1903), the First Symphony (1904), the Second (1911–13), and a violin concerto (1913).

---

[1] His entry into service at the Moscow Conservatory was connected with the semi-political upheaval which also sent Safonov to New York.

[2] G. Bernandt. *Sovetskiie kompozitory: laureaty stalinskoi premii* Moscow: Muzgiz, 1952), p. 26, This is an evaluation made in an environment of Stalin aesthetics. It is not necessarily accepted in full today.

[3] *IRSM*, I, p. 28.

The 'Maori Songs', the 'Exotic Suite' and 'The Garden of Death', as implied in the quotation on page 83 have no influence whatsoever on contemporary Soviet music. Yet it was precisely here that Vasilenko first set foot on the threshold of tonality, where he wavered so long. Like Strauss he seemed about to sever the tonal tie in pursuit of the exotic, erotic, morbid, or even perverse idea. But Vasilenko was never so virile as Strauss. These works, of which only scraps exist, seem pale by mid-century standards. The composer later turned his back on them.

Vasilenko met the 1932 artistic reforms with the following words:

'The decree of the Central Committee of the Communist Party of 23 April, 1932, is the beginning of a new era, opening in our musical art wide horizons of magnificent growth.'[1]

Vasilenko was one of the group of Moscow composers which became the first directorate of the Moscow Union of Soviet Composers.[2] By this time he had fifteen years of Soviet production behind him. He had turned partially to folk song and utility 'mass' music, but had also maintained an appreciation for non-Soviet sources of inspiration. In 1924 he wrote the ballet-pantomime 'Noah' and, in 1924, the ballet 'Joseph the Beautiful'. 'Child of the Sun' was written in 1929 and is operatically concerned with the Chinese rebellion of 1900.

Operas and ballets occupied Vasilenko much as they had Asaf'ev and, to a lesser extent, Gliere. Like Asaf'ev, Vasilenko thought of ballet as a utilitarian, 'business music' vehicle. Among his eight ballets those just mentioned were on religious themes. *Sunlit Lights* (1926) and *Lola* (1926) were made-to-order, derivative, clever but light works. *Lola* was staged in a new edition in 1943. *Triangle* (1935), *Gypsies* (1936), and *Akbiliak* (1942) were Spanish, Gypsy, and Turkmen derived mood settings respectively. *Triangle* was largely a craftsmanlike job of stringing existing Spanish composed music into a danceable whole. Vasilenko's 'investigation' of sixteenth- and seventeenth-century Spanish music for this enterprise helped earn him a doctorate in musicology. Of the five operas *Buran*[3] must be singled out. This was Vasilenko's main contribution to the tradition started by Ippolitov-Ivanov in Georgia and Gliere in Azerbaidzhan. *Buran* is a Tadzhik piece written by Vasilenko with a Tadzhik composer, Mukhtar Ashrafi, in 1938. It lacks the continuity of Asaf'ev's 'middle eastern' works for the stage. The operas

---

[1] *Pravda.* April 24, 1932.

[2] The others were A. N. Aleksandrov, Gedike, Gliere, Goldenweiser, Igumnov, Ippolitov-Ivanov, A. Krein, Miaskovsky, and Feinberg. (*IRSM*, I, p. 72.)

[3] 'Buran' is the name of the Tadzhik hero. Apparently this has somewhere been mistranslated 'Snowstorm' or 'Storm' since a number of English sources thus misname the opera.

Great Canal (1940) and *Suvorov* (1941) were in the nationalistic tradition of the thirties, the first depicting Soviet achievement, the second, a Russian military hero of Napoleonic times.

The third of Vasilenko's four symphonies, the 'Italian' (!) is for an orchestras of domras[1] and balalaikas. The fourth is another monument to Soviet achievement, 'The Arctic'. One of the four concertos is for balalaika. In addition to these genres Vasilenko worked in the area of the art song, writing more than sixty.

To some extent he held fast through this period of creative activity (the thirties and forties) to the feckless expression that had once been called impressionistic and later modernistic. This may have been a defence of an inability to organize his music harmonically. It may, too, have been the product of an easy-going composer hesitating on the harmonic threshold, waiting for permission to enter a new room. The invitation was never issued, and, in fact, Vasilenko's wrists were lightly slapped on several occasions. At the same time, however, he was displayed as a model for the younger composers, largely for his activity on the approved triple-front: use of and development of middle-eastern folk music, use of Russian folk instruments, and the composition of patriotic music.

After 1950, apparently, he tired of waiting. At any rate, his pen dried up. In fact, no significant work is listed for Vasilenko after 1946. It has been suggested that he was unwell. In any case, he was immersed in teaching until 1950 when he retired from the conservatory. His book on orchestration was published in 1952. On March 11, 1956, in Moscow, he died.

Vasilenko was far from a great and, perhaps, not even a good composer. This judgment still leaves him near the top among Soviet composers. He seems to have been deprecated posthumously at the hands of his colleagues. Prokofieff, Gliere, Miaskovsky, and Shaporin are reported as wishing whenever possible to avoid him personally. *IRSM* says of him 'there is nothing new, nothing vital in Vasilenko . . . (his) music did not play a significant role'.[2] If this is Vasilenko's epitaph, then it must be found on many a headstone in the graveyard of Soviet composers.

---

[1] The domra is an old Russian folk instrument, apparently of Turkic origin, first in reported use by the old *skomorokhi*. Modifications and improvements were made on the instrument in 1895 (the Andreev domra) and in 1908 and 1914 (the Liubimov domra) after a century of little use. The instrument is plucked, has three (sometimes four) strings and is tuned in 4ths (sometimes fifths). It comes in seven sizes: piccolo, prima, secunda, alto, tenor, bass, and contrabass.

[2] *IRSM*, II, 305 and 320.

༞༞༞

CHAPTER 9

Boris Asaf'ev

B oris Vladimirovich Asaf'ev was an influential figure in Russian and Soviet music from at least 1908 to his death in 1949. If his composition is discussed only briefly here it is because his influence as a musicologist and critic outweighs his contribution as a composer. One might better say that if Asaf'ev had written no music at all (which is decidedly not the case) an account of his influence as a musicologist must still properly appear in what is fundamentally a document on Soviet composers.

Asaf'ev was actively present at those periods one tends to accept as critical in Soviet music: he was one of the most articulate preservers of tradition over the revolutionary period, a close friend and idea source for Anatole Lunacharsky[1]; at the same time he was at the head of the Leningrad avant-garde group; he headed the teaching division of MUZO Narkompros and was consultant to the latter; he was a member of the Institute of History and Art and founder of its music section, now one of the most important musical archives in the Soviet Union; his ballet works, with Gliere's, became the stereotypes for Soviet ballet; he aided, with misgivings apparently, the 1932 re-formation of artistic groups; he rewrote history in the mid-thirties and, yet, was again active in the liberal movement during the Second World War; he was professor at both the Moscow and Leningrad Conservatories and was the only musician ever named to full membership in the Soviet Academy of Sciences; finally, he was dramatically conspicuous by his absence at the January 1948 Zhandov 'lectures', but made a puzzling appearance in support of Party directives at the All-Union Congress of Composers called to evaluate the new dictums two months later.

His has become the vocabulary of Soviet musical science, although none wield it so well as he.

Asaf'ev was born in St Petersburg in 1884, son of a highly placed

---

[1] Anatole Lunacharsky, 1875–1933; see Chapter 3, p. 33.

civil servant.[1] His native musical talent, appearing early, was in the classical prodigy tradition: absolute pitch, almost total tonal recall, an impressive keyboard technique, self-teaching, etc. Although his parents seemed neither to appreciate nor understand the display of musical talent, there was no effort to block his entry into the conservatory when he was twenty. He had, a year earlier, enrolled in the university and, in the European tradition, continued to a diploma in both institutions.

Stasov's was an important early influence, both in thinking about music and socially. Through Stasov, Asaf'ev became acquainted with Gorky and Repin and with the musicians Chaliapin, Glazunov, and Liadov. Under the latter, Asaf'ev studied composition, graduating from the St Petersburg Conservatory in 1910. He had finished the university in 1908. His precosity marked him,[2] but so did the twin stigmas of dilettantism and an inability to rise, in his original work, above the level of 'accompanist'.

Upon graduation from the conservatory Asaf'ev took the post of repiteteur for the Mariinsky theatre *corps de ballet*. He soon became musical consultant and composer there, continuing until 1937. At the same time his energy and drive to be 'professional' brought out other talents.

From 1911 to 1914 he travelled and studied independently in Germany, France, Italy, and Austria. He returned and began to write about music and to organize music along the lines he had thought so effective in the West. To his list of talents now must be added that of organizer. He founded the Leningrad Philharmonic Association, organized musical and historical exhibitions, organized the history-criticism faculty at the Petrograd Conservatory, reorganized the pedagogical section of MUZO Narkompros, and led, with Iurii Shaporin, the Leningrad branch of the Association of Contemporary Musicians. Throughout his life his talent for organization and leadership was sought at critical moments, ultimately as spokesman for the Party in the reorganization in 1948. He was named to the presidium of the newly constituted Union of Soviet Composers in mid-1948, serving some five to six months before his death.

His first articles, under the pseudonym of Igor Glebov,[3] had appeared

---

[1] An account that he had to help support the family at the age of ten seems spurious.

[2] Stasov, in 1904, had written to his brother, 'Asaf'ev simply amazed me. He is self-taught, has studied with no one, but plays the piano excellently, not as a pianist (this he will never be), but as an excellent musician. He plays the whole Russian school (operas, symphonies, art songs) by heart, is an excellent accompanist and reads with ease. . . .'

[3] The name was assigned him by Vladimir Vladimirovich Derzhanovsky, *Muzyka's* editor.

by 1914 in the Moscow journal *Muzyka*. Here, perhaps, was his genius most evident. With an accurate, rich and inventive vocabulary, and with the maturity and knowledge of a big mind, he discussed and embraced past, present, and future; East and West. He had the ability, rare among European music critics of that time, to accept and encourage the avant-garde on whatever terms, but at the same time to provide the essential ties with, and appreciation for, the past. It is, perhaps, Asaf'ev's greatest tragedy that this unique and vital, creative embracing of contiguous and contradictory musical epochs is dismissed today as a personality 'contradiction'.

Asaf'ev's early writing was specifically in the selective, pro-Russian vein of Stasov: without denigrating Western music he sought an equal appreciation of Russian music. Even when the 'contradictions' had been purged, Asaf'ev's labour of love was that of unpeeling the layers of ignorance around the Russian musical heritage. He clearly sensed a new musical era, but realized that essential to its flourishing was a far broader base, among the people, of understanding creative tradition. His effort to 'spread the base' through schools and easily accessible writings[1] was, of course, no new Soviet tradition, but a continuation of the traditions of the Russian 'Silver Age' in the Arts. Asaf'ev was involved in the editorship of most of the short-lived journals of the twenties.[2] His work with these, especially *De Musica*[3] and his outstanding works of 1929–30, *Kniga o Stravinskom*,[4] *Russkaia muzyka ot nachala XIX stoletiia*,[5] and *Muzykal'naia forma kak protsess*,[6] placed him at the head of Soviet musicologists, both in volume and influence. The last of these, with its companion second volume[7] is the single major influence on contemporary Soviet musicological vocabulary and methodology.

---

[1] Asaf'ev wrote small pamphlets or brochures on Tschaikovsky, Rachmaninov, Liszt, Gluzunov, Rimsky-Korsakov, Stravinsky, Krenek, Berg, Hindemith, and others which were distributed with symphony programmes. These were designed for audience enlightenment before and during the intermission at concerts. The best known series, *Putevoditel' po kontsertam* (Concert guide) began in 1919.

[2] Asaf'ev refused, however, until all other routes to publication were closed, to write for the proletarian art groups' journals.

[3] *De Musica* was published three times, in 1925, 1926 and 1927 in Petrograd. Asaf'ev was editor.

[4] *Kniga o Srtavinskom* (Book on Stravinsky, Leningrad: Triton, 1929, 398 pp.)

[5] *Russkaia muzyka ot nachala XIX stoletiia* (Russian music from the beginning of the nineteenth century, Moscow-Leningrad, Akademiia, 1930, 319 pp.).

[6] *Muzykal'naia forma kak protsess* (Musical form as a process, vol. I, Moscow Mozsektor Gosizdat, 1930).

[7] Volume II of *MFKP* (Intonatsiia-Intonation) was published in 1947 by Muzgiz.

Asaf'ev's career was marked by the now tiresome political ups and downs. At times extravagantly lionized,[1] at times bitterly condemned, he did concede, point by point, many of his positions on modernism and Western musical development. Yet, Andrei Olkhovsky can say of him:

'To anyone who was connected in any way with Asaf'ev or who had carefully read his works it was unmistakably clear that his world outlook and his musical aesthetic conceptions, those which he professed himself and which he persistently . . . implanted in his pupils, did not change one iota during his entire career of almost half a century, half of it under the harsh conditions of Soviet reality.[2]

There was little of the avant-garde modernist in Asaf'ev the composer. With the exception of a rash of operas in the thirties and forties, a few songs and incidental music for the stage, Asaf'ev was *primo* composer for the Soviet ballet. By 1918 he had already written seven. During the twenties he wrote only one; in the thirties he wrote ten, and in the forties, nine, that is, averaging one a year for the last nineteen years of his life. Not all of these were original, not all were finished, but they establish him, from first to last, as a practical man, if not a genius, of theatre music.

The first important ballet was *Plamia Parizha* (Flames of Paris)[3] based on the revolutionary and immediate post-revolutionary scene in Paris of the 1790s. Asaf'ev used popular music of the period: *The Marseillaise*, *Carmagnola*, *Ça Ira*, and, with the aplomb of Handel, fragments from Lully, Gluck, Gretry, Mehul, Gossec, Lesueur, and Cherubini. Asaf'ev was not interested in individuality:

' I worked on the given problem not only as a composer-dramaturgist, but also as a musicologist, historian and theoretician; and as a literateur not avoiding the methods of the contemporary historical novel.[4]

[1] He was named Honoured Art Worker of the RSFSR in 1933, Peoples' Artist of the RSFSR in 1938, and Peoples' Artist of the USSR in 1947. He was also the recipient of a number of Stalin Prizes. See chapter 2, p. 30 for an account of the Soviet creative awards system.

[2] Andrei Olkhovsky, *Music Under the Soviets* (New York: Praeger, 1955), p. 81.

[3] Of the previous ballets, the five pre-1917 scores have been lost. *Solvejg* (based on Grief's music—alternative titles: The Ice Maiden, Ballet of the North) 1918, appeared briefly in 1922 in Leningrad and was just as briefly revived in 1927. Both performances were on the occasion of the revolution's anniversary. The piano score of *Carmagnola* is lost and there was an orchestral version. This ballet, premièred at a Petrograd workers' club, was the model for *Plamia Parizha*. *Eternal Blooms* has not survived in score. It was written as a children's ballet.

[4] From Asaf'ev's article, 'Muzyka "tret'ego sosloviia" ', from the collection *Flames of Paris* (Leningrad GATOB, 1936), p. 6.

The effort was largely lost on his musical colleagues. The usage in *Plamia Parizha* was trite, arrangements pedestrian. Still the initial success of the ballet was undeniable. Asaf'ev knew the stage and was aware of his audience. His dramatic handling, contrasts, relief, dramatic crescendo and decrescendo were those of a master who understood too well that the pit must not interfere with the stage. In view of the by now well established revolt in Western ballet, especially at the hands of the Diaghilev circle, Asaf'ev's *Plamia Parizha* is in itself a radical departure, albeit in a retrograde direction. Asaf'ev, as mentioned earlier, was very aware of himself as a 'dramaturgist'. This theme occurs again and again in his writings. From this, and from his theory of 'intonations' (musical images) grew his governing idea of form as process and form as dramaturgy.[1]

The Fountain of Bakhchisarai, composed in 1932–4,[2] was taken from an early (1824) Pushkin poem. Pushkin, in turn, had concocted the poem from Crimean Tatar folk tales: The Crimean khan, Girei, raids a Polish court making off with, among others, the Princess Maria Pototskaia. On his return to his own court her beauty overwhelms him. He falls in love, to the despair of his one-time favourite wife, Zarema. In harem scenes Girei protests his love, Maria demurs, and Zarema seethes —all on a background of harem dancers. Zarema pleads with, then kills Maria. Zarema is punished in the last act as new beauties and booties from more recent raids are paraded, without avail, in front of the desolate khan. The ballet is preceded and followed by a still scene of the khan appearing alone before the secret fountain of tears he has built to Maria's memory, the Fountain of Bakhchisarai.[3] Again Asaf'ev sought to be historian and musicologist as well as 'composer-dramaturgist', but this time with an intellectual twist. Rather than portray the era of the Crimean khanate, for which he had, at the moment, no research material, Asaf'ev endeavoured to catch musically the time of Pushkin, and, more specifically, the contemporary taste for the pseudo-exotic, no less typical in Russia than in the West during the early Romantic period. As in *Plamia Parizha* historical use is made of period music. Thus, the fountain of tears leitmotif is taken from the art song *The Fountain of the Bakhchisarai Court* by Aleksander Gurilev[4]; Maria's leitmotif is from a

[1] Form, in the Soviet Conservatory, is often taught as dramaturgy.

[2] The libretto was by N. D. Volkov.

[3] The story is no stranger to music. The poem was set in song form by Arensky in 1899, in opera form by Il'insky (date unknown), in opera form by Shaposhnikov (1940) and also in opera form by the Czech composer L. E. Mekhuri (1869, named *Maria Pototskaia*).

[4] Aleksander L'vovich Gurilev (1803–58) was a Russian composer, pianist, and violinist. A teacher himself, his only teacher was his father.

piano nocturne of John Field,[1] and since Maria is the central character, the Field music dominates.

During the periods of intense nationalism just before and during the Second World War, the nationality of Maria was found to be Western Ukrainian rather than Polish. With the exception of that temporary change, the ballet has remained, as written, in the repertoire of the Bolshoi Theatre.[2]

The music is faithfully that of the ballet.[3] As distinguished from *Plamia Parizha*, Asaf'ev uses the leitmotif technique throughout. Girei's motive is one of roughness, even cruelty, which is tempered by his feelings for Maria (Example 1). The image of Zarema is provided by a stereotyped 'oriental' scale. Although not necessarily ethnically accurate, it demonstrates Asaf'ev's feeling for the history of Russian musical practice (Example 2). The actual theme quoted is not repeated as insistently as are those of Maria (the John Field nocturne) and Girei, but demonstrates the pseudo-oriental style used throughout for Zarema and the rest of the harem. In the third act a 'cello announces Zarema's entry into the chamber of the sleeping Maria. The themes of the two female leads predictably combine. Solemn discords presently announce Maria's death from Zarema's knife. Driving home a psychological point, the same music is heard during Zarema's punishment and execution in the fourth act.

The recipe for the *Fountain of Bakhchisarai* was an immediately successful one, and Asaf'ev naturally tended to fix the style and approach, and even the settings. Of particular importance was his process of thorough research before tackling a new ballet. He continued to use 'period' music, leading him, in setting tales of non-European peoples,

[1] John Field (1782–1837) was an Irish pianist and teacher who lived and worked after the turn of the century in St Petersburg, concertizing extensively abroad. It is interesting to note that Soviet discussions of Asaf'ev's *Fountain* ignore its debt to Field.

[2] The ballet received its première in Leningrad at the Kirov (Marinsky) Theatre on September 28, 1934. The conductor was Mravinsky, the ballet master and choreographer, R. V. Zakharov. It was premiered in Moscow in 1936, again with Zakharov and with Melik-Pashaev conducting. Galina Ulanova often danced the role of Maria, Maria Plisetskaia, that of Zarema. The ballet was briefly pulled from the Moscow stage when, in the mid-thirties, the Party launched an orgy of puritanism. The setting was necessarily lush, exotic, and even erotic, a traditional combination re-affirmed as recently as Gliere's sensational *Cleopatra* in 1925. The brilliant Zakharov had dressed his dancers imaginatively. However, the production was halted only for the time necessary to chasten the costumes. There was no overt official criticism and the ballet is presented today as originally—that is, a little something for everybody.

[3] Published only in piano score, Muzgiz, 1939.

Asaf'ev. *The Fountain of Bakhchisarai*

Ex.1   *Girei's motive.*

Ex.2   Zarema's theme.

inevitably to folk music.[1] This practice put new props under the shaky edifice of Russian usage of folk music, at the same time lending more weight to the official doctrine as to what the music of the Soviet minority peoples and their composers should sound like.

If the musical influence of Asaf'ev's method tended toward the stifling, the same method had a far more positive effect on Soviet musical science. Asaf'ev was thorough, careful, and, within limits familiar to most musicologists, accurate. It cannot be said that he created Soviet musicology, but he reopened many doors. He generated interest and subsequently some new understanding of nineteenth-century Russian musical art in his carefully researched ballets based on Pushkin: *The Fountain of Bakchisarai, Caucasian Prisoner, Count Nulin, The Coffin Maker, Cottage in Kolom, The Stone Guest,* and *The Peasant Girl* (or *The Rustic Lady*). He similarly favoured Gogol (*The Night Before Christmas*), Lermontov (*Ashik-Kerib*), and Ostrovsky (*Snegurochka*).[2] His excellent *Russian Music from the Beginning of the 19th Century* is, in a sense, a companion to these works. Each is better understood for knowing the other. The subject of Tschaikovsky, to which Asaf'ev returned again and again in his critical work, was dear to him musically as well, as evidenced by the extensive quotation in *Snegurochka* and *Vesenniaia Skazka* (*A Spring Tale*). The ballets of Asaf'ev the composer took Asaf'ev the musicologist to France (*Spent Illusions*—1935, *Count Nulin*), Spain (*The Stone Guest*), Yugoslavia (*Militsa*), Italy (*Ivan Bolotnikov*), Persia (*Stepan Razin*), England (*The Peasant Girl*), Mongolia (*Lada*), and various other Eastern and Transcaucasian localities. He wrote about and used Russian folk music of the city and country.

For some time Asaf'ev continued to use the 'contrast of peoples' as a, for him, musically generating factor. Of the remaining ballets only

[1] An appreciation of the Soviet view on this matter is revealing. Soviet writers recognize a basic change in Asaf'ev's approach after *Plamia Parizha,* finding 'in his ensuing work of the 30s, starting with the *Fountain of Bakhchisaria* these methods [of using existing music in a new work] were not used . . . with the exception of . . . *Snegourochka,* . . . all Asaf'ev's ballet composition was the original work of the author' (quoted from *IRSM,* II, p. 307). We have seen that this is obviously untrue in *Fountain* . . ., and, technically, it is equally untrue of much of his later work. Asaf'ev's treatment of Tatar or other Eastern folk songs and epics seems no different, given conventional Western harmony, from that of the Field nocturne in *Fountain,* nor the *Marseillaise* in *Plamia.* Direct quotation at length, i.e. ballet potpourri, is not found, but the 'change' in approach would seem hardly more than a matter of degree.

[2] To these one may add Asaf'ev's relatively unimportant operas on works of Pushkin (*Feast during the plague,* 1940; and *The Slavic Beauty,* 1942); Lermontov (*The Paymistress,* 1936); and Ostrovsky (*Storm,* 1940).

Caucasian Prisoner (Kavkazskii Plennik) and the uncompleted *Night Before Christmas* (the latter for seasonal reasons) can even occasionally be found in the repertoire of Soviet Theatres. The 'exotic' ballets (*Radda the Beautiful, Ashik-Kerib, Lada, Sulamif'*) are occasionally revived, especially in the republics. The 'Socio-heroic' ballets (*Partisans, Militsa*) may be staged occasionally for patriotic reasons. Four one-act ballets on Pushkin subjects (the aforementioned *Count Nulin, The Coffinmaker, Cottage in Colom,* and the *Stone Guest*) were written for television and may appear from time to time on that medium. The ballets on historical heroes (*Stepan Razin* and *Ivan Bolotnikov*) were never performed and are, in fact, unfinished.

Thus only *Fountain* and *Caucasian Prisoner* hold the stage on their own merits. It is important to appreciate the role of these two ballets, especially the former, as models for all Soviet ballet. Although the number of ballets written and staged at least once in the Soviet Union is unbelievable by Western standards, only seven have held the stage with any consistency.[1] The idiomatic direction of Asaf'ev's *Fountain* became the definition for the Soviet musical work 'realism'. If Asaf'ev had not appeared as a double threat, gifted in musical potboiling as well as a genius with words, 'socialist realism' might well have another meaning. Composers beset by the problem of writing a successful ballet turn again and again to *Fountain*. Kara Karaev's *Seven Beauties* (1952) pays the Asaf'ev work the tribute of being its exact copy dramaturgically.

The *Caucasian Prisoner*, itself, is a tribute to the success of *Fountain*. This is another of the 'contrast of peoples' ballets. The story is that of a jaded St Petersburg artist taken prisoner by a Trans-Caucasian Cherkass tribe, one of whose young maidens falls in love with him. She sees that he loves another at home, but sets him free and flings herself to her death in the very river which he has just crossed to occidental safety. The material is largely that of Cherkass and Georgian folk tunes. However, at the beginning of the second act the Russian and Cherkass maiden are alone in the large and realistically set Cherkass camp. The area of light narrows finally to show only the couple as he tells her of life and love in St Petersburg. Lo, a rising glow in the centre of the stage reveals not a Cherkass camp anymore, but the statue (full size) of Peter the Great—the Bronze Horseman—ordinarily located on the bank of the Neva in St Petersburg. Symbolically, the monstrous statue occupies the centre of what turns out to be a St Petersburg ball. A string

[1] The seven are: the two mentioned of Asaf'ev, Gliere's *Red Poppy* and *Bronze Horseman*, Prokofieff's *Romeo and Juliet* and *Stone Flower*, and (with much rewriting) Khachaturian's *Gayaneh*.

of stylized city tunes and dances ensue, the lights fade and brighten again on the Cherkass camp. This is the sort of thing that Soviet audiences love and is what Soviet theatres do really well.

Whatever the momentary disposition of other works, the summation of Asaf'ev as a composer must rest with *Fountain*.[1] But Asaf'ev himself delivered the *coup* to any notions that his music can stand by itself. He refused to create suites out of his ballet material, and, indeed, the music could scarcely sustain an independent orchestral work. His four symphonies are not even mentioned in the otherwise exhaustive *IRSM*. Only the First was ever played. The Second was discarded in progress. A second 'Second' was based on an historical peasant uprising, the Third (fourth) on material from an incompleted opera, *Motherland*. He declared his unfitness for the genre in 1946. The sugary whiteness of his harmony, the monotonously thick texture, the absence of originality, and the repetitiousness and inability to find the drama within the music for providing the form are surprising in Asaf'ev, who could discuss these things, their presence or absence in the music of others so brilliantly. He bore the heavy cross of not being a composer; and the younger Soviet composers have borne the cross of having to match him.

The most surprising thing is the dim reflection, when looking at the musicological monument Asaf'ev seems to have left, of what Asaf'ev was earlier: on one hand the champion of Stravinsky, early Prokofieff and even Miaskovsky; the articulate defender of a truly revolutionary music, on the other hand, a strong advocate of a balanced view of Russia's musical heritage—a product of the European cradle. His legacy is neither. He dislodged from the Romantic monolith a brilliant vocabulary which others caught in the period of freedom and used to close doors that should have been opened.

[1] The work was included in the offerings of the Bolshoi ballet troupe in their 1958 US appearance.

꙰

CHAPTER 10

Nıkolai Miaskovsky

Nikolai Iakovlevich Miaskovsky is considered by his most authoritative biographer[1] as the 'greatest Soviet symphonist'.[2] His Fifth she names as 'the beginning of Soviet symphonism'.[3] Miaskovsky's right to this rank rests on his undeniably everlasting pen, his interest in all musical activity, especially teaching, and, perhaps more than anything else, his long life which bridged the years which would allow a man to approach the crucial time of the 1917 revolution with a finished technique, but a still young, malleable taste.

Miaskovsky finished his Twenty-seventh Symphony in November of 1949, nine months before his death, and thirteen months before the work's première performance. In addition to the twenty-seven symphonies, he is the author of thirteen symphonic works in other genres, thirteen quartets, more than 100 piano works, 125 art songs, 17 songs and choruses, and two cantatas. His opus numbers go to 87, and there is a large number of works with no opus assignment.

He taught composition at the Moscow Conservatory from 1929 until his death. Among his students are Victor Belyi, German Galynin, Dmitrii Kabalevsky, Boris Mokrousov, Vano Muradeli, Nikolai Peiko, Aram Khachaturian, Vissarion Shebalin, and about eighty others. He was an active music scholar, contributing regularly to journals in his early years; a member of the editorial board of *Sovetskaia Muzyka*; a member of the editorial collective which published the works of Tschaikovsky and Rimsky-Korsakov; and was, for a number of years, a member of the organization committee of the Union of Soviet Composers.

Miaskovsky was born April 8/20, 1881 at the army fortress Novo-Georgievsky, near Warsaw. He lived there until 1888, in Orenburg until 1889, and in Kazan, where his mother died, until 1893. The family

---

[1] Tamara Livanova (1909–), writing on Miaskovsky in the section on instrumental music in *IRSM*, I.

[2] *IRSM*, I, 233.

[3] *IRSM*, I, 235.

followed Miaskovsky senior who was a military engineer. Miaskovsky has written of these early years and of his years of training and professional activity.[1] He began studying in Kazan, then in Nizhnyi Novgorod (Gorky) and in St Petersburg (Leningrad) in military schools. At the same time he had begun playing the piano under the tutelage of an aunt. He continued the family tradition by entering a military engineering school in 1899, but maintained the musical activity of a dilettante, in the tradition of Cui and Rimsky-Korsakov. From the latter he carried a recommendation to Taneev in Moscow, and Taneev, in turn, recommended him to his pupil, Reinhold Gliere. During the year his battalion was in Moscow, Miaskovsky began his serious study of harmony with Gliere and became acquainted with Taneev and his pupils, Arensky, Ippolitov-Ivanov, and Konius. The first two were the synthesizers, according to contemporary Soviet thinking, of the traditions of Tschaikovsky and the Moscow school, and the 'Mighty Five', or Petersburg school.

On the return of his battalion to Petersburg, Miaskovsky was handed over to Gliere's friend, Ivan Kryzhanovsky. Kryzhanovsky (1867–1924) has the distinction of being damned as one of the evil beasts of embryonic 'modernism' and 'formalism' in Soviet music. Present day Soviet scholars point particularly to his harmful influence on the young Miaskovsky[2] as evidence of his lack of social orientation. Actually St Petersburg was at the time, and was to continue to be for some time after the revolution, a city comfortably within the orbit of European thinking about music. It was this atmosphere that Miaskovsky entered when he returned from Moscow. His own words about Kryzhanovsky and his circle strike middle ground:

'Gliere recommended me to his friend, composer and doctor Iv. Iv. Kryzhanovsky (one of the founders of the "Evenings of Contemporary Music", a student of Rimsky-Korsakov), with whom I studied counterpoint, fugue, form and some orchestration. As a result of these studies and thanks to my return to a circle of temporarily abandoned friends, plus V. V. Iakovlev (a now famous musico-theatrical writer), [and] among whom flourished an enthusiasm for the most contemporary trends in literature, art, etc., my first serious musical experiments were launched—a number of art songs on words of Z[inaida] Gippius. These experiments permitted me to draw near the circle of progressive musicians grouped around the "Evening of Contemporary Music". True, I

---

[1] N. Miaskovsky, 'Avtobiograficheskie zametki o tvorcheskom puti' (Autobiographical notes on my creative path), *Sovetskaia Muzyka*, VI (June 1936). Also reprinted in *Sovetskaia Simfonicheskaia Muzyka* (Moscow: Muzgiz, 1955).

[2] The year of Miaskovsky's return to Petersburg was 1904. He was then twenty-three years old.

4

did not make this circle "my own", since even then the striving for the "last word" in musical technique and invention didn't have, for me, a value in itself. In any case the atmosphere, extraordinarily tense with musical searching, and the supercritical evaluation of results could not but infect me and to compel me to feel that I was, after all, a dilettante and, so long as I was connected with the military service hanging over me, I could not extricate myself from this situation.[1]

Miaskovsky stayed on in Petersburg, successfully finding time enough from his military duties to continue his search for musical style. Towards the end of his term of active duty he took the entrance examinations for the Petersburg Conservatory and in 1906, at the age of twenty-four, he entered that atmosphere dominated by Rimsky-Korsakov and Liadov. For about a year he occupied a 'suspended' category while he first proved his worth at the conservatory and, second, completely freed himself from any military obligation.[2] But he finally entered the reserves in 1907.

Up to this time (1907) Miaskovsky—the soldier, dilettante, and amateur—had a rather off-balance list of compositions behind him. In 1899, 1900 and 1901 he wrote three, two and one piano preludes, respectively. In 1906 he wrote eight pieces for piano, some of whose tunes later appeared in his symphonies. He did the tunes from a set of twenty-five piano pieces written in 1907. From 1903 to 1906, he composed a set of songs to poems of Balmont; and in 1907 he set *Razmyshleniia*, seven poems of Baragynsky. Of all these, only the last was published, and that only partially.[3] His early, controversial songs set to poetry of Zinaida Gippius were composed in two groups, 1904 to 1908[4] and 1905 to 1908.[5]

Miaskovsky said of his first symphony:

'The composition of my 1st symphony (until then I had been afraid of the orchestra) determined my future path. I felt that namely in this area could I always more freely (willingly) express myself. The theatre never attracted me, neither opera nor ballet. In this regard I always

[1] Miaskovsky, 'Avtobiograficheskie zametki', *Sovetskaia Simfonicheskaia Muzyka*, p. 25.
[2] In 'Avtobiograficheskie zametki', p. 27, Miaskovsky ponders the strangeness of a clause in his original release to the reserves which prevented him from enrolling in any civilian academic institution. This would have denied him the conservatory but, 'I was not particularly worried since I was "already" in the conservatory . . . (nobody had asked permission of my military superior)'.
[3] Muzektor Gosizdat, 1922.
[4] Moscow: Zimmerman, 1906; and Moscow: Muzsektor Gosizdat, 1921-2.
[5] Moscow: Muzfond SSSR, 1946.

prefer that which has more the quality of "pure music" and symphonic life in the operas of Wagner and Rimsky-Korsakov.'[1]

The First Symphony (C minor, opus 3) was composed from February to July 27, 1908, and was orchestrated in September of that year. The first performance was not to take place until May 20, 1914 in Pavlovsk, under the direction of P. Anslanov.[2,3] The work is scored for strings and

Miaskovsky. *1st Symphony.*

Ex.1 *Opening theme.*

---

[1] Miaskovsky, 'Avtobiograficheskie zametki', p. 21.

[2] The first symphony was first published in 1929 by the music sector of the State Publishers (Muzsektor Gosizdat).

[3] Serge Prokofieff makes an interesting comment on the first symphony to which Miaskovsky himself never alludes:

'In the summer of 1908 Miaskovsky and I each composed a symphony. During the work (on them) we corresponded and sent one another themes. Miaskovsky's symphony, after a number of rewritings, became his "First Symphony." From mine I saved only the Andante, which later became part of the fourth sonata.' (From Serge Prokofieff's *Iunye Gody* (The early years). A chapter from his autobiography published in *Sovetskaia Muzyka*, 1941, No. 4, pp. 76–78.)

Ex. 2 *I Opening theme, secondary subject.*

Ex. 3 *Transition episodes.*

and...

double winds plus piccolo. The first movement (*Lento ma non troppo*) begins slowly using a theme which will become a part of the main subject of the exposition. This theme, especially its development, becomes important throughout the symphony as unifying material (Example 1). The opening theme of the exposition's secondary subject is also used here (Example 2). Thus the introduction 'exposes' the ensuing exposition. In the exposition both primary and secondary subjects are handled directly and simply with an extended transition section (Example 3) intervening. Both themes are lyric and song-like, characterizing the entire movement. The exposition ends with apparently fresh quotations, actually beginning with an inversion of the theme of the secondary subject (Example 4).

The development refers to all material thus far given: primary and secondary subjects and the exposition's conclusion. The chief attention is given to the main theme which begins to emerge as the primary unifying factor of the entire symphony. Here a rhythmic punctuation alters the cantabile character of the main theme and prepares it for a subsequent entrance in the work's final movement. The recapitulation, however, settles all the material of the exposition into its original form, tonality following the classical pattern. A coda is based on the material used in concluding the exposition.

The second movement (Larghetto-quasi andante) is a complex three-part form in A-flat major with extended tonal excursions, especially to the relative minor. Thus overall tonality seems to be on a line between Ab and f. The general expression is bland and, again, song-like (Example 5), and but for more energetic backgrounds, so are the second (Example 6) and third (Example 7) themes.

The third, and last, movement (Sonata allegro, C minor) is introduced vigorously in an ascending rhythmic pattern (Example 8). The main theme borrows this rhythmic drive (Example 9) and carries it through a vigorous transition (Example 10) to a slower, more lyrical subordinate section. The effect up to this point is strongly reminiscent of the thematic treatment in the development of the first movement. Although the principal theme here is composed of various thematic elements, it is close to that of the first movement in its tension (through augmented sixth chords, ninth chords, etc.) and restlessness (a disinclination to cadence).

The subordinate section is nearly pastoral in nature (Example 11). The strong apparent similarity to the middle movement is not so intentional as it as a product of style. Throughout his work, Miaskovsky frequently retreats to this seemingly neutral or 'tonic' style: broken chords, arpeggiated melodies, and the lulling effect of a slow two against three.

Ex.4   I. *Second theme, inverted.*

Ex.5   II. *First theme.*

Ex.6   II. *Second theme.*

Ex.7 II. Third theme.

Ex.8 III. Introduction.

Allegro assai e molto risoluto

Ex.9 III. Introduction, main theme.

Ex.10 *III. Transition.*

and...

Ex. 11 *III. Subordinate section.*

The formal development section is largely an extension of the final and transition sections from the exposition. The recapitulation is an analogue of the exposition, and only in the coda do all the elements appear in what amounts to a real development. The staggered melodies of the exposition finale (Example 12) appear in varied poses with all the other elements, finally subduing them to close the movement and the symphony.

From the vantage point of 1960 there is little remarkable harmonically in this first symphony of Soviet Russia's first symphonist. As the augmented sixth chords and ninth chords suggest, the harmonic idiom is close to that of late Wagner and of Richard Strauss. Miaskovsky himself acknowledges an appreciation of such a style:

In these (1908) and the following years my affection strengthened toward Western classical and in part (I was not fond of Chopin and Liszt) romantic music, and towards the leading Russian figures, and from among the new impressions the strongest were: 'Kitezh' of Rimsky-Korsakov, Wagner's 'Niebelung' cycle, . . . Scriabin, Debussy, Ravel's 'Spanish Rhapsody' and Schoenberg's 'Pelleas'.[1]

The quotation above, citing Rimsky-Korsakov, indicates the orchestral texture to which Miaskovsky adheres in this and almost all other symphonies.

At the conservatory, Miaskovsky studied orchestration with Rimsky-Korsakov and composition with Liadov. Liadov's pupils at the time included Boris Asaf'ev, Prokfieff, Lazare Saminsky, and Iakov Akimenko (Stepovoi). Liadov's students, and Miaskovsky names himself and Prokofiev as the chief culprits, did not show their modernistic experiments to Liadov. 'Liadov', said Miaskovsky, 'I remember with admiration, gratitude, but also . . . with horror.'[2]

Miaskovsky finished the conservatory in 1911, maintaining the while his fruitful contact with Kryzhanovsky and the 'Evenings of Contemporary Music' group. Through the latter he had repeated opportunities for performance both in Moscow and St Petersburg, including the orchestral performances which were subsequently so important to him. Of undoubted benefit to Miaskovsky was his assignment, in 1911, as the Petersburg correspondent for the Moscow journal *Muzyka*, edited by progressive Derzhanovsky. *Musyka* was the unofficial organ of progressive musical thought in Moscow, and the Petersburg correspondent was important, since he represented the most progressive, and European, city in Russia, the city through which European musical news was piped

---

[1] Miaskovsky, 'Avtobiograficheskie zametki', p. 28.
[2] Miaskovsky, 'Avtobiograficheskie zametki', p. 28.

to the rest of the country. Miaskovsky was probably the last representative of the pre-revolutionary tradition maintained by Borodin, Cui, Rimsky-Korsakov, Tschaikovsky, and others, to combine critical work with composition. Of those on the contemporary scene only Asaf'ev became active, and, in fact, made his musical mark by scholarship, not by his composition alone. Miaskovsky wrote on the classic figures in Russian music, on his Russian contemporaries and on foreign musicians, thereby becoming his own teacher. By comparison with other musical writings of the time, especially in *Muzyka* and its various Petersburg counterparts, Miaskovsky reveals the current of conservative nationalism which was later to engulf him musically.

Miaskovsky continued in Petersburg until 1914. He just managed to complete his Third Symphony when he was immediately mobilized and sent to the front. The war, the subsequent revolutionary activity, civil war, and intervention brought many changes, not the least of which was in Miaskovsky's creative thinking and in the man himself. The war sharply divides his first from his second creative period. He remained in the military service (ultimately with the Red Army) with varying degrees of obligation until 1921. After several assignments at the front, he was re-assigned for a year to (by now) Petrograd and then, in 1918, his regiment was sent to Moscow where he was to remain until his death. Of whatever influence his war years had on him Miaskovsky has the following to say:

Being at war and in several engagements in a significant measure strengthened my democratic inclinations, which were already forming at the conservatory and which became extreme during the February [1917] revolution, although in no definite direction. But the July events in Petrograd reaching Revel [Tallin] through the press, swung me, although in a large measure instinctively, toward a more radical position. . . . The war strongly enriched my supply of internal and external impressions and, moreover, somehow had an influence on a certain brightening up of my musical thoughts. The majority of my music at the front had, if not a bright, at least a more "objective" character. . . .[1]

That his future lay in Moscow rather than in Petrograd/Leningrad

[1] Miaskovsky, 'Avtobiograficheskie zametki', p. 30. The July events to which Miaskovsky refers were civil and military disorders in Petrograd which started spontaneously in military units which supported the Bolsheviks. A rumour circulated by a Socialist Revolutionary cabinet officer to the effect that the Bolshevik's Lenin was a German agent seened to cause a reaction in favour of the government. The Bolsheviks were momentarily suppressed and Anatole Lunacharsky, only recently rejoining the Bolshevik party, was arrested.

Ex.12 *Coda material from codetta.*

etc.

Ex.13 *Miaskovsky. 5ᵗʰ Symphony Ⅱ. Wagner influence.*

Andante

Ex.14 *Miaskovsky. 6ᵗʰ Symphony I. Dvorak style.*

Tranquillo ♩=72

Ex.15 *Miaskovsky. 7ᵗʰ Symphony I. Bitonality.*

was important at the time. Both in Moscow, Leningrad, and elsewhere there had been changes in the cast of characters. Gliere had assumed the directorship of the Kiev conservatory. Rachmaninov, Gretchaninov, Stravinsky, Prokofieff, Cherepnin, and many others were no longer in the country. Kryzhanovsky, in 1918, was to live three more years, and editor Derzhanovsky still held forth in Moscow. Miaskovsky joined Derzhanovsky's household and became once again a member of a progressive group, this one much smaller than its all-embracing Petrograd counterparts. Although Miaskovsky was no longer doing critical writing, his past performances in that area had gained him a name in Moscow. He became a charter member of the Moscow Collective of Composers, and after his complete demobilization in 1921 he joined the conservatory staff with the rank of professor of composition.

By now Miaskovsky's route as a symphonist was well established, and his Fifth (opus 18, 1918) was to be hailed as the first Soviet Symphony. Although he has written extensively in other genres, it is as a symphonist that he will be considered here. Any composer who writes 27 symphonies must suffer some statistical analysis. A composer whose symphonies, moreover, do not seem to have much lasting power, like Miaskovsky's, is lucky to be considered, even statistically. Of the 27 symphonies, 2 are in one movement, 2 in two, 14 in three, 8 in four, and 1 in five movements. Two of the three-movement symphonies (nos. 13 and 22) are played without break. The Sixth Symphony has an optional chorus part; the Twenty-third is based on Caucasian melodies, the Twenty-sixth on Russian. The Nineteenth Symphony (1939) is for band. The distribution of keys is rather even. There are no symphonies in the major keys of Db, G, Bb, and B. The tonalities of three symphonies each are in C major and Bb minor. Otherwise the distribution is one or two symphonies to each of the more usual tonalities. The tonality of C minor is used twice—in the First Symphony, and in the last. There are twice as many symphonies in minor keys as in major keys. As conductors' properties, the early works were frequently performed by Saradzhev; the later ones, including the last three, by Gauk. Alfred Coates conducted the première of the Twelfth (June 1, 1932). The Tenth was first performed by the conductorless *Persimfans* in 1928.

Miaskovsky's work patterns were unique, as one might expect of such a prolific symphony composer. Like most Soviet composers, he separates the functions of composing and orchestration. He finished the piano draft of the Thirteenth on May 29, 1933; on July 1st he finished the piano draft of the first movement of the Fifteenth; on August 18th he finished the piano draft of the Fourteenth; on August 30th he drafted the second movement of the Fifteenth; on October 11th he orchestrated the Fourteenth; on October 26th he orchestrated the Thirteenth. Nearly a year passed. By October 15, 1934, he had finished the piano draft of movements three and four of the Fifteenth. The Thirteenth was premiered on October 27th; the Fifteenth was orchestrated by November 29th. In 1935, the Fourteenth was premiered in February, and the Fifteenth in October. By this time, the Sixteenth was in progress.

The Sixteenth Symphony, one of the best by Soviet standards, was finished and performed in 1936. Miaskovsky was entering his twentieth year as a Soviet composer. He had been mildly avant-garde during the twenties. In general, these early symphonies exhibit more variety of style than the later ones, although they are extremely derivative. Wagner remained a strong influence (Example 13), and the Dvorak-like, 'de-nationalized', Eastern European, symphonic folk style is often heard (Example 14). A bold bitonality was as much Miaskovsky's tool as that of anyone else, as in the Seventh Symphony, in 1922 (Example 15); and perhaps he reached a limit of harmonic tension in the symphonies of this time (Example 16). But this sort of thing is confined to slow, lyric passages. Elsewhere he shared with Prokofieff an early addiction to ostinatos of a vigorous sort (Example 17), or of a stereotyped, romantic cast (Example 18). His works, as in the First Symphony, often open with bass statements of a vigorous (Example 19) or gloomy sort (Example 20). Moreover, he seems to bring many of his ideas 'up from the depths' as in the set of variations contained in the sonata allegro third movement of the Eleventh Symphony (Example 21).

Unfortunately, Miaskovsky's harmony moves only as far and as fast as his fingers could on the piano. Form, even, can be a keyboard product. Turning once again to dry statistics: of the forty-two movements in the Third through the Fourteenth Symphonies, only six escape the grip of the sonata-allegro form entirely. Seventeen are straight sonata allegro, eleven are in a complex, three-part form with governing sonata allegro elements, and eight are in Sonata-rondo form.

The Sixteenth Symphony (1936) seems to mark a slight change in style. The moments of Mahlerish introspection and search, never too frequent, tend now to disappear. An awareness of Shostakovich is evident, but so is that of the demand for 'Soviet optimism'. The work opens in the Shostakovich manner (Example 22) and the secondary subject is a sort of Russian *Old Black Joe* (Example 23). The second movement opens with a similar melody, but continues to a dance-like figure (Example 24). The third movement has a typical Miaskovsky introduction, but one whose promise is immediately diverted by a march (Example 25).

Ex.16 *Miaskovsky. 7th Symphony I. Harmonic tension.*

Ex.17 *Miaskovsky. 8th Symphony IV. Vigorous ostinato.*

Ex.18 *Miaskovsky. 8th Symphony IV. Romantic ostinato.*

Ex.19 *Miaskovsky. 10th Symphony I. Vigorous opening.*

Ex.20 *Miaskovsky. 11th Symphony I. Gloomy opening.*

Ex.21 *Miaskovsky. 11ᵗʰ Symphony III. Low register idea generation.*

Precipitato

Miaskovsky. 16ᵗʰ Symphony

Ex.22 *I. "Shostakovich" opening.*

Ex.23 *I. Second subject.*

L'istesso tempo

etc.

Ex.24 *II. Dance figure.*

Ex.25 *III. Introduction and march.*

The Seventeenth through the Twentieth Symphonies are obviously oversimplifications—mere running water, undoubtedly due to the political uncertainties of the time (1936–40). Miaskovsky had always chosen a route of conformity, simply to be left alone to express himself. The Twenty-first Symphony, though not at all complex, is an example of Miaskovsky's thinking, not of social control. It was awarded a Stalin Prize in 1941 and has been described as his finest.[1] The work is in one movement, although its performance time (twenty minutes) is not beyond the boundaries already set by Miaskovsky.[2] The formal scheme of the work is shown with keys indicated (Example 26). The prologue themes (Examples 27a, b, c) are similar and show a progression from solo utterance through thick, parallel accompaniment. The last of these comes to a quiet cadence on II₇ of the ensuing movement. The sonata form proper begins with an energetic theme in A minor (Example 28),

[1] Bernandt, *Composers*, p. 89.

[2] The symphonies range in duration from twenty minutes (the Twenty-First, Tenth, Eighteenth) to over forty minutes (First through Fifth, Fourteenth, Fifteenth). As indicated earlier, the earlier symphonies tend to greater length.

Miaskovsky. *21st Symphony : formal scheme.*

PROLOGUE

Andante sostenuto

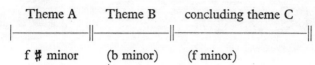

Theme A   Theme B   concluding theme C

f ♯ minor   (b minor)   (f minor)

EXPOSITION

Allegro non troppo, ma con impeto

  Primary subject   Prologue theme B(trans.)   Subordinate subject

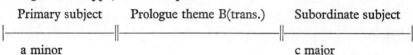

a minor   c major

DEVELOPMENT

                    Piu vivo e poco agitato

subordinate subject: primary subject fugatto on primary material subord.

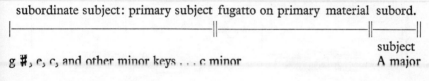

                                        subject

g ♯, e, c, and other minor keys . . . c minor   A major

Prologue themes B and C

RECAPITULATION

Allegro   Poco meno mosso

  Primary subject   Subordinate subject   trans. on sub. subj. material

a minor   D major

EPILOGUE

  Tempo I (Andante)   Lento

  Prologue, theme A analog   Coda-Theme A

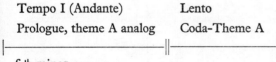

f ♯ minor

Miaskovsky. 21st Symphony

Ex.27 *Prologue themes*

a)

b)

c)

Ex.28 *Exposition, first theme.*

which is passed wholly and in fragments about the orchestra before the transition (on the prologue theme) to the *quasi andante* secondary subject (Example 29). Here the development of the subject is realized on the background of triplets against duplets. The texture of the entire exposition is typically thick with doublings. The exposition ends with this pattern. The development, after a restatement of the primary material in G sharp minor, uses a portion of that theme as fugato material. The outline of the fugato is given (Example 30). A sweeping return to the secondary subject is punctuated by triplets, well established in the fugato; a suggestion of the prologue themes (b and c) leads, as before, into the first subject: the recapitulation. The recapitulation is surprisingly faithful, develops slightly, broadens and ritards on a transition version of the secondary subject, which leads to the andante epilogue. The epilogue is an analogy to the prologue, with a far denser orchestral handling. A coda, based on the A theme, ends the epilogue and the symphony.

During the war Miaskovsky made use of the lessening controls to seek some new symphonic language. His forays were not made in the relatively mild Twenty-second through Twenty-fifth symphonies, but in the *Paticheskaia Overture* (1947) and *The Kremlin at Night* (1947), a cantata-nocturne. It was these works, plus his Ninth, Tenth, and Eleventh string quartets, which set him up as one of the targets in 1948. He was one of the four principals in the Zhdanov attack. Unfortunately, he died so soon after the events, that he was not able to see the faintest glimmer of another future. His Twenty-sixth Symphony seems to have driven him deeper into trouble. It has not yet (1957) been published.

But the Twenty-seventh, his last, won him a posthumous Stalin Prize. This work (opus 85) represents the extreme of orchestral music conceived pianistically, an extreme to which Miaskovsky often went. Chords are thick, the bass ponderous, the texture mostly homophonic. The formal structure is simple, direct, and immediately appealing. The first movement, in regular sonata-allegro form, is introduced with a brief, adagio 6/8 theme over an insistent pedal. The same theme is realized shortly in an allegro 6/8 and becomes the primary material of the exposition. Here again is the sweeping, chordal diatonicism of Miaskovsky's melody. The transition to the secondary subject is achieved through further development of the same material. The secondary subject tends to vacillate in tonality, uncertain about the change to the relative major, finally settling there after another brief tour through C minor. The exposition closes with the primary theme. The development section treats all the material heard so far, including the introductory variant of the main theme—and does so in the original

Ex. 29 *Subordinate subject*

Ex. 30 *Fugato.*

Più vivo e poco agitato

low strgs.

vln.
vla.

etc.

order. The impression is that of a variation recapitulation. The recapitulation itself is standard, and tends to supply the listener with too
much of a good thing. The movement closes with material from the
primary theme. The second movement is an extended three-part form
typically exhibiting elements of the sonata-allegro. The introduction
contains the germs of the first two parts (themes). Each theme is developed after its first utterance. A recapitulation leads to a coda wherein
the two themes mingle. The third, and last, movement is in rondo-
sonata form. The recurrent main theme is simple as are the subordinate
themes. The coda, as in the first movement, combines most of the
elements of the movement, including those of the introduction.

This last symphony of Miaskovsky's has, since its first performance,
been held up as an example of the 'correct' in Soviet symphonism.
Moreover, the forty-second-year development of Miaskovsky's symphonic idiom has been established as a model of creative growth. This
is a difficult thing to appraise. In general, any trend of development
founders in the sheer bulk of Miaskovsky's output. A certain 'progression' from complex to simple harmonies, from chromatic through
diatonic to chordal melody, from 'contrapuntal' to homophonic
texture, from ponderous to more direct rhythms, and even from an
extravagant to a more economical orchestral handling, may be found, if
one looks selectively, and if one stays within Miaskovsky's own limited
framework. Yet, this apparent progression, which leads some Soviet
writers and many of their Western colleagues to speak of the 'old' and
'new' Miaskovsky, is not nearly so marked nor as important as the fact
that the range of difference is small. That Miaskovsky always thought
homophonically is attested to by his laboured polyphony. That his
idiom was always diatonic, chordal, and simple is proved by his aimless-
ness when he tries not to be. There is one Miaskovsky, and this is the
image of the Soviet symphonist.

In a model, one looks, if not for growth, then for consistent elements
of style. First of all, Miaskovsky was a manipulator of form. He was not
a master of form, for he rarely went deeply enough. With thematic
blocks he played chess—a clear, straightforward chess, where the
meaning of each move is immediately obvious. He had an over-dramatic
sense of musical return. His recapitulations and ritornellos wash in with
a pomp that makes the listener feel the least he could do is rise—or jump
out of the way. The composer's avoidance of a third, dance or scherzo,
movement is, possibly, the result of not wanting to be governed by
formal simplicity. Chess players feel confined playing checkers. Miaskovsky's harmony was always mildly modal, and generally dense, even
congested. His frequent polyphonic attempts often led to an unequivocal

bitonality. Seventh chords and augmented sixth chords abound through-out his work, but these creative habits do not obscure an almost total lack of feeling for originality. The model is difficult to follow.

When Miaskovsky died, on August 8, 1950, in Moscow, the Soviet musical world felt a distinct loss. The musicians mourned not the death of a symphonist, but that of a teacher. Nearly 100 Soviet composers had studied with him, many of them now famous men.[1] His teaching style was strict—he felt the classroom was no place for experimentation. His intention was to give his students a conservative basis, his own, from which to build. He never intended to be a model.

[1] And women: Nina Vladimirovna Makarova is a well-known and well travelled Soviet composer. Her travels, and perhaps her fame, are due to her husband, Aram Khachaturian. Mrs Khachaturian finished the Moscow Conservatory under Miaskovsky in 1936, when Khachaturian was Miaskovsky's assistant.

CHAPTER 11

જીજી

Dmitrii Arakishvili

Georgian Western music has had a development replete with fascinating figures, Italian, Georgian, and Russian, which richly deserves close study. Such a study is not within the scope of this paper. In preparation for the discussion here of three Soviet Georgian composers, Dmitrii Arakashvili, Andrei Balanchivadze, and Otar Taktakishvili, a brief word on three of the leading Georgian musical figures of the last 100 years may be useful.[1]

Kharlampii Ivanovich Saveneli (1845–90) founded the first music school in Georgia. He studied at the St Petersburg University and was expelled from that institution for anti-government activity in the 1860s. In 1863 he started studying with Anton Rubinstein at the new conservatory. Among his classmates and friends was Tschaikovsky. Returning to Georgia he found it necessary to support himself by working as a clerk in a bank. Georgians, at the time, had little to do with the more sophisticated music of Tiflis. In 1873 Saveneli organized a chorus which later functioned as a society supporting music classes. In 1876 he was finally able to open the first regular music school in Tiflis. Saveneli's interests lay strictly along Western lines and there was no attempt to incorporate anything natively Georgian into the curricula. The school joined the IRMS network, and this was the organization that Ippolitov-Ivanov directed a few years later.

Meliton Antonovich Balanchivadze (1862–1937) was the father of the contemporary Soviet composer Andrei Balanchivadze, discussed later, and of the Georgian-American choreographer, George Balanchine. Meliton was a composer, ethnomusicologist, singer, and indefatigable publicist of Georgian music. He studied with Rimsky-Korsakov in 1890 at the St Petersburg Conservatory. For many years he worked on his 'Georgian' opera, *Kovarnaia Daredzhan* ('The perfidious Daredzhan', originally 'The perfidious Tamara') from 1896 to 1926.

[1] See also the section on Ippolitov-Ivanov, p. 65.

Among his many songs, 'When I look at you', 'I yearn for you always', and 'Lullaby' (all published 1889) laid the basis for the Georgian art song—a basis not yet overcome. After the war and the political subjugation of Georgia, he wrote a number of Soviet mass works including 'Glory to the Zemo-Avchal'sk hydroelectric station' (1927), a cantata.

Zakharii Petrovich Paliashvili (1871–1933) is considered in the Soviet Union as the founder of Georgian national classic (Western) music. He is the only one of these early three to have studied in Moscow (with Taneev, 1900–3), but his earlier training also included a solid acquaintance with Western European music in the Roman Catholic church in Kutais. Returning to Georgia from Moscow he became active as a musical organizer, composer, teacher, and folklorist. As a composer, opera occupied him principally. His operas *Abesalom and Eteri* (1919), *Daisi* (1923), and *Latavra* (1928) were the Georgian counterparts of Uzeir Gadzhibekov's early operas in Baku, and were preceded in Georgia only by Arakishvili's *Shota Rustaveli*. In *Daisi*, the most effective of the three,[1] extended sections were left merely sketched or with instructions for improvisation along traditional folk lines.[2] Paliashvili's two collections of Georgian folk songs, published in 1909,[3] helped immeasurably to set straight the often brilliant, often bad, fifty-year-old history of endeavour in the Georgian folk music field.

Three of the most important figures among Soviet Georgian composers are Arakishvili, Balanchivadze,[4] and Taktakishvili.[5] They are, respectively, of the first, middle and young generation as loosely defined herein. Arakishvili had the opportunity to Westernize the intonational bases of Georgian music as Gadzhibekov, his close contemporary, had done in Azerbaidzhan. That is, Arakishvili gathered in for a while most of the reins of Georgian musical development. That he did *not* Westernize is undoubtedly his greatest contribution: a contribution to the integrity of Georgian music. Arakishvili developed and

---

[1] *Daisi* was a particular favourite of Stalin's.

[2] Georgia alone of the three Transcaucasus republics has a body of folk music based partly on polyphony. The theory that this is rooted in Western sacred polyphony of the Middle Ages is vigorously refuted in the Soviet Union on grounds of being ideologically (dialectically) impossible. In the mountains of Svanetia, four-part folk polyphonic dances, sacred, and work songs may be heard, although three-part is much more common. Upper Svanetia is the folklorists' dream: a well developed culture, with secular, pagan, and Christian bodies of folk music; but isolated for centuries.

[3] *Eight Georgian Folk Songs for mixed chorus with accompaniment* and *A collection of Georgian folk songs*. The latter included among the Georgian musical 'dialects', Imeretian, Gurian, Ratchan, Svanetian, and Kartalino-Kakhetian.

[4] See p. 269.

[5] See p. 299.

emphasized the critical harmonic basis of his country's music. This was no mean accomplishment in the face of the fact that the Northern 'specialists', Ippolitov-Ivanov and Kastal'sky, had discarded the evidence of their ears and referred to 'out-of-tune' thirds and sixths.

Dmitrii Ignat'evich Arakishvili was born February 23, 1873 in Vladikavkaz (locally Dzaudzhikau, now Ordzhonikidze)[1] to a family whose clan head was a professional beggar and amateur distiller.[2] Young Arakishvili finished the early years of schooling in 1887, in Vladikavkaz, and entered the local church choir. He was forced, however, to leave and travel the North Caucasus in search of work. In Ekaterinodar (Krasnodar), in 1890, he joined an amateur musical group under professional direction. Living there he began to hear more of the world's music. He began to write music on an amateur scale, but some of his early works caught the ears of visiting Muscovites. Finally he found support to go to Moscow. In 1894 he entered the theory and composition class of the Moscow Philharmonic *uchilishche* under Kruglikov. The latter showed Arakishvili's work to Rimsky-Korsakov. In 1901 Arakishvili graduated and stayed on in Moscow, teaching and studying.

By 1897 Arakishvili was already writing learnedly of Georgian culture, and he often interrupted his Moscow regimen with trips to his homeland to gather and record folk music. He wrote rebuttals to Ippolitov-Ivanov's hazy articles on Georgian folk music and otherwise investigated the use of Middle Eastern folk tunes by Russian composers. He gave learned direction to the Musico-ethnographic Commission set up in 1901 by the ethnographic department of Moscow University. His presence among these well-meaning but ill-equipped men[3] at least partly saved Georgian music from the Western harmonic fate suffered by other bodies of Eastern folk music.

[1] Ordzhonikidze is not in Georgia proper but in the Northern Caucasian Autonomous Republic, Northern Ossetia. The area of the Northern Caucasus, including Georgian enclaves, has the densest concentration of ethnic groups on earth.

[2] The family name comes from the Georgian 'arakech'—distiller of spirits.

[3] Other members of the commission included Ippolitov-Ivanov, V. S. Kalinnikov, A. D. Kastal'sky, A. N. Koroshchenko, E. E. Lineva, A. M. Listopadov, A. L. Maslov, V. V. Paskhalov, M. E. Piatnitsky, Taneev, Iu. D. Engel', B. L. Iavorsky, and N. A. Ianchuk. Of these perhaps only Eugenia Lineva proceded scientifically, recording and collecting tunes in Russia and the Ukraine, as well as in Austria and Croatia. Listopadov's work, among the Don Cossacks, was crippled by a romanticized approach. Piatnisky gathered for immediate concert use. Engel' and Iavorsky were interested as composer and theorist, respectively. The latter sought to trace *all* folk music to Russian beginnings and developed a theory of rhythmic modes in a proto-Russian folk music.

During the period 1901–18, although based in Moscow, Arakishvili investigated the Georgian folk melos in great depth. Born and raised in the ethnic welter of the North Caucasus, he became most interested in which of the many music traditions were actually Georgian. This was done not as a nationalistic exercise, but as an ethnographical experiment. As ethnographical research his work had pioneer possibilities and yielded significant results. At first his endeavours seemed fruitless. In Georgia alone there are forbidding differences between the music of the Eastern (homophonic base) and Western (polyphonic base) parts of the country. Arakishvili sought and found the key to kinship of the various Georgian musical dialects in the arrangement of voices to form the 'fourth-fifth chord' and the 'fourth-seventh chord' as independent functions.[1] That the chord, though it exists in other bodies of folk music (Azerbaidzhanian, Russian to some extent), has a uniquely Georgian polyphonic genesis was proved by Arakishvili who found all its forms of development in Kartalin.

Arakishvili might very well have never returned to Georgia to stay. His activity in Moscow fitted well the image of the Russian musician.[2] In 1908 he founded a free elementary music school for poor children. In 1908 he started the journal *Music and Life* which lasted until 1912, an impressive record for the time. He wrote music constantly and was able to shift styles according to whether he was now functioning as a 'Russian' or now as a 'Georgian' composer. In 1911 the overture to his opera *Shota Rustaveli* had its first-draft hearing. In 1916, unable to travel to Tiflis because of the war, he enrolled in the Moscow University archaeological school and took, in 1917, a degree in archaeology. His dissertation, *Georgian folk musical art*, won him the gold medal.

Arakishvili moved permanently to Georgia in 1918, arriving with the status of a near-national hero, although he had not been born in and had not actually lived in his country. His appearance in that year had political implications which may never be understood,[3] but through the

---

[1] Later research (Sh. S. Aslanishvili) has raised considerable doubt about the fourth-fifth chord's functional integrity: it usually resolves to a pure fifth and only rarely stands as tonic. This does not, however, injure Arakishvili's ethnographic theses since the use of the chord remains unique.

[2] At this time and until his return to Georgia, in 1918, Arakishvili used the Russian form of his last name, 'Arakchiev'.

[3] During the war Georgia had been occupied by the Turks, then the Germans through November 1918. The British arrived. Bloody encounters between Georgia and Armenia and Georgia and Azerbaidzhan reflected local tradition as well as the nationalistic urges of each of these countries. Each, tasting sovereignty, fought bitter battles on worthless strips of land over which they hoped to be sovereign. By an overwhelming popular vote the Georgian Menshevik

confusion of the period of independence he functioned admirably as *primo commissar* of music. He had been asked to assume the directorship of the Georgian Musical Society (the old IRMS). This post, from which he was to govern performance and pedagogical activity, suited him well.

On February 5, 1919 Arakishvili's two-act opera, *Skazanie o Shota Rustaveli* ('The tale of Shota Rustaveli') was first performed. This was to remain Arakishvili's most significant contribution, as a composer, to Georgian western music, and the date of its performance in Tiflis became one of the most important in Georgia's musical history. This was not because Arakshvili was ever a great composer: *Shota Rustaveli* is many steps removed in overall quality from even the best Soviet music. But this performance of a clearly Georgian work which was, technically, fully acceptable and performable in the European tradition, and into whose première the musical energies of at least all Tiflis were directed, was a momentous cultural and civic event. This relatively late date for Georgia's first opera,[1] 1919, was the hinge point of Georgian classical music. Arakishvili had begun his opera soon after 1905. Work went slowly: piano excerpts were heard in Moscow, Pavlovsk and Tiflis in 1913, and in 1914 the complete score was submitted to the Italian oriented directorate of the Tiflis Opera Theatre. It was turned down, but when Arakishvili assumed command of that theatre in 1918, the way was clear.

---

party assumed political leadership. Minority Bolshevik uprisings were easily put down. Through the various occupations, border battles and uprisings the thread of desire for self rule remained. An agreement was reached in late 1920 whereby Soviet Russia recognized Georgian independence and sent an ambassador, Kirov. On February 11, 1921, a rebellion broke out in Lori to the south which led to yet another Georgian-Armenian war. The Soviets took the opportunity to attack from the North, under Ordzhonikidze, and appeared before Tiflis on February 17. By the 25th that city was occupied and Georgia fell again into the familiar embrace of her hungry northern neighbour.

[1] Georgia's first opera experience had been only as recent as 1851 when a touring Italian group mounted *Lucia de Lammermoor* in Tiflis. Excerpts from Russian operas were presented in 1855. Full-length operas, with some participation of Georgian singers, began in 1880, and the preference was for the Italian standards, although *Ivan Susanin, Russlan and Liudmilla* and other Russian operas were also staged. During Ippolitov-Ivanov's first Tiflis stay (1885–90) Russian opera was frequently heard. Tschaikovsky visited Tiflis regularly from 1886 to 1890 and heard performances of his operas there. Meliton Balanchivadze's *The Perfidious Daredzhan* had been heard in embryonic form in St Petersburg on December 20, 1897, but this work came to Tiflis only in 1926. Paliashvili's *Abesalom and Eteri*, performable only by Georgians, was staged in Tiflis in 1919, two weeks after the première of *Shota Rustaveli*

Rustaveli[1] was a Georgian poet and folk hero of whom many tales became folk legend. A variant of one of these tales is used by the librettist, A. Khakhanashvili: In the first act Shota takes leave of his childhood beloved, Nina, to travel afar to study; they trade presents. In the second act, after many years, years which find Nina supposedly married to another and the broken-hearted Shota a famous man, the poet is honoured by Queen Tamara on the completion of his famous poem, 'The hero in tiger skin'. During the festivities, which bring some joy to Shota, he is told by a young man unknown to him to travel immediately home. In the company of the young man he does so. He surprises his wife, a surrogate for Nina, in the arms of an Arab servant. Stunned, he turns to the youth and sees that it is actually Nina, who has not married after all. In shock or anger he goes away and Nina commits suicide.[2]

The opera runs to ballads and choruses, all of them separate units. The single, four-measure recitative (Example 1), is the lonely reminder that otherwise Arakishvili makes no use of it. The opera is vaguely motivic, but the composer feels little need for growth in these motives. The most consistently used and developed image throughout the opera is that of the Arab folk song *Urmurli*, a song sung by urban peasants on the road. It is, with the lullaby 'Nana', the most widely known in Georgia,[3] and becomes identified with Nina in the first act (Example 2). The composer all but quotes the melody (Example 3), uses a paraphrase in the introduction to Nina's aria (Example 4), and extends this latter into the simple, effective lament of Nina (Example 5). This all occurs in the youthful scene where the lovers part. In the third act, with the enormity of Giul'chan's crime, Shota's rage, and her impending suicide loading the drama, plus the seasoning tension of many years gone by, this aria returns, embarrassingly identical in every detail. In this, as in most of the arias, Arakishvili does not cite pure Georgian folk music but, rather, the specialized, 'impure' and generally mono-phonic music of the city. In the choruses, on the other hand, the har-monies, if not the polyphony, of the countryside are heard. In the festive

---

[1] 'Shota' is, apparently, a later addition. Rustaveli's dates are unknown. Because his work indicates an association with Queen Tamara, it may be assumed that he lived and worked between A.D. 1190 and 1210. These are the extreme guesses at Tamara's reign. No written record or reference concerning Rustaveli has ever been found. Only his poetry and the many folk legends provide any clue.

[2] The ending in the opera differs from that in the most popular version of the folk legend. In the latter Shota runs the youth through with his sword for disturbing his peace, and then recognizes that it is actually Nina.

[3] Archil Begidzhanov, *Dmitrii Arakishvili* (Moscow, *Muzgiz*, 1953), p. 114n.

Ex.1 *Recitative.*

All here pre-sent, poor and hum-ble, and the rich, and all the home-less.

Ex.2 *"Urmuli" (urban road song).*

Ex.3 *Usage of "Urmurli."*

A - ra-lu a-ra-la — lo — da

etc.

Ex. 4 *"Urmurli" paraphrase.*

Ex. 5 *Nina's lament.*

I am a-lone in lone-li-ness, no dear ones has an or-phan girl

Ex. 6 *Georgian table song.*

Sop.

Alto

Mno-ga-ia   le — ta,   Mno-ga-ia   le — ta,

Ten.

Bass   Mno-ga-ia   le — ta,   Mno-ga-ia   le — ta,

second act a chorus praising Shota is started with a Georgian table song exhibiting the typical fourth-fifth chord (Example 6).

The opera is put together dramatically on two musical axes: the Shota-Nina love and the Arab-Giul'chin affair. The music of these two provides the main two themes of the opening orchestral part (Example 7a and b, Example 8). A third theme, that of the palace pleasures of Tamara, is quoted briefly (Example 9). It figures again in the gala second act.

Shota-Nina

The opera was received as a national triumph. This was due to the intense nationalism of the period more than to the musical qualities of the work. Arakishvili constantly reworked it.[1]

In 1921 Arakishvili became director of the Second Tiflis Conservatory.[2] He was already teaching in the First and, in 1923–4, when the two combined he became director (until 1929) of the composition faculty.

[1] The story and music quoted here are from a three-act edition completed some time after 1919.

[2] The Second Conservatory was expressly for gifted peasants and workers and was based with the Philharmonic Society of which Arakishvili was director. This was the Tiflis solution to the problem solved in Moscow by admitting such talent to the established conservatory, the latter with disastrous results. The Tiflis Second Conservatory had, by 1922, 1,638 students.

Ex. 7b. *Arab-Giul'chin theme*

By now Arakishvili's training and position were no longer unique. A large musical cadre of Georgian nationality had replaced Russians. Moreover, being a sort of Georgian 'Renaissance Man', Arakishvili found it difficult to specialize as narrowly as a conservatory often demands. He moved from composition to musical ethnography to children's pedagogy fitfully and, finally, became professor in name only in

Ex.8 *Arab-Giul'chin theme*

1929. In one way or another he had been the teacher, at times, of Shalva Azmaiparashvili (1903–), Andrei Balanchivadze (1906–), Ivan Gokieli (1899–), Grigorii Kiladze (1902–), Shalva Mshvelidze (1901–), and Iona Tuskia (1901–). In 1932 he became First Secretary of the Georgian USC for two years. He turned again to folk music and wrote folk-based choruses and songs during the thirties. Ideological imperatives from the centre interfered with due scientific process until the war. But Arakishvili again delved deeply into folklore, this time impressing the

5

Ex. 9 *Tamara's palace*

Georgian Academy of Sciences sufficiently to inaugurate a department in that field. Arakishvili himself became a member in 1950.

As indicated earlier, Arakishvili's composition was insignificant during the last third of his life. Most of the songs and choruses are unpublished. He wrote three symphonies (1932–4, 1940–2 and 1948–51), also unpublished, which had one or two hearings each. His most valuable legacy remains his work in the folk field. No one could resist the Stalinist demands made on ethnographical research, especially in Stalin's native Georgia. So one can say that some of Arakishvili's late work is distorted, or even false. He died in Tbilisi in August 1953, six months after the death of the dictator, and was unable to make the corrections one feels sure he would have made. That work has gone well since. Impressive Georgian forces, well-equipped, are at work on the Georgian ethnomusicological gold mine, carrying on Arakishvili's life-long labour.

CHAPTER 12

ᡞᢛᡞᢛ

Uzeir Gadzhibekov

In a consideration of Azerbaidzhanian music it is difficult to avoid entering the ideological dispute about the absence or existence of a genuine, ethnically and culturally 'pure' Northern Azerbaidzhan history. The idealized Soviet image is that of Northern Azerbaidzhan as one of a trio of nations (with Armenia and Georgia) whose people have always venerated one another and worked together in the face of cultural pollution from Turkey or Iran; three nations that have borrowed the best from one another, each maintaining, however, its cultural purity; three nations whose people, although their leaders may be at war, still hold and held one another in high regard, and whose tendencies toward unity and peaceful co-existence were periodically strengthened by the benevolent intervention of Russia; and, finally, three nations of demonstrably deep antiquity. Unfortunately the historical facts of politics and geography make the case a shaky one. Culturally, based on surviving literature and evidence both linguistic and ethnic, the point is far easier made in the case of Armenia and Georgia than in that of Azerbaidzhan. The Azerbaidzhan language is a Turkic variant, the Azers are an ethnic mix of Turk and Iranian, and the 'Azerbaidzhanian literary heritage' exists only in Iranian (Persian) or, later, in Osmanli Turkish; i.e. in the minds of Soviet theorists.

The integrity of the Soviet Azerbaidzhan musical tradition, in the absence of records, rests on the 'integrity' of the Soviet Azerbaidzhanian *mugam*. Here, again, the attempt to isolate the Northern[1] Azerbaidzhanian *mugam* from similar if not identical types of *mugams*, *maqams*, and *makams* in the arabo-turkic-Iranian musical heritage is mere nitpicking; at best guessing. The first great modern Azerbaidzhanian musician, Uzeir Gadzhibekov, laid a foundation for study of the *mugam*,

---

[1] The reference must always be to 'Northern' or 'Soviet' Azerbaidzhan since most Azerbaidzhanis live outside the Soviet Union in Iran, just as most Armenians live not in Soviet Armenia but in Turkey.

but not as a musical phenomenon exclusively Northern Azerbaidzhan-ian.[1]

Gadzhibekov is, in some ways , the Azerbaidzhanian Komitas (*q.v.*). He had, however, no legacy of research, no tradition upon which to build as Komitas had. Nor was Komitas so concerned as Gadzhibekov about Westernizing or bringing up to date a supposedly 'outmoded' system. Gadzhibekov was truly the originator of his country's music: He wrote the first Azerbaidzhanian opera, founded the first Azerbaid-zhanian music school, the first 'Western' choir, and began the research into his country's folk heritage which has continued, for better or for worse, to the present.

Uzeir Abdul Gusein ogly Gadzhibekov was born on September 5, 1885 in the city of Agdzhabedy. His father was a member of the small Azerbaidzhanian intelligentsia: a clerk for the Russian government. By comparison with its nationalistic neighbours, Armenia and Georgia,

---

[1] *Mugam:* Through usage the term has come to mean three things: (1) Through early Russian misunderstanding, and in the light of indifferent research, the *mugami* were thought to be the equivalent of the Byzanto-Russian *lady* of the *znammenyi rospev*, just as the arabic *maqam* was occasionally mis-takenly identified with the early Western church modes. (2) A genre with formal traits of the rhapsody and suite, improvisational in style, on texts by classical middle Eastern poets (but also now with Soviet texts); performed by an en-semble which may include a singer, *khanandist* (high drum), *tarist* (six-stringed, long necked, plucked instrument, originally with frets placed just smaller than the interval of a half tone) and *kiamanchist* (3 to 5 stringed, bowed instrument with a possible tuning: B, G, d, a, e; a small, ball body; requires a virtuoso technique). (3) (The definition important here) A raga-like melody type. Although usually illustrated as scales, each *mugam* has, or had, characteristic

melody patterns. In the classification that has gone on in Soviet Azerbaidzhan there is a strong resistance to this factor, first because of the ridiculous Stalinist tenet that the *mugam* was derived, if not from the *znammenyi rospev* itself, at least from its intonation (*popevka*) and, more importantly, through Westerniza-tion of intervallic content which has emasculated the patterns. The most important of the *mugami* (Soviet musicology insists on 70) are the *rast* (cf. arabic *rast*), *shur* (from the Iranian *avazat: shur*), *segiakh* (*avazat: sihgah*), *shushter*, *chargiakh* (*avazat: chahargah*), *baiati*-(place name) (*avazat: bayat-i*-(place name)), and *khumaiun* (*avazat: humayun*). Note, in the above example (a) the presence of both B natural and B flat.

Azerbaidzhan was a backward, thinly settled[1] grazing area whose people were only dimly aware of the notion of sovereignty. The small corps of the urban intelligentsia was strongly Russian oriented: this was the only possible 'window on the West'. The rural land holders, workers and peasants were, depending on location, Persian or Turkish oriented.

Gadzhibekov spent his early youth in Shusha, reportedly surrounded by folk musicians, and in 1899, at the age of fourteen, was sent to the teacher's seminary in Gori (Georgia) where he first studied musical theory, violin, and 'cello. He steeped himself in 'Western' ways. In 1905 he returned to Azerbaidzhan, to Baku, and began an intense intellectual activity. Gadzhibekov was an exceptional person. He easily became a leader in many ways other than musical. He concerned himself with the literacy of his country and worked among the new 'proletariat'—the oil workers—to stamp out illiteracy and improve their status. He translated Russian classics into the Turkic dialect spoken in most of Northern Azerbaidzhan and compiled an Azerbaidzhanian arithmetic text and a Russo-Azerbaidzhan dictionary. He was aware of and dissatisfied with the state of social and economic development he saw around him, and, although he resented Russia as the oppressing imperialist power, he saw a solution in contemporary liberal Russian thinking, or such is the claim of Soviet historians.

In 1907 he wrote the first Azerbaidzhanian opera, *Leili i Medzhnun*. This work is still the closest to a truly Azerbaidzhanian opera any composer has written. The story is a classic middle-Eastern folk tale.[2] Scored for Azerbaidzhanian folk instruments as well as some European ones, the opera includes *mugams* in 'pure' form: only the directions implicit in the given *mugam* are supplied by the composer; the performer was expected to improvise in the traditional style. *Leili i Medzhnun* was first presented in 1908 in Baku. This highly personal opera form, so dependent on the consistency of the performer,[3] became the standard for a short time only. Gadzhibekov himself continued with the genre for a while[4] as did his brother Zul'fugar (1884–1950) with *Ashug Garib* (1916),

---

[1] Azerbaidzhan has been extensively colonized since the revolution. Although most Azerbaidzhani are still sheep herders, their percentage of the population has dropped far below 50 per cent. The newcomers are mostly Russian and Ukrainian.

[2] For more on this fable and its use by Azerbaidzhanian musicians see p. 313.

[3] Since the *mugam* (the rhapsodic form) is not exclusively a vocal work, some of the orchestra parts were also in part improvisatory. Gadzhibekov played the violin in a number of performances.

[4] Other *mugam* operas by Gadzhibekov: *Sheikh Senan*, 1909; *Rustan and Zakhrab*, 1910; *Shah Abbas and Khrshid Banu*, 1911; *Asli and Kerem*, 1912; *Garun and Leila*, 1912–15. Up to this time Gadzhibekov was his own librettist.

and Gadzhibekov's long-time friend and associate Abdul Muslim Magometovich Magomaev (1885–1937). Magomaev's first such opera was *Shah Ismail* (1919).

Whatever Gadzhibekov's contribution and whatever his sincerity, he was fanatically possessed of the idea that Azerbaidzhanian music must correct its 'mistakes', i.e. the non-Western scalar structure and apparent lack of harmony. To him, the naive mathematics of Western diatonicism was irrefutable logic. Just as it was not difficult to persuade him of this, it was equally easy to persuade him of the primitive level of the *mugam*-based music of his people. Only much later, when it was too late, did he suspect that he had tampered with the fragile distillate of centuries of sophistication. By that time authoritative Western ears, notably Gliere's (see p. 70) had accepted and capitalized on Gadzhibekov's monster.[1] Gliere's *Shah Senem* (1927) was a point of no return for the new Azerbaidzhan music. Nor could it become the new focus: something else had to take its place as well. Magomaev had been opposed to Gadzhibekov in the matter of 'westernizing' Azerbaidzhahian music, but his was the last authoritative Azerbaidzhanian voice, until very recently, to speak for what was tagged 'bourgeois orthodoxy' in native music.

In 1911 Gadzhibekov went to Moscow to study in the musicodramatic preparatory school to the conservatory. He studied there with Ilinsky, but moved on to St Petersburg in 1913 where he studied with Kalafati.[2] A number of his pre-revolutionary operas (see above) were written there, and he became adept, as we have seen, at what Asaf'ev called 'Russian music of the East'. His studies, on their completion, however, stilled his operatic pen for many years. The period from 1915 to 1922 seems untraceable. No two references are consistent: It has been suggested that he led a music section of the Red Army[3]; another source indicates simply that he left the Petersburg Conservatory for financial reasons.[4] It must be remembered, of course, that Azerbaidzhan maintained a separate course of independent government until 1921. Gadzhibekov's role, even his whereabouts, during this intense period can only be guessed at.

In 1922 Gadzhibekov founded Azerbaidzhan's first music school, in Baku. During the ensuing decade he originated orchestras and choirs

---

[1] See p. 73.

[2] Vassilii Pavlovich Kalafati, 1869–1942, taught at the St Petersburg Conservatory. As mentioned elsewhere, he is the one time mentor of Igor Stravinsky.

[3] *Sovetskie Kompozitory*, p. 126.

[4] Groves, III, 540, fifth edition. The credit for the article on Gadzhibekov is given to the Society for Cultural Relations with the USSR—a monumental dunghill of misinformation in Groves.

and generally occupied the centre of responsibility for musical development in his country. His views seem to have coincided comfortably with those of the Party in matters of the cultural integrity of Azerbaidzhan. So far as any records show he approved the scrapping of the old Azer (Turkic) alphabet and the substitution of the Latin; and, when Ataman of Turkey latinized the Turkish alphabet, and the confusing switch was made from Latin to cyrillic letters, Gadzhibekov was a staunch advocate. That the move tended to isolate Northern Azerbaidzhan culturally (except from the USSR) rather than purify it, was, apparently, of no concern to Gadzhibekov. It must be admitted that Gadzhibekov, a man of influence in many fields, was one of the keystones of the Russification of his country.[1] At the same time, and in Gadzhibekov's defence (if indeed he needs one), it must be pointed out that backward, illiterate, disease-ridden Northern Azerbaidzhan seemed, after a slow start, to explode into the twentieth century. In view of this undeniable progress, Gadzhibekov, during the troublesome times of collectivization and genuine national independence movements, threw his considerable weight to the Soviet side. If he was a bell-wether, it was in the spirit of Boris Godunov who after the initial murder did his best to do what was right.

By the early thirties it became obvious that Gadzhibekov's prolific days as a composer had stopped with the revolution. The opera style he had originated with *Leili i Medzhnun* was a dead issue: competent performer-improvisers had all but disappeared from the scene. His last big work was the opera *Ker-ogly*, written from 1932 to 1936 and performed in Moscow in 1938. This opera, his last, had librettists G. Ismailov and M. Ordubada, who carefully nurtured a story of Azerbaidzhanian struggle against oppression through the historiographical morass of the early thirties. When the opera was finally shown in Moscow (with a Russian translation by L. Zaltsman) Stalin was well pleased. A reception was arranged and the dialogue between Stalin and Gadzhibekov took its place in that short, curious series of such confrontations given world-wide publicity by Soviet propaganda organs. Gadzhibekov was one of the first Stalin Prize winners.

Among Gadzhibekov's other works are four cantatas, the last two being *The Motherland and The Front* (1943), and the *Hymn to Victory* (1945); works for folk orchestra[2] including two fantasies, one each on

[1] Azerbaidzhan's population is now more than 50 per cent Russian and key posts have been held for years by Russians.
[2] In 1932 Gadzhibekov had worked out systems of tuning, notation and instrumentation for orchestras of Azerbaidzhanian folk instruments.

the *mugams chargiakh* and *shur* (both in 1932); and a number of folk settings.

Gadzhibekov's *magnum opus*, however, was the monumental ethno-musicological work *The Bases of Azerbaidzhanian Folk Music*, finally published in Baku in 1945. His work had begun on this before the revolution, and afterwards most of his efforts were directed towards it. This work, like any work whose creation spans a good bit of Soviet history (for example, Shaporin's *Decembrists*, Livanova's music history, Pasternak's *Dr Zhivago*), carries scars of the ideological battle. The year 1945 was a year of liberal publication, and it is fortunate that the book appeared then. The amount of work is impressive, and it is standard academic fare now in most of the Soviet near and middle East.

Because of its 'narrowness' and 'rigid nationalistic' approach and its 'historical inaccuracy' the book was criticized in February 1948 in Moscow, and later that year more completely in one of the rash of imitative, fledgling forums in the periphery, in Baku. But the criticism never reached Gadzhibekov who died on November 23rd.

꙳꙳

CHAPTER 13

Sergei Prokofieff

O f the composers considered here, Sergei Prokofieff is the most significant. Of all music written since 1900, Prokofieff's is the most played today throughout the world. Of Soviet composers, Prokofieff's style is, perhaps, the most consistently and identifiably individual. From the first to the last of his works this idiomatic unity holds, even in the attenuated combinations of his later works. He was a prolific composer and wrote in all media. His works include nine operas, eight ballets, seven symphonies, as well as a number of works for chorus, orchestra and soloists, five piano concertos, two violin and two 'cello concertos, piano sonatas, piano cycles, and music for the stage and films. At the time of his death much of this music was still under official condemnation. Among the major works excluded from perfor- mance in the Soviet Union were the piano concertos numbers two (1913), four (1931), and five (1932); the symphonies numbers two (1924), three (1928), four (1930), and six (1945–47); the ballets Le Pas d'Acier (1925) and Prodigal Son (1928); Scythian Suite (1914–15); and, perhaps most sadly, the operas Gambler (1915–16), Love for Three Oranges (1919), Flaming Angel (1919–27), Semyon Kotko (1939), and Story of a Real Man (1947–48). Chamber works, songs, and other works of smaller proportion were also not performed. Many, but not all, of these works have since returned to the Soviet repertoire.

One balks at assigning this significant composer to a national or nationalistic niche. Technically, Prokofieff was a Soviet composer, and, so far as we know, he was so by choice, but he alone of the composers considered here transcends that definition and its limitations.

Through sloppy scholarship, opportunistic and sensational journa- lism, revolutionary heat, and bewildering politics, all intensified by the stature of the man, traditional misconceptions have surrounded Prokofieff. These involve not only his music, personality and attitudes, but even such facts as dates, including the one of his death. One resists the temptation to deal with Prokofieff through review and correction of the published materials concerning the composer. This would yield the story of Prokofieff and his music, and it would also provide a revealing, perhaps disquieting, view of certain aspects of both Soviet and Western musical reporting.[1]

Prokofieff was born on April 11/23, 1891 in Sontsovka in the Ekaterinoslav Gubernia of the Ukraine. His father was, and would continue to be until his death, the manager of the Sontsov estates.[2] In his

[1] The basic secondary source on Prokofieff is, by default, the biography by Israel V. Nestyev, *Prokofiev*, published in Moscow by Gosmuzizdat in 1957. The same is available in English, published in Stanford by the Stanford University Press in 1960. The excellent translation is by Florence Jonas. This volume is a considerable enlargement and revision of an earlier work by Nestyev, also available in both Russian and English. The two editions differ significantly in interpretation and vocabulary. The later, enlarged version suffers from restraints on musicology of the mid-fifties in the Soviet Union. Two easily available 'primary' sources are (1) *S. S. Prokofiev, Materialy, Dokumenty i Vospominaniia*, compiled and edited by S. I. Schlifstein, and published in Moscow by Muzgiz in 1961. Parts of an earlier (1956) edition of the same have been published in English under the title *Autobiography, Articles and Reminiscences* by the Foreign Language Publishing House, in *c.* 1958 (references in this chapter are to *Materialy* in the 1961 edition, with a slash separating the page citation from that of the English language edition, if that citation appears in the latter); and (2) a similar compilation by Nestyev and G. Ia. Edelman, *Sergei Prokofiev, 1953–1962: Stat'i i Materialy*, published in Moscow by Sovetskii Kompozitor, first edition in 1962, second edition in 1965. Contents of the two editions do not precisely coincide.

Western biographies abound in most Western European languages. Those by Michel Hoffman (French, 1963), Claude Samuel (French, 1960), and Friedbert Streller (German, 1960) may be of some use to the recreational reader, but not to a specialist. Two published recently in English by Lawrence and Elizabeth Hanson (1964) and Victor Seroff (1968) were best avoided altogether.

Authoritative, scholarly, responsible scholarship is being done by Malcolm H. Brown, whose *Symphonies of Prokofiev* will shortly be published. The many references to the work in this chapter are to pages of the manuscript which Professor Brown has kindly loaned me. He is at present working on a definitive biography.

[2] The smallness of the village, the post-revolutionary tradition of changing place names, and the relatively late attention paid to Prokofieff's early years caused scholars (and cartographers) to 'lose' Sontsovka until 1960. M. Babkov, in the Stalino Radians'ka Donechchina (Soviet Donbass), published the results of his research: Sontsovka is now Krasnoe, a fact heretofore unknown to biographers and, reportedly, to Prokofieff himself. Nor, until this time, were the villagers aware of their famous countryman, although Babkov did find two old residents who remembered the Prokofieff family. Plans, as of 1960, were afoot to erect a Prokofieff House of Culture on the site of the old Prokofieff home, and there was talk of changing the village name once more—to Prokofievo. However, since Prokofieff visited Sontsovka at least as late as the Autumn of 1910, at the age of nineteen, some of Babkov's story may be exaggerated. Mira Mendelson, Prokofieff's second wife, speaks of the composer's concern in 1942 when the battle front moved near Sontsovka. (*Materialy*, 377/171.)

autobiographical notes,[1] Prokofieff dwells on his childhood surround-
ings. He mentions works of Beethoven, Chopin, (easy) Liszt, Tschaikovsky and Rubinstein as among those he used to hear his mother play.
He was precociously talented, and he was indulged. By the age of ten,
when he had his first personal, professional contact, he had written a
number of childish pieces including an opera, *Giant*. He was displayed
by his anxious mother in Moscow before Taneev in 1902, and, during the
succeeding two summers, Reinhold Gliere was dispatched by Taneev
to Sontsovka to see to the child's formal musical training. In 1904, at
the age of thirteen, Prokofieff was enrolled in the St Petersburg Conservatory. The choice of St Petersburg over Moscow was critical: it has
been suggested elsewhere that Gliere, who was at home in either city,
recommended the Northern capital. In any case, Gliere did not argue
for Moscow, as at least one Western account says. Moreover, young
Prokofieff's maternal relatives were Petersburgers, and the Conservatory
Director, Glazunov, after an initial lukewarm reception, urged the
choice upon the boy and his mother. Thus Prokofieff moved from
Gliere, the first of his most important musical relationships, to Liadov
and Rimsky-Korsakov. These conservatory professors he judged dull
and ineffective. He 'got much more' from his older fellow student,
Nikolai Miaskovsky.[2]

During the conservatory years, 1904 to 1914[3] Prokofieff entered the
St Petersburg modern music circles with enthusiasm. The enthusiasm
was returned by Ignatz Kryzhanovsky and Viacheslav Karatygin who
were organizers of the important 'Evenings of Modern Music) (see
p. 22), and, significantly, by close supporters of the Diaghelev circle.
With one of the latter, Walter Nuvel, he travelled in June of 1914 to
London—a graduation gift from his mother. The Diaghelev troupe was
appearing there, and, for the first time, Prokofieff savoured something of
the musical world outside the two Russian capitals. This visit had many
consequences. Here began his long association with Diaghelev. The
visit implanted firmly in his mind the Russian composer's notion of
success abroad. Most importantly, it tended to fix his own musical ways.
As to the latter, it is significant that Prokofieff himself, as well as many
musical commentators, felt that his lifelong store of musical idioms was
assembled early and was to undergo no basic change. Proportionate
usage and assembly rather than changing idiom was to delimit his

[1] *Materialy*.
[2] *Materialy*, 136/22.
[3] Prokofieff graduated in composition in 1909 and returned for piano training
until 1914. In 1915 he re-entered, as an organ student, in order to avoid military
service.

creative periods. Returning at the end of a month to Petersburg,[1] with a commission from Diaghelev, Prokofieff set about the composition of the ballet *Ala and Lolli*.[2] The score shows with every page that he was reeling under yet another London impact—that of Stravinsky.

Prokofieff became well known in Moscow as well as Petersburg modern music circles. He reports that his progress in the contemporary direction was appreciated neither by his professors in St Petersburg nor his old acquaintances at the Moscow Conservatory. Through 1918 he received important orchestral performances in Moscow under Koussevitsky and 'in St Petersburg/Petrograd under Siloti. An enviable publication record began in 1911 with the Jurgenson publication of his *Piano Sonata No. 1* (op. 1) when the composer was only twenty. Jurgenson and Gutheil published most of his early piano music, including the first four sonatas, two piano concertos, and *Sarcasms*, as well as some songs. The Russian Music Publishers (Koussevitsky)[3] at first ignored the young rebel on the advice of a board which included Sergei Rachmaninoff.

Prokofieff moved abroad in 1918. One must be clear about the reasons, since most sources ascribe his leaving either to discomfort with or misunderstanding of the revolution, or to an immediate desire for money. The revolutionary events were so dramatic, and so much general attention is focused on these early years, that both Soviet and Western writers naturally seek therein the things that moved Prokofieff.[4] But, it is most probable that Prokofieff's mind was made up well before 1917, and, in any case, the force of tradition had long since carved the path: All Russian musicians of accomplishment went abroad. The late nineteenth and early twentieth centuries found Russian composers, conductors, and instrumentalists situated in many Western musical posts. They were prominent on the concert circuits. Russian music and Russian musicians were 'exportable' items even before Diaghelev. The

[1] Prokofieff narrowly missed the outbreak of the war.

[2] *Ala and Lolli* appears as opus 20, i.e. the suite derivative, *Scythian Suite*. Gutheil: Petrograd, 1923.

[3] In 1914, Koussevitsky bought out Gutheil. In 1916 Prokofieff broke with Jurgenson and went over to Koussevitsky. He remained with Koussevitsky, in Russia and subsequently abroad, for some twenty years.

[4] Indeed, few of the many musicians, as such, who left Russia during these times were 'avoiding' the reality of the revolution as both Western and annoyed Soviet reports still say. Moreover, few of them anticipated permanent estrangement. The revolution's grip on men's minds in the early days of the Soviet Union is so taken for granted that we must constantly be reminded to the contrary. The musician was apathetic and disinterested. His knowledge of the situation and of its leaders was absent or distorted. The diaspora took place simply because, for the last time, the opportunity occurred.

pattern of success for a Russian musician, then and, curiously, now, included, as a matter of course, the quest for a prolonged personal impact abroad. By the end of the first decade of the new century, and certainly during and immediately after the war, America seemed to offer the most rewards. Prokofieff was totally engrossed in his music and with himself as a musician. His concern with Russian politics was, and was to remain, negligible unless it interfered with his muse. He did not want particularly for money. He was naive in many things, frankly self-centred, and still very much the *enfant terrible*. Prokofieff later told of how he made up his mind to leave for America while sojourning in isolated Kislovodsk during the last months of 1917 and first part of 1918. But, as early as mid-1917 he had negotiated with the visiting American, Cyrus McCormick, about financial arrangements in Chicago.

By the close of this, Prokofieff's early Russian period, his most important works were the *Scythian Suite* (op. 20, 1914–16), the *First Violin Concerto* (op. 19, 1916–17), an opera, *Gambler* (op. 24, written in 1915–16, but not appearing in its final form until 1927), a cantata *Seven, They Are Seven* (op. 30, 1917–18), and the *Classical Symphony* (*Symphony No. 1*, op. 25, 1916–17), the latter a significant, not altogether representative work. There were also the numerous works for piano ranging from short sets of pieces of which *Sarcasms* (op. 17, 1912–14) and *Fugitive Visions* (op. 22, 1915–17) are the best known, through the piano sonatas one through four, to the piano concertos numbers one (op. 10, 1911–12), two (op. 16, 1913, reconstructed in 1923 after having been lost), and three (op. 26, 1917–21, finished abroad).

The *Scythian Suite*, as mentioned earlier, derives from *Ala and Lolli*, the ballet suggested by Diaghelev. The plot involves the struggle between the forces of the Sun God and the Evil God. The latter, after one abortive attempt (thwarted by moonbeams), succeeds in carrying off Ala, the sensuous fertility idol whom the ancient Slavs (Scyths) worship. Lolli, a Scythian warrior, fights the Evil God for her release and is at the point of defeat when the Sun God intervenes (by rising) to destroy the Evil God, and saves both Ala and Lolli. Primitivity, savagery, the orgiastic, barbaric sensuality, and paganism were the identifying characteristics of 'Scythianism', a concept which held a strong place in many movements in art and literature of the time. Scythianism clearly dominates Stravinsky's earlier *Rite of Spring*. Prokofieff heard and saw this work in London[1]; Nestyev is amusingly overcautious when he says, 'It (*Rite*) seemingly had some effect on the style of *Ala and Lolli*'.[2] The *Scythian Suite* is scored for a large, full

[1] Prokofieff had heard the Stravinsky work in a concert version in Moscow under Koussevitsky earlier in 1914.   [2] Nestyev, *Prokofiev*, p. 92.

orchestra with augmentation which brings the specified force to 140 players. Indeed, the work is a *tour-de-force* in orchestration. Quasi-experimental combinations, heavy brass and percussion, sound-effects, and poly-choral and poly-rhythmic devices predominate to the exclusion of any sustained melodic interest. The complex scoring is meticulously and laboriously worked out, and Prokofieff admits to having spent an inordinate amount of time on orchestral detail, especially in the last two movements. The suite is very like a symphony—perhaps more of a piece with the symphonies two through six than is his first, *Classical Symphony*. If it is argued that the thematic treatment and formal structure falls short of symphonic 'dignity', then much the same case can be made for the other symphonies as well.

The first movement places in contrast the energetic and heroic (the Sun God) with the lyric, mellow, and exotic (Ala). The second movement is a dance movement among dances. Representing the Evil God and his powers, it exhibits intentionally rude and incessant rhythms and a generally blazing pace. The third, slow, movement is a nocturne with a simple melody which is ultimately lost in shimmering effects of strings, flutes, oboes, celeste, and harp. The movement is interrupted by ominous ejaculations reminiscent of the second movement. All orchestral powers are assembled in the last movement and point dazzlingly to the longish conclusion or coda—a tonal sunrise which must certainly be included as one of the more successful members of the sub-genre of musical sunrises. Nestyev likens this finale to that of Scriabin's *Poem of Ecstasy*.[1]

The reason for the work's appearance in a four-movement concert form stems from Prokofieff's second trip toward the radiance of Diaghelev early in 1915. Diaghelev met him in Milan, absolutely rejected *Ala and Lolli*, mollified the composer by arranging a concert of his works in Milan, and sent the bewildered young man home with a 3,000 ruble contract for another ballet, the *Buffoon*. Prokofieff remained loyal to his rejected *Ala*, rewriting very little to put it into four-movement form. The work had many performances before Prokofieff left Russia, and its preparation and reception were not without incidents self-consciously similar to those attending the première of Stravinsky's *Rite of Spring*, in 1913, in Paris.

A superficial comparison of the *Scythian Suite* and the *Classical Symphony* might reveal two composers. The 'Scythian' orchestra of 140 becomes, in the symphony, a modest classical orchestra: pairs of winds, strings, and tympani. Prokofieff subsequently spoke elliptically of his first symphony, sometimes in the spirit of dismissal, sometimes

[1] Nestyev, *Prokofiev*, p. 107.

in its defence. He avoided the 'neo-classical' label and explained his approach as one in which he tried to commit himself directly in full score. He thus avoided both the piano stage of composing and the separation of the phases of composition and orchestration which latter procedure is still standard for the Soviet composer. The four-movement result is only superficially classical, but altogether delightful. Malcolm Brown suggests that the work is a divertimento. Brown further points to a 'basic insensitivity to the manipulation of form',[1] which characterizes this and other work of the composer. As we have seen and shall see further, this characteristic, perhaps expressed more positively, is seen throughout Russian and Soviet music.

The symphony's first movement is an Allegro in conventional sonata-allegro form. The development is accomplished through repetition and repetition of sequences. Piquant and brash in close handling of harmonies, the overall harmonic scheme can yet be called conventional. An elegant, reserved slow movement follows. Whereas melodic motives were broadly spaced in the first movement (e.g. two-octave leaps), now an aloof melody moves at some distance from its humble accompaniment. The most nearly lyric moments in the work occur in this movement. Here, too, the archtypical 'Prokofieff Shift', or unexpected displacement of the tonal centre, is heard at such serene leisure as to expunge the notion of the grotesque so often associated with it. The third movement is the Gavotte, often played separately, to Prokofieff's annoyance. Perhaps Prokofieff catches here more accurately the essence of the pre-classical dance than he does that of classical flavour in the other movements. The merriness, abandon, and heavy footedness are reminiscent, even, of the early dance before the sophistication of the late Baroque. A musette-like middle section is used to provide an ABA structure. The generally conjunct melody seemingly casts its tonal moorings off in the A sections: the B section is tonally more cautious. The last movement moves off briskly and is replete with tonally blunted cadences and abrupt stops all carefully, if not altogether successfully, handled.

Whereas the *Scythian Suite* received many performances prior to Prokofieff's departure, the *Classical Symphony* received but one. This one performance was probably very important to the composer, since the agent for his release from the Soviet Union, the powerful Anatole Lunacharsky, was in the audience.

Prokofieff became an international figure for twenty years, and for nine years he did not visit the Soviet Union. Leaving the USSR by the

---

[1] Malcolm Brown, *The Symphonies of Prokofiev*, p. 17.

Eastern route,[1] he missed connections for a projected South American tour and waited in Japan, where he gave recitals of his works, for a US visa. He arrived in New York via Honolulu ('delightful') and San Francisco in September. He remained in the United States for nineteen months with one concert tour to Canada. He concertized, attended and performed concerts of his own music, and composed. His activities centred in New York and Chicago. Still very much the idol-smasher, his impact was made even sharper by colourful newspaper coverage. Of these two years in the US, Prokofieff wrote somewhat disparagingly in his autobiographical notes. He ridiculed the *naïveté* of the American public and the American Mammon worship. Above all he lamented the crushing burden of performances. But, these views and judgments must be tempered with the knowledge that they were expressed in auto-biographical notes of *c.* 1940 whose reliability in discussing the West is suspect. Virulent anti-Western bias was politically demanded at the time.[2]

Although he seemed most anxious to court the New York public, Prokofieff found more promise in Chicago where he soon repaired to accept Cyrus McCormack's earlier invitation. Fitful negotiations with the Chicago Lyric Opera brought him a commission for and, finally, performance of his *Love For Three Oranges*.[3]

[1] Formal permission for leaving—and exit papers—were provided by Lunacharsky and the Commissariat of Education. Alexander Benois, a 'World of Art' painter, and Maxim Gorky introduced Prokofieff to Lunacharsky after the Petrograd première of the *Classical Symphony* on April 21, 1918. By May 7th, Prokofieff was on his way to Vladivostok. Prokofieff recalls the encounter with Lunacharsky in his autobiography. Writing, probably in 1940, he says, '(I intended) to return within a few months.' Lunacharsky remained a loyal adherent of Prokofieff's throughout the early period of criticism of *émigrés*. In *Zhizn' Iskusstva*, no. 22, for June 1926, p. 16, he cautions, 'Stravinsky has, in a signifi-cant measure, already fallen into the clutches of glittering artifice. Prokofieff, in order fully to develop, must return to us before the devil of Americanization overwhelms him.' Soviet historiography holds Prokofieff's decision to leave a tragedy. As Nestyev puts it (p. 159), 'The decision to leave Russia was a bitter and irreparable mistake for the young musician, for nothing could ever compen-sate for his prolonged separation from his motherland, which had entered upon the path of revolutionary construction.'

[2] Dmitri Kabalevsky, editor of *Sovetskaia Muzyka*, solicited the autobio-graphical notes to honour the composer on his fiftieth birthday on April 23, 1941. The first instalment appeared in the April issue, the next not until April 1946, when monthly publication was resumed after the war.

[3] The commission for *Love For Three Oranges* was given in January 1919 for production in the Autumn. Prokofieff finished the music through the summer of 1919, but Cleofonte Campanini, the conductor who had enthused over this setting of a libretto by a fellow Italian (Carlo Gozzi), died in mid-season. The Chicago directorate had invested liberally in the production ($80,000 by then,

In 1920 Prokofieff left for Paris and divided his time for the next two years between Western Europe and the United States. His war-induced break with Diaghelev was soon patched, but the friendship seems never to have been as close as is frequently reported. In 1922 Prokofieff settled in Ettal in the Bavarian Alps with his mother, and near his bride-to-be, Carolina Nikolaevna Codina. In 1923 he married Miss Codina, a sophisticated, cosmopolitan beauty who sang under the name of Lina Llubera.[1] Until the birth of their sons, Carolina accompanied him everywhere, and she did so frequently thereafter. They often appeared together in concert in Europe and in the United States.

Ultimately, the Prokofieffs made Paris the centre of his *émigré* activity until the 1936 return to the Soviet Union. The years abroad were productive years.[2] Prokofieff finished a number of works begun in Russia and substantially revised earlier works such as the ballet *Buffoon* and the opera *Gambler*. In addition, the Western years[3] saw the completion of the ballets *Le Pas d'Acier* (op. 41, 1925), *Prodigal Son* (op. 46, 1928), and *On the Dnieper* (op. 51, 1930); the operas *Love For Three Oranges* (op. 33, 1919), and *Flaming Angel* (op. 37, 1919–27); a number of vocal works; the piano concerti numbers three, four, and

---

reportedly $250,000 by December 1921), but, suddenly bereft of the conductor, and with the composer abroad, they nervously halted preparations for the remainder of the season. Resuming plans the following Autumn, the interim director was faced with an obdurate composer: in order to stage the opera they must pay him indemnity for the year's delay. And, so, in Prokofieff's words, 'again the opera was not staged, but this time, I must confess, the fault was mine'. By the 1921–2 season, Prokofieff had withdrawn his unusual demand, a new contract was made, and the opera produced.

[1] The first Mrs Prokofieff had been born in Russia; her mother was half Russian. But her schooling and career had been international.

[2] A tenet of Soviet musical history is that these were unproductive years for Prokofieff.

[3] The year of Prokofieff's return from the West is argued, as will be seen. For purposes of this listing the author is guided by location of publisher (either Gutheil or Koussevitsky's Russian Music Publishers in the West, or, in Russia, the State Music Publishers). Difficulties arise with works like *Lt. Kije*, conceived for a Soviet film audience, but worked into a five-movement suite published by Gutheil in 1935. Prokofieff's first Soviet publication was a set of mass songs (op. 66) in 1935. Thereafter, cautiously, the Soviet State Music Publishers published some music for children (1936) and *Peter and the Wolf* (1937). Nestyev, in his list of Prokofieff's works, shows the pre-1918 cantata *Seven, They Are Seven* as first published by Gutheil in 1925. But, the music sector of the State Publishers had issued the score in 1922, and Prokofieff acknowledges this in his autobiography (*Materialy* 173/63). Thus, although it was never performed in the Soviet Union, this cantata has the honour of being Prokofieff's first Soviet publication.

five (the second was entirely rewritten in the West), as well as numerous other piano works; chamber works, including opus nos. 34, 35, 39, 50, and 56; and, most impressively, orchestral works numbering over twenty. Prokofieff, though a concertizing pianist, was apparently overwhelmingly drawn to the orchestra. Not only did the Western period produce the Second, Third and Fourth Symphonies,[1] but Prokofieff turned an astonishing number of works in other mediums into orchestral pieces.[2] Thus, from the Western period, orchestral suites were made from *Buffoon* (1922), *Le Pas d'Acier* (1926), *Prodigal Son* (1929), *Gambler* (1930–1), *Love For Three Oranges* (two suites, 1922 and 1924); and full orchestra pieces from the Andante of the *Fourth Piano Sonata* (1934), the (chamber) *Overture on Hebrew Themes* (1934), the Andante from the *First String Quartet* (1930), and even from the *Overture for Seventeen Performers* (1928). The glaring exception seems to be Prokofieff's favourite, the opera *Flaming Angel*. But one need look no farther than the *Third Symphony* for the orchestral expression of that work.

Flaming Angel meant much to Prokofieff. He worked on it for an unusually, for him, long period, 1919 to 1927,[3] and his failure to see it produced vexed him until the end of his life.[4] Plans and promises had been made by the Berlin opera for the 1927 season,[5] and towards this

[1] The *Fourth Symphony* (op. 47, 1930) was written on commission for the Boston Symphony whose directorship Koussevitsky had assumed. The work was substantially revised and given a second opus number (112) in 1947.

[2] Revision and transcription were distinctive characteristics of Prokofieff's creative ways. Although the process of transcription usually cast the work into the orchestral medium, this was by no means the exclusive route. Opus 35, *Five Songs Without Words for Voice and Piano*, 1920, became, in 1925 (as op. 35-bis) *Five Melodies for Violin and Piano*. Later, the same music appears under op. 52, *Six Transcriptions*, as part of a work for piano alone.

[3] Parts of *Flaming Angel* (Renata's theme, the convent theme) were taken from music destined for a quartet in 1916. The quartet was not finished, but its characteristic 'white key' themes became a part of the opera and, later, the *Third Symphony*. So, the period of composition embraces the years 1916 to 1927. These are the dates given in Nestyev's catalogue of works.

[4] The work was given a concert performance on November 25, 1954 in Paris and was finally staged in September of 1955 in Venice. These dates are, of course, after that of the death of the composer. The opera was produced subsequently in Milan (1956), Basle (1956–7), Spole (1959), Trieste (1959), Cologne (1960), and Brno (1963). Brno's production was the first (and only, to date) staging in a country of the Warsaw pact and was typical of Czechoslovakia's growing attitude of liberality towards the arts.

[5] The early writing of the opera went swiftly: Prokofieff had his performers in mind. Mary Garden, a performing champion of contemporary music, had assumed directorship of the Chicago company in the spring of 1921. This compelling woman, who had created the role of Mélisande in Debussy's *Pelléas and*

performance Prokofieff finished the opera. However, plans were cancelled because, says Prokofieff, the parts arrived too late. There were doubtless other reasons.[1]

Prokofieff came upon Valery Briusov's novel written at the turn of the century, in 1919, perhaps earlier. The original title, like the story, was a period piece; it describes the plot at as great a length as is necessary here:

The Flaming Angel or a Truthful Tale in Which the Story is Told of a Devil Who More Than Once Appears to a Maiden in the Form of a Shining Spirit and Seduces Her to Commit Various Sinful Acts: of Godless Dealings in Magic, Astrology, and Necromancy; of the Trial of the Aforementioned Maiden Presided Over by His Holiness The Archbishop of Trier; and Also of Meetings and Conversations of a Knight with the Triune Doctor Agrippa von Nettesheim, and with Doctor Faustus, written by an eyewitness.

Although the elements of religious morbidity, murky rites, torture, and the heroine's erotic travail are implicit, the action depends, not altogether successfully, on the psychological reaction of the characters to these grisly events, not on the events themselves.

The opera contains some of Prokofieff's most memorable music. If there was, with Prokofieff, an intellectual drive to re-assemble his creative work into the idiom of the full orchestra, then so was there a strong, basic inclination to seek his creative starting point, and to solve creative problems, in the dramatic—in opera, and, less often, in ballet. Malcolm Brown speaks of Prokofieff's youthful infatuation for opera, pointing to the evidence of works in that genre written when the composer was yet a child.[2]

Mélisande, was to be Renata in *Flaming Angel*. At the time Prokofieff did not have Nina Koshets in mind for the role, as reported, although Miss Koshets had sung the Fata Morgana role in *Love For Three Oranges* and was later to sing fragments from *Flaming Angel* in a concert performance in Paris in 1928. When Mary Garden resigned her post, within two months of having staged *Love . . .*, and after less than a year's tenure, Prokofieff saw no opportunity for immediate performance. The creative world of Diaghelev, into which he had moved, accommodated ballet, but not opera.

[1] Prokofieff says (in *Materialy* 166/55), 'The subject is partly to blame (for "never having any luck with a performance"); it does not fall easily into a libretto, as is the case with all stories told in the first person; that character (the knight, Ruprecht) never leaves the stage, and the others are left so vague that one has to invent situations for them.' Plans for correcting dramatic faults suggested by New York Metropolitan Opera artists in 1930 were not realized.

[2] Malcolm Brown, *Symphonies of Prokofiev*. *Giant* and *On Desert Islands* (both 1900) were written to similar libretti concocted by the nine-, ten-year old

Flaming Angel demands of the soprano everything from broad, open lyricism through imperative ejaculations to husky declamation not unlike *sprechstimme*. Prokofieff built much of his musical drama out of the humblest of elements: the inflected half-step. It appears as an element of melodic tension and mutation, as the actor in wry modal change, as a factor in numerous ostinati, and, in its occasional obvious elision, as a settling factor. Dramatically, it is largely the property of Renata. But, just as her unhappy fate engulfs that of the other characters, so does her music, and her half-step, colour that of the others. This is a *leit-motif* opera and a clearly delineated one. The early music for Ruprecht is stately, although it grows complex as his hopeless affection for Renata waxes. Elsewhere, Prokofieff displays other wares. In Act III Renata finds Heinrich whom she has been seeking because she thinks he is the embodiment of Madiel, the angel who loved her and whom she loves. But the lecher now cruelly rejects her. Her mood and her music go grotesquely awry. Her love motive for the angel undergoes a psychotic change by means of tense octave interpolations and the intrusion of the ubiquitous half-step. When this music appears as the basic material for the third movement of the *Third Symphony*, Malcolm Brown says of it, '(It) is one of the most astonishing and demoniacal movements Prokofieff ever wrote', and, further,

Prokofiev invents acoustic combinations which vie in originality with the unearthly, teratogenic sounds manufactured today by electronic means. And he does it with only the string section of an ordinary orchestra. The achievement is unique.[1]

In Act V, after a tranquil opening, a group of nuns is whipped into a frenzy by the real or imaginary presence of evil. Prokofieff's orchestra blazes. Not unlike some moments in the *Scythian Suite*, this section accomplishes more without the excessive expense of the suite. The nuns' pacification is accomplished, musically, by a sloping off into simple triadic diatonicism and the abandonment of extreme ranges in the voices and instruments.

---

author. *Feast in Time of Plague* (1903) was based on Pushkin, and *Undine* (1904-1907) on de La Motte-Foqué's poetic setting. A young Petersburg poetess, Maria Kilschtedt, prepared the libretto from V. Zhukovsky's Russian translation. *Undine* is important. Miss Kilschedt's setting was brushed lightly with the *avant-garde* flavour of the time. The settings and events in *Undine* are akin to those of the later *Ala and Lolli*, *Seven, They are Seven*, and *Flaming Angel*— dark, sensuous, and exotic. Nestyev, predictably flails the young poetess with the epithets 'cheap', 'pretentious', and 'decadent'. None of these early operas bear opus numbers.

[1] Malcolm Brown, *op. cit.* p. 211.

The opera, dramaturgy aside, is formally of a piece. Malcolm Brown points out that not only was every major musical idea in the opera included in the symphony, but, 'The genesis of each (thematic) transformation is found in the *Flaming Angel* (speaking of the first movement)', as well.[1]

Flaming Angel represents one of Prokofieff's most industrious searches in his push for an effective style of creative communication. It has been suggested that his creative vocabulary was assembled early. In *Flaming Angel* it was arranged and tested. The composer of *Flaming Angel* must be considered personally and in the context of the twenties: He was yet young, he was proud and rebellious, he wanted to succeed in the best sense of the word, but he wanted to lead, not follow. Yet, he was hobbled by having burned some useful bridges to the past during his stormy years at the conservatory. Emotional rejection of what others were doing and had done was an adolescent practice which had become an unshakeable habit of the man. The Western musical milieu of the twenties resounded with the blows and counterblows of creative ideas generating still further creative ideas. Prokofieff was aware of and excited by them all.[2] But he was unable to learn from them, much less ape them; and his fear of doing so extended even to older music. In any case, Stravinsky had pre-empted the path pursued in the *Scythian Suite* (*Ala and Lolli*). Any sort of apprenticeship to a master, as obtained superficially in the Viennese circle, was prohibitively distasteful to him, and, again, he was too proud to risk copying from a distance. *Flaming Angel* was his sustained effort[3] to assume some kind of creative leadership in Western music—that leadership he so envied in Stravinsky and Schönberg. But the effort failed. *Flaming Angel's* cripplingly inflected half-step, the unexpected shifts in tonality, and in form and melody as well, the ostinati designed to propel, but which often hamstrung—these elements could not support Prokofieff's effort in a milieu which demanded the new at whatever expense. The bi- and poly-tonal chords were used without consistent system, yielding no

[1] Malcolm Brown, *op. cit.* p. 225.

[2] The paucity in Prokofieff's (and other) writings of mention of Schönberg, Berg, and Webern is deceptive. Prokofieff knew these men and knew of their works as well. He had met Schönberg for the first time in St Petersburg in 1911. He had played the St Petersburg première of Schönberg's three *Klavierstucke* (op. 11) in the preceding year.

[3] In addition to the pre-Western work on the aborted 'White Quartet', Prokofieff devoted significant amounts of time to *Flaming Angel* in 1921, 1922–3 (at Ettal), in 1927, in 1928 (the recasting into the *Third Symphony*), and in 1930. He mentioned publicly his intention to return to it in *c.* 1940–1, but there is no record of his having done so.

sustained poly-harmonies but, rather, colour, texture and embellishment. The impudent aloofness which had kept him from serious analysis of the music of his contemporaries and his predecessors left him bereft of equipment. Perhaps most lamentably he failed, as did many of his colleagues then and later, to appreciate any but the outermost layers of the deep legacy of Debussy. One may conjecture, as we shall here, about the reasons for Prokofieff's return to the Soviet Union, but, if a musical reason alone is sought, then it must be the failure of *Flaming Angel*. His move, he certainly knew, was not to an atmosphere where *Flaming Angel* could succeed. It was a retreat.

In January of 1927 Prokofieff had overcome some doubts, and the pull of his homeland had become strong enough so that he and his wife visited the Soviet Union. This was the first step of a series lasting through 1938 at the conclusion of which Prokofieff was clearly in place as a Soviet composer. These years span a complex period in the political and cultural development of the Soviet Union. To Prokofieff, apolitical to the end, only certain features of this development were evident. Had he been more acute in matters other than the musical, or more interested, he might have opted for remaining an *émigré*. The 1927 visit was a creative triumph. All elements of Soviet life welcomed him and received his music with enthusiasm. This adulation came to a man who frankly enjoyed and sought acclaim, but to a man for whom that acclaim had been waning in the West. Moreover, these were years when seductive nets were spread from Moscow to recapture some of the Russian talent, brains, and creativity that had scattered in 1917. Reports have Prokofieff dickering, in 1927, with highly placed Soviet authorities, perhaps with Stalin himself, over the conditions for his return to the Soviet Union.[1] Underlying Prokofieff's reception in early 1927 were the principles of the NEP period (see p. 47). The ACM was in its late period of glory. Prokofieff could not have forgotten the success of this visit.

His second visit, in November of 1929, was, however, like the second act of a cheap melodrama. The villain appeared in triumph—this was the RAPM at its most savage. Prokofieff was brutally treated in the RAPM press, and the ACM had ceased to publish. Proposed performances were aborted. His inclinations to return to Russia must certainly have been shaken. He carried away from his 1929 visit an apparently clear image of one of the evils of a creative life in the Soviet Union. But, in the melodrama, the villain is overwhelmingly defeated and everlasting happiness follows. The RAPM was thoroughly discredited and dissolved

[1] Such reports have never been and perhaps can never be confirmed. Their incidence and sources, however, are impressive. Prokofieff sat with Anatole Lunacharsky at the 1927 première of *Love For Three Oranges*.

in 1932, and the major part of Prokofieff's fears dissolved, too. He saw no further than the RAPM. Collectivization and its particulars had no meaning for him. He saw no portent in the swift manipulation of cultural organization from the political centre.

Still, he approached his November[1] 1932 visit with caution. He was not attacked, 'proletarian' cultural remnants seemed few, and his old friends, Gliere, Miaskovsky, and Asafi'ev, were reassuring. He was taken in only in the sense that most Soviet artists as well as many Western observers were taken in. Hindsight provides us now with dazzlingly reasoned analyses of this period, but misjudgment was the rule of the time, and for some time thereafter. The demands of Soviet reality in the early thirties brought conditions to musical life which coincided with what Prokofieff desired at the moment.

Final decision was delayed a bit longer. Prokofieff was in Paris for premières of his ballet *On the Dnieper* and his *Sonata for Two Violins*, and was then on his way to America before the year was out. Nevertheless, Soviet historiography sets 1932 as the date of Prokofieff's return to the Soviet Union. To have established such a date fits the importance attached to 1932 in Soviet thinking. Nestyev says,[2] '(Prokofieff) spent the greater part of 1933–4 in the USSR although he did make occasional trips abroad, including visits to his family in Paris . . .'. Nestyev's final clause casts some doubt on Prokofieff's residence in Moscow. The Paris apartment was not shut down, nor was his family moved to Moscow, until the spring of 1936. In that connection Malcolm Brown says, 'He was probably advised to sever obvious personal ties outside of his native land.'[3]

Such quibbling about dates casts little apparent light on Prokofieff and his music, but it does illustrate Soviet historical imperatives. In Prokofieff's case the illustration does not end there. It seems clear that an agreement had been reached between Prokofieff and Soviet authorities—at some high level. A good guess would be that the agreement included, for Prokofieff, protection from RAPM-like attack and interference, relief from certain USC obligations (such as submission of work in progress to adjudicating committees of peers), possibly financial security,[4] and, clearly, the freedom to travel abroad. His immunity

---

[1] Malcolm Brown, *op. cit.*, says December.

[2] Nestyev, *op. cit.* p. 246.

[3] Brown, *op. cit.* p. 389.

[4] That Prokofieff returned to the Soviet Union solely for financial gain is an accusation made but not valid. That he welcomed, at least, freedom from concertizing to compose is a far more generally accepted argument, but one which the author finds also suspect. In Soviet writings, and even in Prokofieff's statements of *c.* 1940, a great deal is made of the unwelcome, nagging chore of

from official censure in 1936, when he was a far more likely target than Shostakovich, probably reflects conditions of the agreement. Even later, in 1939, when officially sanctioned tragedy visited his friend and co-worker (on *Semyon Kotko*), Vsevolod Meyerhold and his wife, Prokofieff was not touched. Indeed, evidence indicates that Prokofieff was initially shielded from some of the details of the Meyerhold affair. And he continued, for a while after his return, to travel abroad. In the winter of 1935–6 he toured Spain and North Africa with the violinist, Soetens. In the 1936–7 season he concertized in Europe and the United States. In 1938 he again toured Europe and the United States and made commitments for further appearances through 1940. But, he never travelled abroad again. Nestyev and other writers say simply that the war intervened. No demand is made so urgently of the Soviet historian as that to rationalize (or ignore) the facts of the 1939-mid-1941 period in Soviet history. From a low point in relationships between Germany and the USSR in 1936 and 1937, a fitful conciliation was taking place. Hitler accelerated it with an important speech in April of 1939, terminating a 1937 non-agression pact with Poland. In May, Stalin replaced foreign minister Litvinov with the German-leaning Molotov, and, in August, Molotov and Ribbentrop signed the German-Soviet pact. In September Stalin signed a similar agreement with Japan which both negated the German-Japanese 'Anti-Comintern' pact of 1936 and released Soviet soldiers to Europe from the Eastern frontiers. Military action by both allies followed: jointly against Poland and, in the appropriate sphere, unilaterally against Finland and France. By June of 1940, military occupation of most of Europe had been accomplished by that improbable, ephemeral, but effective Moscow-Berlin-Rome axis. Prokofieff's country was in military, trade and cultural alliance with Nazi Germany, and the rest of the West was the enemy. The Popular Front, of which Prokofieff had been a prominent if unaware feature, collapsed overnight. With that collapse the existing market for creative export was destroyed, and none took its place.

By the eve of the Nazi onslaught on the Soviet Union, which dissolved the partnership, Prokofieff's list of Soviet works displayed certain departures from his earlier creative ways. Committed, now, to his role as a Soviet composer, he was once again arranging and testing his composer's vocabulary. He wrote no symphonies, nor was he to

---

appearing as a pianist and conductor in order to make a living in the West. Yet, until his injury in 1945, he continued to appear as a conductor, and his second wife testifies that his piano concertizing did not diminish until 1942. Even on his first Soviet trip, in 1927, he appeared as a pianist in at least twenty two concerts throughout the country.

venture into that genre until 1944. He appeared in print as early as 1934 with arch-doctrinaire statements about the need for and production of music for the broad masses, and even characterized the sort of music appropriate as 'light-serious' or 'serious-light'.[1] At the time of that statement he named his suites on *Lt. Kije* and *Egyptian Nights* and the 'collective farm songs'[2] he was then writing as examples. To this list he subsequently added *Songs of Our Days* (op. 76, 1937), a set of topical, brave, patriotic subjects whose final, transcribed version was for soloists, chorus, and orchestra; another set of *Seven Mass Songs* (op. 79, 1939); *Cantata for the 20th Aniversary of the October Revolution* (op. 74, 1936–7) set to a text consisting of the writings of Marx, Engels, Lenin, and Stalin[3]; and *Zdravitsa: Hail to Stalin* (op. 85, 1939), a work written to honour Stalin on his sixtieth birthday, and which used contemporary 'folk' material from several republican sources. All but the last were ideological failures, and, musically, *Zdravitsa . . .* is, too. Nestyev says of the sets of songs that they are dull and colourless, 'the composer unable to express a contemporary theme successfully in the simple and accessible forms of the mass song'. But, of the dreadful *Zdravitsa*, the same author can say, 'In these folk verses, a feeling of love and respect for the Communist party is interwoven with thoughts about the new socialist life.'[4] These early Soviet years, however, were years when Prokofieff adhered to a common notion of the time in Europe: that more than one 'style' was possible for, perhaps even demanded of, the contemporary artist,[5] wherever he was. Hence his non-programmatic, textless ventures including the three piano sonatas begun in

---

[1] *Izvestiia*, November 16, 1934. Reprinted in *Materialy* 215/100.

[2] Prokofieff probably referred to opus 66 (1935), *Six Mass Songs for Voice and Piano*.

[3] This unpublished, unperformed work shows the depth of Prokofieff's early Soviet effort and commitment. The work was scored for 500 performers; the two choruses were specified as one amateur and one professional, and the normal full symphony orchestra was to be augmented by a brass band, a large percussion ensemble, and an accordion band. Among the ten sections were a setting of part of the opening of the Communist Manifesto ('A spectre is haunting Europe . . .'), a setting of Lenin's *What Is to Be Done*, a setting of Stalin's *Vow* (at Lenin's bier), and a Chorus (Part Ten) dedicated to the 1936 Stalin Constitution and using texts therefrom.

[4] Nestyev, *op. cit.* p. 309. The cautious and adroit Nestyev gets high marks for this statement. It satisfies two demands: first, that for the socio-political identification with creative thrust—old and obvious; second, the displacement of the object of reverence (Stalin) by another (Communist party). If, as Nestyev told Malcolm Brown, the copy for his book was finished in 1955, then he was a pioneer in the development of the ritual vocabulary of de-Stalinization.

[5] Nestyev, p. 293, finds Prokofieff abandoning this view by 1937, which seems unlikely.

1939, and the *Cello Concerto* (op. 58), begun in 1933 and finished in 1938.[1]

Other works, however, are strangers in either category. The ballet *Romeo and Juliet* (op. 64, 1935–6), *Peter and the Wolf* (op. 67, 1936), the incidental music for the film *Queen of Spades* which evolved into music for Pushkin's *Boris Godunov* (op. 70 and 70-bis), the cantata *Alexander Nevsky* from the film music (op. 78, 1938–9), and the operas *Semyon Kotko* (op. 81, 1939) and *Duenna* (op. 86, 1940) are among them. Perhaps Prokofieff himself would assign some of these works to the 'accessible' category, but they do not all share the cheap conception and/or pomposity of most items therein. Of these, *Romeo and Juliet*, *Peter and the Wolf*, and *Alexander Nevsky* were immediately successful upon performance, although difficulties of various sorts in staging *Romeo and Juliet* prevented its Soviet première until two years after its world première in Brno, Czechoslovakia (December 1938). Of the operas, *Duenna* had a modest success at its war-postponed première (November of 1946) and the earlier *Semyon Kotko* was attended by unprecedented difficulties.

Valentin Kataev's story, 'I, Son of a Working People' (Semyon Kotko), was suggested to Prokofieff by a mutual friend, Alexei Tolstoi. Kataev, a Ukrainian, and a revolutionary writer, poet, and soldier, had been shown some documents[2]: 'orders of General Hoffman, commanding the German Army of Occupation in the South of Russia, 1918; dispatches of partisan companies of the time; many extracts from the German and other presses . . .'[3] This material and his recent knowledge of the Spanish Civil War, plus the then current fears of further war with Germany, moved the author to write a novel of 1918 including, as characters, bolshevik sympathizing peasants in the Ukraine, unreconstructed kulaks, 'white' counter-revolutionaries, and roving German army elements. Kataev admits to some historical manipulation

---

[1] Curiously, Nestyev (p. 238) calls this work, which was finished in 1938 and first performed in that year in Moscow, one of the 'last works Prokofieff composed in Western Europe'. The work was included in an all-Prokofieff programme honouring the twentieth anniversary of the October Revolution. The cold reception of this and other works on the programme was a rebuke to the composer. Some of the concerto's material was to re-appear near the end of the composer's life in opus 125, *Sinfonia Concertante* (originally the *Second Cello Concerto*).

[2] A. Ehrlich, at the time editorial secretary of *Pravda* provided Kataev with the hitherto hidden documents. Kataev served Pravda from time to time as a correspondent, and he and Ehrlich had worked together earlier on another newspaper.

[3] Liudmila Skorino, *A Writer and His Time*, Moscow: Sovetskii Pisatel', 1965, p. 291.

for colour's sake, but the tenor of the years permitted it[1]: Semyon comes home from the front in 1918, freed by the Bolshevik revolution, but not fully understanding it. He re-enters with enthusiasm the life of his agricultural community, but all is not well: kulaks emerge, including the father of his beloved Sophia, and marauding Germans burn the village, including the Kotko hut, and beat Semyon's mother and sister. Semyon joins the partisans, returns to thwart the forced marriage of Sophia to an old landowner, and kidnaps the girl. He is captured and sentenced to execution, but is saved by the partisans. Prokofieff, Kataev, and director Vsevolod Meyerhold worked together closely on the opera. Kataev complained of Prokofieff's demanding, machine-like habits, and Meyerhold, according to Kataev, was in a constant state of alarm, demanding of Prokofieff that he hurry.

Once again, Prokofieff was setting great store by an opera, his first since *Flaming Angel*. In this favourite genre he wanted to score with a Soviet subject. Kataev's stereotypes: an awakening hero, noble Bolshevik partisans, a greedy kulak, an adolescent heroine (Frosya), mischievous youths, a sailor, etc., seemed to provide reason for great musical range and contrast. Prokofieff introduced Ukrainian folk songs for Kotko's young sister, Frosya, comic gallops for Frosya and her playmates, broad, lyric melody with a large range for Sophia. The kulak, Tkachenko, is treated with wry humour; Lybochka, who had loved the executed Bolshevik, Psarev, goes mad in music palely reminiscent of that music used for the distraught Renata in *Flaming Angel*. The more adventurous essays portray the Germans: here are the violent tonal twists, discords, rhythmic jolts and orchestral extremes used by Prokofieff at his most imaginative. Aside from, and even including, these musical portraits, the opera leans heavily on recitative. Prokofieff, Kataev, and the replacement director, Serafima Birman, in different places, reflected on the necessity to keep recitative to a minimum. Prokofieff said before the opera's production, 'I have avoided dry recitative (recitativo secco?) as the least interesting element in opera',[2] yet, he has not.

All but the orchestration was finished by June 28, 1939, and Prokofieff left his co-workers, Meyerhold and Kataev, for Kislovodsk to complete the orchestration. He did, but a nightmarish period in Prokofieff's life began that summer. First came the news of Meyerhold (which occasioned his reluctant collaboration with Serafima Birman.[3] The Nazi-Soviet

---

[1] The story was published in 1937. Incidental music for a staged version was written by Tikhon Khrennikov in 1938.   [2] *Materialy* 237/119.

[3] Birman said in 1955, 'I will not pretend to flatter Prokofiev in these remembrances (He was often harsh to me, sometimes unjustly so) . . .', *Materialy*, 505/269.

Pact caused his plans for going abroad to be cancelled. He was separated from his cosmopolitan wife, Carolina, and his two sons. It then became clear that *Semyon Kotko* had to be radically altered before its première. Political demands of the most unavoidable sort now intruded on Prokofieff's work. With the Nazi-Soviet pact, said Kataev much later,[1]

'. . . There came a pause. The opera's trappings had to be subdued. The Germans were even redressed (or disguised) as Austrians. And even then there were diplomatic unpleasantries . . .'

With many last minute changes, and under pressure for still further adjustment, the opera had its première on June 23, 1940. It remained uncomfortably in the repertoire of the Stanislavsky Theatre for that season. But, with the Nazi invasion in June of 1941, there was no hope for the now all but pro-German work. It disappeared from sight.[2]

The war years took Prokofieff and his second wife, Myra Mendelson, first to Nalchik (August 1941), then to Tbilisi (November 1941), Alma-Ata (May 1942), briefly to Perm (then called Molotov, June 1943), and back to Moscow (October 1943). He remained in Moscow until the end of the war and until his retreat for reasons of health to Nikolina Gora in mid-1946. In Nalchik, the first evacuation stage for Moscow's musical community, Prokofieff worked on his opera *War and Peace*. The work was to occupy him for eleven years. Here, too, he wrote the ill-received symphonic suite *The Year 1941*, and, attracted by local folklore, collected materials part of which he used in his *Second (Kabardinian) String Quartet*. His six months in Tbilisi, where he was still in the Moscow evacuee contingent, saw further work on *War and Peace* (leading to the first of the unacceptable 'final' versions), the *Seventh Piano Sonata*, and a spate of concertizing in the Caucasian cities, his last.

Prokofieff left the Moscow group for Alma-Ata where he worked for a year with the Moscow and Leningrad Film Studios which had been evacuated to the Central Asian city. He further experimented with style in music for the films *Lermontov, Tonya, Kotovsky, Partisans in the Ukrainian Steppes*,[3] and, with Sergei Eisenstein, part of *Ivan the Terrible*. With the exception of the latter, none of these have opus numbers, and none of them are published. Work on *War and Peace* continued in

---

[1] 1963, in an interview with Liudmilla Skorina and quoted in her *op. cit.* p. 306.

[2] In its original anti-German form, the opera first reappeared in Brno and Ostrava, Czechoslovakia, in 1959, and, in 1960, in Perm and Leningrad.

[3] *Partisans* . . . was written for the Ukranian Film Studio evacuated to Semipalatinsk. The score was delivered there by the composer in December 1942. It contains elements of *The Year 1941*.

Alma-Ata. The Kirov (Leningrad) Ballet summoned him to their evacuation centre in Perm to make arrangements for the postponed *Duenna* and *Cinderella*, the first finished, the second begun before the war. Again in Moscow in late 1943, he finished *Cinderella*, prepared a concert performance of *War and Peace*, completed the last of the three sonatas begun in 1939, and wrote his *Fifth Symphony*. The symphony had its première on January 13, 1945.

Prokofieff, though sheltered by evacuation and hard work during this period, still shared much of the horror of the war with his countrymen. Creative problems of at least equal difficulty forced him to conclusions which seem, finally, to be reflected in the successful, slick *Fifth Symphony*. During the war period a concentration of effort by the composer to find a place for the uncompromising idiomatic combinations he had developed prior to his return to the Soviet Union is heard, first in *Semyon Kotko*, and continuing through *The Year 1941*, the suite from *Semyon Kotko*, the *Ballad of an Unknown Boy*, and the film scores, *Kotovsky* and *Partisans*. . . . In agreement now that these combinations did not form an acceptable style for depicting positive dramatic factors in Soviet fashion, he developed their use in portraying the unattractive and the inimical: in these works the German and/or Nazi. This creative line is reflected to a lesser degree in the earlier *Alexander Nevsky* (the Teutonic invaders); and his struggle to resolve the impasse he reached (in the *Fifth Symphony*, for instance) is seen in the prolonged rewriting of the film score for *Ivan the Terrible*, Part II, and the early troubles with the much altered opera *War and Peace*. Perhaps he had felt most free in the *Ballad of an Unknown Boy*. *Ballad* was published as a poem by Pavel Anatolsky in the journal *Literature and Art* while Prokofieff was in Tbilisi. The composer was immensely moved and sensed the dramatic propriety of the work: a young boy sees his mother and sister killed by the Nazis. As the invaders retreat he throws a hand grenade into a staff car. What then happens to the boy—and who he is—is unknown. The Nazis provide Prokofieff with the opportunity for inventive, innovatory exercise. Though tonal, the cantata brings Prokofieff close to dodecaphonic usage. The theme of the invading Nazis shows a near-row, quoted but, apparently, unobserved by Nestyev:

(12 - c♯)

This march-like theme is treated canonically at the unison and gives way in later entries to extravagant orchestral noises. The theme for the boy is in sharp contrast: lean diatonicism with a wistful and ingenuous air. Elsewhere, Anatolsky's language is blunt and seems chosen to jar the reader in the Mayakovsky manner. Prokofieff is sympathetic to the effort and provides music to match. The work is superficially well within the line of development of the Soviet cantata form, but tastefully avoids running the doctrinaire gamut and ordering of emotional stereotypes required thereof. Hence, the tension and pathos are unrelieved—and they need not be, given the theme.[1] But, *Ballad* was ill-received after its première in Moscow on February 21, 1944. And the same reception met the other works in which Prokofieff pursued this line. Many years later Nestyev and others advanced the reason that these works were too one-sided in their use of intonations; that the mood was unmitigated by any more cheerful elements. But, although he backtracked along several lines, Prokofieff never accepted the criticism of *Ballad*. In the last few years of his life, even after 1948, he insisted on the work's worth.

The rejection of many of his works at the time of *Ballad* began to fall into a recognizable pattern: well before the calamitous events of 1948 it had become clear, at least to others, that Prokofieff was no longer enjoying that full immunity from sanctioned censure that had protected him in the late thirties. Perhaps the unavoidable pandemonium surrounding *Semyon Kotko* had first breached that protective mantle. He had been exempt from the system of punishment *and* reward. He became officially subject to the system, characteristically, with awards: the Order of the Red Banner of Labour in 1943, and a Stalin Prize, the latter for the *Seventh Sonata*, in 1944. But big guns were trained on him simultaneously. It was new to Prokofieff to be criticized in formal meeting as he was in 1944. It was doubtless shocking to consider the source of the criticism. Dmitrii Shostakovich, high atop the Soviet musical establishment with the unencumbered success of his Fifth and Seventh Symphonies behind him, joined others in criticizing Prokofieff. At a meeting of the Plenary Session of the Organizing Committee of the USC, called to weigh the musical product of the war years so far, Shostakovich singled out the *Ballad*, noting the absence of 'a solid, constructive base'. He called the work formless, and insisted on the impossibility of creating a large-scale work using Prokofieff's illustrative methods. Prokofieff's reply was loftily oblique:

---

[1] The author has not seen the score of *Ballad* but has relied on fragments seen and on recollections of those who remember the music. The work was never repeated after the première, nor was it published.

he spoke generally of the composer's art, which requires, 'creative imagination . . . inventiveness', and of the need for the new in new times.

In this setting Prokofieff began work on his *Fifth Symphony* (in July of 1944). He was still fitfully at work on *War and Peace*, and *Ivan the Terrible* was scheduled for release later in the year.[1] In the *Fifth Symphony* Prokofieff set out to develop the heroic element—that element critics found lacking in his works. Malcolm Brown speaks, indeed, of the work's 'heroic stride', and also of the (now) comic 'wrong' notes, harmonic twist, and 'virtuosic manipulation' of the orchestra. Again, Prokofieff had rearranged his vocabulary and added to it the 'heroic' formula. For that formula he needed to look no further than Shostakovich's Fifth and Seventh Symphonies. That he did so is discouraging on many counts, and the *Fifth Symphony* suffers from a shallowness which its superb craftsmanship emphasizes rather than hides.

From 1945 through early 1948 Prokofieff continued working on *War and Peace*.[2] He reworked his *Fourth Symphony* considerably, trying to apply the 'success' lessons he had learned from the *Fifth Symphony* without destroying the work. He worked also on the *Sixth Symphony* and on Part II of *Ivan the Terrible*, on his *Ninth Piano Sonata* (op. 103, 1947), on his *Ode to the End of the War* (op. 105, 1945), and on the opera *Story of a Real Man* (1947–8).

An illness—hypertension resulting from a fall in 1945—caused Prokofieff to pace himself carefully for the eight remaining years of his life. Conducting was ruled out, and he had given his last public performing tour during the war. His composing habits were changed, and, especially towards the end, he was restricted occasionally to mere minutes of work a day. Prokofieff and his wife established a quiet retreat at Nikolina Gora in mid-1946.[3] Short periods of immobility and hospi-

---

[1] *Ivan the Terrible*, Part I, was released on January 18, 1945. For this work Prokofieff was awarded another Stalin Prize. Part II was not released, on Stalin's orders. The dictator had long been drawn to the subject matter. Sufficient evidence and testimony exists to conclude that he identified himself with the sixteenth-century ruler.

[2] Concert performances of parts of *War and Peace* took place in 1944 and 1945 in Moscow. A 'première' of the first eight scenes was staged in Leningrad on June 12, 1946. The 'final' version of eleven scenes was premiered in Prague on July 25, 1948. Another concert performance, presumably of the eleven scenes (second edition) was heard in Moscow in June of 1953. A somewhat changed version was staged in Leningrad in April 1955, and a version of '13 scenes with cuts' was produced in Moscow on September 8, 1957. Much, though not all, of the rewriting and delay stemmed from the routine USC auditions and criticisms to which Prokofieff was subject during the last years.

[3] Prokofieff had tried vacationing at Ivanovo, the Moscow USC retreat during parts of the two previous summers. Nestyev speaks of the comradely warmth

talization punctuated these years. One retreat to Nikolina Gora removed him from the immediate, if not the subsequent, pain of part of the Party and government proceedings against the composers in 1948.

Prokofieff, as we have seen, was prominently placed among those most severely taken to task in 1948 by Andrei Zhadnov.[1] Prokofieff could not, now, ignore the criticism, as he had that uttered by Shostakovich in 1944. No trace of official protection was left, although his startled initial reaction indicates that Prokofieff thought himself still shielded. His subsequent apology[2] and expression of gratitude to Stalin and the Party was doctrinaire but defensive enough to elicit further attacks—now from the jackals. The lion, Zhdanov, had retired from the field.[3]

Prokofieff's *Story of a Real Man* had been started before the 1948 Party attack. With his apparently unflagging optimism he thought the opera would both solve some personal creative problems and satisfy the Party's demands. In the aforementioned letter of apology he had said as much. After admitting to the 'sickness of formalism' (while cautioning against banality and 'rehash' in seeking 'instantly comprehensible melody'), he pointed to those works wherein he had already sought a clearer language: *Alexander Nevsky, Toast to Stalin, Romeo and Juliet*, and the *Fifth Symphony*. In opera he justified his use of recitative on dramatic grounds: 'In connection with the (Party) resolution', he concluded that certain opera situations call for aria, others for recitative, and that certain situations allow either. In the latter, the composer must decide. Tschaikovsky inclined toward aria—and, said Prokofieff, he would follow suit in *Story of a Real Man*. Once again Prokofieff had been strongly attracted to a Soviet theme: he and Myra Mendelson prepared the libretto from Boris Polevoi's book. Prokofieff worked hard, both before and after the Party resolution, and finished the opera by August. He wrote without benefit of collective auditions at the USC, sticking to his old notions of creative privacy. It was to be the last time he could do so. The Leningrad Kirov Theatre had encouraged him from the beginning of the opera, and the work was in rehearsal by the

---

between the composer and his colleagues in residence in the cabins and main house at Ivanovo. But eye-witnesses found him curt and unapproachable. He ridiculed others, snubbed Shostakovich, teased Kabelevsky, and would not acknowledge the likes of Khrennikov and Belyi. Indeed, he tolerated only his two old companions, Gliere and Miaskovsky.

[1] See p. 56.
[2] The apology was in the form of a letter to P. N. Lebedev and Khrennikov, and was read to an assembly of composers in Moscow. Prokofieff had retreated in ill health to Nikolina Gora.
[3] Andrei Zhdanov died suddenly and unexpectedly on August 31, 1948.

beginning of the 1948–9 season. Officialdom attended an unusual (for Prokofieff) private, full dress[1] hearing on December 3, 1948. The scheduled appearance for the public was promptly scrapped,[2] and once again the cultural press heaped abuse on Prokofieff's head. *Story of a Real Man* was not to be heard in the Soviet Union until the 1960–1 season, more than seven years after the composer's death.

Story of a Real Man was Prokofieff's last opera. Of his last works the oratorio *On Guard For Peace* and the *Seventh Symphony* were official successes during his lifetime. The pale, tuneful, but dreadfully banal oratorio represents, for Prokofieff, the ultimate retreat from, and abandonment of, previously held principles.[3] One must understand these years to understand *On Guard For Peace*. Prokofieff was racing against failing health, and he was desperate to break through the official sanctions against his music. These were severe: theatres and orchestras would not, indeed could not programme Prokofieff's music. The USC attitude was ambivalent, and he remained under public, publicized attack from the USC leadership, especially Khrennikov and Kabalevsky.[4] His only champion among his fellow composers was Miaskovsky, himself under a cloud. Moreover, Miaskovsky died in 1950. His few partisans were largely performers, certain elements in the Bolshoi and Kirov directorates, and writers and poets. Sviatoslav Richter and the twenty-two (in 1949) year-old Mstislav Rostropovich were unflagging adherents. They performed together the première of the *Cello Sonata* (op. 119, 1949) in late 1949.[5] Richter gave the delayed première of the *Ninth Piano Sonata* (op. 103, 1947) in 1951. And, in a unique arrangement, Richter and Rostropovich pushed through the first performance

---

[1] The scenery was only suggested.

[2] Nestyev, without comment, lists the December 3rd trial performance as the première.

[3] In yet another example of the 'Nestyev Shift': (p. 407) 'A brilliant expression of . . . increased social orientation . . .'

[4] But this must be considered carefully. Such attacks from colleagues may well have saved Prokofieff far greater punishment, given the times. Shortly after Prokofieff's death it became apparent through articles and journals that Kabalevsky had maintained a certain relationship with the composer—'a strong friendship', in Kabalevsky's words. Since Prokofieff had earlier shown little respect for Kabalevsky, one seeks another answer about Kabalevsky's role: he was the USC assigned caretaker, after 1948, for Prokofieff. He was on the panel that condemned *Story of a Real Man*; he policed, subsequently, the propriety of Prokofieff's composing procedure, i.e. he saw to it that Prokofieff's work came before the USC *obsuzhdeniia*. He oversaw arrangements with performing bodies. Kabalevsky explained his assignment to this author in 1958 as 'taking care of this ill genius', an obligation assumed in a brotherly spirit by the USC.

[5] Nestyev gives the date of March 1, 1950.

of Prokofieff's *Second Cello Concerto*[1] in February of 1952. Rostropovich played, and Richter made his debut as a conductor with the Moscow Youth Orchestra.

Youth, in many ways, dominated this last period of Prokofieff's activity. A predeliction for portrayal of the young has been noted before. But, that Prokofieff returned to his own youth and sought creative outlet through youthful channels is not due to this alone. The only official routes to performances open to him were through establishments devoted to Soviet youth: hence, the Moscow Youth Orchestra; and, hence, the sponsorship of *On Guard For Peace*, *Winter Bonfire* (op. 122, 1949), and the *Seventh Symphony* as well as suites and resetting from the as yet unfinished *Stone Flower*, by the Moscow Children's Radio Division.[2] *On Guard* found Prokofieff going too far in the quest for accessibility. He clearly runs afoul of the very dangers he earlier warned against in 'seeking instantly comprehensible melody'. Forced again to seek musical solutions to, for him, incomprehensible political problems, he fastened on Shostakovich's successful answer to 1948: *Song of the Forests*. The need for emotional over-simplification, pomp, and topicality confounded the composer, and the music sometimes stops in favour of pure narration. Embarrassment rather than drama is thereby achieved. The bulk of the work is in discreet, five- to ten-minute sections. Elsewhere a continuous musical description is provided as background to narrative. Orchestral passages establish a limited and obvious 'intonation' leitmotif vocabulary. Yet, *On Guard For Peace* is, with all its manifold weaknesses, impressive evidence of the consistency of individual traits in Prokofieff's style. For, even here they come through, albeit in the artificial manner of the less talented among those who imitate him. The work, which was awarded a Stalin Prize,[3] was premièred in the Moscow Hall of Columns. There, two years earlier Prokofieff and his wife had attended the opening session of the USC congress.

An ever increasing proportion of Prokofieff's time in the last years was devoted to reworking earlier pieces. A number of projected revisions

---

[1] Reworked, the concerto appears in the list of works as op. 125 *Sinfonia Concertante for Cello and Orchestra*.

[2] While wishing to avoid a conclusion, the present author would point to an interesting aspect of the Soviet penal and rehabilitation system: adults deemed through boards or the court as chronically 'anti-social' are often set to work with children in camps, orphanages and clubs. The experiment was broadly carried out in the mid-fifties and had its legal beginnings during the Soviet period. The roots of the idea reach back into the nineteenth century.

[3] The Prize, one of the second degree, was awarded for *On Guard For Peace* and the suite, *Winter Bonfire*.

remained undone. One pair of new works, of importance in the Soviet Union, remained. These are the ballet *Stone Flower* (op. 118)[1] and the *Seventh Symphony*. As in the past, a stage and symphonic work were idiomatically paired. The *Seventh Symphony* was originally conceived as a symphony for youth, then a work about youth, and, finally, a symphony expressing and containing many aspects of youth and youthfulness. Simplicity, charming moments, directness, tunefulness, and uncomplicated form and drama both characterize and weaken the work. The result is much in the vein of the *Fifth Symphony*. The only factors escaping naivety are the solutions to technical problems: smooth transitions and, especially, extravagant orchestration. The latter is maintained at such a high level of facile sophistication as to ridiculously overpower other aspects. Prokofieff was well aware of the dangers of forcing simplicity. On the basis of the symphony's occasional descent into unbelievable banality (e.g. the finale) some Western observers have guessed that Prokofieff was deliberately baiting the ideological censors. A better case could be made for such irony in *On Guard For Peace*, however.

On March 5, 1953, a month short of his sixty-second birthday, Prokofieff died. He had never stopped working; he had never given up, so one may assume that he was still fighting, in spirit, the fight of the *Flaming Angel*, as he had throughout his career. His last finished work, the *Seventh Symphony*, was pushed emotionally into prominence after his death. It was an unfortunate legacy left to those, mostly Soviet, young composers who sought to follow the path started by Prokofieff. Gradually, as controls were lifted and official indignation forgotten, the available items in that legacy became more numerous. Yet, although his position on the concert stage is emphatically assured, Prokofieff left little to excite today's aspirant composer. No crueller thing could be said, for this was the point of much of his life's struggle: a success that transcends the concert hall or opera theatre. For many reasons, both political and personal, it was denied. He would have been the Mussorgsky of his century: he was its Borodin—no small accomplishment.

[1] Nestyev gives the completion date as 1950. Yet, Prokofieff was still revising, with a performance pending, at his death.

PART THREE

The Middle Generation of Soviet Composers

Introduction

The middle generation of Soviet composers is here arbitrarily defined as including those composers whose training and creative periods begins after 1917. There is no direct musical significance to this date. The composers considered run from Shaporin (1887–) to Sviridov (1915–), so the old generation is overlapped. Again, the criterion is that of period of creativity, yet, it is interesting to note that, despite the overlap of generations, all members of the middle generation represented here are still living, whereas no one of the older generation, chosen similarly, is now alive.[1]

A qualitative factor, however, divides the middle generation. Reference will be made to the first and second groups of middle-generation composers. The first group includes Shaporin, Shostakovich, Shebalin, and, perhaps, Balanchivadze; it is that group directly affected by training in the liberal twenties. The second group, including Khrennikov, Kabelevsky, Khachaturian, and Sviridov, either finished their training later or were not so affected by pre-1930 musical thought as they were by the new notion of Soviet success. They were, in various ways and to various degrees, all affected by Shostakovich, his music, his success, and his adversity; although two were older, two younger than he.

Typical of both the first and second groups is technical mastery. Typical of the first, but not the second, is an individuality of approach, which, one way or another, precludes most political considerations. Common to the members of the second group is an appreciation and accommodation of political reality as a natural component of creativity. Hence the change in style and approach of group two is often blinding and bewildering. Style change in group one is complex and laboured. Extra-musically, the members of group two are the perennial standard bearers for Soviet doctrine. The members of group one are, generally, those most severely criticized for violating that doctrine, although the categorization is not that simple in practice. Shaporin, of the first group, has never received official criticism, nor has he ever been led to public apology. Khachaturian, of the second group, has shared criticism with Shostakovich and Shebalin, although it has been due, largely, to his zeal in copying Shostakovich—an attempt to equal the success abroad of the latter.

[1] Vissarion Shebalin died in early July, Iurii Shaporin in December of 1963, after this was written.

CHAPTER 14

Iurii Shaporin

Of the group of composers chosen here to call the middle generation. Shaporin is by far the oldest. Chronologically he belongs to the older group, but his musical career was late starting: His first professional work, incidental music to *Much Ado About Nothing*, was written in 1919, eleven years after the performance of Prokofieff's first symphony. If today Shaporin represents the conservative bridge between the first and second generation—even the first and third—the apparently retrograde development is a personal and honest one. Shaporin was at the barricades of modern music in the twenties. Given a nation of composers committed, and almost totally limited, to nineteenth-century traditionalism as an unarguable premise, then Shaporin is a good composer. His gifts appear in many areas: he is a masterful melodist, he understands and manipulates harmony expressively, and he instinctively understands what is appropriately 'Russian'. His sense of form and drama is keen. Under the circumstances, his economy is his greatest gift. He alone among well-known Soviet composers is a slow writer. His reputation is founded on but a handful of works, not because they are the best among many, but because they are the only ones.

Iurii Aleksandrovich Shaporin was born November 8, 1887 in Glukhov in the Chernigovsk area of the Ukraine. His Russian parents were artistically oriented[1]; his mother had been a classmate of Rachmaninov and Scriabin under pianist Zverev at the Moscow Conservatory. On a dilettante scale Shaporin studied piano and 'cello and even tried his hand at salon composing. Under the influence of his stepfather, he enrolled in Kiev University as a student of history. He became pianist-accompanist for the excellent student choir and began studying composition and theory in classic Russian dilettante style with Liubomirsky. However, Nicholas Lysenko, the great Ukrainian representative of the ideas of 'the Five', suggested Shaporin's removal to the more

---

[1] The *Bol'shaia Sovetskaia Entsiklopediia* states that both Shaporin's parents were artists. Elsewhere no mention is made of his father, but of his stepfather who was a Kiev University professor of literature.

stimulating atmosphere of the capital. In 1908, at the age of twenty-one, and with the backing of his family, Shaporin went to St Petersburg to continue his study of history at the University there.

His studies did continue. A tentative attempt to enroll concurrently in the conservatory foundered on Shaporin's lack of sight reading ability at the keyboard, and on his seeming 'gentleman-dilettante' approach—anathematic to the Rimsky-Korsakov-trained Glazunov.[1] Shaporin's naive compositions, shown at the time to Glazunov, had enough promise, however, to make the latter remember the former at a later, significant date.

Shaporin's years at the University of St Petersburg (1908–12) were valuable. Among his fellow students were Alexander Gauk,[2] and Alexander Kas'ianov. Shaporin wrote knowledgeable papers on the relationships between Tsar Nicholas I and the revolutionary Decembrist, Speransky: He was to return to the time and activity of Speransky for inspiration for his opera, *The Decembrists*. Shaporin's upbringing and outlook were in the deeply religious, conservative Russian tradition. Midway through the university he considered entering the clergy. The summer before his graduation from the institution, at the age of twenty-four, he vacationed in Yalta as the guest of a priest, F. Fcodori. A local singer, a friend of Feodori's, sang a song recently composed by the young Shaporin as an encore to a concert. The concert was attended by Glazunov, also vacationing in Yalta. Glazunov inquired if this might be the 'same Shaporin'. They met, and the path to the conservatory was opened for the young historian. Thoughts of becoming a priest were shelved.

In 1913, after finishing the university, he entered the conservatory, studying composition with Sokolov and orchestration with Steinpress. His work with Cherepnin he remembers with particular gratitude. Cherepnin had an encyclopaedic mind which went far beyond the bounds of the class in score reading.

Shaporin was typical of the St Petersburg educated, middle class youth in the early 1900s. He was deeply convinced of the need for political and social change.[3] Critical friendships grew with other

---

[1] Glazunov had himself been a student of history (in 1875), and Rimsky-Korsakov, of course, had a military career. These very contradictions had made both men extremely sensitive about career-mindedness.

[2] Gauk, too, later concentrated on music and became one of the best known Soviet conductors. For many years he was director of the Moscow Philharmonic. He died in 1963.

[3] Typically, Shaporin knew little or nothing about the Bolshevik factionists. His ideas for reform were based on legal procedures. Although he belonged to no group formally, he was in sympathy with the Constitutional Democrats.

6*

members of the young intelligentsia. He entered army service in 1916, serving with the Finnish guard, and was demobilized and returned to finish the conservatory in 1918. The October revolution seemed to Shaporin, as it did to many at its very centre, a phase. Out of the conservatory he directed the Baltic Fleet summer band and became attached to Petrograd drama theatres as an accompanist.

In the Petrograd Bolshoi Drama Theatre he wrote the incidental music to *Much Ado About Nothing*, *King Lear*, and to Schiller's *The Robbers*. In 1920 he went north into Petrozavodsk for two years. There he not only supplied music for the drama but also conducted a local symphony. Here, too, he indulged in his last overt act as a religious man by building and conducting a magnificent church choir. He crowned his stay in Petrozavodsk with a performance of the Mozart *Requiem*, conducting his chorus and orchestra.

The next two years were confused for any artist in the Soviet Union. Many of them, mostly poets and authors, gathered in Petrograd and tried to express themselves through their art about the confusing maelstrom around them. Shaporin was among them. Donald Treadgold says of them, 'On the morrow of the October Revolution few of them adhered to the Bolshevik regime.' Shaporin became one of the last important figures in a strong Russian literary and creative tradition: that of the rapprochement of composer and writer. He alone of Soviet composers is identified by intimate friendship with Alexei Tolstoi,[1] Aleksandr Blok,[2] Evgenii Zamiatin,[3] Vyacheslav Karatygin,[4] Maiakovsky,[5]

[1] Aleksei Nikolaievich Tolstoi (1882–1945), a count and the nephew of Leo Tolstoi left Russia in 1917. His return in 1923 marked a political milestone in the arts. There were subsequently a number of such returnees. He had known Shaporin well since 1912.

[2] Aleksandr Aleksandrovich Blok (1880–1921) is today the most beloved (according to Guerney) of the poets identified somehow with the revolution. His poetry, like some of Maiakovsky's, is in no way orthodox Bolshevism, but is highly personal. Classified as a symbolist, Blok easily breaks the bonds: he is less terse but as effective as Maiakovsky, not so clever but more accurate than Zamiatin. Blok and Shaporin met in 1918 and were the closest of friends until the poet's death. In the concluding lines of Blok's *The Twelve* may lie the clue to Shaporin's synthesis of revolution and religion. The poem is concerned with the progress of a twelve-man Bolshevik patrol in revolutionary Petrograd. Their march has been a grim, pragmatic mirror of thoughts and scenes and fragments of the horror around them: they have shot, perhaps accidentally, the prostitute lover of one of their members and . . .

> Thus they their sovereign march pursue
>
> Behind them skulks the hound half dead;
> Ahead (with flag of sanguine hue)—
>
> Invisible within the storm
> Immune from any bullets' harm

Konstantin Fedin[1] and others. Although many composers have set the words of these poets (except Zamiatin), only Shaporin really knew them. Opus 1, number two is a ballad for voice and orchestra to a text by Alexei Tolstoi. Shaporin also wrote the incidental music for Tolstoi's *Ivan the Terrible* (perf. 1944), and Tolstoi was the original librettist for *The Decembrists*. Shaporin composed the highly complex music for Zamiatin's drama *The Flea* (after Leskov's *The Steel Flea*) and set some of the author's terse poetry. These settings are listed as lost. Actually they fill in Shaporin's 'missing' opus number, four, and are settings for voice with orchestra. Shaporin's bent toward modernism reached its height in the Zamiatin music. A six-part suite on *The Flea* is scored for woodwinds, horn, trumpet, trombone, 16 domras, 3 baians (accordion-type), piano, double bass, flexaton, xylophone, tympani, and other percussion instruments.[2] Shaporin's opus nos. 12 (1939), 18 (1940–45), 18a (1946) and 19 (1948) are all settings of Blok's poetry. The most important is opus 12, *Dalekaia Iunost'* (Faraway Youth), a set of

---

> Walking with laden step and gentle
> In snowy, pearl strewn mantle
>
> With small white roses garlanded
> Jesus the Christ walks at their head.
> (transl. by Gilbert Guerney)

[3] Evgenii Zamiatin (1884–1937) was a literary 'Balakirev' to the Serapion Brotherhood—a remarkable and neglected man. Although once a Bolshevik and a revolutionary himself (he was imprisoned at the age of fifteen for his activity in 1905), he became outspokenly disappointed with the Bolshevik regime. He met Shaporin in 1922. He is not acknowledged in the Soviet Union today (his name is not even mentioned in the *Bol'shaia Sovetskaia Entsiklopediia*), and he occasionally glimmers in the West in the reflected light of Orwell's *1984*, a romanticized copy of Zamiatin's novel *We* (c. 1920). With Maxim Gorky's intercession he received a passport to tour in the West in 1931. In Paris he, like his fellow 'tourist', Glazunov, stayed aloof from both 'red' and 'white'. He died in Paris in 1937, just one year after the death of Glazunov, one of his few friends in exile.

[4] Viacheslav Gavrilovich Karatygin (1875–1925) was a literary figure, music critic, and sometimes composer. An enthusiastic champion of progressive music, he had known Shaporin since late conservatory days. He worked with Shaporin and Asaf'ev in the Leningrad group out of which grew the Association of Contemporary Musicians.

[5] Vladimir Vladimirovich Maiakovsky (1894–1930) is now called the poet of the revolution. He was excited about the revolution's possibilities, but his later poetry reflected disgust at the graft and perversion of his dream. His poetry was direct, rough, and often cruel. He committed suicide.

[1] Konstantin Aleksandrovich Fedin (1892–) was a German prisoner in 1916–17 and became a journalist and poet—a member of the literary Serapion Brotherhood. He knew Gorky and Romain Rolland.

[2] The work was published by Gosmuzizdatel'stvo in 1935.

ten poems. Opus 14 (1937) is the symphony-cantata, *Na Pole Kulkova* (In the Kulikov Field) on words of Blok. Maiakovsky's *Ode to Revolution* was the inspiration for Shaporin's only symphony (opus 11, 1930–3). The symphony retains the Maiakovsky epigraph:

O Zverinaia, O Detskaia	O Savage, O Childlike
O Kopeechnaia, O Velikaia! transl.	O Petty, O Great!

The four movements (The Past, Dance, Lullaby, March) are scored for four performing units: band, orchestra, choir, and piano. The whole tends to give the piano concerto prominence. The choir sings without words. The work is grandiose and of an heroic proportion which reminds one of the *Bogatyr Symphony* of Borodin, the Russian composer whom Shaporin most nearly resembles. The work has also, if contradictorily, been called an epic of an artist meeting life. About this time Shaporin's novelist friend, Konstantin Fedin, published his *Brothers*. The hero of the rather commonplace novel is the composer, Karev. One chapter, 'Nikita Karev's Symphony', is an analysis both technical and emotional of the imaginary work and was written by Shaporin himself at Fedin's request.

Shaporin had known Gorky since the days of the Leningrad Bolshoi Drama Theatre and worked with him again starting in the early thirties. One source indicates that this friendship continued strong and that Gorky's death, violent and mystery-wrapped, was a hard blow to Shaporin.[1] There was no musical issue. Their joint project had been an opera on Gorky's *Mat'* (Mother), but Gorky's death, coinciding with one of Shaporin's periods of silence postponed the work. Khrennikov preempted with his Party-lining *Mat'* in 1957,[2] and, in any case, Shaporin was no longer interested in the caponized image Gorky had become.

Nor did Shaporin neglect the classic Russians. He was particularly devoted to Pushkin (opus 10, 1949) and Lermontov (opus 3), and also set Tiutchev (opus 6).

Shaporin's musical contacts were also many and varied. Most important in the Leningrad period were his friendships with Asaf'ev, with whom he formed the Association of Contemporary Musicians, and with some of the younger composers, especially Shostakovich. It is interesting to remember, when reflecting on Shaporin's seeming status today as a living example of the value of romantic orthodoxy, that he was the head of the Leningrad ACM. This creative musical organization was the most progressive in Russia, if not in all Europe. For a brief span of years, those of Shaporin's tenure, the best of the parallel lines of musical

---

[1] V. Vasina-Grossman, *Iurii A. Shaporin* (Moscow: Muzgiz, 1946), p. 107.
[2] See p. 260.

development in Russia and in Europe vectored in the Leningrad ACM. Its noblest and most characteristic virtue was its indiscriminate embrace. This was no narrow circle, no clutch of hot-eyed men bound by some dogmatic manifesto. If early twentieth-century Russian music was spared the fate of her literature—that of fragmentation into ideological 'isms'—the Leningrad ACM provided the refuge from the musical literateurs. It is, of course, no accident that Boris Asaf'ev was Shaporin's partner. It is stated of Asaf'ev elsewhere herein:

'He had that ability, rare among European music critics of that time, to accept and encourage the *avant-garde* on whatever terms, but at the same time to provide the essential ties with, and an appreciation for, the past.[1]

Much the same could be said of Shaporin.

The demise of the ACM in 1929 and of the comic-opera RAPM[2] in 1932, and the ensuing formation of the Union of Soviet Composers in 1932–3, coincided with the end of what might be called Shaporin's instrumental period. This had started with the effective but naive piano sonatas of 1924 (in b minor, opus 5) and 1927 (opus 7), continued with the *Blokha* suite (1928, opus 8) and culminated with the Symphony (opus 11). Shaporin's path changed considerably in the thirties. His writing continued at a slow pace: three major works, or rather, their completion lay ahead of him. He became, in 1935, a statistic in Moscow's artistic rape of Leningrad. In that year he moved, on an irresistible commission from the Moscow Bolshoi, to Klin, living in Tschaikovsky's *dacha* and working on *The Decembrists* (by this time in its fifteenth year of creation). The tale of the progress of the *Decembrists* is resumed later. Shaporin never returned to Leningrad.

In the Kulikov Field has been mentioned. Although first heard in 1939,[3] the collaboration with Blok had begun in 1918. Some of the verses were cast by Blok in a metre assigned by Shaporin. During the final polishing period, so characteristic of Shaporin, he enlisted the literary aid of the poet, M. Lozinsky. The battle in the Kulikov field is that Russian historical milestone, 1380, when the Moscow Prince Dmitrii met the Tatars on the field near the confluence of the Nepriadva and the Don (hence: Dmitrii Donskoi). The musical language is simple,

---

[1] See p. 88.

[2] RAPM—Russian Association of Proletarian Musicians. See p. 49.

[3] In lists of Shaporin's works the date of *Kulikov* is given as 1937. It was, however, finished only in 1939 and was performed by Shaporin's old Petersburg University classmate, Gauk, on November 18th of that year in the Bolshoi Hall of the Moscow Conservatory. The confusion in date is undoubtedly due to Shaporin's drawn-out writing habits.

honest and effective. Its performance abroad further provided Shaporin with a modicum of that essential for Soviet domestic success: foreign recognition. This was Shaporin's first of a set of epic-heroic works connected with the tense drama of the war. It was followed by the historical films *Minin and Pozharsky* (1939), *Suvorov* (1941), and *Kutuzov* (1943). From the first two of these he fashioned vocal-symphonic suites.

Shaporin and his family were evacuated to Tbilisi during the height of the war. This was considered a prestige retreat. Here Shaporin, amidst other wartime musical duties, worked on *Skazanie o bitve za russkiu zeml'iu*, opus 17. Even the title, 'Tale of the battle for the Russian land', shows Shaporin's reluctance to leave a formula already successfully tried. The multipartite work was clearly concerned with contemporary goings-on, but was saved from outdating by its lack of specifics and by a constant reference to the past. Thus the sections 'On the Volga Banks' and 'On the Don Steppes' reflect the battle of Stalingrad without naming that city. The work, musically very like the earlier *Kulikov*, was written in two years, a Shaporin record. Its first performance was at the Bolshoi Hall of the Moscow Conservatory, under Gauk, in April 1944. Both *Kulikov* and *Skazanie* were awarded Stalin Prizes of the first degree.[1] This set of 'battle 'works concluded with the relatively unsuccessful *Dokole Korshunu Kruzhit*: ballads of War and Peace. Also set for chorus, soloists, and orchestra, the work has never been published. Shaporin uses poetry from both world wars: Blok's from 1914 and that of Konstantin Simonov[2] from 1941. This work, with the others mentioned since the late thirties, demonstrates the composer's slow turn and penetrating glance toward the past. Even his treatment of the present is in allegorical terms, a practice which places him with Mussorgsky and especially Borodin. More than anything else, his technique and style show no trace of the 'new'. Shaporin, the dramatist, simply feels no need to struggle with a new mode. This does not mean that his music is always comprehensible; there is plenty of room in nineteenth-century Russian music for obscurity. But his idiom is always approachable. Just as Pasternak, whom the composer knew and admired, is '. . . the very last of Russia's (literary) intellectuals',[3] so is

[1] *Kulikov* was published in score by Muzgiz in 1946; *Skazanie*, in piano score only, by Muzgiz, and not until 1950.

[2] Konstantin (Kirill) Mikhailevich Simonov (1915–) is a popular Soviet publicist and novelist. His writing falls in the categories of love stories and historico-patriotic novels. One of the latter, *Days and Nights*, is an account of the Stalingrad battle, and is well known in the West.

[3] Bernard Guilbert Guerney, *Anthology of Russian Literature* (Random House: New York, 1960), p. 417.

Shaporin the last of the musical intellectuals in the nineteenth-century Russian tradition.

For those who embrace the mathematics of cause and effect relationships for their own sake, Shaporin's life and creative activity presents a pretty pattern of preparation for his final assault on *The Decembrists*. His early stage music provided the understanding of drama, an understanding that matured with the years; the instrumental period of *Blokha* and the First Symphony prepared his orchestra. His vocal-symphonic works, especially the cantata *Kulikova* and oratorio *Skazanie* were a giant step towards synthesis. There remains only his activity in the art song. To those already mentioned we can now add the settings of eight elegies by Russian poets[1] (opus 18), Ten Romances and songs on words of Soviet poets[2] (opus 21, 1948), the tenor and orchestral ode *To Chaadaev* (on Pushkin, 1949), the *Burlatskaia pesnia* (Boatman song) after Gorky (1951), and some folk song arrangements (1951). Of these *To Chaadaev* may be singled out as another, final, stylistic synthesis.

To Chaadaev[3] is a totally unassuming musical work in length, idiom and text. Pushkin's early lines are deceptively direct:

Poka svobodoiu gorim	While we burn for freedom
Poka serdtsa dlia chesty zhivy	While our hearts quicken for honour
Moi drug, otchizne posviatim	My friend, exalt our native land
Dushi prekrasnye poryvy!	The soul's splendid passions!
Tavarishch, ver'; vzoidet ona	Believe me, comrade, she will ascend
Zvezda plenitel'nogo schast'ia	That star of charming happiness
Rossiia vsprianet oto sna	Russia will leap from her slumber
I na oblamkakh samovlast'ia	And on the wreckage of autocracy
Napishut nashi imena.	They shall write our names.

The tenor solo is gentle harmonically and lies in the most effective range. Representative excerpts are in Example 1. The orchestra, which is small but for the presence of piccolo and tuba (with three trombones), is sparingly used. It begins to blaze in the middle section with brilliant

[1] Lermontov, Tiutchev, Iazykov, Ogarev, Fet, Annensky, Bunin, and Blok.
[2] Rozhdestvenskii, Surkov, A. Tolstoi, Isakovsky, Sal'nikov, Shchipachev; and two folk poems.
[3] *K. Chaadaevu*: the last nine lines of Pushkin's poem are used by the composer. Peter Iakovlevich Chaadaev (1794–1856) was a Pushkin classmate, a 'Decembrist' who left the secret organization before the December events, and a critic of the absolute power of the autocracy. His bent for criticism, if not reform, led many later Russian liberals (Belinsky, Herzen, Plekhanov, etc.) to seek in his thinking a Russian rather than a Western source and history for their own ideas. Grounded deeply in religious thought and processes, Chaadaev's legacy is less useful to the Bolsheviks.

scoring and firm duplets against the 12/8 triplets, subsides momentarily, and ends in a triple forte climax. The chorus in the *tutti* passages fairly well exhibits the harmonic direction; the sound of the male voices is well calculated. Both these observations are exhibited in Example 2. The work is a well-wrought miniature and bears surface resemblance to many another Soviet work.

Shaporin. *To Chaadaev.*

Ex.1 *Representative excerpts: vocal writing.*

Po-ka svo-bo - do-iu go - rim, po-ka serd-tsa dlia ches-ti

zhi-vi   To - va-rishch, ver' vzoi-det o-

- na zvez-da ple - ni - tel'-no-go scha - stia

Ex.2 *Chorus excerpt.*

S.

A.

i na ob - lom - -

T.

B. Ros-si - ia vspria-net o - to sna   i na ob-

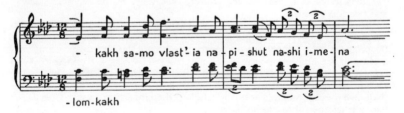

- kakh sa-mo vlast'-ia na - pi-shut na-shi i-me-na

- lom-kakh

The Decembrists embraces all of Shaporin's creative work, both in time and style. To anticipate, it is not a great opera, but it is a popular one, and it is the only contemporary Soviet fixture in the repertoire of the Bolshoi. There were a number of Shaporin 'Decembrists'. *Paulina Goebl'* was a first version. The Goebl' (Goebbel) story is a sidelight of the Decembrist uprising: Pauline Goebbel was a leftover from the Napoleonic visit and retreat. She married the Decembrist Annenkov and followed him into exile. Two scenes from this early essay, with libretto by the historian P. E. Shchegolev and Aleksei Tolstoi, were given in 1925 on the hundredth anniversary of the uprising. Through the years Shaporin rewrote and shifted the focus of the story, seeking advice from various writers and from Asaf'ev, but always clinging fast to historical accuracy. It was largely through Asaf'ev's persuasion and his intervention with the Bolshoi Theatre, that Shaporin renewed his assault on the Decembrist problem at Klin in the thirties. This assault resulted in some scenes on the Moscow stage in the thirties, but there was no formal presentation. The story and the dramatic emphasis continued to change. The last period of intensive effort, early 1953, was sparked by close collaboration with a final librettist, Vsevolod Rozhdestvensky. Unfortunately the *dénouement* of the drama of the creation of the opera is disappointing. The love story remains, but is secondary. The character of Pestel' was introduced at the last minute, and much of the plot bears on him. The plot and fate of the Decembrists themselves becomes central. These are not the disappointing changes: they seem logical and even necessary if the opera is to bear the name Decembrists. But, apparently, Rozhdestvensky persuaded Shaporin of the necessity of including the ideologically correct 'masses'. For this to have been Rozhdestvensky's main task would not be at all unusual in the Soviet Union.[1] The inclusion of the masses as protagonists is historically inaccurate and unconvincing on the stage.[2]

The story of the uprising itself begins with the mustering of forces and ideas, north and south, and the crescendo of anger against the Tsar. It culminates in a battle scene of proportions possible only with a huge stage, unlimited supernumeraries and budget for sets. It ends with the dispersion of the Decembrists. Those to hang meet their fate bravely;

[1] There is a type of functionary in the Soviet Union who provides ideological direction for authors and others. These are skilful hacks whose services may be bought by the artist or, at least in the past, assigned by ideological authority.

[2] The Decembrist uprising in 1825 was a revolt of the young élite, most of them serf owners in a country where serfs and owners were of the same race. There is no doubt of the liberal flavour of the event, considering the antique medievalism of Russian royal philosophy at the time. But this was a palace revolt in which commoners figured only as mercenaries for their masters.

and the others bring the opera to a Dostoevskian close on the road to exile in Siberia. Laid upon that is the love story of Decembrist Dmitrii Shchepin-Rostovsky, a prince, and the poor neighbour daughter, Elena Orlova. The forbidding difference in station makes their love a tragic one at first. But, after Dmitrii is sentenced to Siberia, Elena tricks the Tsar (at a masked ball) into granting her permission to join him.[1]

This is also a folk (narodny) opera in the same sense as Boris Gudonov. In fact, many superficial parallels can be drawn between the two operas: There is even a Tsar's monologue, in which he sings of the troubled times during which he has taken the throne (Example 3). But the Gudonov balance of good and evil is lacking. The Tsar is evil overdone: he says, when informed of the sentencing of the Decembrists:

'What! Shoot every fifth one? Why? Why? I'm not a bloody man. Really, Benkendorf, don't you know my feelings? Punish them, but without bloodshed! Hang them!'

Shaporin betrays no wish to push his idiom into untried areas. His expressive stock is large and eclectic. If at times his harmony sounds like a grousy Grieg or an attenuated Wagner, then he is merely calling on his vast knowledge of music literature to express exactly what he wants. In a quartet whose participants are variously motivated by love, despair, mortification, and indignation, Shaporin provides a Wagner-like motivic underpinning (Example 4). Nor does he hesitate to quote himself. The penultimate scene, with the condemned Decembrists, ends with the music and last five lines of poetry from Shaporin's *To Chaadaev*.[2] In characterizing Olga Mironova, Dmitrii's mother, who cruelly disowns him because of both Elena and her own devotion to the Tsar, Shaporin exhibits a sharp harmonic tongue (Example 5). On the other hand he is prepared for tenderness when depicting Elena's yearning. Her leitmotif involves the characteristic of an ascending 7th (Example 6a), and Dmitrii's thoughts of her (Example 6b) are a reflection of this image. Another Dmitrii love motive, his protestations of love, is cast in an 8/4 metre, fervently divided 3/4, 2/4, 3/4.

Shaporin is reluctant to quote folk material. Rather, his idiomatic choruses are originals which soon assume a folk popularity. One such chorus graces the dramatic peak of the opera: the arrival of the Moscow regiment in St Petersburg to aid the Decembrist's cause (Example 7).

If Shaporin understands these things, he also understands the

---

[1] This is the mutation of the Annenkov-Goebbel story.

[2] See p. 175. The prophetic Pushkin lines were written seven years before the December events.

elements that reconcile a Soviet audience to the dramatically or musically obscure. The ballroom scene is tricky dramatically. Musically it
must portray the viciousness of Dmitrii's mother, Elena's lament, and
the Tsar's capricious cruelty on the background of, in order, a Mazurka,
Waltz, and Polonaise. The complicated music barely reaches the mind
of the listener who has been stunned since the curtain by the set.
Massive columns, great doors, complex chandeliers (graduated to give
depth), and costumes blaze in white and gold. The actual battle is

Shaporin. *Decembrists.*

Ex. 3 *Tsar Nicholas's aria, and aria from Mussorgsky's "Boris Godunov."*
(excerpts)

Nicholas:

V ne dob — ryi chas v stu — pa — iu ia na tron. ___

Boris:

Ex. 4 *Accompaniment to quartet.*

Ex.5 *Olga Mironovna's aria*

similar in proportion: On the stage, at left and right, are the St Petersburg Synod and Senate buildings; in the centre background is a huge
replica of Peter's statue; beyond that the Winter Palace is dimly seen.
Along the left the river Neva flows; in the middle distance, right, is the
façade and part of the dome of the Cathedral of St Isaac.[1] The Moscow

Ex.6

a) *Elena's theme.*

b) *Dimitri's thoughts of Elena.*

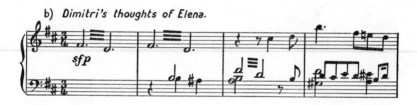

regiment appears before the assembled Decembrists who then summon
their own troops. A sympathetic Navy regiment joins them. The people
of the town gather to watch and exhort. A Metropolitan enters with an
entourage of priests and choirboys. The Tsar's army, preceded by a
general who is shot off a horse, moves up with cannon and the battle
rages. The Bolshoi and Mariinsky stages are, of course, among the largest
in the world.[2] Standard battle music is punctuated by familiar sounds,

[1] Actually, St Isaac's could not be seen from the vantage point indicated.
[2] The première of Shaporin's *Decembrists* took place in Moscow at the Bolshoi
Theatre in June 1953, Melik-Pashaev conducting. It was first presented in
Leningrad in June of that year, Khaikin conducting, at the Mariinsky (Kirov)
Theatre.

Ex.7 *Chorus of the Moscow regiment.*

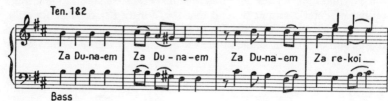

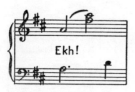

Ex.8 *Battle music from 'Decembrists' and fragment from*
                                        Soviet national anthem. -

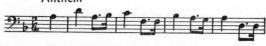

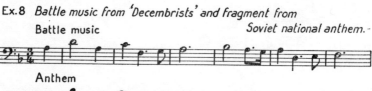

Ex.9 *Heroism motive*

  a) *original form*

including a strong intonation of the Soviet national anthem (Example 8). Here, too, the opera's unifying intonation, the motive of the heroic Decembrist idea, is sounded (Example 9). This motive also opens the opera and occurs whole and in fragments throughout the work.

Perhaps with the completion of *The Decembrists*, Shaporin's career-long project, the creative web has been woven. He has written only one

Ex.9 *Battle Scene*

short, as yet unpublished song cycle since then. His teaching activity at the Moscow Conservatory continues. As a teacher he also departs from the Russian norm. Whereas most Soviet composers demand imitation and try to reproduce themselves in the old European tradition, Shaporin gives full rein. Among his students are the usual Party-lining poetasters, but there is also the slick, successful Rodion-Shchedrin and even Russia's lonely serial composer, Andrei Volkonsky. As the last of his generation, Shaporin is held in high regard at both the conservatory and the Moscow Union of Soviet Composers. For the latter he is usually the ceremonial toastmaster, opening composers' meetings, greeting foreign delegations, and dedicating memorial concerts.

Shaporin has never been attacked by the Party,[1] and for this reason has never gained the Western notoriety which seems to be the quickest way to Soviet fame. But, neither has Shaporin ever indulged in the elaborately pitiful 'confessions' and maudlin displays of humble gratitude to the Party that others have. He is not a Party member, nor has he ever extolled the Party as some non-Party artists do.[2] His only work of political title was for the film *Three Songs of Lenin* (1934). He has never touched the Party axe.

Shaporin's honest, old-fashioned music is buried under the equally old-fashioned but cynical and contrived regurgitations of the Khrennikovs, Kabalevskys, and Khachaturians. If he is already a cipher in music history it is because he has taken the punishment due these, his brethren, the *canaille* of twentieth-century Art.

[1] At the 1948 discussions a Party speaker had just put the head on his vitriol by reading the roll of offenders. Rhetorically he demanded 'Have I left anyone out?' The stenographic report reads, 'voice from among the listeners: "Shaporin!"' An anecdote concerning this interruption is in the form of a dialogue between two musicians: 'And who was it who called Shaporin's name?' 'Don't be silly, it was Shaporin himself!'

[2] A recent example is that of the anti-Stalinist, independent, one-time abstract painter Martiros Sarian. The Soviet press, in early 1962, with heady saturation, printed paeans of praise for the Party and Khrushchev by Sarian. The Armenian artist, as late as mid-1960, had said, 'What Party? What Khrushchev?'

❧❦❧

CHAPTER 15

Dmitrii Shostakovich

O n May 12, 1926 the first symphony of Dmitrii Shostakovich, a recent graduate of, and now a graduate student at, the Leningrad Conservatory, was premiered by Nikolai Mal'ko with the Leningrad Philharmonic. The time of the première is critical. Stalin's struggle with Trotsky had ended with the former the victor. Kirov had assumed Party leadership in Leningrad six months earlier, bringing considerable authority to that disillusioned city. Western interest in Soviet events was high. By means of his First Symphony, Shostakovich was to be the first Russian composer 'of an age with the revolution' to receive sustained acclaim abroad. This was the first opportunity for the new system to display its own product musically.

Shostakovich was born in St Petersburg on September 5, 1906. His parents were enthusiastic if occasional music patrons, and young Shostakovich first took piano lessons from his mother at the age of nine. He was placed in the Glasser school and there made his first attempts at composition. These were trifling sketches, but were founded emotionally on the events around him: the war in 1914, the 1905 revolution, whose bitterness still lay heavy in St Petersburg minds, and the more immediate atrocities of the revolutionary events of 1917–18. In 1919 his parents sought advanced training for their son at the Petrograd Conservatory. Glazunov accepted the boy immediately, personally granting him a scholarship, and Shostakovich began studying piano with Leonid Nikolaev and composition with Maximilian Steinberg. Shostakovich finished the piano course brilliantly in four years and continued with Steinberg. The atmosphere still reeked heavily of the past. To avoid Rimsky-Korsakov's self-conscious horror of dilettantism, the course in free composition was begun only in the last year or two, after solid grounding in harmony, counterpoint, fugue and orchestration. But Shostakovich, like Miaskovsky and Prokofieff before him, rebelled in private. His First Symphony, then, was already opus 10. Of the previous opera (Shostakovich began numbering in 1919) only number 5, *Three Fantastic Dances for Piano*, 1922, was published.[1]

The First Symphony, composed in 1924-5, was Shostakovich's diploma work. One need not look too closely to see the various influences: obviously this was a student well acquainted with Tschaikovsky, Scriabin, Rimsky-Korsakov, and even Prokofieff; and also with Debussy and Gershwin. But more important are the elements of individual maturity and craftsmanship. It is a remarkable work for a boy of nineteen. On the strength of the implied promise, and certainly, in part, to satisfy the Western hunger for any Soviet cultural news, the symphony began immediately to be played abroad. The Association of Contemporary Musicians[2] used its foreign channels actively to propagandize the work of the young Leningradite.

The work is in four movements, beginning with an Allegretto whose introduction supplies, in embryonic form, much of the material of the whole work. A trumpet fanfare opens the work, losing its stridency as it competes with comments, first of the bassoon, eventually the 'cello, which become richer and more sonorous. A sarcasm of idiom, at the moment frankly borrowed but eventually to be Shostakovich's personal property, is evident. The principal theme, a march-like, idiomatic response to the original fanfare, is a development of intonations of the introduction. The fanfare figure separates theme A and B. The latter is a waltz with no brass instruments. The woodwinds handle the melody against a wryly pedestrian string accompaniment. The theme is not much different in character from theme A. The nearly mathematical formal construction of the sonata makes this similarity of subjects, by contrast, surprising. This much discussed problem is solved by Shostakovich in an obvious contrast, even conflict, between the whole of the exposition (straightforward, dance and march rhythms) and its introduction (terse, mystic, portending). The development is a successful demonstration of the young composer's mastery of the devices, if not the texture, of polyphony, although here the art or dramaturgy of the movement seems, if not lost, temporarily suspended. The recapitulation is considerably shortened and cryptically paraphrases the exposition in reverse order of themes. The quotations become fragmentary, episodic and give way to the fanfare which is in turn superseded by a dying theme A figure in the flutes, with wisps of the fanfare in the clarinet to end the movement.

The scherzo (second movement) has often been called the most successful part of the symphony. It is the only movement free from the

[1] Muzgiz, 1926.
[2] See Introduction, p. 49, for discussion of the ACM.

direct influence of the first, and it is a dazzling *tour de force* in orchestration. The harmonic underpinning is in constant motion, opening with a brief, disjointed canon at the octave between 'cello and bass. The first part includes a melodious, humorous theme which emerges into a passage of melodic play that has been likened to the sound of a street crowd.[1] A 'trio' section features two flutes on the background of violin tremolo.

It is comparatively lyric, thin and unfocused. The Scherzo concludes with a facile combination of these elements. The movement is important. The first theme exhibits the balance of melodiousness, humour, and sarcasm which are to become Shostakovich trademarks. The orchestration, especially the inclusion and use of the piano, is probably the most original element of the work, although, certainly, one cannot imagine the accomplishment without the Rimsky-Korsakov background. Unusual combinations of instruments, including piano as a melodic instrument, are explored with effect; there seems little inclination, as will appear in some of Shostakovich's later works, to avoid risks. The form is put together mathematically with no loss of dramatic impact, a fact not quite true of the first movement.

Shostakovich turns in the Lento to a lyricism inflected with or affected by an uneasy grotesqueness. The oboe handles the melody against a string background. The second part is a Scriabinesque orchestral treatment of the same material with a more contrapuntal texture.

The finale grows out of a short Largo introduction connected with the stage-setting third movement. The 'A' theme of the Presto proper begins unexpectedly with a fast, low, clarinet passage. This chromatic passage bears a strong tonal and colour relationship to the bassoon figures in the introduction and elsewhere in the work. But the relationship is obscured by a dynamism and perpetual motion character which recalls the Scherzo movement. Also, as in the scherzo, the orchestra takes on brilliant colour. The piano is used effectively as before, but with the additional colour of martellato octaves in the very high register.

The Symphony, though still played with some frequency, has suffered unfairly from the passage of time. Eclectic to begin with, its genuine innovations have since been copied many times, even by Shostakovich himself. The self-conscious, melodic grotesquerie has now become a tiresome stock item. The truly ingenious use of the piano (and in any account of the use of the piano as an orchestral instrument, this work must occupy an important place) has been a guide for far too many imitators. High, martellato octaves would be almost conspicuous

[1] I. Martynov, *D. D. Shostakovich* (Moscow: Muzgiz, 1946), p. 10.

by their absence in contemporary scores, as would the richly melodic sound of the 'tenor-baritone' octave. These considerations, however, don't detract from the importance of the work for its time. What does detract, and what provided fuel for the few critics who reserved doubts in the mid-twenties and early thirties, is that with all the trappings of maturity, the symphony is not a profound work. One cannot avoid the word 'slick' in considering the structure. Although the work is replete with the 'images' so beloved of Soviet critics, Shostakovich never shapes these to anything approaching their potential in depth. The First Symphony remains what it was: a cracking good graduate work, imaginative though eclectic, which, through the coincidences time brings, provided its composer with an international reputation.

Shostakovich entered the intense musical life of Leningrad energetically. The success of his symphony sharpened the conflict in his mind between this form and the stage, to which latter he was more naturally drawn. Nikolai Mal'ko's voice was a powerful one. He had conducted the First Symphony's première, but he was the principal conductor at the Mariinsky Theatre, and he urged Shostakovich to turn to the stage.[1]

For the moment he immersed himself in keyboard activity[2] and began familiarizing himself with music literature—a weak spot then and now in Soviet conservatories. He was most intrigued by the developments in music of his contemporaries abroad. Leningrad had a strong Western outlook and the country was enjoying the liberal flush of the post-civil war NEP.[3] Shostakovich, in predictable rebellion against the conservatism of his training, chose from Leningrad's international selection, Berg, Stravinsky, Prokofieff, Krenek, and Hindemith, rather than Miaskovsky, Gliere, and Glazunov, as his aesthetic comrades.

Shostakovich found much to do in the two years following the First Symphony other than composing. The works during this period were two string octets,[4] a piano sonata,[5] *Aphorisms* for piano,[6] and the beginning of his first opera. Of these the Second Symphony[7] may be dismissed: where the First Symphony was formally accurate, this is formally stiff; where the first is eclectic, this is shallow imitation.

---

[1] Shostakovich himself mentions the strong influence of Boris Asaf'ev at this juncture.

[2] In 1927 Shostakovich competed with honour in the Chopin piano contest in Warsaw.

[3] See p. 47.   [4] Opus 11, published by Muzgiz, 1927.

[5] Opus 12, published by Muzgiz, 1927.

[6] Opus 13, published by Triton, 1927.

[7] Opus 14, dedicated to October. The work was first performed by Mal'ko with the Leningrad Symphony on November 6, 1927. It was published by Muzgiz in 1927.

The Second Symphony is significant as an indication that Shostakovich was investigating.[1] The one-movement piano sonata, called his 'last tribute to the past.[2]' is another eclectic work, unsuccessful largely due to its difficult technical problems. This was composed back-to-back with the radical and surprising *Aphorisms*. This is a set of ten short piano pieces with convenient rather than accurate subtitles: 'Elegy', 'Lullaby', 'Recitative', 'Serenade', 'Scherzo', 'Nocturne', etc. Scorned now by the composer himself, the set of *Aphorisms* is quite clearly a forecast of the dull pedanticism of the sets of preludes and preludes and fugues. The fact emphasized by Soviet critics that the latter are closer to life[3] is lost on the Western listener, and the reasoning seems to have an ideological rather than a musical basis. The *Aphorisms* are mostly two-part exercises in contrast and counterpoint. The 'Scherzo' is uncompromisingly difficult. Of the set only 'Elegy' and 'Lullaby' escape the dryness born of the naive and visible effort to be abstract. Still, the awkward melodic lines are a strong clue to the enchanting grotesqueries Shostakovich was to achieve subsequently.

This relatively quiet period preceded a furious burst of activity which saw progress in the direction pointed out by Mal'ko, Asaf'ev, Shaporin,[4] and Samuil Samosud[5]—that of the stage and films.

The opera *The Nose*, with a libretto by A. Price, covers, essentially, the Gogol tale of the man who lost his nose while shaving and the subsequent search for and finding of the nose. But the current formalistic stream of literature could not leave it at that.[6] The libretto contains incidents and characters from *Dead Souls*, *Taras Bul'ba*, *Old Fashioned Landlords*, *Memoirs of a Lunatic*, and *The Wedding*, all by Gogol, but even refers to a character, Smerdiakov, from Dostoevsky's *Brothers Karamazov*. The number of characters, then, reaches seventy. Whatever reasons of 'not being accepted by the people' are given now, it is rather the unwieldy cast and difficult orchestral part that were the reasons for the opera's initial disappearance from the repertoire. *The Nose*, with all its variety, provides a catalogue of current expressive

---

[1] The third movement 'investigates' the fugato principal. At one point thirteen independent voices sound. The work calls for chorus in the last movement. [2] Rabinovich, p. 22.

[3] In this case, 'life' = 'zhanrovoi' (the adjective for the French *genre*. The art term 'genre-painting' is used extensively in Soviet music criticism.

[4] Asaf'ev and Shaporin (which see) were the leaders of the Leningrad Association of Contemporary Musicians.

[5] Samosud was musical director from 1918 to 1936 of the Leningrad Malyi (Small) Opera Theatre.

[6] Formalism: the legitimate literary movement is referred to here, not the Soviet epithet.

devices. The ideas of realism were strong in all the arts,[1] and Shostakovich was quite literal in his ideas of musical imitation of natural
sounds. The trot of a horse (celeste and percussion), the hiccoughs of an
inebriate (harp, violin, and woodwinds) and the sound of shaving
(double bass harmonics) are portrayed with startling accuracy. The
work is, as a matter of fact, far more interesting orchestrally than
vocally. The vocal work, fragmented among so many performers, tends
to awkward, curious recitative, fading often into pure speech. The
orchestra is chamber size, one of each instrument being present. There
are many independent orchestral episodes using the resources of the
chamber group in various combinations. The *entr'acte* to scene two, for
example, uses percussion alone. It is a difficult work to play, but its
first performance[2] was such a brilliant reading that the work ran for a
rather longer period than the one or two performances anticipated, due
to public demand. Thereafter Shostakovich had to be content with
concert excerpts, as no other Soviet theatre was provided the funds to
mount the cumbersome work.

The Nose may not be a serious work. Shostakovich's comments on it
were always in the vein of ridicule. There is only farce and slapstick,
with no attempt at the depth to which Shostakovich was to probe in
Lady Macbeth. The use of the orchestra sets it apart, and, indeed, from
this juncture on, Shostakovich broke from the tradition that still holds
true among Russian composers. He does not write for piano and later
orchestrate in the Russian manner as epitomized by Rimsky-Korsakov.[3]
Rather he thinks and writes in score, including all details which he
rarely changes. This practice separates a small handful of post-1917
Soviet composers from their fellows.

By the time the opera had made its impact, Shostakovich was immersed in opera, ballet, films, and music for plays. In the interval
between *The Nose* and the Fifth Symphony, Shostakovich wrote the
abortive Third and Fourth Symphonies, one set of six songs (opus 21), two

---

[1] Mosolov's ballet, *The Factory*, had been premiered in Moscow in 1926.

[2] January 12, 1930 at the Malyi Opera Theatre under Samosud.

[3] It is conventional in the Soviet Union for the composer to present his work
in 'black' (chernyi) (i.e. 'piano') form to his colleagues in the regularly scheduled
meetings of the Union of Soviet Composers. Collective judgments are then made
about the future, if any, of the work, after which the composer proceeds to the
orchestration. This practice, based on the usual procedure, amounts to a difficult
problem for Shostakovich, since he writes in score away from the piano. Always
anxious to accommodate due process, Shostakovich at first, and later the usc
itself, paid for other hands to make piano reductions. Thus the Eleventh
Symphony was already in orchestral rehearsal in 1957 when it was given its
'black' hearing before the symphony section of the usc.

short orchestral pieces (opus 23), the twenty-four piano preludes (opus 34), a concerto for piano and trumpet (opus 35), a jazz suite (opus 38), and a 'cello sonata (opus 40); but he wrote two operas, three ballets, music to seven plays and six motion picture scores. Of the opus numbers 15 through 33, only five were not for films or the stage. This was precisely the period most criticized in later years, yet it was the period when Shostakovich was most intimately and comfortably in contact with the classical 'proletariat'. Shostakovich worked and was known in a number of Leningrad theatres from 1927 on, but his basis activity was as musical director for the Leningrad Theatre of Working Youth (TRAM— Teatr rabochei molodezhi). He wrote for this unusual theatre a great many musical fragments. These, plus three extended works with suite possibilities (*The Shot*, opus 24, 1929; *Virgin Soil*, opus 25, 1930; and *Rule Britannia*, opus 28, 1931) may be considered, with *The Nose*, as preparatory ground for his principal and last stage works, *Lady Macbeth of Mtsensk* and the ballet, *The Sparkling Brook* (opus 39, 1934).

Lady Macbeth of Mtsensk (*Ekaterina Izmailova*), opus 29, was written in 1930–1 on a Leskov story with a libretto by Price. It is the story of the relatively sophisticated Ekaterina who is withering intellectually and morally on the farm where her merchant-farmer groom has taken her. Though urged by his father (who sometimes imagines himself capable of taking care of the matter of heirs) to act more like a husband and less like a piece of farm machinery, the husband apparently feels that having married and established Ekaterina in his house he has fulfilled his social obligation. A new hired hand, Sergei, promptly discovers the tension and takes the classical steps to relieve at least a part of it. The resulting affair is jeopardized by the father and son, so their grisly removal is effected. Ekaterina and Sergei enjoy the brief, uneasy stewardship of the farm, but, under the pressure of the fact that all concerned know perfectly well what happened, they betray themselves.

On their way to prison in Siberia, Sergei reveals his basic fickleness by becoming infatuated with another member of the prisoner group (Sonja), a prostitute. He procures Ekaterina's warm stockings for the shivering Sonja, but any hope of reward is lost when Ekaterina kills Sonja and herself.

It is a significant and often missed point that this was Shostakovich's first essay at expression of something other than humour on the stage. Despite the ironic grotesqueries of *The Nose*, the sarcasm of *The Golden Age*, and the serious propaganda nature of *Bolt*, Shostakovich had never brought his tools to the task of sheer drama, classical tragedy. In *Lady Macbeth* comic relief exists, as it does in most tragedies, involving the person of Aksinia, an older woman servant of the farm. But now

Shostakovich was to portray musically, as vividly and realistically as he did soccer in *The Golden Age* ballet, flogging, physical humiliation, peasant roughness, rape, and murder. *Lady Macbeth* was, of course, the fulcrum for levering creative music into the position of government control,[1] but in the mass of verbiage about the well controlled and calculated official reaction and propaganda, some basic conflicts and original, even unique, factors in the work itself have been ignored.

The influence, both dramatic and musical, of *Wozzeck* is unmistakable. Iurii Shaporin, Shostakovich's companion at a Leningrad performance of *Wozzeck*, has discussed the excitement of the young composer. The work is one of Shostakovich's best and refuses to die; indeed it is periodically given new life by its would-be detractors: Inevitably, in Soviet journals and reviews, when the time comes for discussing *Lady Macbeth*, the author can't stop.[2] That part of the controversy that is creatively legitimate stems from the title character, Ekaterina Izmailova, whose aspect is as bewildering, as good and evil, as naive and complex, and as capable of radically varying portrayals as that of her 300-year old namesake. The establishment of Ekaterina as a sympathetic, beset woman of potentially noble proportion is accomplished in the first act by a simple lyricism denied the other characters and, indeed, heard rarely elsewhere in the work. And yet, ample dramatic room is left, as it is in the case of the original Lady Macbeth, to make of the 'Lady' either a witch or a martyr throughout. But more perplexing is that the character can be variously adapted to increase from pettiness to a spiritual nobility via the same route as Raskol'nikov in *Crime and Punishment*, or to degenerate from the nobility all women share by virtue of being a woman, to a tawdry image, something less than human from the lower depths. Again the parallel with the original Lady Macbeth, and her conflicting history of portrayals, is brought to mind.

Considering the dramatic structure, it is difficult to decide what Shostakovich had in mind. The work was to be the first of three such operas, each depicting the situation of Russian woman in three different eras.[3] Ekaterina is, of course, the woman of recent feudal times. As such it may be proper dramatically for her either to increase or diminish in stature. But drama demands, no less than does Marxian ideology, a hint if not of salvation, then of its potential source. The traditions of

---

[1] See p. 52.

[2] In vol. II of *IRSM* the author, still under the strictures of 1936 and 1948, discusses and quotes from *Lady Macbeth* for twenty pages (195–215). Even the Fifth Symphony is not given such detailed coverage (cf. pp. 416–29).

[3] Shostakovich outlines this plan in the article 'Tragedy-Satire' in *Sovestkoe Iskusstvo*, October 16, 1932.

nineteenth-century Russian opera, especially those of Mussorgsky, and again to say nothing of the implications of Marxist-Leninist revolutionary thinking, would turn the seeker for some ray of hope to the people, the 'masses' or their representatives as depicted in the opera. But the colours of gloom, deceitfulness, and hopelessness extend in heightened hue to the workers and peasants portrayed in the opera. At no time can the listener identify sympathetically with the petty, misshapen, and squalid figures that abound in the work. Other lines of reasoning find the sought-for source of deliverance in the attitude of the mass of convicted prisoners on their way to Siberia with Ekaterina and Sergei.[1] Yet close scrutiny reveals nothing but shock and pious 'tuttutting' on the part of the unhappy company.[2] Moreover, the humiliation and remorse of Ekaterina pervades the last act, to the dramatic exclusion of other elements. Indeed, if hope or exaltation is to be found it may be imagined in Ekaterina's last cries; although even here the basic conflict reigns supreme, since the final humiliation, murder, and suicide seem grounded not so much in Dostoevskian remorse as in carnal jealousy.

Shostakovich in this, his first approach to tragedy, could not leave his satirical tools idle. In discussing *Lady Macbeth*[3] he announced that his intention was to 'create a satire, a revealing satire, tearing away the masks of, and generating hatred for, the whole terrible arbitrariness and mockery of merchant life'. The music of the opera can be categorized with no detrimental effect. First is the cantabile character of vocal line. In this is found the most radical departure from vocal usage in *The Nose*. Although Ekaterina has most of the sympathetic cantilena, the other characters depart from cantabile style only to the degree demanded by their roles.

Recitative is similarly balanced. A second category would be the naturalistic music already mentioned. The third category is found almost exclusively in the accompaniment: the grotesque and sarcastic. If the vocal parts are singable and dramatically straight-forward, the instrumental parts are decidedly not. A firm and inviolate distinction may be drawn between the two elements. On the instrumental side is Shostakovich of *The Nose*, on the vocal side, one might say, there is no 'Nose' at all. Thus, Shostakovich is able to say, '*Lady Macbeth* is a continuation

[1] *IRSM*, II, 209.

[2] In what one suspects is more than mere coincidence, Dostoevsky's Raskol'-nikov finds himself in exactly the same position as Ekaterina just before her suicide: on the way to Siberia with a nondescript pack of fellow prisoners. Dostoevsky's 'ray of hope' was unavailable to Shostakovich—a religio-spiritual rebirth.

[3] See n. 3, p. 192.

and consolidation of those musical positions which I laid out in the opera *The Nose*,[1] and at the same time to say, 'The musical material of *Lady Macbeth* differs strongly from my previous operatic work, *The Nose*—my deep conviction is that in opera one must sing',[2] without being in the least contradictory. This third category has been aptly labelled 'grotesque scherzo'.[3] These 'scherzos', often sarcastic and/or brutal parodies on more lyric sections of the opera—principally the part of Ekaterina—underscore the focal points of tension and drama such as the flogging of Sergei, the rape scene, the murder of the father-in-law at Ekaterina's hands, and the chorus of prisoners when they are chiding Ekaterina into her final crime. Their development and use are epitomized in a particular progress of events noted also by the authors in *IRSM*[4]: Aksinia, an old peasant woman, is beset by scoffers, among them Sergei, who handle her roughly.[5] Ekaterina protests, finally with success, and fixes the achievement with a lyric aria concerning the dignity of woman. The tense, yet simple theme is handled mockingly in the ensuing *entr'act*. At the climax of the rape episode the theme is heard again in caustic dress, depicting 'the triumph of Sergei, not only in "mockery of the peasant woman [read: 'womankind'—SDK]" but in effecting her [woman's] submission to him.'[6]

The opera was successful at home and abroad. It was received as revolutionary and exciting by the Russian musical world and stayed continuously in the repertoire of many theatres until early 1936 when it was finally with drawn for good. The opera and its success generated a new area of thinking in Soviet music. One looks in vain in Soviet newspapers and journals of the time for any adverse criticism of the work—until January 26, 1936. Thereafter the one-time acclaimers became verbiferous. Lady Macbeth portended great things. The obvious faults: a certain mechanical form, some unintended awkwardnesses, an occasional lack of sympathy for the voice, have all been overcome in later works of different genre. If Shostakovich had not been separated from the stage he could easily have progressed to a *Wozzeck* or *Peter Grimes*.

The next work to cause any impact was the Fifth Symphony. Again, this is an example of a combination of fame and notoriety. The Fourth was in rehearsal (under Fritz Stidry) at the time of the Party attack on

[1] In *Vecherniaia Moskva*, December 21, 1932.
[2] See n. 3, p. 192.
[3] *IRSM*, II, 200.
[4] Pp. 201, 202.
[5] This tormenting scene is also, and incidentally to the progression being discussed, a scherzo of the type mentioned.
[6] *IRSM*, II, 202.

Shostakovich and was withdrawn.[1] The Fifth (opus 47), subtitled 'A composer's answer to just criticism' was finished in 1937, first performed on October 21, 1937, and published in 1939.[2]

This work, with the first String Quartet (op. 49), inaugurates a new period in Shostakovich's creative path. That it is new is, at least, a conclusion easily arrived at and agreed to by all. The musical content and value of the new period is, however, a great area for debate. At this point Shostakovich's work takes two tacks: one is that of the facile, clever, melodic, often pompous, but 'successful' style found in the Seventh, Ninth, Eleventh, and Twelfth Symphonies, in the *Leningrad Suite* for chorus and orchestra (1942), the cantata *Song of the Forests* (1949), the suite *The Fall of Berlin* (1949), the *Party Cantata* (1952), and the *Holiday Overture* (1954), and to a lesser extent in the Fourth and Fifth quartets (1949 and 1952). The other tack is that of a laborious, often overwrought, prolonged style of working out supposedly conflicting but not always obvious ideas. Here one would mention especially the Mahlerish Eighth Symphony, the Twenty-four Preludes and Fugues, and the Second and Third quartets. The Tenth Symphony, the violin concerto, and the 'cello concerto (1959) are, for the moment, specifically withheld from this dichotomy.

The two styles, neither of which, to be sure, dominates exclusively any one work, are the fruit of Shostakovich's severing his ties with the stage, and particularly with the idiom he had previously fancied appropriate thereto. The depth of the conflict lies in the fact that the decision was Shostakovich's own, regardless of the fact that external factors would have forced such a decision in any case. When official reasoning in the mid-thirties indicated that Shostakovich's music was ideologically and socially wrong, there is no indication that Shostakovich did not immediately try to understand and adopt, as well as he could, that line of reasoning, criticizing himself and apologizing sincerely. The image of a bloody but unbowed, bolshevik, neo-Beethoven is the false product of interpreting an essentially Russian

---

[1] The fact that Shostakovich's Fourth Symphony has recently had its 'première' performance, in April of 1962, with Mravinsky conducting the Leningrad Philharmonic, has little or no bearing on the period under discussion, i.e. twenty-six years previous to the première.

[2] This première, in Leningrad, was the first of Shostakovich's works to be presented under the baton of Eugene Mravinsky. This was a double debut, Mravinsky assuming the permanent directorship of the Leningrad Philharmonic in 1938. Since then Mravinsky has enjoyed a monopoly on Shostakovich premières with the exception of that of the Seventh Symphony. The latter was first performed by Samuil Samosud, Mravinsky and the Leningrad Philharmonic having been removed to Siberia during the German encirclement.

phenomenon by non-Russian standards. Shostakovich is no Khrennikov or Kabalevsky to whom accommodation of socio-political demands is a comfortable and legitimate factor in the creative process. He is a Russian, though—one to whom such matters involve a bit of spirit wrestling. Shostakovich 'accommodated', and ultimately it was his own decision, but that the accommodation was and is uncomfortable is amply indicated in the further course of his career.

The String Quartet, opus 49, 1938, was a tentative, light, but not necessarily trivial first quartet. The Sixth Symphony (The 'Lenin') was one of his shortest. It suffers being overlooked between its neighbours, but at the time aroused some controversy: it was thought to be 'time left over' after the Fifth. That is, it contained nothing expressly new. More important, for 1948 critics, was the apparent irreverence, in one of the 'heroic' symphonies,[1] of Shostakovich's having his wry way with a sarcastic gallop in the *Lady Macbeth* style in the last movement. A piano Quintet, opus 57, 1940, is altogether serious with a certain classical austerity of line mixed with Bizet-like bustling. An early movement of the five includes a prelude and fugue. Shostakovich's habit of quoting, carefully, certain short stereotypes is developed in this work. He chooses certain melodic combinations as another would a chord.

The war years brought to many Soviet composers the international recognition, however brief, that Shostakovich already enjoyed. Shostakovich's activities were duly reported upon as he played with his children during bombing or mounted the Conservatory roof to watch for fires. In three months he was ordered out of the city. He went first to Moscow, and by December was in Kuibyshev with other figures of the Moscow cultural world.[2] He had begun the Seventh Symphony, so it is said, in besieged Leningrad; it was first performed in Kuibyshev in March of 1942 under Samuil Samosud and the Bolshoi orchestra.[3] This performance was followed within a few days by one in Moscow.

The Seventh became, perhaps, the most played symphony by a contemporary composer. It had all the ingredients for success: a birth in the thick of well publicized fire, supra-national patriotism at a patriotic time, an idiom and programme easily acceptable to any audience, and even a nasty row among three prima-donna American conductors about

---

[1] The Fifth, Sixth and Seventh are the 'heroic' symphonies.

[2] In retrospect, Shostakovich's having been assigned haven with the Moscow rather than the Leningrad cultural evacuees has significance.

[3] Although *IRSM*, vol. II, gives this date, place, orchestra, and conductor, it also mentions (p. 5) a *first* performance in early March with Stoliarov conducting the Moscow Conservatory Orchestra in a programme for the evacuated Leningrad group.

who should be first to conduct it. The work's US performance on July, 19, 1942, was the first outside the Soviet Union. It was performed in its official, legal version sixty-two times in the 1942–3 season[1] and many more times in adumbrated, arranged, or pirated form.

The war period and the ensuing two to three years, with the lessening of Party attention to artistic affairs, afforded more freedom for Soviet artists. This 'freedom', as we have seen elsewhere,[2] provided an atmosphere for the emergence of the specific works to be condemned by Zhdanov in 1948. In Shostakovich's case these works were the Eighth and Ninth Symphonies, and the Second and Third Quartets. The settings of Jewish folk poetry and the violin concerto, although finished in 1948, were not heard until 1955 and figured only briefly in the 1948 discussions.

The two symphonies, the Eighth and the Ninth, form, with the Seventh, the trilogy of 'War' symphonies, thus dovetailing with the 'Heroic' symphonies of which the Seventh is the last. The original idea was, according to Rabinovich, that the Tenth, then, would be a 'Peace' symphony-epilogue. Ignoring the obvious reasons for abandoning the Tenth in 1948, that of a literal Party ban, Rabinovich says that Shostakovich could not write a Tenth because 'as a humanist and an artist, Shostakovich felt that the forces of evil had not been completely destroyed . . .'. The two symphonies are not alike: The Eighth is reminiscent of Mahler in its endless presentation of themes and their working out. The idiom is not so obvious as that of the Seventh and its general tone is murkier. The Eighth was finished in 1943 and performed in November of that year by Mravinsky. Again, in matter of sheer sound, a comparison with Mahler is suggested. The bulk of the work is thoughtfully slow, low pitched, and chromatic. Similar handling in the Seventh is considerably shallower than it is here. The Eighth, too, is spared the bombastic 'comic' relief so blatant in the Seventh. Perhaps the best moments in the Eighth occur in the last two movements where the texture lightens at times to near-chamber quality, and episodic comments impart a personal philosophical tone. The fourth movement (there are five movements, three, four and five being played without break) is actually a passacaglia to whose 'hopelessness' Soviet critics reacted adversely. This is followed by a brighter finale—a pastorale.

The Ninth Symphony is—and was—a surprise. There is little attempt at depth, so when none is reached there is no disillusionment. Rather than being a symphony, the work is a *pastiche* of a symphony. There are five movements, each necessarily short. The elements of symphonism, even Shostakovich symphonism—emotional contrasts,

[1] Rabinovich, p. 72. [2] See Chapter 1.

orchestral exploitation and display, linear grotesqueries, and sarcastic, grotesque juxtaposition of moods—are present in a form so capsulized as to be parodies. One toys, perhaps groundlessly, with an idea strong in Russian tradition about the ominous portent of a *ninth* symphony; i.e. Beethoven's last![1] Was this Shostakovich's way of getting over the fatal hump . . . by writing a non-symphony?

The Third String Quartet reveals what has now become a Shostakovich characteristic: the tendency toward five movements. This is not to say that all pieces in sonata form are of this length from now on; the Tenth, Eleventh, and Twelfth Symphonies, for example, are four-movement works.[2] The extra movement usually appears between the standard third and fourth movements and is usually slow, differently orchestrated and extremely personal. The Third quartet is a case in point. Here the fourth movement's adagio, lyric, disjunct theme contrasts strongly with the ostinato patterns of the third movement. The quartet, especially the first movement, is as uncompromising harmonically as anything since *Lady Macbeth*. Concerning a harmonically 'tough' passage in the first movement, the composer was challenged rhetorically during the 1948 Party sessions to say that he actually heard such harmonies.[3]

One of Shostakovich's most intimate works was finished on the eve of the 1948 denunciations: the song cycle of Jewish folk songs (op. 79, 1948).[4] These were not performed until well after Stalin's death. Eight of the eleven songs are touching laments; three depict happy Jewry in the Soviet Union. They are, unfortunately, unpublished and, in view of traditional Russian anti-Semitism, rarely heard.[5]

[1] Miaskovsky, for instance, wrote his Ninth and Tenth simultaneously, to insure that his Ninth would not mean the end as it had with Beethoven.

[2] The fourth movement of the Tenth, however, is divided between a long, Andante 6/8 introduction and an allegro 2/4.

[3] From interviews with Soviet composers.

[4] Rabinovich says 1949, erring by one year. In any other context this could be charged to mere error and would hardly require a footnote. The confounding thing about Soviet music is that whether the songs were written before or after the 1948 denunciations is of utmost importance. 1948 was a grim year for composers: it was sheer hell for Soviet Jews. A genocidal policy against the Jews on the part of the Party and government was in ugly crescendo in 1948–9. No composer, gentile or Jew, would have dared set Jewish poetry in 1949. Rabinovich's wrong date would indicate that a composer could. So, is it an error?

[5] The Thirteenth Symphony lies beyond the scope of this paper (January 1963), and has not yet been heard in this country (as of March 1963). It is pertinent here in that Shostakovich returns to the theme of oppressed Jewry. There is included, in the choral last movement, a setting of Evgenii Evtushenko's *Baby Iar*, a protest at continued anti-Semitism in the Soviet Union. The work

Shostakovich's assumption of teaching duties at the Moscow Conservatory in 1943 ended an era at the Leningrad Conservatory: the move symbolized the Moscow victory. Shostakovich was still listed at Leningrad, but had no more students there. He was a good teacher and an influential one, as the rest of this discussion indicates.[1] As mentioned earlier, Shostakovich is one of a handful of Soviet composers who both write and analyse in and from score, away from the piano. Since his teaching was influential, and since, in 1948, his influence was found to be pernicious he was relieved of his professorial duties in that year and has not taught since.[2]

The period 1948 to 1953 was a suspended one in Shostakovich's musical development. His concert music of this period reverted to the idiom and style of his music for motion pictures: a special idiom in Shostakovich's mind. Shostakovich has scored from twenty-five to thirty motion pictures. His first was the deriding 'silent' *New Babylon* in 1929, and his last, at least until 1959, was the 1955 *Ovod* (The Gadfly). The number averages about one a year from 1929 to 1955, but his work is concentrated in the period 1937-40 with ten of the total number, and again in 1948-9 with six. Quite obviously he turned his unstoppable energy into this field at times of crisis.[3] Thus he seeks time for larger artistic decisions. His most significant films have been *Zlatye Gory* (The Golden Mountains, op. 40, 1931), *The Passer-By* (op. 33, 1932), *The Great Citizen* (in two parts, opera 52 and 55, 1938 and 1939), *Meeting on the Elba* (op. 80, 1948-9), *The Fall of Berlin* (op. 82, 1949), *Unforgettable 1919* (op. 89, 1951) and *Unity* (1954). In these films Shostakovich's main concern is accessibility: There are no problems, no complex images. Bad is bad, and good is good, the latter usually triumphant. The scores are tuneful and have provided popular songs for Soviet citizens.

---

has been withdrawn once for a change of text (which Soviet Premier N. Khrushchev says *he* suggested) and a second time, within days of this writing for reasons as yet not explained.

[1] Among his students were Gadzhiev, Galynin, Karaev, Sviridov, Karen Khachaturian, and others.

[2] However, sometime after mid-1960 there is evidence that Shostakovich, with none of the usual fanfare, has resumed the training of graduates at the Leningrad Conservatory. In mid-1960 there were no Shostakovich students at the Leningrad Conservatory. In the April 29th issue of *Sovetskaia Kul'tura* there is an historical layout honouring the Conservatory's 100th anniversary. Among the pictures is a small one of Shostakovich with students which was so captioned. The picture is unmistakably that of Shostakovich of very recent years.

[3] This is true of enough other Soviet composers to make of it almost as standard a practice as that of Soviet writers, under stress and pressure, turning to translation.

The idiom of non-film works such as *Song of the Forests* (op. 81, 1949) and *The Sun Beams on our Native Land* (op. 90, 1952) was not, then, new to Shostakovich. Of these two oratorios the first, *Song of the Forests*[1] has had the widest hearing. Its idiom is not complex. In all honesty, one must give the work credit for overall dramatic effect. Drama as we have noted earlier, comes naturally to Shostakovich. Certainly it took a dramatist sure of himself to handle the scene wherein Stalin goes to a map, imperiously indicates an area and says 'Let there be trees!' The work was awarded one of the very last Stalin Prizes.

The twenty-four preludes and fugues (op. 87, 1950–1) relieve this picture somewhat. Though they cannot, in comparison with other works, escape the charge of superficiality, they are, as mentioned before, a reference to the early, equally superficial, experimentations in *Aphorisms*.

The doldrums of 1948–53 were passed for Shostakovich in late 1953 with the Tenth Symphony. The liberal movement in Soviet Art grew swiftly to a climax in late 1956 and early 1957,[2] was squelched then, and has lain more or less dormant since, save for a brief flood and ebb in 1962–3. The Shostakovich Tenth Symphony served as the fulcrum for discussion of the conservative versus liberal traditions in music until 1957, when, with Party intervention, the conservative, neo-Stalinist view momentarily prevailed. The reactionary victory was fixed by Shostakovich's maudlin, acquiescent, programmatic Eleventh Symphony.

The gap between the Ninth and Tenth Symphonies was one of eight years. Perhaps this accounts, in part, for the differences found in the latter work. Although it is a work of superb craftsmanship—one could say, even, that the symphony is laboriously overwrought—there is not the sureness nor the articulate comfort of the Seventh and Ninth. Personally convinced of the need for Art's reflecting the contemporary, Shostakovich seems unclear about the ethics and morality of the present. Perhaps this very questioning, leading as it does to deeper probing, is what lifts this symphony several notches above his last five. That he was unable to draw clear lines between the optimistic and the evil (the former triumphant, of course), led to the adverse criticism of the Tenth.

The opening theme in the low strings is used as a source not only in

[1] The working title of the oratorio was 'An ode to Stalin's reforestation programme', a reference to an immense programme in the lower Volga in which thousands of people planted millions of trees with donated time on vast acres where trees had never grown. The trees died.

[2] The name for this liberal period, roughly coincident in all the arts, has became a part of the common vocabulary: The Thaw (after a novel of that name by Ilya Ehrenburg).

the first movement, but throughout the work. One is reminded immediately of the similar formula in the First Symphony. The tritone often recurs. This movement ends with abated tempo and a return (in the coda) to the introductory material. The second movement, marked 'Allegro=116' is a short, frenetic, march-like ejaculation sustained through 90 per cent of its length at a double-forte dynamic level. Aside from one hushed, tensely muted passage, the dynamics subside only occasionally to softer values and only then in order to get a good run at some sforzandi. The movement opens with utterances of the two basic 'images' which exhibit as much contrast as possible under the circumstances. These elements join with various fragments, mostly rhythm characters, in developing approximately the first third of the movement. A new, chromatic theme joins the rush with a Neapolitan key shift. The rushing, headlong pace and accompaniment do not subside. One of the first themes now reappears and continues, in various instrumental combinations, in an augmented form, until near the movement's end. There follows the only sustained quiet passage, mostly scrubbing, with staccato punctuation. From there the texture and dynamics swell to a close: the last dynamic indication is 'sffff'.

The third movement (allegretto) refers immediately to the introductory material of the first movement with a 3/4 minor theme. The similarity of idiom to the third movement of the Fifth Symphony is noticeable. The theme exhibits a variety of character. In a subsequent development, lacking only the characteristic head, it becomes a catalogue for further material. The movement develops on the meandering lines indicated until a solo horn states a remaining, non-related, element. On an underpinning of first-movement introductory material and light, homophonic string chords, this theme and its diminutions are firmly established. The original material returns in various forms including the contrapuntal, augmented, and 'dismembered'. The horn call again intervenes and alternates with urgent utterances of the primary material until the end. The ending itself is a quiet, scantily accompanied statement of the head of the first theme followed again by the horn call and a delicate comment in the flute and piccolo.

The fourth movement, beginning without pause, is a step in Shostakovich's solution of the problem of a sonata's ending. The introductory andante 6/8 almost assumes the proportions, dramatically, of a movement. Elsewhere, as we have seen, a thoughtful, personal fourth movement precedes a Shostakovich finale. In this, apparently, Shostakovich finds balance. In this work the balance is not yet achieved. One feels, in retrospect, that the non-related horn episode in the third movement is the beginning of the breakdown of the form in the

7*

composer's mind. The 2/4 allegro is a firm, busy, but not optimistic finale to the work.

The Tenth Symphony, as mentioned before, belongs to a different style, sharing this small pigeon-hole with the violin concerto and 'cello concerto. This report ends with a brief consideration of the latter.[1] Premiered in November of 1959, the concerto may be considered a 'joint' work. Shostakovich and Mstislav Rostropovich, the 'cellist for whom the work was written, collaborated on the cadenza which is the fourth of the five movements. The work is extremely difficult to play,[2] and, among the larger works of Shostakovich's last twenty years, must be given the edge in sharpness of harmonic idiom. The solo part is lyric only in the second movement. Elsewhere its utterances are of universally unpredictable length, now short ejaculations, now awkward stridencies which use the instrument's entire range. The fourth movement (cadenza), for 'cello alone, is an awesome technical display, hovering on catastrophe, and leads into the driving fifth movement wherein the 'cello, at dazzling speed, maintains what would be recognized as an ostinato if it could be heard above the noise.

Shostakovich is a man of many styles, to all of which he tries to bring sincerity of expression. His laboured progress from style to style may well be related to the tightening and relaxing of external controls but, nevertheless, remains an extremely personal thing. Of the styles abandoned the most lamented must be that of the operas, especially of *Lady Macbeth*. The abandonment of the style of the Fourth Symphony ('unrelieved gloom') brings up a curious point: To Shostakovich the work has always been his deepest and most personal, but at the same time he recognizes the atavistic qualities of such an expression of personality in his socialist milieu. Elsewhere, in every work but the Fourth, the approach to the highly personal, be it the gentle lyricism of which he is capable, or the brooding of the Eighth Symphony, is tempered and even shattered by the much puzzled-over idiom of the grotesque. The grotesque and the personal are eternally mated antidotes for one another in Shostakovich's vocabulary. He must use but mistrusts the latter and punishes his personal expression with the former.

Moving on, one finds a Shostakovich free of that conflict—perhaps

[1] The short interval since the première of the Eleventh Symphony (The '1905 Symphony', premiered in November of 1957) has found most critics in agreement: that it deserves scant consideration. Although awarded the Lenin Prize, the highest Soviet honour, it is rarely heard. The Twelfth Symphony is its twin. The Twelfth and Thirteenth Symphonies lie, arbitrarily, beyond the scope of this dissertation.

[2] In performance Rostropovich shifts his tiring hold on the bow to a hatchet grip just before the fury of the fifth movement.

regrettably free. This is Shostakovich the super-stylist or technician. The quality is found in the two concertos and in the Tenth Symphony, although certainly not exclusively. The motion-picture style has been mentioned; another, that of his music written for children has not: it is obvious, effective music. Finally, though the personal idiom of the Fourth Symphony seems abandoned, there is the intimate, reflective, relaxed manner of his songs, starting with the 1948 Jewish cycle—a manner almost unknown outside the Soviet Union.[1]

What, then, can be the judgment of Shostakovich as a composer? To delay the answer, and to introduce a new and final theme—one which must be heard—one proposes without detracting from the possibility of his greatness, that Shostakovich is an 'over-rated' composer. This is simply because, with all his well-publicized official criticism, he is easily the most honoured and lionized composer of his time, if not of all time, within his country and without. His list of honours is long and peculiarly mixed for a composer. He has an honorary doctorate from Oxford (1958) and is an honorary member of the St Cecilia Academy in Rome, the Swedish Royal Music Academy (1954), and the German Academy of Art. He is a holder of the Sibelius Prize, the French Order of Commander in Art, and, for his Eleventh Symphony, the Lenin Prize (1960). Among his other awards at home are five Stalin Prizes. He has held the rank, since 1954, of Peoples' Artist of the USSR, the highest designation in this particular scale; and is also holder of the Orders of Lenin and the Red Banner. To this list of, at least, music-related honours one must add that he is a winner of the International (Lenin) Peace Prize.[2] He is an active member of the Soviet Committee for Defence of Peace, in which capacity he has been honoured at international meetings in New York (1949), Warsaw (1950), and Vienna (1952). In a recent trip to Berlin with Iurii Shaporin, he was again awarded a peace prize and spoke for total disarmament. He has been a Leningrad deputy to the High Soviet of the RSFSR and is currently an unopposed candidate as deputy of the High Soviet of the USSR. (Elected political posts in the Soviet Union are honorary rather than functional.) Long

[1] Shostakovich's recent vocal works, as well as some of Ekaterina's songs from *Lady Macbeth*, are most effectively performed by Galina Vishnevskaia, accompanied on the piano by her husband, the 'cellist Rostropovich.

[2] The Lenin Peace Prize was inaugurated in 1955, and recapitulates, although it pointedly ignores, the Nobel Peace Prize structure. No Soviet has ever won the latter, and indications are that the Nobel Committee never considers the members of the Russian bloc. The Lenin Peace Prize is awarded to several persons a year, unlike the Nobel Prize. The latter has never been awarded to an artist with the exception of Alfred Schweitzer, whose award was for his humanitarian work.

active in the governing body of the Union of Soviet Composers, he is now chairman for the RSFSR. He has established the image of the composer engaged in social work and has received high honours for this work. It is said of him, 'It [social work] is necessary for him, like air; as a most important condition for the development of his talent.'[1] It should be emphasized here, without trying to nag, that this is simply a useful image: Shostakovich's hermit-like habits and his discomfort around, and even fear of, people is well known in Moscow and Leningrad.

He has had two signal honours recently. In Novorossisk there is a statue with a flame eternally honouring heroes (in general). On the hour, from somewhere within the statue, by means of a tape recording, there sounds a brief orchestral piece of Shostakovich's, *Novorossisk Chimes*. Finally, the first Soviet cosmonaut, Iurii Gagarin, during his orbit through space around the earth, sang Shostakovich's 'The Motherland hears, the Motherland knows'.

Again one comes to the postponed judgment. Shostakovich is easy to criticize, as are all superb craftsmen. It is also easy, and tempting, to read into the man's work the pernicious influence of a malevolent government, although it has been indicated above that Shostakovich's shortcomings are peculiarly his own. It is certainly safe to say that Shostakovich is a prolific composer. This paper indicates that he is also an honest composer, within limits that bind most creative artists and men.

But history sweeps away all these considerations and others that are 'easy' or 'safe' at the time. The road should now be cleared for the answer: the judgment will not come here. When a future audience is separated from the present by a period equal to that separating us from eighteenth-century Vienna, *then* the judgment can be made between Shostakovich-Salieri and Shostakovich-Mozart.

[1] *Sovetskaia Kul'tura*, no. 31, March 13, 1962, p. 2.

꓅꓅

CHAPTER 16

Vissarion Shebalin

Shebalin's life and training closely parallel those of Dmitrii Kabalevsky. It is interesting to compare the two composers: they were born within two years of one another (Shebalin is older), they both graduated from the Moscow Conservatory under Miaskovsky, Shebalin in 1928, Kabalevsky in 1929. Each had before him the image and model of the successful Leningradite, Shostakovich. Both, during and after their years at the Moscow Conservatory, worked with young musicians. Both became docents at the conservatory in 1932, and both were professors of compositions by the end of the 1930s. The collective works of both men are studded with important works for the dramatic stage. But the main interest in the comparison of the two lies in a few striking differences: The principal one is that although Kabalevsky is a prominent example of the politically aware, ideologically deft, and creatively opportunistic group of middle-generation composers, Shebalin, his twin in so many other ways, does not or cannot accept easily the conservative canons of Soviet orthodoxy as an integral part of the creative process. Thus Shebalin is aligned with that middle generation group of Soviet composers which includes Shostakovich and Shaporin. Comparatively independent creatively, Shebalin suffered, perhaps, the most extreme penalties of the composers criticized in 1948.

Vissarion Iakovlevich Shebalin was born June 11, 1902 in Omsk. His father was a teacher who instilled in his son a love for poetry: some of Shebalin's first works (around 1920) were settings of the work of both Russian and Western, ancient and modern poets. By the age of ten, Shebalin had already shown marked musical aptitude, and his formal training began. He was enrolled in an Imperial Russian Music Society school and, in 1920, was in the recently converted Omsk music *uchilische*. There he studied theory under Nevitov,[1] to whom he later

---

[1] Mikhail Ivanovich Nevitov (1887–) was a Gliere and Taneev pupil in Moscow. For many years he had a peculiarly mixed career in, on the one hand, law and management, and, on the other, music. Occasionally these functions were

dedicated his first quartet (1923). In 1922 his first numbered work appeared—two settings of R. Demel's poems, 'The voice of evening' and 'From far away'. He immediately set to work on the setting of some excerpts from Sappho. He finished these and the three-movement quartet in Omsk in 1923.[1] Shortly thereafter he moved to Moscow and enrolled at the age of twenty-one in the Moscow Conservatory. His study continued there under Miaskovsky. During the years at the conservatory he wrote three more sets of songs on poems of Anna Akhmatova (op. 5, 1925), Blok (op. 7, 1925) and Sergei Esenin (op. 9, 1926–7); a trio, a piano sonata, and the first symphony. As was the case with his classmate, Kabalevsky, Shebalin was pushed and encouraged[2] to provide competition for the internationally famous products of the Leningrad Conservatory. Shebalin, however, was not as politically acceptable, nor did he personally care as much as Kabalevsky. Shebalin's course through the conservatory was as a mature musician, Kabalevsky's as a gifted *enfant terrible*. Shebalin joined none of the ideological groups and refrained from joining those choristers protesting the nature of Leningradite Shostakovich's success abroad.

While studying at the Moscow Conservatory, Shebalin also taught theory at Moscow music technicum: at Stasov school from 1923 through 1924, and at the Rimsky Korsakov school, 1925 to 1928. In 1928 he graduated from the conservatory with highest honours. His diploma work was the First Symphony, already performed outside of Moscow,[3] but now publicly heard in Moscow for the first time—on two pianos, eight hands.[4] The work is in three movements. One is struck by the intonational influence of Borodin. The nervous melody which supplies the material for much of the first movement (Example 1) and fragments thereof (Example 2) recall the similar figure in Borodin's First Symphony (Example 3). Elsewhere, in the opening theme (Example 4), for example, he shows the influence of his teacher, Miaskovsky. The opening of the second movement (Example 5) again emphasizes the previously heard

---

combined as business manager and organizer of composers' and artists' groups and music schools. His list of works reads like a progressive list of Soviet propaganda projects: *From February to October* (cantata, 1924), *October* (cantata, 1926), *First of May Song* (1925), *October Rain* (1929), *Against War* (1930), *In Memory of M. V. Frunze* (orchestral poem, 1938) and others.

[1] The songs (opus nos. 1 and 2) were published by Muzsektor Gosizdat in Moscow, 1926. The quartet was published in international edition by Muzsektor in 1928.

[2] All but a few of Shebalin's early works were soon published.

[3] The principal performance was in Leningrad, October 1926, under Saradzhev.

[4] The first Moscow orchestral performance was in 1929 under Golovanov.

Shebalin. *First symphony.*

Ex. 1 *First movement melody.*

vlns.

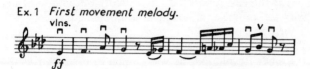

ff

Ex. 2 *Melodic fragments.*

and

Ex. 3 *Excerpt from Borodin, 1st Symphony.*

Ex. 4 *Opening theme.*

Bb cl.

Ex. 5 *II. opening theme.*

Bb cl.

Borodin intonation. Shebalin's devotion to fugal appurtenances is heard here in staggered entries. The harmony suggests at times a Scriabin approach. Examples 6 to 17 trace the intonations through the last movement. This movement breaks the orchestra into soloists and chamber groups, as the examples show. Admittedly eclectic, the First Symphony shows the promise, although in a different direction, that Shostakovich's First Symphony did.

In Shebalin's graduating year (1928), while teaching at the Music School of the October Revolution, he was chosen as instructor at the conservatory. A bit later he added a third post at the Gnessin Institute. Such split responsibilities were not unusual, for at this time the Soviet Union was still suffering the effects of the diaspora of its musical cadre during and after the revolution.

With relatively little fanfare Shebalin grew solidly as a teacher and composer. His Second, Third, and Fourth Symphonies were composed in 1929, 1934–5, and 1935, respectively. These remain his only symphonies, but he composed a number of symphonic overtures, suites, and tone poems. The symphonic poem 'Lenin' (1931) is for orchestra, chorus, and soloists, and is a setting of Maiakovsky poetry. The third symphony is of interest because of the finale, a passacaglia, fugue, and coda. The Fourth Symphony was one of his rare gestures to political orthodoxy: it is dedicated to the Soviet Army and depicts the storming of Perekop, in two movements.

But Shebalin had grown to question the symphonic form. His most successful substitutes were the clever *Variations* (1940) on the Russian theme *Uzh ty pole moe*, the *Overture on Mari Themes* (1936); and suites such as opus 22 (1935) in eight sections: Waltz, Tarantella, Waltz, Mazurka, Song without words, Potpourri, Waltz, Galop. Of these the *Overture on Mari Themes* (op. 25) has been singled out as representing his best.[1] The work is plotted in sonata-allegro form, however the expected key relationships are lacking. This is in line with Shebalin's abandonment at this time of the tonal restrictions of the form. The interest of the work lies not in the form nor in the harmony which is predictable if not prosaic. But the various themes, lifted bodily, are engagingly put together. The opening theme (Example 18) provides a lyric introduction. The material is, however, repeated later. Varied forms (18a and 19) grow in tension until a trumpet figure (Example 20) announces the simple main theme (Example 21). This theme provides the unity of the work, appearing throughout in various guises and functions. In the same brisk tempo, a second theme (Example 22) appears and flirts

[1] Shebalin's *Overture on Mari Themes* was first performed in December, 1936 by the Moscow Philharmonic under Golovanov.

Ex.6

Ex.7

Ex.8 *Oboe fragment.*

Ex.9 *Fugal fragment.*

Ex.10 *Horn call.*

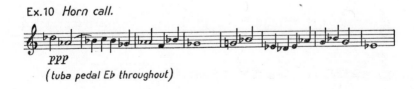

Ex. 11

Ex. 12

Ex. 13

Ex. 14

Ex. 15

Ex. 16

Ex.17

Shebalin. *Overture on Mari themes.*

Ex.18 *Opening theme.*   a) *variant*

Ex.19 *Opening variant.*

etc.

Ex.20 *Trumpet figure.*

Ex. 21 *Main theme.*

Allegro assai

Ex. 22 *Second theme.*

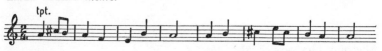

Ex. 23 *Third theme.*

Ex. 24

with the first. The trumpet call intervenes to prepare for a third theme (Example 23) which is developed at some length, subsiding finally into a *piano* utterance with four solo violins in harmony. The opening, introductory figure returns as codetta and bridge to the development section. This is in five parts, or three parts if the last two are accepted as recapitulation. But a curious twist in the emphasis in the development has seen the abandonment of the old second subject (Example 22) and its replacement by the theme shown in Example 6. A comparison of the two themes shows that '22' is readily absorbed by '23', and this is, indeed, what happens. Further comparisons of the various themes and their variants reveal Shebalin's source of unity and explains, in large measure, why this work deserves being singled out among dozens, perhaps hundreds, of similar potpourris of folk songs by Soviet composers.

If constant, direct reference to the body of folk art as a source is accepted as part of the creative process, and it certainly is in the Soviet Union, then creative ability begins with the artist's behaviour at this source. The mature work is half completed with the initial selection of themes. The judgment must be a skilled one, the choice, a creative one, if the finished work is to be good art. When Soviet works are heard that combine the *Varsovienne* with the *Internationale*, or an Uzbek pipe tune with the Soviet National anthem *and* the *Internationale*, one suspects that the bases for judgment are not entirely musical or creative. Shebalin's themes here are organically related—as related as if they had been worked out in the nineteenth-century Mahler style. Let it suffice merely to mention the pentatonic intonations pervading most of the themes. All but one (Example 21) of the themes exemplified begin with the melodic interval of a third, up or down. The pattern of leaps and skips is significantly compatible. Shebalin has said of the process:

'We know well that the incessant dialectical process of change is going on in the development of folk melody. [Before us stands the problem of] knowing how to develop the elements of folk melody, to turn [these melodies] into brilliant, dynamic images, to create from these images works of large proportion.[1]

These themes were not got out of a book of Mari tunes. They were not collected like plant specimens during a Muscovite, mass ethnomusicological invasion of the Mari countryside. Among Shebalin's close acquaintances in the mid-thirties were the Eshpai's, father and son.[2]

[1] Vissarion Shebalin, 'Dorogu Podlinnomy Novatorstvu', *Sovetskaia Muzyka* (no. 7, 1940).
[2] Iakov Andreevich Eshpai (1890–1963) was a violinist, conductor, teacher, and pioneer in Mari folk song collecting. His original formal training ended

Eshpai senior generated in Shebalin an interest about the Mari background he and his son shared. The younger Eshpai was, in turn, affected by Shebalin's enthusiasm. Together they collected tunes and went over much of the ground already covered by the older Eshpai. Shebalin accompanied the son on the latter's ethnomusicological assignments to his homeland. The *Overture on Mari Themes* is a result of this intimate approach.

In 1932 Shebalin had become docent, in 1935 professor at the conservatory. His reputation of quiet, competent authority grew. In 1941 he was granted the Doctorate of Arts degree without having to defend a thesis. The honour was due him as a composer, but his scientific work on nineteenth-century Russian music was also mentioned. He had orchestrated and finished the Mussorgsky opera *The Sorochinsk Fair* in 1933. In 1937 Shebalin disinterred, finished, and orchestrated in appropriate style the Symphony-Overture upon which Glinka had ceased to work in 1834. This 'first Russian symphony' promptly entered the repertoire of many Soviet orchestras. In 1940 Shebalin completed his violin concerto. In 1942, during his evacuation to Sverdlovsk, he wrote a three-act musical comedy, *The groom from the embassy*, and the fifth of seven quartets. This latter was the 'Slavonic' quartet. It is in five movements and uses Russian, Ukrainian, Polish, Slovakian, and Serbian folk intonations, although there are few direct citations. Written in the heat of the war's early stages, the work occasionally falls into the pitfalls of contrivance generally avoided in the *Overture on Mari Themes*. The quartet was awarded a Stalin Prize. Shebalin had, by this time, turned to chamber music, although his cantata *Moscow* was awarded another Stalin Prize in 1946.

In 1942, upon his return from Sverdlovsk, Shebalin assumed the directorship of the Moscow Conservatory. These were the days of great honours. He attained the rank of honoured art worker of the RSFSR in 1942, and, in addition to the Stalin Prize already mentioned, received a number of minor awards and prizes. Finally, in 1947, he became a People's Artist of the RSFSR.

Perhaps because he had risen so high, because he hadn't the protective buffer of international fame Shostakovich and Miaskovsky had, and because of his extremely vulnerable position as the conservatory's

---

before 1917. He resumed it later, finishing the Moscow Conservatory in composition, under Konius, in 1930, and continuing graduate work in 1933. Andrei Iakovlevich Eshpai (1925–), the former's son, finished the Moscow Conservatory in 1953 under Golub'ev. He continued into graduate work and has won some minor honours. The music of both Eshpais is routine handling of Mari and other bodies of folk literature in elaborated pianistic style.

director, Shebalin's tumble from favour in 1948 was a great one. His chamber music, including even the Stalin Prize-winning *Fifth Quartet*, was condemned. In the face of his stony silence about the teaching merit, or lack of it, at the Moscow Conservatory, he was dismissed from his director's post and from the conservatory faculty. He was handed a humiliating assignment at the Moscow Red Army Band School where he languished for three years before rejoining the Moscow Conservatory faculty. Perhaps cruellest of all was the machinery that managed all this. At the controls was the student whom Shebalin had housed and fed in the thirties, Tikhon Khrennikov.[1] Khrennikov, needlessly, handled his old teacher brutally.

In 1949 a Shebalin string trio, a sinfonietta on folk tunes, and an unaccompanied choral work, *Winter Road*, were heard, but they were pre-1948 works. Otherwise the years 1949–51 found Shebalin silent. In 1952 he wrote music for a (second) film on Glinka and another a capella chorus number, *The Cliff*, on words of Safronov, Barto, Tanka, and Isakovsky. The following year he did another film (*Sadko*). By now he had resumed a teaching post at the Moscow Conservatory and was working, as he had been since at least 1945, on his last important opus, an opera on Shakespeare's *Taming of the Shrew*. The libretto boils the play down to some extent. The leitmotives are associated almost exclusively with Catherine and Petruccio. Characteristic of Shebalin are the economy of orchestration and the lightness of his humorous touch. The opera uses recitative far more than most Soviet opera, and folk songs are conspicuously absent. The choice of subject, of course, demands this. In sum, unfortunately, the work seems like an exercise. It is not successful stage, although it has been done a good deal in theatres around the Soviet Union. It is almost too easy to say that the creative talent which could have made *The Taming of the Shrew* a fine opera was broken in 1949. Yet, one searches in vain for technical evidence of extra-musical influences. The harmony is less astringent than in some of his chamber music of the mid-forties, but it is bound to be in such work. However, the creative momentum which had carried Shebalin logically to chamber genres had obviously been stopped. It is not so important that *Shrew* followed the ideological events of 1948 as it is that the opera followed 1948 *and* a spate of film music, mass choruses, light songs and the like.[2]

The Taming of the Shrew has been the highpoint of Shebalin's latest

[1] For more on Khrennikov see p. 257.
[2] A piano score (the duplicated manuscript) was published by Muzfond in 1956 in an edition of eighty copies. In 1958 Sovetskii Kompozitor brought out of a piano edition in 580 copies.

creative years. His health seems to have curtailed his activity at the Moscow Conservatory. A second opera, *Sun over the steppe*, was performed with piano in late 1958. It is a three-act work of medium to short length on a revolutionary theme involving Cossack partisans and White troops. It is decidedly 'sovietized' in its bad-guys *v.* good-guys portrayals and in the massive use of the chorus representing the people. There is no overture, nor is there any use of the orchestra alone at any point in the body of the opera. This demonstrates how much Shebalin has changed. The original hearing was not enthusiastically received and Shebalin withdrew the work to rewrite it.

In a final analysis it is difficult to avoid comparison with Prokofieff. Shebalin took the care and had the workshop approach typical of Prokofieff. Vladimir Protopopov mentions but denies[1] the frequent criticism that Shebalin is exclusively a workshop technician and not an artist at all. Those who accused him of extreme formalism in the late forties and early fifties travelled this critical route to their conclusions. Shebalin's harmony is often colourful without the thickness characteristic of his countrymen, and this again puts him in Prokofieff's good company. Both composers have a harmonic tap-root in the music of Borodin. Vladimir Blok, an ex-student and enthusiastic biographer of Shebalin, is excited about the insight to be gained from a comparison of the respective creative lines of development: Borodin-Prokofieff and Borodin-Shebalin.[2] Shebalin is not so complex harmonically as Prokofieff often is, or was, but the former more consistently employs a complex, light textured polyphony. Rhythmically, Prokofieff is the more savage and unpredictable of the two.

Shebalin's next step is perhaps the most critical of his career. *Sun over the steppe* has apparently convinced him of the futility of the operatic genre. The door to chamber music has been reopened for some time, and perhaps once again Shebalin will pass through.

Shebalin died in Moscow (soon after the foregoing was completed) in late May or early June 1963.

---

[1] Vladimir Protopov, 'O muzyke V. Shebalina', *Sovetskaia Muzyka*, November 1958.

[2] Vladimir Blok, 'Kamernye Sochineniia V. Shebalina' (Chamber works of V. Shebalin), *Sovetskaia Muzyka*, November 1960.

CHAPTER 17

⅊⅋⅊

Aram Khachaturian

If the musical activity of one man could be said to form an important cornerstone of Soviet musical creativity, the man would not be Sergei Prokofieff, nor Dmitrii Shostakovich, but would have to be Aram Khachaturian. This is obviously not a qualitative musical judgment. Khachaturian is, musically, a Russian composer; for purposes of Soviet example he is a sometime Armenian composer—an Uzbek composer, or a Georgian composer, or an Azerbaidzhanian composer. He epitomizes, in solid Russian style, the republican composer of ultimate, and imaginary, greater Soviet maturity. Actually Armenian by descent, Khachaturian will often use Armenian tunes in his music. He is just as apt to use Russian, Uzbek, or Ukrainian tunes. But the essence of his importance is that all these, including the Armenian, are handled in the same manner: in the St Petersburg tradition. Understandably hazy about his folk roots, Khachaturian has suggested that his predilection for percussive harmonic seconds and his inclination to pedal and organ point have an Armenian basis. These are rarely encountered in Armenian music.[1] Contrapuntally approached seconds are heard in *Georgian* folk music, as is vocal pedal point,[2,3] but Khachaturian is certainly not a Georgian composer. With his technical prowess, his canny ear for sounds, and his energetic momentum, he embraces the whole of Soviet musical orthodoxy with more success than any of his contemporaries.

Soviet ideological demands fettered Khachaturian as an 'Armenian' composer in the mid-thirties. The indications are that this designation was appreciated neither in Armenia nor by Khachaturian. That he was lionized as Armenian (*in absentia*) was due not so much to his name as to his remarkable talent and impressive energy.

Although famous for his ballets *Gaiane* and *Spartak*, it is the suites from these, plus the two symphonies, and the concertos for piano,

---

[1] Armenian folk music is largely monodic.   [2] See p. 122.
[3] Khachaturian was born in Tiflis.

violin, and 'cello that have carried Khachaturian's name around the world. He is a symphonist above all, understanding the texture, colour, and rhythmic possibilities of the orchestra as well as any contemporary composer, but, perhaps, exhibiting the depth of the least of them.

Aram Il'ich Khachaturian was born in Tiflis on June 6, 1903. His family is reported to have loved music, although his father was a book-binder. Aram was the third of four brothers. The oldest, Suren, was to play an important part in Khachaturian's training. Although Soviet biographers dwell on the folk dancing and singing indulged in by the Khachaturians, it seems clear that Aram was not destined for a musical career. He attended the Tiflis Commercial School, the family plan being that he would become a doctor or engineer. While there he played in the band, and he was already a self-taught pianist of some accomplishment. In 1910 his older brother, Suren, left for Moscow. Suren worked there, with success, with the Moscow Art Theatre. Suren also started the drama section of the Armenian House of Culture. In 1918, when Aram was fifteen, the desire among Georgians for independence was strong. Since, to Georgians, ideas of independence seemed to include clearing all Armenians from the face of the earth, the years 1918 to 1921 were precarious ones for the Khachaturians in Tiflis. A move to Armenia was not considered because that was a notoriously unhappy land at the time, and, moreover, the Khachaturian family had already edged far away from their Armenian background, yearning for the North. In 1921, on the heels of the Red Army, Suren was sent, with other Moscow Transcaucasian figures, to bring national cadres to the centre. He included his brother, Aram. Both brothers now used the name Khacha-turov.[1] Suren introduced Aram to the exciting artistic circles of MKhAT, but also saw to it that the younger brother's proper schooling was continued. Accordingly, Aram took preparatory courses for entrance into Moscow University, and, in 1922, entered the biology department of that institution. At the same time, he approached the officials of the Gnessin School, and, in spite of his utter lack of formal training, was accepted as a student of violoncello, an instrument he had not yet played. Studying at both institutions, he leaned more and more towards music. In the middle of his third year at the university he was quite happy to be expelled from the biology faculty. In 1923, Mikhail Gnessin[2] had joined his sister at the school. When Khachaturian

[1] Suren's son, the Soviet composer Karen Khachaturian, has changed his name back to the Armenian style, but is considered a Rusisan composer.

[2] Mikhail Fabianovich Gnessin (Gnesin), 1883–1957, was a 1909 graduate of the St Petersburg Conservatory under Rimsky-Korsakov and Liadov. His work ranged from the deeply religious to Soviet propaganda. He taught all over

severed his connection with Moscow University he immediately entered Gnessin's composition course. Thus, at the age of twenty-two, he first began his formal acquaintance with the creative tools of music. His first work of significance was still nine years in the future. He began writing in small forms: the earliest works were 'Dance' for violin and piano (1926), a 'Waltz-Caprice' (1926), and 'Poem' (1927) for piano, and an 'Allegretto' and 'Song-Poem' (1929) for violin and piano. The latter was written in honour of the *ashugi*.[1] Of these works, all but the Allegretto were published. Two marches (1929 and 1930) and an unpublished string quartet (1932) rounded out the effort of the first few years, but these were already works written as a student of the Moscow Conservatory. In 1929, Gnessin assumed teaching duties at the conservatory and Khachaturian was brought in tow. He continued with Gnessin for another year and then switched to the class of Nicholas Miaskovsky. Miaskovsky at first emphasized small forms with this mature student, leaving Khachaturian to come to his own conclusions concerning his folkish harmonies. Miaskovsky was bemused by the supposedly Armenian sound of Khachaturian's music, and was under the impression that he was giving rein to a clearly national spirit: so, perhaps, was Khachaturian. In any case, the situation provided the composer with an unusual opportunity almost independently to pursue and develop his own tastes. This opportunity was rare for a Miaskovsky protégé. His work included a number of songs—a genre he never abandoned. In 1932 he wrote his first work for chamber ensemble,[2] a piano trio. The work is usually listed as being for piano, violin and clarinet, however, the clarinet was a subsequent substitution for the 'cello. This work was heard by Sergei Prokofieff on one of his visits (1933) to the Soviet Union, prior to his permanent return. Because of the merit of the work, and as a gesture of regard for his old classmate, Miaskovsky, Prokofieff took the trio with him when he returned to Paris. It was played there for a Russian *émigré* audience, but its conservative sound failed to make much impression in *avant-garde* Paris. In the work, in its clarinet version, Khachaturian attempted to duplicate the sounds of

---

the Soviet Union: 1908 St Petersburg, 1908–13 Ekaterinodar (Krasnodar), 1914–21 Rostov-on-the-Don, 1923–5 Gnessin School, 1925–35 Moscow Conservatory, 1935–44 Leningrad Conservatory, and 1944–51 the Gnessin School again. Boris Kliuzner, Aro Stepanian, Tikhon Khrennikov, and Vadim Salmanov are among his other students.

[1] The *ashugi* honoured were the Azerbaidzhanian folk bards who wandered the Caucasus.

[2] This excepts the string quartet which was actually a counterpoint exercise—a double fugue.

certain Transcaucasian folk instruments. Such attempts, and there are many among Soviet composers, merely nibble at the edges of the vast area of instrumental sound exploited by Western composers in this century. Soon after the trio, Khachaturian completed his *Dance Suite* (1932–3): five short dances which worked out Armenian, Georgian, and Uzbek tunes. The work was more important, however, as Khachaturian's first sustained essay at using the orchestra. Otherwise, in his undergraduate years, Khachaturian wrote more songs and short piano pieces. Some of these were said to be based on Armenian, Uzbek, and Ukrainian tunes, but one begins to suspect that this became a game with Khachaturian, just as Kreisler's 'discoveries' of forgotten works for violin were with him. Khachaturian's next work for symphony orchestra, and his first work of significance, was the *First Symphony* (1934), written as a graduation requirement.

As a whole the symphony does reflect one Transcaucasian characteristic: the formless, rhapsodic progress of an *ashug* tale. Elsewhere, the massive orchestra, the length and the ornamented melodic lines place the work squarely in the Great Russian tradition. Lush melody dominates. The introductory theme and the two contrasting main themes grow rhapsodically into and out of one another. The first movement has no formally placed development. The themes are developed, melodically, from their first hearing. This first movement is supposed to represent the composer's 'homeland', Armenia. Perhaps one can find touching the rather wild melodic rapturousness with which Khachaturian paints that homeland he has never known. The second movement is a variation development of a nocturne melody. The passing of this theme from instrument to instrument is interrupted by a lively dance tune, a mountain folk dance if one heeds the publicity. The 'A' section returns to close the movement. The third and last movement is rather obviously based on the Georgian lezghinka (*lezginka*). The interest is no longer on the melody as in the first two movements, but on the intricate cross rhythms and the occasionally polyphonic texture of the orchestra. The work is a remarkable testament to Khachaturian's understanding of the orchestra. It is interesting to note in this connection that he is one of the few Soviet composers to write originally in full score. Although he is not so consistent in this as Shostakovich, it is quite clear that he can break the tradition by which most Russian and Soviet composers have always been bound: that of writing for piano first, and later orchestrating by formula.

Khachaturian continued into graduate school under Miaskovsky, serving his teacher as assistant until 1937. During this time his rate of composition slowed somewhat. He became fascinated by the music of

Prokofieff, just returned, and eagerly attended the discussions of contemporary music at the home of Derzhanovsky. Here, Prokofieff expounded his views on the West. In 1936, apparently with some encouragement from Prokofieff, Kabelevsky finished his Piano Concerto. If the First Symphony was the work of an accomplished student, the concerto is that of a mature composer. Khachaturian's style, although marked by variety, was set. In this he is the exception among the middle generation of composers who accept political awareness as a component of creativity. Although Khachaturian, in a latter day, became properly aware, his style has not undergone the bewildering changes also characteristic of this group. The Piano Concerto remains one of his best works. One wishes to lay to rest the dogmatic nonsense of this being an 'Armenian' concerto, or a concerto of any other nationality. Khachaturian, though he seeks, cannot really single out what is Armenian, Georgian, etc., etc. In an article on folk music,[1] he discusses a theme from the second movement of the concerto as having been developed from, 'a simple little Armenian song'. Gustave Schneerson later quotes this in the foreword to the published score.[2] Apparently, it was immediately discovered that something was amiss. In a book on Khachaturian, published in 1958,[3] Schneerson again refers to the Khachaturian article, with some Orwellian rewriting:

Khachaturian tells how by means of developing the melody of a *simple little urban song*, which one always heard in old Tbilisi, he arrived ... at this theme (italics mine—SDK)[4]

The concerto contains some themes developed from Transcaucasian tunes, but this makes it precisely as Armenian as Dvorak's *New World Symphony* is American, or as Mendelssohn's *Scotch Symphony* is Scottish. The work abounds in the intricate rhythmic fabric, brilliant orchestral sound, and mildly experimental instrumental combinations typical of Khachaturian. A small step forward is heard in the piano part: the instrument undergoes an exploitation surprisingly fresh in some instances. The first theme of the first movement has the rhythmic drive that characterizes most of the work (Example 1). In Example 1,

[1] Khachaturian, 'Kak ia ponimaiu narodnost' v muzyke' (How I understand the folk element in music), *Sovetskaia Muzyka*, no. 5 (May), 1952.
[2] Khachaturian, *Concerto for piano with orchestra* (Moscow, Muzgiz, 1957), with a foreword by Schneerson.
[3] Gustave Schneerson, *Aram Khachaturian* (Moscow, Sovetskii Kompozitor, 1958), p. 27.
[4] In the *Sovetskaia Muzyka* article from 1952, Khachaturian also complains: 'It is curious that even Georgian and Armenian musicians, with whom I conversed, did not recognize this theme and its folk basis. . . .'

measures four through seven are written in full to show some of the
details of texture and harmony. The two themes of the first movement
have clear cut entries and are duly opposed in character (see Example 2
for second theme), but here, as in the First Symphony, Khachaturian
develops immediately. The responsibility for the second theme, after an
oboe statement, is assumed by the piano. This theme is developed
rhapsodically by the piano alone in a quasi-cadenza which leads into the
development proper. The art of Khachaturian polarizes most frequently
in ostinato. Less kindly, one would call him a slave to the ornamented
beat: and he enslaves his audience as well. A case in point is the development of the movement under discussion, based melodically on the
original theme. The accompaniment changes only with the substitution
of one ostinato for another. Khachaturian occasionally writes contrapuntal lines, but he obviously never feels safe without his ostinato
drum. The recapitulation begins with a mutated form of the first theme
—a mutation easily recognized. The reappearance of the second theme,
with some development, leads to the cadenza proper. Khachaturian
introduces this with a flash of his orchestral wit, posing bass clarinet and
double bass in duet (Example 3). The double bass provides the predictable pedal. The orchestra, after an unusually long cadenza, supplies
a short, loud coda on first theme material.

The second movement is a theme with variations. The theme is the
one verbally belaboured by Schneerson and Khachaturian. Its first
treatment, by the piano, shows Khachaturian's use of major and minor

Khachaturian. *Piano concerto.*

Ex.1   *First theme.*

Ex. 2 *Second theme, first statement and piano entrance.*

Ex. 3 *Introduction to cadenza.*

Ex. 4 *Theme from second movement.*

seconds (Example 4) mentioned earlier.[1] But the non-Transcaucasian has little difficulty in assimilating them into Western harmonic patterns. A refreshing feature of the movement is the choice of textures. The most obvious is the use of a whistle-flexaton in unison with the first violins. The five, more or less, variations exploit the orchestra, with the piano often heard in brief comments and ejaculations. Pedal and ostinato usage is almost as frequently heard here as in the first movement. The penultimate variation brings the piano part close to the intonations of the first theme of the first movement (Example 5). The last variation is short and ends the movement with a thematic fragment identified throughout with the variation endings (Example 6).

The last movement, like that of so many Soviet symphonies and concertos, is a glittering string of dance-like tunes. The relentless energy of the rhythmic ostinato presents the various tunes like a skilful card sharp dealing a hand of stud, face up. The ultimate ace is the return of the first theme of the first movement, after an extended section for piano alone. The seeker after formal logic has no problems, unless he reads Schneerson on the last movement:

'We hear anew the inspired improvisation of the folk singer, telling of the past sufferings (?) of the motherland (Armenia? Georgia? Tannu Tuva?—SDK), of the struggle (?) of the people for happiness.' (questions mine—SDK)

and one returns in confusion to the score for a fruitless search.

Grounds, drones, pedals, and ostinatos can support blinding rhythmic tricks and exciting or intense contrapuntal and harmonic forays; they can underpin the fierce, gay, morose, or tender; they can excite or lull, but they can also stupefy and paralyse. It is doubtful that the primary unifying factor of any work of symphonic proportion can be ostinato, without running the risk of the latter. In the concerto, Khachaturian delights on occasion. In general, he mesmerizes. Again, he demonstrates a free and articulate knowledge of the orchestra.

The successful première of the concerto[2] found Khachaturian caught

[1] While disagreeing that the work has some sort of 'nationality', the author cannot resist pointing out the similarities, here, to Georgian folk music. The seconds are frequently the by-product of the ubiquitous, Georgian fourth-fifth chord. See p. 127. Moreover, the parallel fifth progressions are to be found in Georgian native music. Surprisingly, no Soviet analysis points this out. Khachaturian's Georgian background usually gets consideration only in fifth place, after Armenian, Azerbaidzhanian, Uzbek, and Russian.

[2] The piano concerto was first performed in the Maly (small) Hall of the conservatory in late 1936 by pianists Bertha Kazel' and 'Aleksei Klumov'. Klumov was actually Khachaturian-Khachaturov. The première with orchestra took place July 12, 1937 at the ten-day Festival of Russian Music. The soloist was Lev Oborin to whom the work is dedicated.

in the mighty, surging tides of nationalism which swept through the thirties. He had, soon after the concerto, written his 'Song of Stalin'.[1] The concerto moved him to the front rank of Soviet composers; the 'Song' was a sure-fire ideological credential. Klumov-Khachaturov-Khachaturian began to double back on his ethnic tracks, with official encouragement. Within a year of his success as a Russian composer, during the ten-day Festival of Russian Music, Khachaturian was famous as an Armenian composer. His task most closely associated with the title was the composition of a ballet for the upcoming (1939) Moscow Ten-day Festival of Armenian Music. He was accorded various Armenian honours, and, finally, went to Armenia for the first time in his life, in the spring of 1939. He was then thirty-six years old. This began his tenure as an Armenian composer and also began the long story of his ubiquitous ballet, *Gaiane*.

Ex. 6 *Ending, last variation.*

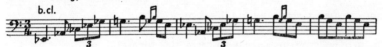

The first version of *Gaiane* was the inoffensive *Schast'e* (Happiness) he wrote for the Armenian festival. The story was that of a borderland Armenian kolkhoz: the young men were being drafted. Armen, the hero, tangles with border violators, is wounded, but returns at last. He is happily married and settles back to kolkhoz life. The story is simple, with little conflict and very little ideological didacticism. The ballet is mostly an excuse for mounting a series of energetic and largely captivating dances. Khachaturian composed seven dances on Armenian models, a Russian round dance, a Ukrainian hopak, and a Georgian lezghinka. This was his contribution to the otherwise all-Armenian festival.

A year later, after two suites had been formed from *Happiness*, and after the violin concerto, he began *Gaiane*.[2] The story is somewhat the same with a bit more strife and Russian patriotism: the same scene, during the war, finds the kolkhoz woman Gaiane unhappily married to Giko. The latter is evil, rude, and dislikes the kolkhoz and Russians.

[1] The 'Song of Stalin' became the concluding episode of the subsequent (1938) *Poem of Stalin* for chorus and orchestra. It is written to the words of the Azerbaidzhanian *ashug* Mirza from Tauza. The epigraph reads, 'Leader of the land, thy glory is exalted among the people higher than the mountains. . . .'

[2] The name of the ballet is that of its heroine. The name comes from an Armenian saint, traditionally connected with the establishment of Christianity in Armenia.

He later betrays his country. Armen, Gaiane's brother, is in love with Aisha; Nuneh, Gaiane's friend, with Karen; and Gaiane finds love, the solution of the Giko problem, and inspiring political direction from Kazakov, a Russian border guard. Musically the new ballet was *Happiness* with the addition of several new dances (including the sabre dance) and some orchestral colours of evil hue to depict Giko. In 1952 Khachaturian again turned to *Gaiane*. The result was much more than a revised edition. About one-third of the score was changed. The story is a postwar one, at the same kolkhoz, but now the various love stories become interracial, and the theme is that of the love and brotherhood of man united under the banner of happy labour. The conflict involves a newly emerged (Russian) hero, Georgii. He expels himself from the kolkhoz because a dishonest deed of his nearly leads to the death of a friend. He subsequently finds peace through open admission of his guilt.[1] This last version was performed at the Leningrad Kirov Theatre in 1952, but underwent further extensive revision prior to its reappearance at the Moscow Bolshoi Theatre in 1957.

Thus *Gaiane* has occupied Khachaturian from 1939 to at least 1957. In 1940 he wrote his second concerto, that for violin and orchestra. The work is in awesome debt to the first piano concerto. Khachaturian, like many composers before him, does not intend to abandon a successful formula. The second theme has a phrygian modal cast (Example 8) as does the nocturnal theme of the second movement (Example 9). The finale is, again, a set of slightly developed dances. Once again, in this work, the melodic and rhythmic ostinatos tend to overpower. In the violin concerto the form is far more riven than unified by this element.

As the war's back-lash of liberality in the arts increased, Khachaturian felt free to move away from his ethnic pigeon hole. He made the mistake of trying to move away idiomatically: his idiom, as we have seen, was not nationalistically Armenian, but was essentially his own. When he moved away, in the Second Symphony, from the orchestral sheen and compelling rhythmic drive, he was severing no ties other than those with his own bag of tricks. He was forsaking his controls. During the work on the Second Symphony, Khachaturian was living at the USC resort at Ivanovo. His comrades there included Peiko, Muradeli, Shaporin, and Shostakovich. These men, excepting Muradeli, had impressive creative arsenals. Khachaturian tried the lyric, unfettered melodic style of

---

[1] One wonders about the degree of truth in a Moscow anecdote: Khachaturian is rewriting *Gaiane*: A small, borderland kolkhoz in Armenia has been chosen as the launching site for the first orbit, ever, of a musician—a Soviet violinist who can high jump over seven feet. But Giko, Gaiane's evil uncle, in league with the American nuclear rocket bases across the border in Turkey. . . .

Shaporin, the formal tension and harmonic toughness of Shostakovich, and the self-disciplined, intellectual approach of Peiko. But he was ill equipped. The Second Symphony and the Cello Concerto, which suffered the same approach, became grist for Zhdanov's mill in 1948.

Khachaturian. *Violin concerto.*

Ex.7 *Primary rhythmic motive.*

Ex.8 *Second theme.*

Ex.9 *Nocturne theme, second movement.*

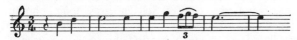

That criticism affected Khachaturian very little. Since it was 'depersonalized' in 1958, Schneerson can now say, '(Khachaturian) correctly accepted this criticism as the fatherly concern of the Communist Party and the people for the flourishing of progressive musical art'.[1]

Khachaturian turned to film music for a while after 1948. The most successful scores were those to *Vladimir Il'ich Lenin* and *The Stalingrad Struggle* (1949). From the former he developed the work which, aside

[1] Schneerson, *Aram Khachaturian*, p. 47.

from the 'Sabre Dance', has been most widely heard in the Soviet Union—the *Funeral Ode to Lenin*. The Ode is a curious keystone to Khachaturian's career: it is in line with the prevailing philosophy, and it was immensely popular. Just as the 'Sabre Dance' writhed in the West through all forms of performing torture, so does the funeral ode— but within the Soviet Union. One of its tunes has even been heard wailed by the mourners in an Orthodox funeral procession in a small town near Leningrad.[1] Khachaturian has not budged from the musical position of the time of the Ode. The work uses nearly every stereotype of lament known to music. If the author were not saving invective for the ballet, *Spartak*, he would unburden himself on the Ode. A few musical examples should suffice: the opening displays the familiar pedal (Example 10). A clarinet sounds the following theme (Example 11). These finally work through a *feroce* passage into the ultimate in passionate statement (Example 12). The film from which the Ode was disinterred won a Stalin Prize.

In 1950, Khachaturian began his teaching career, filling the gaps left by Shostakovich and Shebalin in the Moscow Conservatory and at the Gnessin Institute. At the latter he became director. His teaching has been limited by his other activity, but among his students have been Eshpai and Oganesian. Khachaturian was rapidly filling all the contours of a Russian musical *deiatel'*. It is interesting to compare his course at this time with that of Kabalevsky. In addition to teaching and composing Khachaturian now began a career as conductor, and he is a good one. He began to travel abroad with delegations, and he has become a perennial visitor to South and Central America. Since 1951 he has appeared quite frequently in print. Less loquacious and argumentative than Kabalevsky, Khachaturian is still more often to the point. He is horrified, in print, at the number of 12-tone composers he meets outside the Soviet Union: 'Even in Iceland, with ten or twelve professional composers, there are some adherents of Schoenberg's dodecaphonic system.'[2]

While on a trip to Italy in 1950, one of his first abroad, Khachaturian became interested in the story of Spartacus. He worked on a ballet from 1950 to 1956, when it was presented, on December 27th, at the Leningrad Kirov (Mariinsky) Theatre. Suites, and a published piano score, had appeared *before* this première. When it was finally staged in Moscow,

[1] The tune in question could be considered intonationally close to a certain Russian church music style of the late nineteenth and early twentieth centuries: a music sharing the colour, if not the content, of the religious painter, Vrubel'. For a note on the Orthodox trappings of Communist burial, see pp. 237, 238.

[2] *Sovetskaia Muzyka*, no. 3, 1951, as quoted in Schneerson's *Aram Khachaturian*, p. 57.

in March of 1958, it was hailed as a new departure in Russian ballet—the first since 1917. The talents of Igor Moiseev as choreographer and Maia Plisetskaia as Aegina did lend some sparkle to the dancing. But the music and libretto were both of a banality and triviality that bordered on illness. Edmund Stillman says of *Spartak*:

Ex.10 *Opening.*

Ex.11 *First theme.*

Ex.12 *Climax.*

'... the mind which can conceive the monumental vulgarity of a "Spartacus" ballet has the imagination of a disinherited Russian housemaid—a housemaid below stairs in one of those vicious parvenu households which Russian fiction, from Gogol to Kuprin, recorded up to the very eve of the deluge.'[1]

Vulgarity is the unifying element of both libretto and music. The endless ostinato becomes physically unpleasant: the Russian word *grubyi* (rude, coarse, pronounced groo-bwee) is an adjective of the proper sound. This, of course, is not successful music in any environment. The ballet has already left the regular repertoire, failing, even, to supply the touch of burlesque often associated with Soviet ballet.

The comparison with Kabalevsky suggested earlier reveals other points the two composers have in common. Already heavily laureate, and busy with travelling, delegations, speeches, and State occasions, Khachaturian, like Kabalevsky, has little time left to compose. Having understood their environment, each has travelled a creative path into triviality; by doing so they have each 'betrayed' that understanding with later works of little or no success. In the thirties, the period of their most interesting works, one could compare them with enthusiasm. Now, one is not attracted nearly so much by the question, which is the better, as by, which is the worst.

Khachaturian, and Kabalevsky, for that matter, are still several cuts above Khrennikov and Sviridov. It would not be fair to call Khachaturian an opportunistic hack, like Khrennikov. It may be that an artist who understands, accepts, and who is in creative sympathy with his total environment, is no artist at all. Khachaturian's firm belief is that the artist, not the system, must be wrong in the Soviet Union, and has honestly strived to be in tune with that system. Khachaturian's gift should have given him comfort as a writer of short dances and ballads. In his *milieu* where quality is often commensurate with proportion, Khachaturian's gift does not suffice.

[1] Edmund Stillman, 'Moscow: 45 years', *Show*, November 1962.

CHAPTER 18

ᕽᕽᕽ

Dmitrii Kabalevsky

D
mitrii Kabalevsky is a composer supremely conscious of success
—in the better rather than worse meaning of the phrase. As a
Soviet Composer he is well within the realm of established
thinking to equate awards, popular acclaim, and performances abroad
with creative quality. Moreover, he is clear-headed and articulate about
his stand and ideas.[1] His writings are among the clearest Soviet expressions
of ideological orthodoxy and the one-to-one relationship between ability
and popularity or reward. His career, then, has been geared to what
success is in the Soviet Union; this is to say, success has been his guide-
line to quality. Since musical success often depends on non-musical
machinery, Kabalevsky is not without strong, covert critics.[2] Thank-
fully, he well understands that the basis of excellence, built thereafter

---

[1] Kabalevsky speaks almost unaccented (Oxford) English, a phenomenon
rare among Soviet composers.

[2] Kabalevsky's behaviour during the unfortunate, 1948 blanket condemnation
of composers (since rescinded by the Party) revealed a personal evaluation so
cynical and yielded results so unsavoury as to cause an estrangement between
him and his fellows. The Party attack opened against Muradeli and continued
with Shostakovich, Prokofieff, Khachaturian, Shebalin, Popov, and Miaskovsky.
As Andrei Zhdanov presented the Party's case it became clear that Kabalevsky
alone of the better known composers was being left out of this illustrious circle.
Taking the floor early, Kabalevsky briefly echoed the points made by Zhdanov
and then began a detailed attack on his own opera *The Taras Family*. The work
had not been heard and was not even finished, although the first part was
allegedly in rehearsal at the Stanislavsky, Nemirov-Danchenko theatre. With
frequent references to comrades Zhdanov and Stalin, the Party, and the Soviet
people, Kabalevsky *apologized contritely and thanked the political leadership for
its direction*. The two surprising things about the 1948 conference were, first,
the fact of political interference and, second, the apologetic and appreciative
posture of the affected composers. Kabalevsky set the pattern for the latter.
Ostentatiously, Kabalevsky withdrew his opera to make changes. When ultimately produced (1950) it won a Stalin Prize. By his actions at the 1948 conference and congress Kabalevsky shared the notoriety of the condemned without
the risk of providing a material basis for real criticism: but he also established
himself as an ideological leader—a leading composer, hardened by the 1948
fire, now off on the right foot.

8*

by whatever means, must be solid technical mastery. Bearing this in mind, and granted a certain gift, Kabalevsky has naturally become well known through his two operas, the Second Symphony, the concertos dedicated to youth, and his other work in music literature for children. If his struggle to escape the shadow of greater contemporaries, notably Shostakovich, had not driven him to certain musical and extra-musical extremes, however, the listener might have been spared the Kabalevsky codex of banality.

Although he was never to be identified artistically with that city, Kabalevsky was born in St Petersburg on December 30, 1904. His father was a burgeois functionary, a mathematician and graduate of the St Petersburg University. Young Kabalevsky was exposed to the liberal, 'expressive' education favoured for sons of such families and wrote poetry and did illustrations while still quite young. His schooling included piano lessons. Extremely well coordinated, of which he made a great deal later, Kabalevsky excelled in certain sports. In 1918 when Kabalevsky was fourteen, the family moved to Moscow. Perhaps to augment the family income in these immediate post-revolutionary times, Kabalevsky began to give piano lessons when he himself was only fifteen or sixteen. As a matter, to him, of course, he composed simple works for his students to play when he could find nothing suitable elsewhere.

By tradition destined for mathematics, law, or economics, Kabalevsky, for the moment, found the Arts preferable for a number of reasons. He entered the Scriabin Institute in 1919, at the same time studying painting and drawing. In 1922 he finished the technikum (gymnasium) and took the exams for entrance to the Engels Socio-Economic Science Institute. The next three years are ill-explained. There is no accessible record of whether or not he passed the examinations. It could very well be that his bourgeois background prevented his entrance into such a critical study. In any case, for three years he continued to teach young pianists, played piano for silent movies, and continued intermittent work with his Scriabin Institute piano teacher, V. Selivanov. Selivanov showed Kabalevsky's work to George Catoire[1] who was then teaching composition at the Scriabin School as well as at the Moscow Conservatory. Selivanov also interceded on Kabalevsky's behalf with Goldenweiser at the Moscow Conservatory.

In 1925 Kabalevsky enrolled as a piano and composition student under Goldenweiser and Catoire, respectively, at the Moscow Conservatory.

[1] George Catoire, 1861–1926, studied mathematics in Moscow, then piano and composition with Klindwort and Vilborg, with the former in Berlin. He later studied with Liadov, Arensky, and Taneev.

Upon Catoire's death Kabalevsky entered the important student-teacher relationship with Miaskovsky. In 1925 a loose federation of composition students was formed. The organization was a perpetuation of that group of young composers who had competed in 1925 for a prize for a work in Lenin's memory. They assumed the name *Proizvodstvennyi Kollektiv*, shortened in the manner of the time to PROKOLL. The group, actually the youth arm of the RAPM[1] (which they entered formally in 1929), took on the predictable anti-Leningrad cast, and Kabalevsky appeared in print criticizing certain highly vulnerable Leningrad tendencies.[2] But Kabalevsky was, even this early, ready to jump in the direction of opportunity: He was also a member of the Association of Contemporary Musicians, as well as of other organizations. His biographers are confused, and understandably.[3]

The initial success of Shostakovich's first symphony in 1926 and its subsequent fame abroad, reflected so characteristically in Shostakovich's position at home, was a matter of some concern to the members of PROKOLL. A conservatory bulletin from late 1929 contains an article criticizing 'writing for Western taste', citing the Shostakovich work. It was signed 'PROKOLL'. Nevertheless such recognition, by an identical route, was incumbent on young Moscow composers, and Kabalevsky seemed best fitted, musically and ideologically. His earliest published work was a set of songs to words by Aleksandr Blok. This was already opus 4. The three earlier numbers were (1) a piano prelude in 1925, (2) two pieces for 'cello and piano in 1927, and (3) a collection of children's pieces for piano, 1927. These have never been published. The Blok settings represented Kabalevsky's farthest excursion into musical modernism and were decidedly tame by 1927 standards. Vissarion Shebalin's setting of one of the same poems[4] had a far sharper impact and was finished and published before Kabalevsky's version. Until the success of the Second Symphony in the mid-thirties, Kabalevsky found the most consistent route to performance lay in piano and vocal miniatures. The first String Quartet (op. 8, 1928) is an immature attempt at combining depth and a certain folk style. The ensuing piano concerto (op. 9, 1929) is uninteresting not because of any 'modernistic influences', the usual charge, but because Kabalevsky had not yet the maturity for such a work. Nor did he demonstrate in the concerto the

---

[1] See p. 49.

[2] *Sovetskii Muzykant*, organ of the Association of Contemporary Musicians, no. 1, 1927.

[3] Grosheva in her *Dmitrii Kabalevsky*, p. 12 says Kabalevsky never entered the ACM although he was '. . . close to some of its members'. In *IRSM*, p. 64, the author says that Kabalevsky quit the ACM in 1931.

[4] 'Svirel' zapela na mostu' (The pipe began to sing on the bridge).

knack for large-form compromise that proved so successful in his later concertos. Nevertheless, this was the work that was hailed in advance as Moscow's answer to Leningrad's Shostakovich.[1] A similarly bleak judgment of Kabalevsky's 'Poem of Struggle' for orchestra and choir (op. 12, 1930) and a similar lack of success, leaves the aforementioned piano and vocal works, plus an unpublished work for radio (op. 15, 1931) by which to judge the young composer. In writing for young performers, or at least for young listeners, Kabalevsky was exercising practical experience, whereas in the other works he was not. His natural inclination toward youth, as performers or audience, was the first such sustained effort in Soviet music and provided a guide for other composers including Shostakovich and Prokofieff. To this period, and to this genre, belongs the ubiquitous *Sonatina in C Major* (op. 13, 1930, published by Muzgiz, 1932). This three-movement work, rather than a larger effort, was the vehicle by which Kabalevsky's name first became known abroad. Perhaps the only other works worth mentioning during this early period are the eight songs for children's choir and piano (op. 17, 1932). These are still in the repertoire in the sense that the less difficult among them are still sung in schools. They are short, mildly onomatopoetic impressions of a train, a street, a birdhouse, the First of May, city gardens, a verdant city, a boat, etc.

At the crossroads of 1932, the recent graduate had a rather limited accomplishment behind him. Shostakovich, two years his junior, was already through three symphonies, one an international success, two successful operas, and two ballets. Kabalevsky, at twenty-eight, was faced with difficult choices: he could emulate Shostakovich; or he could stick with the proletarian conservatives and, in tearing down the image of Shostakovich, build up his own; or he could ignore Shostakovich and retreat to those very few areas and forms in which he would not compete directly with the Leningrad competition. He tried all three. Particularly, during the period 1931–7, when Shostakovich seemed to have forsaken the symphonic form, Kabalevsky wrote his set of three. But

[1] Both the concerto and Shostakovich's First Symphony were diploma works, each by the outstanding member of a graduating class. Kabalevsky's concerto was staged to suit the advance publicity in 1931 at the Bolshoi Theatre, with Shirinskii conducting the house orchestra and the composer at the piano. Shostakovich's First Symphony had been performed earlier in the year (March) by Toscanini in New York (the third American performance) with good reviews. The natural question, why so weak a work, advanced so late, can be answered with a look at the Moscow Conservatory situation at the time. Because of the drastically lowered entrance requirements, the barring of almost all but the proletarian class, and the lack of political qualifications of better student composers, such as Shebalin, there was no one but Kabalevsky to serve in the role.

with Shostakovich's Fifth Symphony, and his coincident abandonment of the stage in 1937, Kabalevsky reversed himself: he stopped writing symphonies[1] and his opera, *Colas Breugnon*, appeared almost immediately.

One problem of immediate importance to Kabalevsky was solved by the Party's dissolution of all musical organizations and formation of the all-embracing Union of Soviet Composers. Kabalevsky figured prominently in the conservative and policy-determining Moscow branch as a young organizer.[2] By this time he was also editing for Moscow's Muzgiz and the Moscow radio. The period from 1932 to 1937 was not a particularly prolific one for Kabalevsky, but it was the period of his three symphonies, the second of which seemed to be the instrument for realizing his desire for foreign acclaim.[3]

The First Symphony was dedicated to the October revolution on its fifteenth anniversary. Kabalevsky felt the occasion demanded simplicity and that the work should be approachable by the largest number of listeners. A programme was in order: the first movement portrays the people in the pre-revolutionary yoke of Tsarism. The gloom is achieved by combining double-bass, 'cello, and bassoon in extended sepulchral passages. Yet, elements of 'the people' are present in folk-like melodies. The second, and last, movement represents the uprisings of the people and their joyous victory. The composer develops a folk theme whose subject is Lenin. The work had been intended as a symphony-cantata based on V. Gusev's verses, 'The Year 1917'. However, Kabalevsky abandoned the idea of chorus and word-setting, retaining only the programme idea. The work has not remained in the repertoire.

Work on the Second Symphony was interrupted by the advent of the tenth anniversary of Lenin's death to which Kabalevsky, as well as many other composers, dedicated his work.[4] Kabalevsky's contribution was his Third Symphony ('Requiem'). This time Kabalevsky used a chorus, setting the words of N. Aseev: that poet's response to the leader's

[1] The unsuccessful Fourth Symphony was produced twenty years later.

[2] As an active and articulate member of the Moscow USC, Kabalevsky quite naturally took part in the wide-spread negative discussions of Shostakovich's *Lady Macbeth of Mtsenk* and *The Sparkling Brook*. For the same reasons, and since he had been particularly tart about the Shostakovich stage works, as the machinery of official pardon was applied to Shostakovich's Fifth Symphony, Kabalevsky found himself a prominent spokesman in favour of the work.

[3] The Second Symphony was actually finished after the Third. The symphonies and pertinent dates: I, in C sharp major (two movements), 1932, published by Muzgiz in 1934; III, 'Requiem' with chorus (two movements) 1933, published by Muzgiz in 1935; II, in C major (three movements), published by Muzgiz in 1937.

[4] Lenin died in January 1924.

death. The two movements are played without break, and nearly identical thematic material further binds the two. The work is full of expressions of (in order) alarm, deep grief, funeral march music, recitative, and Orthodox Slavic mourning.[1] An ode of lamentation, heard in the introduction, is transformed into a heroic image that engulfs the work in the finale. This work, as well as the First Symphony, and even the second, is little more than story telling, a naive attempt at the depth required in a symphony. Kabalevsky's natural inclination to make the music accessible results in its being simple-minded, a characteristic which works to his advantage only in his children's music.

The Second Symphony was ostentatiously without programme, although the composer thinks of it as 'autobiographical'.[2] Soviet criticism classifies this as the life-asserting (*zhiznutverzhdaiushchii*), happy, dynamic symphony typical of the mid-thirties, the rapid growth of industry, and of the period inaugurated by Stalin's decree that 'Life is brighter, gayer . . .'.[3] The symphony was played abroad during one of the periods of intense Western interest in anything Soviet. In music this period was the result of the impact of Shostakovich's First Symphony. Thus the popularity of Kabalevsky's Second was not so much a challenge but a tribute to Shostakovich. The work is classically formed. A thrice repeated, dramatic principal subject contrasts with a lyric, 'pretty' tune whose intonations carry into the second movement. This movement, requiring no more depth of purpose than an extended song form, is the most acceptable in balance of intent and effect. The third movement is designed as both scherzo and finale and earns the epithet of the time, 'happy music'. The mood is festive, the rhythm insistent, and the lyricism overpowering. The Second Symphony must join its predecessors on the librarian's shelf. Nevertheless, although these works cannot aspire to the grand designation of 'symphony', within them is the distillation of Kabalevsky as a stylist: ostinato of a piercing, compelling sort, a real gift for lyric, melodic line of 'intimate' length, an equally striking gift for the fleeting harmonic *mot juste*. Kabalevsky's gift, in short, is that for the most appropriate, the most obvious: a gift that would have made a third-rate composer of even Beethoven. The last of

[1] Joseph Stalin's intoned oration over Lenin's body in the form of a church litany, the long, solemn display of the body in Moscow's Hall of Columns, and the erection of a shrine on Red Square in which the body is displayed (under glass) in the manner of an Orthodox saint generally provide the mood and trappings with which Lenin is remembered in contemporary Soviet art. Religious symbolism is strong.

[2] Grosheva, *Dmitrii Kabalevsky* (Muzgiz, 1956), p. 22.

[3] A phrase contained in various speeches of 1932.

Kabalevsky's three symphonies[1] was completed on the eve of the new historical and folk doctrines of the government. Troublesome to other composers, the new doctrines were to prove to Kabalevsky's advantage.

During the thirties Kabalevsky worked as a senior editor at Muzgiz. He was hard working, expert technically, and was hailed in this capacity as a Stakhanovite. His works were published consistently by Muzgiz. Of the seventeen opera (13 through 29) written in the thirties, only 15, 20, and 29 are unpublished.[2] Of those published only two works for children were published by an agency other than Muzgiz.

Colas Breugnon was Kabalevsky's first stage success. The Romain Rolland story of a seventeenth-century artisan was used by Kabalevsky and his librettist, V. Braginym, as allegorical material for the present.[3] The opera is in three acts of two scenes each. Breugnon is first seen among the people of Clamecy,[4] participating in dancing and revelry which are interrupted by the arrival of Breugnon's Mycaenas, the Duke. In the second act the villagers are decimated by a plague brought to them by the Duke's soldiery. The people stage an uprising, and Colas is killed in the third act. Mass scenes predominate: the grape harvest, village merry making, the uprising, etc. In these choruses Kabalevsky sought to catch the French folk spirit. In traditional Russian fashion he studied collections of folk songs. In the opera direct quotation is the exception: rather Kabalevsky's notion of the French folk idiom distilled is employed. The symphonic episodes are important. The music of the overture and the entr'actes was later formed into a suite which carried *Colas Breugnon* abroad. The suite thus joined the Piano Sonatina and the Second Symphony as an international traveller.

In 1939 Kabalevsky became a full professor at the Moscow Conservatory; in 1940 and continuing to 1946 he was the principal editor of *Sovetskaia Muzyka.*[5] Also in 1940 he joined the Communist party.

---

[1] The Fourth was premiered in 1956. Little attention was given to it, nor will much attention be given here. The established custom of a favourable review from a 'name' colleague was ignored, and only Kabalevsky's old PROKOLL associate and a classmate, the happy hack, Vladimir Fere, could be called upon for a lukewarm comment in *Sovetskaia Kul'tura*, October 27, 1956.

[2] Opus 15, 'Galician Zhakeria' (1931), for orchestra, chorus and soloists, is a radio work. Opus 19 (1933–4) is a set of four piano preludes and opus 29 (1940) is a set of four piano preludes and opus 29 (1940) is a suite for jazz orchestra.

[3] The Rolland work was in the form of fourteen separate tales of Breugnon. Breugnon was an artistic Robin Hood who met various situations with an optimism so disproportionate as to cause his death at the hands of his snobbish, royal patrons.

[4] The opera was originally entitled *Master from Clamecy*.

[5] *Sovetskaia Muzyka* was discontinued as a monthly during the war. Kabalevsky was responsible for an annual issue only, from 1942 through 1945.

His oratorio, *The Motherland is Great* (1942) was based on the works of various poets and is in the popular, heroic vein of the time. Other works during the war included, on one hand, many songs of light or patriotic nature,[1] a suite for chorus and orchestra, *Narodnye mstiteli* (The folk avengers, op. 36, 1942), which was written with the poet E. Dolmatovsky while both were at the front; an unsuccessful opera, *V Ogne* (In the flame, op. 37, 1942), which was withdrawn after one or two hearings, but much of whose music was used later in *The Taras Family*; and, on

Ex.1 *Use of simple tune*

the other hand, works of a more serious or abstract nature like the 24 Preludes for Piano (op. 38, 1943) and the Second String Quartet (op. 44, 1945). The five-movement quartet contains some of Kabalevsky's most complex music, and his simplest. The course of development in the work is from complex to simple, a fact that leads one to assume it may be autobiographical for the time. Since this period, which was a crossroads for Kabalevsky, the composer has put complexities behind him.

Each of the twenty-four Preludes has a folk song as a generating point,[2] although this is not always obvious. Most of the folk songs are taken from the Rimsky-Korsakov collection *100 Songs*. The key

[1] These include the 'Brevi Song' and 'Sea Song' (opus 32, 1941), the vocal monologues 'Order for the son', 'We cannot be defeated', and 'In the thick, dark grove' (opus 33, 1941), and three songs on poetry of Marshak (opus 34, 1941).

[2] At the beginning of the work, after the dedication to Miaskovsky, Kabelevsky quotes from the Lermontov *Notes*: 'if I want to inject the folk element into writing, there is truly no place for me to seek it other than in Russian songs.'

arrangement is through the circle of fifths in major and minor pairs. The ultimate prelude, in D minor, is the only one that changes key, bringing the whole work to a close in D major. The idiom ranges from that of simple tune quotation (Example 1) to a rather complex harmony and texture (Example 2). The work is unlike the superficially similar works of Shostakovich or of Bartok in the insistence on the piano style. There

Ex.2 *Harmonic and textural complexities*

is a close affinity with the sound of Schumann (Example 3). Elsewhere folk rhythms are pressed into service (Example 4).

Kabalevsky's most important work within the Soviet Union's boundaries was to be the opera *Sem'ia Tarasa* (The Taras Family). The work was premiered in Leningrad on November 7, 1950. The whole concept of the opera brings again to mind Kabalevsky's understanding of the ingredients of success. He chose a Stalin-Prize winning story, B. Gorbatov's *The Unsubdued*,[1] which had been published in Pravda in 1942. The title hero is old Taras. His sons and daughter are partisan fighters in the recent war. The Germans are present in all their evilness,

Ex.3 *Schumannesque piano style.*

having overrun the area where the Taras family lives. The opera depends strongly on leitmotives and their development. Nothing is complex but the maze of motives. The music, the characters and the story are all painted in primary colours. The work is exhaustingly emotional, so overwrought that only the philosophy that prevails in any country during wartime can support it. Although the Soviet Union was not, technically, at war in 1950–1, the nervous tenor of these years, Stalin's last, easily provided the bellicose background. In a limited sense this is a children's opera. No such intention has ever been expressed by Kabalevsky, but the emotional level of the drama is distinctly immature, and the pen the composer used was the one with which he has always been most successful: that of the many works for children.[2]

[1] The opera itself won Kabalevsky a Stalin Prize. Moreover, in an unusual move, the collectives mounting the premières in Leningrad and Moscow were also awarded Stalin Prizes for their performances. The first performance, in Leningrad, was at the Kirov Theatre with Boris Khaikin conducting. The Moscow première was at the Stanislavsky, Nemirov-Danchenko Theatre on March 11, 1951.

[2] The scene where Nastia is caught, grilled, mistreated, and sent to her death by the Nazis is so disturbing to children that the Stanislavsky, Nemirov-Danchenko Theatre production abridges the section.

Ex. 4 *Folk rhythms*

The leitmotives, as indicated, are many and are so densely used that the work affords a theorist a complex puzzle. The main abstract images are those of struggle, victory and the unsubduable nature of the Soviet people. This last (Example 5) is also identifiable with Taras and with his daughter, Nastia, the real hero of the opera. Nastia is a school girl, a child who becomes a woman through the fire of war and the flame of her child's love for Pavka. Her themes are many, including that of her love (Example 6) which tells of her approaching womanhood, and her regard for her school (Example 7) which emphasizes her child-like nature. Her defiantsong when she faces death bears the intonations of the 'unsubdued' theme (Example 8, compare Example 5). The opera

Ex. 5 *Unsubdued theme.*

ff pesante

Ex. 6 *Nastia's love.*

has many characters and many situations which were a test for Kabalevsky's cleverness. The Nazis are portrayed in orchestral sound of alarm (Example 9) andunrelieved evil. At one point the ominous intonations of the enemy combine with a lullaby tune (Example 10) later sung by Nastia's sister-in-law. A chorus of young women, forced into shameful service to the invaders, is set in the style of a Russian folk song of grief (Example 11). There is a tendency to suspend the dramatic flow during the choruses more than during the arias. In one instance the Komsomols gather near their old school houses intending to blow it up, since it has become a German command centre. Stealth is important since the guard stands not thirty feet away. Nevertheless the youths sing a lusty song of their own bravery that has an effect amusingly similar to the *Pirates of Penzance's* 'With Cat-like Tread!'

Ex. 7 *Nastia's school song.*

Expressivo e dolce

la se - vo-dnia so shko-loi pro-shchat'sia be-ga-la

so svo-ei par-toi so shkol'nym sad-om, *etc.*

Ex. 8 *Nastia's song of defiance.*

A es-li kto i byl, ni-che - vo ia ne ska - zhu vsë rov - no!

Ex. 9 *Nazi theme.*

Ex. 10 *Enemy theme: lullaby.*

(and 8va)

Ex. 11 *Women's chorus of grief.*

Oi, _____ sto - ro - na mo-ia, _____ oi, sto-
Sto - ro - na ____ sto-

-ro - nush - ka, _____ ty na - vek, __ pro-
-ro - nush - ka, ty pro - shchai, __ na - vek, __ pro-

-shchai... Pro-shchai, mi - la-ia, oi, ro - di - ma-ia
-shchai... Pro-shchai, mi - la - ia, __ ro - di - ma-ia

In general, one can say of the work that Kabalevsky was ashamed of nothing. This, dramatically and musically, is a shallow sort of flag waving, At a point where Taras, as spokesman for a group of old men who refuse to rehabilitate a destroyed factory, is shot, the *Internationale* is suddenly sounded. It closes the scene and is not heard again. But there is no denying the technical gift of the composer. He succeeds through the tangle of themes in making each heard and many understood. This was the work he ostentatiously withdrew in 1948 for revision. What those revisions, if any, were will remain a question. It has been suggested, however, that the libretto was at fault in following too intimately the love story of Pavka and the juvenile Nastia. If so, Kabalevsky had adopted another means to popular success frequently encountered between 1940 and 1948 in motion pictures and novels as well as in opera and ballet, that of frank handling of love affairs.

The post-1948 Kabalevsky was again revealed in the set of three concertos dedicated to youth. These are for violin (op. 48, 1948), 'cello (op. 49, 1949), and his third piano concerto (op. 50, 1952). Of these the violin concerto has generated the most interest both in the Soviet Union and abroad, where it is sometimes included in the repertoire of mature violinists. It was written for young instrumentalists. The work, however, is difficult, and only such a young violinist as the prodigy Igor Bezrodnyi could give a convincing reading.[1] The work is in the standard three movements, each formally traditional. The themes are direct with some chromatic flavour (Examples 1 and 2) and are developed largely by repetition. The secondary subject of the first movement is a popular Ukrainian folk song (Example 2). This is developed lyrically, whereas the first theme undergoes some treatment in rhythmic fragments. The first two measures of the first theme alternates among the various solo instruments. A standard recapitulation, wherein the second subject receives some further development, is followed by an energetic coda based on the first subject. The Andantino Cantabile second movement treats melodies akin to the secondary subject of the first movement (Example 3). This is a fairly standard practice with Kabalevsky. Harmonically lush but simple, the generally thick texture is only occasionally lightened with quasi-polyphonic fabrics (Example 4). The third movement (Vivace giocoso) is full of happy sound. The form, rondo-sonata, amounts to a chain of dance tunes. The main theme (Example 5) is based on Kabalevsky's 'A foursome of friends', and a secondary tune is that of the Komsomol chorus from *The Taras Family*. A short cadenza, based on the first theme (Example 6), and partially

---

[1] The work was premiered by Bezrodnyi in 1949 in honour of the thirtieth anniversary of the Komsomol.

Kabalevsky. *Violin Concerto.*

Ex. 1 *Theme*

Ex.2 Secondary subject (Ukrainian folk tune)

II. Melody resembling previous material

x. 4   II *Quasi polyphony*

Ex. 5 *Third movement, main theme.*

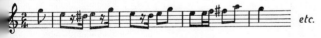

etc.

Ex.6 *III. Cadenza on first theme.*

accompanied, sets off a short coda. The work as a whole is facile with no attempt to penetrate intellectually or emotionally.

One of the most remarkable aspects of Kabalevsky's career is the rapid drop of productivity dating from about the time of the violin concerto. The Western observer is often quick to lay this to the ideological controls imposed about that time. This, however, is clearly not the case with Kabalevsky. He has become the image of the Soviet musical figure: the musical *deiatel'*. With Khachaturian, he has most faithfully served as missionary for his country's creative ideology. The tradition of the *deiatel'* is difficult to understand in the Western musical framework. Kabalevsky perennially leads, hither and yon, delegations, another Soviet tradition. He addresses mass workers, he appears with Mongolian collective farm workers, he writes articles for the domestic and foreign newspapers and journals, he appears on television panels where he argues his view in articulate Russian, French, or English, he both receives and presents awards on festive and solemn occasions. He does not have time to compose. Moreover, if, as has been suggested, popular acclaim is identified with creative success in Kabalevsky's thinking, then fresh creative effort may not seem necessary. If the drive for recognition is a dominant part of the creative process, and if that drive is fully satisfied, then part of the creative urge is torn away.

As spokesman for official policy, and as the 'champion of youth', Kabalevsky had, in 1956, embarrassingly to display the double-think expected of his group and generation of composers. In a lead article in *Sovetskaia Myzyka*,[1] he took the initial step in wiping away the personal criticisms of 1948. The step was obviously that of the Party—in Kabalevsky's shoes. He decried the vulgar criticism, by 'certain persons', of many of the young composers of the time, and names some of them as highly esteemed today. He speaks of the ridiculous extremes to which 'they' went in condemning these youths, still innocently within the conservatory walls. He insists that the old matter needs bringing up and cites, as reason, instances in which 'they' are continuing their vicious practice. One such case he mentions is that of Andrei Volkonsky, who was expelled from the Moscow Conservatory in 1954. Of course, the 'certain persons' and 'they' include thriving Party leaders as well as Khrennikov, and Kabalevsky himself. Kabalevsky is reliably reported, from various sources, as being instrumental in the expulsion of Volkonsky, the latter a would-be serial composer.

The violin concerto was followed by the less successful concertos for 'cello and piano. The latter two, with consecutive opus numbers 49 and

[1] Dmitri Kabalevsky, 'Creativity of young Moscow composers', in *Sovetskaia Muzyka*, no. 1, 1957.

50, were written two and a half years apart. Of Kabalevsky's subsequent works only a few have pretensions beyond those of his work for children: a third opera, *Nikita Vershinin* (op. 53, 1954), the Fourth Symphony (op. 54, 1954-4), and one may include the *Symphonic Poem* (op. 65, 1961?).[1] The Fourth Symphony has been mentioned as unsuccessful. It was performed abroad, mostly in the United States.[2] The opera is dramatically nearly identical with *Taras*: Nikita Vershinin embodies characteristics of both old Taras and of Ivan Susanin. The locale of the opera is the Far-Eastern Siberian province during the civil war,[3] and it deals with the attempts there to establish Soviet power. Enemies of the people, mostly white-guardists, overrun the area where Vershinin lives with his family. The family includes a young girl, Katia, who loves the fighting Bolshevik, Peklevanov, etc., etc., etc. The role of the masses is even greater than in *Taras*, so chorus music and choral texture tend to dominate. As in most of his stage work, Kabalevsky uses the orchestra alone a good deal. Although the work borrows the dramatic ingredients successful in *Taras*, it is musically dull and trivial. It is now (1959) in process of revision.

Kabalevsky is still one of the most published of composers in the Soviet Union. But a brief survey of the publication of the last few years (averaging ten to thirteen items a quarter) shows that over 90 per cent is republication of old children's works, inclusion in graded children's albums, rearrangements of old works for folk instruments and ensembles, and arrangements for dance band. This is trivia, and it seems to have become the setting for Kabalevsky as a composer in his latest period. A superb technique, and an unusual insight into the nature of immediate popular success are his two creative weapons. The essential third weapon, a personal depth which must, at times, ignore the first and second, has always eluded him.

[1] The other assigned opus numbers: 55, *Two Songs* (1955); 56, incidental music to *Romeo and Juliet*; 57, *Songs of morning, spring, and peace* for children's chorus with orchestra; 58, *Spring sings*, a three-act operatta; 59, *Rondo for piano*; 60, *Four rondos for piano*; 61, *In the magic forest*, for narrator, piano and chorus; 63, *Lenintsy* (roughly: Lenin's lads and lassies) for orchestra and three choruses (children's, youth and mixed); 67, a game-chorus for children, chorus, and piano; 69, Rondo for violin and piano. Other works after 1954 include many short, popular songs on topical subjects which often appear in the daily press, and an unassigned (as yet) work in memory of Patrice Lumumba, *The last hour tolls*.

[2] The first US performance of the Fourth Symphony was by Mitropoulos and the New York Philharmonic, October 31, 1957.

[3] A Far-Eastern republic was established east of Lake Baikal in April 1920. That it was merely a clever Bolshevik administrative device became clear in late 1922 when, after enlisting sympathetic pressure from the United States to clear Japanese troops from the mainland, it dissolved overnight into the Moscow government.

꙳꙳꙳

CHAPTER 19

Tikhon Khrennikov

Tikhon Khrennikov is a composer of insignificant talent. In the usual course of things a study of this sort would include no consideration of such an inferior figure. Khrennikov, however, holds a unique position, that of first secretary of the Union of Soviet Composers, a post to be gained and held only by a master politician, in the Soviet sense, and, nominally, a post to be held by a producing composer. Time will deal with Khrennikov in one of two ways: it will damn him as the bell-wether of Soviet music, or it will forget him. In either case his music will not be an issue.

Tikhon Nikolaevich Khrennikov was born on June 10, 1913, in El'tsa in the Orlov district midway between Moscow and the Black Sea.[1] A flair for music developed early,[2] and he entered the Moscow Gnessin institute in 1929 at the age of sixteen.[3] In 1932 he switched to the Moscow Conservatory, studying with Litinsky, a Gliere student, and finally with Shebalin[4] under whom he graduated in 1936.

By this time, in the prodigy tradition, Khrennikov had already

---

[1] Ordinarily Soviet biographers either ignore a composer's class background or, if it is properly proletarian, overemphasize it. In Khrennikov's case, however, it is bluntly stated that he was the last of ten children born to a petty bourgeois (*meshchanskii*) family.

[2] Khrennikov read and wrote at the age of four and was a mathematical prodigy, according to Soviet sources. His first work, a piano etude was composed when he was thirteen.

[3] One author (L. Kaltak. *Tikhon Nikolaevich Khrennikov*, Moscow: Muzgiz, 1946, 45 pp.) reports a hard decision for Khrennikov after he finished school: should he continue in music or should he go to the country and become the managing secretary of an agricultural *soviet* (council)? He was much drawn to the latter and had prepared himself for such work, specializing in school in soviet administration. Gnessin himself persuaded Khrennikov to take the former course.

[4] Khrennikov, leading the Party's musical offensive in 1948, was especially vicious toward Shebalin and effected his removal from the directorship of the Moscow Conservatory.

9

accumulated some local fame. A 1933 Piano Concerto and his First Symphony (1934–5) were received with interest. These were skilful copies of Shostakovich and Prokofieff. Khrennikov has remained a particularly apt cook of a broth which blends a borrowed idiom with a keen awareness of the current Party taste. His first successful opera, *V. Buriu (In the Storm)*[1] (1936–9) demonstrates this quality. By this time Shostakovich had been officially admonished and the hack Dzerzhinsky praised for *The Quiet Don. In the Storm* copies the idiom and dramaturgy of the Dzerzhinsky work, in fact, Khrennikov's is a better piece of writing. The magical ingredients are a bowdlerization of the original Virta novel by A. Faiko and Virta himself, and the inclusion, for the first time in the history of the musical stage, of Lenin as a character. The opera bears no stylistic resemblance whatsoever to the earlier works mentioned.

A Second Symphony was written during the period 1940–3, undergoing extensive rewriting after its premier performance under Golovanov in Moscow on January 10, 1943. The symphonies and concertos of Khrennikov have never had much impact. His best is for the stage, and his earliest sustained experience was with incidental music for plays. Khrennikov's situation and activity during this period in Moscow was important in his later career and development. However the important aspects are less musical than they are political and social. The writer views with distaste their discussion here, however a peculiarity intimate, if not scholarly, view of Khrennikov in the thirties is given by the Soviet expatriate Juri Jelagin in his *Ukroshchenie Iskusstv*.[2] Khrennikov worked on theatre music at the Vakhtangov Theatre in Moscow where Jelagin was also a member of the collective. Jelagin refers to Khrennikov as originally gifted, but then spells out, in sordid detail, Khrennikov's moral and aesthetic conversion into a political monster. The account, rendered dispassionately, and even with humour, is highly readable and convincing.

By the beginning of the war Khrennikov, although prominent politically, was virtually forgotten as a composer. During the war years he wrote a few songs including 'There's a little town in the North' and 'At six o'clock in the evening, after the war'. L. Kaltak, in 1945, provides an analysis of part of his style, uncannily anticipating the Party formula laid down in 1948:

---

[1] *In the Storm* was dedicated to the famous Nemirovich-Danchenko who supervised its staging.

[2] Juri Jelagin, *Ukroshchenie Iskusstv* (New York: Chekhov, 1952) with 434 pages is also published in English: *The Taming of the Arts* (New York: Dutton, 1951), 333 pp.

'Khrennikov's music never sounds passive or indifferent. It is pervaded with active, life-asserting principle and passion. Khrennikov's heroes are full-blooded, healthy Soviet persons, comprehensively perceiving the world, reworking it, struggling for the happiness of their people, their motherland. They know clearly how to love and how to hate'.[1]

Khrennikov occupied two critical positions during the war: positions that brought him under official eyes. He was head of the music section of the Red Army Central Theatre (until 1954) and an active member of the All-Union Organization for Cultural Relations with Other Countries (VOKS). In 1948 he headed the music section of VOKS. In these posts, while writing little music, he proved to be the man the Party sought in 1948. As chief musical spokesman for the Party,[2] he shared with the Party Central Committee member, Andrei Zhdanov, the responsibility for the attack on the composers Shostakovich, Khachaturian, Miaskovsky, Prokofieff, and Shebalin, and on certain musicologists, principally Gruber and Livanova. It seems certain that he collaborated in the subsequent party music codex. Although he had previously held no position in the Union of Soviet Composers, he was now elevated to first secretary. That he has continued to hold that post (for fifteen years) is no less remarkable than his originally gaining it.[3] As a composer, however, Khrennikov was in need of refurbishing. *In the Storm* was remounted and received a good deal of publicity in the post-1948 period. A new comic opera *Frol Skobeev* was unsuccessfully premiered in February

[1] L. Kaltak, *Tikhon Nikolaevich Khrennikov*.

[2] Khrennikov had joined the Party only in 1947.

[3] Khrennikov's most brilliant political *coup* as first secretary derived from his knowing when to be quiet. The second All-Union Congress of Composers in 1957 was borne in on a crest of liberalism, enthusiastically endorsed by Dmitrii Shepilov, ex-director of *Pravda* and, at the time, a fast rising star on the exclusive Party Central Committee. Shepilov was even mentioned in the Western press as the heir apparent to Khrushchev, just as Zhdanov had been to Stalin in 1948. Khrennikov, his works, and his leadership of the Union of Soviet Composers underwent a prolonged liberal attack before the Congress in the pages of *Sovetskaia Muzyka*, and during the Congress in most of the never-ending speeches. Khrennikov's support came largely from two arch-reactionary Leningrad musicologists, Iurii Keldysh and Iulii Kremlev. Khrennikov remained passively silent throughout. But when Shepilov delivered the final talk, strongly agreeing with the liberal majority, the assembled musicians, and at least all Moscow, awaited the news of the removal of Khrennikov, Keldysh, and Kremlev from authority. Instead, of course, Shepilov was suddenly 'removed' from the Central Committee in a routine purge of the leadership. Kremlev and Keldysh assumed the choice academic and editorial positions abruptly vacated by the most outspoken members of the liberal group, and Khrennikov emerged all powerful.

1950. Finally, in October of 1957, his opera *Mat'* ('Mother', after the Gorky story) was premiered simultaneously in Moscow, Leningrad, and Gorky, a unique tribute to a man who had just triumphed in the political area as well.[5] *Mat'* obviously does not hold the stage on its own merits. The very performance of this style-less, miserably derivative music is the most damning evidence of musical and political blackmail.

[5] See n. 3, p. 259.

꩜

CHAPTER 20

Georgii Sviridov

G eorgii Sviridov is a composer typical of that group among the middle generation which is most aware and sensitive ideologic- ally. He is the youngest of the middle-generation composers considered here. At one time a student of Shostakovich's, he had neither the depth nor, ultimately, the desire to sustain his teacher's approach to creativity. Superficially, he is stylistically close to Shostakovich. With the socio-political keenness of his group, he quickly discovered his musical base, developed it, and achieved the pinnacle of Soviet success: the Lenin Prize in music for his 1959 *Pateticheskaia Oratoria*. He was, and is, the youngest composer to receive the honour.[1]

Georgii (or Iurii) Vasil'evich Sviridov was born December 16, 1915 in Fatezh in the Kursk *gubernia*, midway between Moscow and Kiev. His early schooling was constantly interrupted, a phenomenon not at all uncommon during the time. At the age of fourteen he entered a Kursk *tekhnikum* specializing in music and the other arts, majoring in piano. After two years, he was chosen, as were many exceptional talents outside the metropolitan centres, for further training. Sviridov, in 1932, accordingly moved to Leningrad, continuing in the Central Musical Tekhnikum. He finished the composition course under M. Iudin in 1936.[2] When Iudin went to the Leningrad Conservatory, he brought

---

[1] The Lenin Prize was re-instituted in 1957 when it became clear that the Stalin Prize name, if not the structure, could no longer be used. Much more selective and far fewer than the former prizes, the Lenin Prize was first awarded to Prokofieff (posthumously) in 1957, to Shostakovich in 1958, to Solov'ev-Sedoi and Aram Khachaturian in 1959, and to Sviridov in 1960.

[2] Mikhail Alekseevich Iudin, 1893–1948, studied at St Petersburg University and later at the conservatory under Zhitomirsky. He began teaching in 1918, well before he finished the conservatory (1923). In 1936 he joined the staff of the Leningrad Conservatory and became full professor of composition in 1939. He left Leningrad during the war and was unable to meet the competition to resume his old post thereafter. In semi-retirement, he taught choral conducting in Kazan' until his death.

with him the promising provincial talent: Sviridov continued there under P. Riazanov.[1] In 1937, Shostkovich, riding the crest of the success of his Fifth Symphony, joined the staff of the Leningrad Conservatory to teach orchestration. Not to study with Shostakovich in the late thirties was unthinkable. Sviridov, with many others, was attracted and managed to switch teachers. He finished under Shostakovich in 1941 and was evacuated to Novosibirsk,[2] where he remained through 1944.

Twenty-six years old at the time of his graduation, Sviridov already had a fairly impressive list of works. These included his first Symphony (for strings, 1940), a musical comedy and film music (1939), song cyclec on Pushkin (1935) and Lermontov (1938), and an early piano concerto (1936). Mentioned in various earlier sources, but not in the official biographical-bibliographical publication of the Union of Soviet Composers, are a suite for string quartet, a set of piano preludes, a Second Symphony, and, in collaboration with Ivan Dzerzhinsky, a work for the Red Army chorus and dancers, *Soviet Cossacks*.[3]

During the war years, Sviridov had already abandoned his attempts at following in Shostakovich's footsteps. It was clear to him that sociopolitical understanding was essential in creative work. It was equally clear in the pertinent Party circles that Sviridov was an undeniably talented person, one who, with good results, could be accelerated in his career. The system of punishment and reward in the arts had deteriorated during the war, when such energies were expended elsewhere. During the lull, Shostakovich reigned supreme, largely on the strength of the international success of his Seventh Symphony. But, in 1946, Sviridov's 'acceleration' began with his winning a first degree Stalin Prize for his piano trio of 1945. This was an unusually high degree for

[1] Petr Borisvich Riazanov, 1899–1942, was a violin student in one of the prerevolutionary St Petersburg People's Folk Conservatories—low or no cost musical preparatory schools which were converted into uchilishches and tekhnikums after 1918. Riazanov served both sides in the civil war, a common occurrence, and returned to finish the Petrograd Conservatory in 1925 under Zhitomirsky and Shteinberg. He taught periodically at the conservatory and, in 1935, became dean of the composing faculty. Evacuated to Tbilisi, he taught there until his death. His most successful students were Ivan Dzerzhinsky, A. Machavariani, Solov'ev-Sedoi, Hodge-Einatov, Otar Chishko, and Sviridov.

[2] Novosibirsk was one of the Leningrad cultural evacuation centres. One Leningrad source indicates that Sviridov was in the army, but was demobilized in order to join the evacuation. No mention is made of this elsewhere.

[3] For some reason, obviously at the wish of the composer, the USC Bibliography (see bibliography) significantly omits other Sviridov works. These include, in addition to those mentioned, a number of piano works a musical comedy, and the Third Symphony.

one so young, and unusual in any case, considering the prize work.[1] This unusual awarding of the prize may be considered one of the first important Party steps to the *denouement* of 1948: a political move to which Sviridov may have been but an unwitting pawn.

In the nature of a pawn in the middle of the game, Sviridov stood more or less immobile during the fray of the late forties. Before this, during the war, he had written, in addition to the trio, a second piano concerto (1942), a musical comedy (*The wide sea stretches away*, 1943), a piano sonata, and some Shakespeare song settings (1944), and a piano quintet (1945). The Stalin Prize success spurred him innocently to more chamber music, with two quartets in 1946. Then, starting with two piano partitas in 1947, one has the picture of the bewildered composer, pen stilled, wondering whence and whither his fleeting fame.[2] With the exception of two short groups of art songs (1948, 1950), the years 1947 to late 1950 are blank.[3] By 1950, however, it was apparent that Sviridov had been engaged for some time in a marathon setting of poems of the Armenian Stalin Prize winner, Avetik Isaakian. By this time he had completed seventeen extended art songs on words of that poet. Unimportant and tentative in themselves, they are, in retrospect, the beginning of a new creative crescendo which carried him from that point through a similar setting of Robert Burns' poetry,[4] an unfinished oratorio, *The Decembrists*,[5] and the orchestra-choral poem *In memory of Sergei Esenin* (1956—the date is incorrectly given in the USC Bio-bibliography), to the slick, successful Lenin Prize winner, *Pateticheskaia Oratoria*. The young Georgian composer, Otar Taktakishvili, keys this last period of Sviridov's development to '[his credo] love for the people, for its simple, strong and exalted feelings'.[6] This, upon reflection, is

[1] The trio was subsequently found unsatisfactory by Sviridov himself who revised it in 1947 and again (for a new published edition) in 1955.

[2] Even the 1948 storm passed him by. He was brushed aside as '. . . one of Shostakovich's other pupils'. (From the stenographic report of the 1948 All-Union Composers' Conference.)

[3] There is no documentation, or other evidence, to justify a jump at what seems the natural conclusion: that these were the years of the works omitted from the USC Bio-Bibliography. See n. 3, p. 262.

[4] The Burns poetry was set in the early fifties and published by Muzfond in a limited edition in 1955. In an article, 'Notes on Georgii Sviridov's Style' in *Sovetskaia Muzyka* (no. 10, 1960), p. 46, L. Poliakov reasons rather cryptically, 'It is characteristic that the composer gradually, from afar, approached the theme of revolutionary Russia in the twentieth century (a reference to the subsequent Maiakovsky setting) through the imagery of Armenia and Scotland (!) . . .'

[5] Sviridov discontinued work on *The Decembrists* in 1955. The Decembrist theme is a Soviet favourite. For a more successful treatment see p. 177.

[6] Otar Taktakishvili in *Sovetskaia Muzyka* (no. 9, 1957), p. 71, in an article, 'On the music of Georgii Sviridov', p. 71.

extremely well put. Taktakishvili traces the evidence back to some early settings of Blok's poetry (1940, unpublished), as well as to the Isaakian and Burns settings. There can be no argument that the works starting with the Isaakian cycle represent a new departure. Indeed, Sviridov identifies himself with the already mentioned 'second group' of the middle generation by an abrupt, mechanical style change. There is little evidence in a comparison of the prize-winning trio and the Isaakian cycle even to suggest that they are the work of the same composer. The 'style' they do share is a Shostakovich flavour common to many younger Soviet composers.

If the first work of the new style is the Isaakian cycle,[1] and if the *Pateticheskaia Oratoria* is the altogether predictable culmination,[2] then the quasi-oratorio, *In memory of Sergei Esenin*, is the key. The massive means, the topical subject, safe in the liberal slump of 1955, the careful culling of Esenin's poetry for the ideologically acceptable,[3] the painfully accessible idiom, with appropriate sound effects, and the overpowering balance of optimism and bravado coincide in the work. It treats nine of Esenin's poems in ten settings. The scoring is for tenor solo, large chorus and augmented orchestra. Immediately, one would say the orchestra plays a markedly subsidiary role, but, extending the analysis a bit further, one is tempted to some such statement as, *all* the elements are secondary. The solo part tends at times to be sing-song, not so much in the character of folk song, but, rather, in that of popular dance balladry. Example 1 is the opening page of the piano score of the work: the theme flirts with the pentatonic. This theme and those in Examples 2 and 3 hover in the tonic or dominant area of the scale. Rather than answering any poetic demand, this seems instead to be an attempt at peasant *genre* painting. Where the melody is of another type it is almost always that of Example 4. The metre markings here seem to be an affectation. The chorus is used homophonically almost exclusively. It

---

[1] This consideration leaves out the earlier Blok settings. They are unavailable and not performed now.

[2] See n. 1, p. 268.

[3] Sergei Aleksandrovich Esenin belongs to that trio of 'great' revolutionary poets which includes Blok and Maiakovsky. Originally inspired by Blok, the peasant-sprung Esenin became one of the Moscow Imaginists. He is best known in the West for his marriage to, hilarious, world-touring debauch with, and divorce from Isadora Duncan in 1922. As a poet he was a 'peasant oriented' Bolshevik who became articulately discouraged with the suffering and with the failure of the peasant mind to unshackle itself. Of his suicide in Leningrad in 1925, Maiakovsky (himself to be a suicide) wrote:

> In this life it is not hard to die.
> To mold life is far more difficult.

plays a single rather than diverse dramatic role, although occasionally the men alone, or sopranos alone are heard. Curiously, the soloist and chorus coincide only in the first part, 'Ah, my cast-off land'. The tenor solo alone is heard in parts three (In those parts . . .), six (The night before Ivan Kupal—I), and nine (('I am the countryside's last poet . . .').

Sviridev. *In memory of Sergei Esenin.*

Ex.1 *Opening*

Ex.2 *Tonic oriented theme.*

9*

In the remaining six parts, the chorus and orchestra do without the solo voice. Part eight ('Peasant buddies') is a rollicking, mass folk song (Example 5). The ostinato accompaniment is typical for many other sections as well, and if that does not wholly characterize the texture of the orchestral part, it does typify the overall level of extreme simplicity.

Ex.3 *Dominant oriented theme.*

Ex.4 *Theme and tenor solo.*

Ma - tush-ka v ku-pal'-ni- tsu   po - le - su— kho- di - la

This is a work for hearing: analysis yields little but disappointment, but the dramatic pacing, the drama-as-form, is the area in which Sviridov shows his ability. Any complication of harmony or texture, any moments of introspective formal depth would have ruined the effortless sweep of emotional thinking, from beginning to end, for Sviridov's audience. Sviridov is quite properly concerned about that audience. He does not care to educate nor to inspire in any sense other than to move emotionally. He provides fifteen or twenty minutes of effective, refreshing laxative. He differs from composers like Shostakovich, who also has the audience in mind, in his abhorrence of the controversially instructive. The Esenin poem shows the hand of Sviridov's teacher, Shostakovich, but only the superficial hand of style.

In memory of Sergei Esenin, then, is no tribute to Sviridov's teacher. Sviridov has again identified himself with the 'second group' by being socially realistic. The urge to write another 'Seventh Symphony' had died, and in any case, Sviridov's personal doldrums of the 1947–50 period had convinced him to abandon the deeper Shostakovich image.

Much more telling to this observant mind was the success of Shaporin's oratorio-cantata series: *On the Kulikov field* in 1938, and, especially, *The story of the battle for Russian land* of 1944. At the time of their initial success, Sviridov was a youthful, sneering critic. Ten years later, when time had both mellowed Sviridov and proved the hardiness of the Shaporin works, Sviridov paid him the honour of imitation. Sviridov had re-established residence in Leningrad in 1944, but became more and more identified with the capital. Although still listed as a Leningrad composer, he spends most of his time in Moscow.

Ex.5. *Peasant buddies.(Mass song)*

Finally, there is the *Pateticheskaia Oratoria*.[1] This work differs little in idiom and imagery from the Esenin settings.[2] It is longer. The expressions of grief which are heard in the earlier Isaakian poems and diminishing thereafter in Sviridov's work, are here totally lacking. Maiakovsky's poems were selected with the care already noted in the Esenin settings.[3] Maiakovsky,[4] a physically big man, writing in a rude violent time, used the outsized image, the vulgar, and the coarse among his palette colours:

B'et	A man
muzhchina	smashes
damu	a woman
v mordu,[5]	in the snout,

He carefully calculates their use. Sviridov's music is born in crudeness and vulgarity, steeped in it, saturated with it. When the poetry demands coarseness, Sviridov is coarse; when it demands imagery, Sviridov apes; when it suggests bravery, Sviridov blares; and when it is beautiful, Sviridov supplies the pathetic, mawkish prettiness of a Moscow prostitute.

Sviridov is cleverer, musically, than Khrennikov. He is natively safer than Kabalevsky or Khachaturian. He is at least the equal of these technically. For such reasons as this, he is a good composer in his environment, and he deserves a Lenin Prize.

[1] A rare opportunity for observation of the manipulation of the Soviet ideological system of awards was afforded the author in 1959. Long before the performance of the *Pateticheskaia Oratoria* it was earmarked for the Lenin Prize. Its premier performance was obviously a gala celebration in advance. On the day the review appeared in the Soviet press, the review's author was approached concerning the work and its performance. His comment: 'I was sorry to have missed the performance; I shall have to read the review.' The mystery of such engineered creative goings-on is a mild one for the Soviet intellectual. In the first place, such a work *has* been heard before the première, in piano form, at a session of the appropriate review board of the USC. There, decisions for its performance, and as much as possible, for its level of reception are made. In the second place, it is clear to the Soviet mind that it is not desirable to leave such things to chance. Such an important matter as a Lenin Prize is much more meaningful if the 'surprise' is well prepared.

[2] The work has been heard in performance by the author. The score has not been consulted. It was published by Muzgiz in late 1961, in Moscow, with a parallel English text.

[3] The poems used: (1) 'March'; (2) 'The tale of Wrangell's rout;' (3) 'To the heroes of the Perekop battle'; (4) 'Our land'; (5) 'Here will be a garden-city!'; (6) 'Conversation with Comrade Lenin'; (7) 'The sun and the poet'.

[4] For a short biographical account of Maiakovsky see p. 171, n. 5.

[5] From 'The tale of Wrangell's rout'.

CHAPTER 21

꙰

Andrei Balanchivadze

The career of Andrei Balanchivadze overlapped and complemented rather than continued that of Arakishvili.[1] Where Arakishvili probed Georgian history for subject matter, Balanchivadze looks to his own time; where Arakishvili was mainly concerned, as a composer, with vocal music, Balanchivadze tends to instrumental genres; and where Arakishvili is manifestly steeped in Georgian folk music, Balanchivadze exhibits a more personal idiom, a transformation of the folk melos which often moves far from direct quotation. In all these things, Arakishvili is typical of his generation, Balanchivadze of his, in Georgian music.

Andrei Melitonovich Balanchivadze was born June 1, 1906 in St Petersburg. His family was a famous musical one. Andrei studied piano from the age of five, and, with his older brother, George, tried his hand at composition. The Balanchivadze children went to regular schools, George graduating into the Mariinsky Ballet School. Andrei would have followed him, but the family, leaving George behind, moved back to Georgia (Kutais) when the war started. In Kutais, under the culturally benevolent Menshevik dictatorship, the senior Balanchivadze started a music school. There Andrei studied piano and 'cello and played first 'cello in the municipal orchestra. He remembers with gratitude the organist Vikhovsky, with whom he first studied theory. In 1921 the Bolsheviks closed the school, and Andrei went to the Tiflis Conservatory, studying there with Cherepnin, Barkhudarian (in 1922) and Ippolitov-Ivanov (1923). His earliest, serious works were composed there. His style was at first derivative along Chopin-Scriabin lines. To this underpinning he self-consciously applied Georgian chordal harmonies without, apparently, understanding them. It is interesting to speculate, when considering the external similarities of Scriabinesque and Georgian folk harmonies, what the result would have been had the

[1] See p. 119.

young Balanchivadze had a more mature understanding of both. Balanchivadze's diploma work was a dance suite in two parts wherein he dropped the 'foreign' influences and derived his music from two folk tunes.

After graduating, Balanchivadze worked as a pianist for Tiflis theatres. In June 1927, half of a concert was devoted to his music: a march, a concert waltz, an adagio, and the suite mentioned. Good reviews helped make him a candidate for participation in a unique socio-cultural experiment being conducted by the Soviet Government at the time. As a part of the first five-year plan, it was felt necessary to impress Russian cultural patterns firmly on the republics. Cadres of specialists and would-be specialists in all fields were sent from the republics, including Georgia, to the North for study. Balanchivadze was included in the group of young composers from Georgia who were sent to the Leningrad Conservatory.[1] To Balanchivadze, of course, this was a return to his birthplace. He studied there from 1927 to 1931 under Zhitomirsky. He became an enthusiastic participant in the Leningrad Association of Contemporary Musicians, enjoying prolonged contact with contemporary Western music. This aspect of his musical training was later brought to Georgia where it had much to do with shaping that republic's musical future. Balanchivadze's graduate work in Leningrad was a chamber work for string quartet, harp and oboe. The Western influence was strong, and particularly that of Hindemith, with whose music Balanchivadze had recently become familiar. There is in the work the additional use of Georgian folk cadence formulas, now applied with a surer hand. This sextet, however, probably represents the peak of abstract development with Balanchivadze. He, like other republican composers, developed two styles. The sextet represents one. The other is characterized by tunefulness, homophonic structure, heavy, but brilliant and adept orchestration, Eastern scale colouring and motoric rhythms. These were the works for consumption at home. One of Balanchivadze's 'mass' works of the time, 'For the Harvest', was sung appropriately by a 10,000-voice chorus at the Fourth Leningrad Municipal Olympiad of *samodeiatelinosti* groups.

In 1931 Balanchivadze returned to Tbilisi and assumed the post of musical director and composer at the Mardzhanishvili Theatre. He also

[1] On June 3, 1926 an historical conversation took place between Meliton Balanchivadze and Joseph Stalin during an intermission of one of the former's operas at the Tiflis State Opera Theatre. The gist of Stalin's conversation was that the influence of Russian music on Georgian was noticeable and beneficial; that an organic unity existed and should exist between the two. These observations were widely published and, in the oblique way of the times, assumed the force of directives. See I. Stalin, *Works*, Vol. 8, biographical chronicle, p. 396.

worked with TRAM,[1] and received his intense practical training in the theatres of Kutais, Telavi, and Tbilisi. In 1934 he wrote the first of three piano concertos. Himself a pianist of the Lisztian persuasion, Balanchivadze does not escape the Hungarian composer's pianistic idioms. Again the folk influence is heard in certain ostinato rhythms: ♫♫♫♫in the first movement and metres such as the 7/8 dance of the second movement. The harmonic progression I_7–II_7—III_7–IV_7, all with absent thirds, is found repeatedly in the second movement and has a folk basis. The success of the concerto made Balanchivadze's name a wellknown one.

In 1935 Balanchivadze met and worked with Vakhtang Chabukiani[2] on what is considered the first Georgian ballet, *Serdtse Gor* (The heart of the Mountains, originally 'Mzechabuki').[3] Chabukiani mingled classic ballet with Georgian folk dance which he had developed to classical stature. Balanchivadze's music is utilitarian in the Soviet ballet manner. The ballet was uncommonly popular in the Soviet Union and is still performed in Tbilisi.

In 1937, after two years apprenticeship in the *rabfak*,[4] Balanchivadze joined the Tbilisi Conservatory staff. He became professor there in 1940. During and immediately after the war he composed a First Symphony (1944), his second piano concerto (1946), and a second ballet, *Rubinovye zvezdy* (Ruby Stars, 1947). A curious fate befell these works. When the 1948 Party criticism of music and composers began to reverberate in the Caucasus[5] these three works fell under fire. The ballet was never staged and the concerto did not enter the repertoire.

[1] TRAM—Teatr rabochei molodezhi (Theatre of working youth).

[2] Vakhtang Chabukiani is one of the small handful of Soviet artists who, with no fanfare, stand with the world's greatest. As a dancer he has no equal among Georgian men, traditionally the best male dancers of the Soviet Union. As a choreographer and balletmaster he is largely responsible for the rare glimpse of intimate, exquisite taste seen in the Kirov and Bolshoi theatres. He is extremely individualistic and refuses any permanent position in the northern theatres in spite of strong official urging. Occasionally he stages and/or dances in a Georgian opera, usually with the Leningrad Kirov Theatre. For a composer to work with Chabukiani is tantamount to success. His *Otello*, to the pallid score of Machavariani, has the finest staging and choreography, and the greatest male dancing (Chabukiani as Iago) in the Kirov repertoire.

[3] Previous Georgian attempts at ballet, Tamara Bakhvakhishvili's pantomimes and *Liubovnoe zel'e* (The love potion, 1930) and Gokieli's *Vitiaz' v tigrovoi shkure* (The hero in tiger skin, *c.* 1935) are generally ignored as being, respectively, amateurish and formalistic.

[4] Rabfak—rabochii fakul'tet, workers' faculty or school.

[5] The opening wedge of the 1948 criticism was an attack on the opera *The Great Friendship* of the Georgian composer-hack Vano Muradeli.

These were, apparently, weak works, but the symphony, far superior, was most critically attacked. The point of attack was the harmony which was actually Balanchivadze's most successful synthesis to date of Western and Georgian. The Northern inquisitors failed altogether to recognize the ethnographic achievements and the strong bond with folk harmony. Like Ippolitov-Ivanov sixty years earlier, they referred to systematic out-of-tune-ness. Balanchivadze withdrew the work, and it was not heard again until 1954. The symphony is in the heroic style of Shostakovich's heroic trilogy, replete with battles, dirges, and a positive hero image.

In his Third Piano Concerto (1952) Balanchivadze added a new Soviet dimension to his music, that of the 'children's genre'. In the Soviet Union this does not mean, necessarily, music playable or to be played by children, nor does it mean music that condescends to children's tastes. It is, rather, music with Soviet youth, its spirit, striving and future in mind. Prokofieff, Shostakovich, Kabalevsky, and many others have frequently written such music. The Balanchivadze Third Piano Concerto is singled out here, too, because it is a post-war, post-1948 work. Balanchivadze nowhere indicates officially that this is a programme work, but this simply follows Soviet custom: that of withholding the programme for explanation in articles and interviews later. Upon application, Balanchivadze readily supplies the information that the movements are: I. Pioneer Life; II. Conversation with grown-ups: children in the out-of-doors, and III. Scenes from camp life. The composer uses nearly direct folk material in the second movement; the folk song, 'Salami chitunebo'. Elsewhere in the intensely melodic work he uses Georgian modes and melodic formulas. In some instances he imitates the sound of Georgian folk instruments. The first theme of the first movement (Example 1) is lyric, but with the possibility of march-like development. The possibility is subsequently realized. This theme is broadly developed, in one instance augmented along the lines of Georgian folk melody (Example 2). The subordinate subject (Example 3) is sounded only briefly and does not figure in the development. It finally assumes, in significantly different character (Example 4), the function of wrapping up all the ideas just before the extended reprise-coda. The latter contains a short cadenza and the movement ends, after subdued suggestions of first and second themes, with a loud cadence. The second movement, after a trilling introduction in the high strings and a disjunct melody in the piano (Example 5), quotes the folk melody mentioned (Example 6). The simple harmonization shows traces of folk harmony (parallel thirds and triads and fifth-seventh chords) as well. The last of the three variations of which this movement is formed changes to an introspective minor sound, and the folk melody is pressed into a more disjunct form, reminiscent of the opening theme, with some polyphonic interplay (Example 7). The whole is on a background of piano arpeggios in triplets. The last movement is more restricted than freed by the subject matter: youth at camp. The themes duly contrast (Example 8), and that sums up the third movement. There is no real development of either of these themes, only their repeat and return on slightly varying accompaniments.

Balanchivadze is today, at fifty-eight, one of the ceremonial fixtures, musically speaking, in a highly ceremonial country. His honours include

Balonchivadze. *Third piano concerto.*

Ex.1 *First theme.*

Ex.2 *Disjunct, folk variant.*

Ex.3 *I. Subordinate subject*.

Ex.4 *I Substitute subordinate subject*

Meno mosso

Ex.5 *II. Opening piano statement.*

Ex. 6 *II Folk melody.*

Ex. 7 *II Folk melody, with disjunct elements and counterpoint.*

etc.

Ex. 8 *III. Themes.*

Theme 1

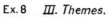

Theme 2

Stalin Prizes[1] and the rank of People's Artist of the Georgian SSR. He is active in the Georgian USC and still looks after the training of the Georgian younger generation.

The past years have been difficult ones for Georgian pride.[2] Neither Stalin nor Beria were particularly solicitous of their homeland, but their deaths and subsequent dishonour seemed to deprive the Georgians of national heroes. As recently as 1960 Georgians in high station bragged of Stalin, and a monument was being erected to him in Stalin Park, atop the mountain on whose flanks part of Tbilisi is situated. Such things are impossible after the 22nd Party Congress. At present, Georgia's over-all cultural niche in the Soviet Union is not clear. There are those, like Balanchivadze, who with encouragement could create a school of independent, contemporary music. There are others, like Muradeli, who could lead his country's culture into the already crowded swamp of Russification. The course of the careers of the young composers, like Otar Taktakishvili, will probably carve the route in this generation.

[1] One Stalin Prize was granted in 1947 for the Second Piano Concerto, but this did not save the work from subsequent condemnation.

[2] Aside from hurt pride, Georgia has escaped many of the social and economic troubles that have beset the rest of the Soviet Union. Georgia is one of the most economically successful areas of the Soviet Union. Her land is fertile and her people energetic. The incredible beauty, variety, and magnificent climate of Georgia undoubtedly gave rise to the Georgian folk saying, 'God got his idea for heaven from Kartvelia (Georgia)'.

PART FOUR

The Young Generation of Soviet Composers

Introduction

As with the preceding generations, various factors have been considered in choosing composers for discussion as members of a 'young generation'. The six chosen range from Karaev (1918–) to Shchedrin (1932–); two are Russian (Galynin, Shchedrin), and three are republican: Taktakishvili is Georgian; Karaev and Amirov, Azerbaidzhanian. Four of the six are graduates of the Moscow Conservatory, the others of conservatories in their home republics. Their dates of conservatory graduation span but eight years, and this is one of the most critical factors governing their inclusion here: their training was completed, and in most cases started, after the war. An additional chapter covers, briefly, certain other composers whose achievement is of a minor, or particular, sort.

These younger composers have enjoyed the maturest fruit of the Soviet system: the system which the preceding generation built. To them, certain things are a matter of course: support while studying, rather regular performances and commissions, and the economic shelter, for a while, of the USC upon graduation. They have expected and, showing promise, have received the propaganda services of the USC and the cultural press. These organizations, and the State in the form of the Ministry of Culture, have tended, nurtured, and otherwise invested heavily in this younger generation of composers. As the products of the finished machinery, they must succeed. The six chosen here have succeeded, to various degrees. For those who do not succeed, the largess[1] of the USC ends about the third year after graduation. They go to work, having had their chance, and room is made for the fresh crop of hopefuls. The effective, if mechanical, process creates a problem for the seeker of 'young talent' among a nation's composers. Those young

[1] The support of the USC takes the following form: the graduates' state required obligation to work is suspended by the USC. The USC can, instead, place the composer in a part-time job, or it can relieve him entirely of labour obligation for one or two years. He is allowed the various home and rest facilities maintained by the USC. His wife, if he is married, is given a dispensation on her labour obligation, which allows her to work in the geographical area of her husband's activity. This avoids conjugal hardship and provides the necessary money, which the USC does not.

Soviet composers who, measured by the publicity and performances they receive, seem already to have achieved an eminent position, may, within a short space of time, be forgotten teachers in a provincial *uchilishche*, or directors of remote *samodeiatel'nost'* groups.[1]

There are no Shostakovich's or Prokofieff's among the younger generation: indeed, there could not be. The occasional rebel is usually a young Turk seeking a momentary sensation before subsiding into obdurate conformity. None have the training to sustain creative search; few have the conviction that such search is morally right. Departure from musical convention requires more tools and more time than does departure from, say, the conventions of painting. There is no 'underground' school of musical composition analogous to the widely publicized 'underground' school of art. The techniques of music are too remote. Some possibilities have been considered for inclusion, but rejected. One such hopeful disintegrated before the author's eyes. A single exception, differing from his colleagues because of his early, Western European training, is considered in the last chapter.

[1] The composer-student is encouraged, and recently required, to develop a secondary, teaching skill. In almost all cases, because of the already strong keyboard orientation of their training, the secondary emphasis is piano.

CHAPTER 22

ɔⱴⱴ

Rodion Shchedrin

B y the time of the creative maturity of Rodion Shchedrin, assuming
for the moment that he has reached a certain stage of maturity,
the central path of development of Soviet music had diverged so
far from that of the rest of the West that an observer from the latter
milieu must judge on two levels. He is bound by common sense to a
critical, Western judgment, and he is bound by a sense of fairness to a
judgment within the composer's world of values. A Soviet composer of
Shchedrin's age has not had the choice that Kabalevsky or Shostakovich
had, although he can capitalize on the experience of these two men.
Born after the administrative reformation of artistic groups, he has no
notion of the wealth of styles in the twenties. He was just entering
kindergarten when, in 1936, the Party indicated what opera should be.
He lived through the period when Soviet children were conditioned to
revere Stalin as a god and father. So, the 1948 Party directives, when
Shchedrin was but sixteen, were unshakeable imperatives. His notions
of liberalism are connected with the brief interludes of 1954 and 1957,
and in each case the *dénouement* was the expected, and welcomed, push
back into line by the Party.[1] Shchedrin writes now in a style one must
call traditional—that of twentieth-century Soviet music. A Western
analysis, then, is all but automatic: impressive technical mastery,
preoccupation with sheer sound, use of a folk idiom, eclectic harmony,
avoidance of introspection and formal depth, an overwhelming emphasis
on programme music and vocal-symphonic genres, and point blank
communicative aim at the mass audience. Further, one might judge
with such adjectives as 'trivial', 'crude', and 'sensationalist'. Shchedrin's
curious dilemma is that he hears these words *within* his milieu as well.
He has found a logical point of departure that irks the urban, Soviet
intellectual. But, in spite of his training in the Soviet game of musical
chess, he may have prepared an escape square.

[1] One may now add the date 1962–3. Significantly, Shchedrin has, so far,
never been linked with the rebellious youths of whom poet Evgenii Evtushenko
is a famous leader.

Rodion (or Robert) Konstantinovich Shchedrin, the youngest of the composers considered here, was born in Moscow on December 16, 1932. His father was a minor Moscow musical figure, a theorist and occasional writer on musical subjects. Shchedrin began music lessons (piano) at an early age. He displayed a certain precocity, but enough, apparently, to gain him entrance to the ten-year music school administered by the conservatory. As it was, his early schooling was interrupted by evacuation during the war. In 1948 he was enrolled in the Moscow Choral Uchilishche. There he first began to compose. These early works have been described as brave, noisy attempts to say too much, with too little experience and technique.[1] Such a judgment cannot be considered unusual of one so young, but the quality of having much to say is still Shchedrin's. In 1951 he entered the Moscow Conservatory and studied there with Iurii Shaporin. Shaporin's student's have always displayed more divergence of style and technique than those of any other well-known Soviet teaching composer. This is a testament to the older composer's refreshing acceptance of almost anything in the spirit of search and experiment. Shchedrin, already well along in creative quantity,[2] was guided immediately by Shaporin into a string quartet (1951) and the piano suite *Holiday on the kolkhoz*. He uses folk themes liberally, especially in the quartet, but it is in the last movement of the piano suite that he displays, for the first time, a characteristic that has become Shchedrin's constant creative companion: that of the melodic and rhythmic intonations of the Russian *chastushka*.[3] The notion of the

---

[1] A. Lesnikov, 'Rodion Shchedrin', in *Sovetskaia Muzyka: Articles and Materials* (Moscow, Sovetskii Kompozitor, 1956), p. 281.

[2] Shchedrin had just finished his symphonic poem, *Story of a Real Man*, prior to his conservatory entrance. The work was instrumental in gaining him admission.

[3] The Russian *chastushka* is a two- or four-line folk verse, light, usually, but not always, humorous, and often topical. The double entendre is common. The *chastushka* style is akin to the American nonsense chants of children. But in its widespread use, content, and popularity, it has no equivalent, the limerick being, possibly, the closest form. The following is a *chastushka* used by Shchedrin in his opera *Not Just Love:*

V lesu rodilas' elochka,	In the woods was born a Christmas tree,
V lesu ona zhila-byla,	In the woods her life she spent,
Potom vliubilas' v mal'chika,	Then she fell in love with a little boy,
I v gorod s nim ushla.	And to town with him she went.

Or, in the double meaning used by Shchedrin in his opera:

In the country lived a merry lass,
With a beauty fully blown,
By and by, she loved a lively lad,
And she left with him for town.

chastushka as unifying creative material for large forms is a curious one, or even a contradictory one, but as an element of the piano suite, it was successful.

In the summer of 1951, Shchedrin participated in a folklore expedition—by now an ordinary and required part of conservatory curriculum. This, his first of two such trips, was to Byelorussia. There, he recorded folk songs which he used in the second movement of a piano quintet (1952) and in the vocal-symphonic suite *Twenty-Eight*[1] (1953). A second expedition, to Vologda, in 1953, provided further material which he used in the piano concerto (1954). The concerto is in four movements; the third movement is an unusual, for Shchedrin, passacaglia. In the first movement, Shchedrin develops and varies some children's songs. Two *chastushki* again provide the material for the fourth movement. From the inclusion of these simple tunes in the concerto stems the criticism of some of the Moscow sophisticates mentioned earlier. In truth, one must reconsider the definition of 'concerto' before making a judgment.

Shchedrin's first widely publicized work was the ballet *The hunchbacked horse*. This traditional children's tale was a natural for Shchedrin's *chastushka* style, although he uses it less here than in later works. As a ballet, however, it is much too long, for children and grown-ups alike. The work was written on commission for the Moscow Bolshoi Theatre and was started before Shchedrin's graduation from the conservatory (1955). The work was brought to a conclusion in 1956, with insufficient editing, and was presented at the Bolshoi. It was not successful and was withdrawn for more work, appearing at the Bolshoi again in 1960. An orchestral suite from the work had existed since at least 1956. It was performed in the United States by Leopold Stokowsky, to whom Shchedrin's music had been introduced on a visit to the Soviet Union. It is in suite form that the work is discussed here. The influence of simpler Prokofieff and early Stravinsky is obvious, that of Rimsky-Korsakov and Rachmaninov less so. The suite consists of nine parts, the last containing an Adagio and Finale. The orchestra is full size, with augmented percussion. Shchedrin exhibits two melodic styles beyond which, possibly for reasons of unity, he rarely goes. The first of these is an energetic, declamatory *marcato*. Example 1 shows three samplings from as many parts of the suite. The other style is lyric (Examples 2a and b) and repetitive, amounting at times to a brief ground bass (Example 2c). Very few ideas are sustained for more than a few repetitions: organic development is absent. The nine pieces are necessarily

[1] The 8th (Panifilov) rifle division defending Moscow in 1942 included twenty-eight heroes.

short, each painting a mood or singing a simple song. Dissonant harmonic combinations run to seconds and sevenths and are percussive rather than harmonically functional (Example 3). Although Shchedrin is impressively adroit with the orchestra, the work is still clearly founded on the piano idiom. From Shchedrin's score, a Martian could easily deduce that humans have ten fingers—the Martian would have to know about the piano, of course (Example 4). Shchedrin is, after all, one of the last of the three inbred generations of Soviet composers, to whom the keyboard is a creative essential. Shchedrin, and the rest of

Shchedrin. *The Humpback Horse Suite.*

Ex.1   *Marcato thematic style.*

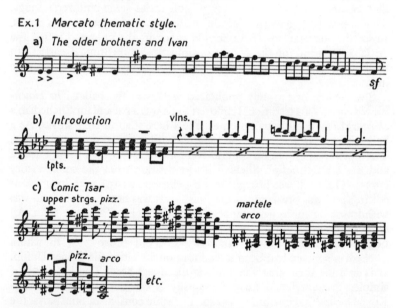

his Soviet generation probably understand the relationship of piano sound to orchestral sound better than any group from any other nation.[1] In the general absence of twentieth-century techniques, they must.

In *Konek-Gorbunok*, Shchedrin's faith in the Russian *chastushka* is exhibited largely in the quatrametric or pentametric near-ground.

[1] In belated academic recognition of the special importance of the technique of conversion from the palette of the piano to that of the keyboard, Soviet conservatories now divide the composition faculty into three sub-faculties: composition, theory, and orchestration. The practice of such division long preceded the academic adjustment.

Ex. 2

a) *Lyric thematic style*

upper strg.

vcl.

pizz.

b) *Revival of the Tsar-maiden.*

c) *Grief motive*

Example 2a is a remote example; Example 5 is typical. Elsewhere, real grounds and ostinati abound. The non-Russian listener is not able, in the suite, to pick out all the intonations of the *chastushka* without a guide—nor is it sensible to do so. In this sense, the ballet is severely,

Ex. 3   *Percussive dissonance (Comic Tsar).*

Ex. 4   *Pianistic idiom.*

Ex. 5   *Chastushka - based near ground.*

prohibitively national. But the ballet, and its suite, pushed Shchedrin to the forefront of his generation in a manner not seen since the emergence of the young Shostakovich, thirty years earlier.

Shchedrin has been a model of proper deportment for young Soviet composers. For those less orthodox, hence deprived of the machinery of success, he has offered righteous words of advice:

'The Party today, more than ever, is permeated with the spirit of Leninist humanism. The person, his destiny, his talent, his character— are the centre of attention [of the Party] ... and now I have become accustomed to this. But I cannot but marvel at and regret how the life of some members of my generation has taken shape. I will name some: Grant Grigorian, Aleksandr Kondriat'ev, Aleksei Artem'ev. They are rarely discussed now. And yet, in their time, in the years of conservatory study, these were the class leaders.'[1]

As one might expect, Shchedrin has the overall aspect of orthodox morality—and an apparent lack of real humour. Wit, however, he does possess: and once again we face his use of the *chastushka*. In a sense, Shchedrin's *chastushka* intonations and rhythms have always been close to Soviet music. Shchedrin has consolidated the process and given it a name. But the wry, simple, Shostakovichian plays on tonality, over a dominant-tonic bass; the Prokofieff 'shifts', potentially far ranging, but couched in four-bar logic; and even the Stravinsky rhythmic ploys, so complex on paper and in execution, but, for the ear, so closely tied to even, short phrases, may all be forbears of Shchedrin's *chastushka* style. This, of course, is the reason for comparing the young composer to these older masters. Shchedrin can be daring in his style: the harmonies of Shostakovich and Prokofieff have drawn criticism, at times, for being too harsh, too remote from the people. But now can any harmonic or rhythmic digression, no matter how wild, be unacceptable when it remains in the controlling embrace of the *chastushka*?

Shchedrin's *Ne tol'ko liubov'* (Not just love, 1961), is an exercise of his idiom, revealing both its possibilities and its failings.[2] The opera, to a libretto by V. Katanian, quotes actual folk tunes only twice. But the easily distilled intonation of the *chastushka* is heard throughout. The story is a variety of love triangle: Barbara, an older, single, seemingly stable woman, is kissed on an innocent lark by the younger, devil-may-care Volodia. Volodia is actually in love with, and intends to marry, Natasha. The innocent kiss brings out Barbara's latent feminine instincts. Volodia, in confusion, tries to straighten things out painlessly, and Natasha gets jealous. So far, the *chastushka* serves. The path to an operetta or an opera-farce is clear. But this is no operetta. The story goes beyond the triangle: Barbara is the efficient energetic president of the successful *kolkhoz*; Volodia is a youth of great socialist potential, just returned from study in the city, lightly contemptuous of farm life and

---

[1] Rodion Shchedrin 'Train the young assiduously', in *Sovetskaia Muzyka* (no. 1, 1962), p. 13.

[2] *Ne tol'ko liubov'* is no one-performance opera. Shchedrin has reaped the rewards for orthodoxy. Widely publicized, pushed by the USC, *Ne tol'ko liubov'* has received performances all over the RSFSR. Both it and *Konek-Gorbunok* are candidates for the most widely publicized work of a young, Soviet composer.

those who live it; Natasha is the eager, unspoiled, inwardly beautiful image of Soviet girlhood. Elsewhere are the healthy, productive *kolkhozniki*. Their work norms, Barbara's efficiency, Volodia's potential, and Natasha's purity are endangered by the flare of emotion—and, by God, the fields have not been sown. The *chastushka* no longer suffices, for these are powerful, dramatic elements. So long as the *kolkhozniki* dance and sing, so long as Volodia flirts, and so long as Natasha is merely piqued at his city ways, the *chastushka*, in Shchedrin's hands, is refreshing and communicative. But when the *kolkhozniki* become alarmed, when Volodia becomes deeply involved, and when Natasha truly suffers, the *chastushka* does not do the job. It could. Musical drama is full of examples where the simple is used to define the complex, the trivial to set off the serious, and the playful to delineate horror: While Cio-Cio-San commits suicide in the background, her child toys happily with a flag. The music of *Pélleas and Mélisande* swells to sweetness and beauty under the sordid triangle it supports. In one of opera's grisliest moments, in *Wozzeck*, Maria's child sings 'hop, hop, hop' on his hobby horse, as the horrified citizenry rush by him to the nearby lake wherein his questionable parentage has been solved by murder and drowning. And one remembers vividly, in the 1936 Shostakovich *Lady Macbeth*, the mocking, flippant, musical parodies that underlie the scenes of humiliation. Therein, perhaps, lies the clue to Shchedrin's lack of success—aside from popular success. Irony, hopelessness, the severely and personally emotional, the impractical, the grotesque, the perverse, and the illogical have been exiled from the Soviet musical scene, especially from the stage. Shchedrin can milk the *chastushka* dry, but he dare not pervert its basic function. As a result, the listener is not touched by the pathos of the scene between Barbara and Volodia at the cowbarn; instead, he is warmly assured by the music that all will have a successful ending. Not even Shchedrin can keep *chastushki* going incessantly. In between, there are extended moments of what must be called musical filler—chords, runs, and arpeggios. There is, in the opera, a good bit of spoken dialogue. And occasionally, the music slopes off disappointingly into brief, operatic stereotypes. Thus one hears Tosca, Ivan Susanin, Kashchei, and others: the unprepared auditor can easily, and mistakenly, fasten on the framework of derivation rather than the essentially trivial *chastushka*. Presumably, the Soviet audience is not unprepared. The opera has no overture. In Perm, if not elsewhere, the function of overture was filled by the recorded roar of tractors. Certain other touches demand notice: in two scenes, an offstage choir chants background words which occasionally retreat from meaning. A quartet of tractor drivers plays dominoes to staccato utterings like, 'Move!'

'Your turn,' and 'Let me think'. They are waiting out a rain, cleverly represented by a jazzy, pizzicato fugue.

Shchedrin, in spite of some unofficial criticism by the urban sophisticates, is a successful Soviet composer. Moreover, his use of the *chastushka* has opened rather than closed an escape hatch, as yet untried, but through which he can leave his cramped, creative environment. He is young, and it bears repeating that he has much to say—much that is quite serious. Maturity may bring him humour, without which little serious has ever effectively been said.

꙰꙰

CHAPTER 23

German Galynin

A unique feature of the Soviet educational system is the *detdom* (detskii dom) or children's home. Wars, revolution, collectiviza-tion, famine, and purges have created within the Soviet Union an unusually large number of parentless and illegitimate children.[1] The *detdoma*, which seek to correct this situation, were established on the basis of nationalized orphanages, and they became, in many instances sociological laboratories. The children receive, by law, regular schooling through their seventeenth year. There is a marked emphasis on the Arts, and there are special *detdoma* for children with an unusual musical gift.[2] The Soviet composer, German Galynin, was raised in a *detdom* in Tula, near Moscow.

German (Herman) Germanovich Galynin was born March 30, 1922 in Tula. Considering the times, it is altogether possible that his parents

[1] The official reasons for such orphanages is given in *Information USSR*, Macmillan, New York, 1962, page 410, as follows: '. . . child neglect . . . in pre-revolutionary Russia, . . . the frequency of poor harvests, . . . and the difficult conditions of life in towns gave rise to a situation where hundreds of thousands of children were roaming the countryside like beggars.' This source adds the post-revolutionary reasons of foreign intervention and civil war of 1918–20. Still, the number of *detdoma* in 1958 was 4,065 and the children therein num-bered 367,000, according to the same source.

[2] From their Soviet beginning (or rather, resumption) the function of the *detdoma* has been considered that of producing especially 'creative' adults. This is a traditional Russian conceit in the handling of parentless and illegitimate children that stems, probably, from well before Catherine's reign. But it was Catherine who, in 1763, issued a manifesto which put into practice the plan of Ivan Ivanovitch Betsky: the establishment of homes which would turn the (illegitimate) children into useful citizens, forming a new social class, which would enrich the arts, sciences, and professions. At the age of sixteen, boys would either continue in the homes as masters, or, given talent, could enter the Imperial Academy of Arts. The plan was a grisly failure: the homes became known as 'angel factories' because of the great mortality rate. (See Bernice Madison, 'Russia's illegitimate children, before and after the revolution' in *Slavic Review*, vol. XXII, no. 1, March 1963, p. 82).

died in the famine of the period of war communism. In any case, nothing is known of them. Galynin showed special musical promise. Although the *detdom* where he was raised was not one of the special musical ones, he found time to teach himself to play the balalaika, domra, and piano. In 1938, at the age of sixteen, he was sent by the authorities to Moscow for musical training.

Galynin's most impressive qualification seemed to be desire. Fiercely individualistic, he entered the music *uchilishche* attached to the Moscow Conservatory. He accepted his fellow students only as challenges to meet and overcome. He was a bit older than his classmates, and was rather far behind them in training. His ability with the balalaika and domra, he felt, was laughed at and he soon refused to play. Under the direction of Professor Sposobin, Galynin's desire helped him catch up with his class. He immediately plunged into composition: his first public performance was one of incidental music to Cervantes *Salamanskaia Peshchera* (Salaman Caves). This work was completed in his first year at the *uchilishche*, and, though predictably derivative, it showed amazing learning ability. He concentrated, however, on piano works. In these he sought constantly the most 'professional' trends: complex harmonies and textures, Scriabinesque melodic lines of infinite, rhapsodic length, and contrived imbalance of form. He disdained the lyricism of Russian melodic tradition as 'too simple'. In short, he was moving as far as he possible could from the domra and balalaika. If the influence of Scriabin was strong, so, occasionally, was that of Schumann, and Liadov. But, as the oldest of the young generation considered here, he still had some contact with the memories of the twenties and early thirties in music. By 1941, his graduation year from the *uchilishche*, he had put aside Scriabin and Liadov, and the influence of Prokofieff was emerging strongly. The idiom of Prokofieff's *Mimoletnosti* ('Fugitives') was increasingly discernible.

In 1941, prepared now for the conservatory, Galynin chose instead to enlist in the army. Attempts while in uniform at mass songs were unsuccessful, and his tendency since has been to avoid them as sincerely as he once approached them. He lead military *samodeiatel'nost'* groups until his mustering out in 1943.

He immediately entered the Moscow Conservatory and resumed his study of composition with Dmitrii Shostakovich. Under the latter's guidance, he continued to write for piano; a set of variations (1943), a suite (1944), a fourth piano sonata (1945—in one movement like the preceding three), and a concerto (1945–6). The last three of these were criticized subsequently as being formalistic: the concerto, dedicated to youth, was not performed until 1955. The sonata, still reflecting the influence of Prokofieff, had certain Bach-like organization and rhythms. In 1946–7 Galynin wrote a first string quartet. This was a highly chromatic, dissonant work, quite reminiscent of Shostakovich's Third Quartet, also written in 1946. Galynin employed curiously awkward ostinatos, and only the lyric third movement escaped condemnation later. A piano trio, written on the eve of the 1948 denunciations, remains unperformed. This is a neo-baroque experiment in polyphony. The movements are: I Prelude, II Toccata, III Passacaglia, and IV Fugue.

As an already well advanced pupil of Shostakovich's, Galynin was well covered by Zhdanov in 1948. The viciousness of the means employed for attacking all of Shostakovich's supposed weaknesses wreaked havov on some of his pupils, especially Boris Chaikovsky, Aleksandr Chugaev, and Galynin. Kabalevsky was chosen, in 1957, to quash the verdict:

'I cannot but recall how crudely and falsely the criticism in 1948 dealt with G. Galynin, whom we all—musicians and ordinary music lovers—, esteem now as one of the outstanding representatives of the young generation of Soviet composers. In the lead article of *Sovetskoe Iskusstvo* for February 21, 1948, it was said that G. Galynin, and with him two others—B. Chaikovsky and A. Chugaev—, had developed in their art (and all three were only twenty-some years old and were still studying at the conservatory!) the principles of anti-people formalism, and that their work "contradicts the spirit of the Soviet People!"'[1]

The immediate results, for Galynin, were a long stop to any performances, the loss of his teacher, and a hiatus in his student status which may have lasted as long as a year. He resumed at the reorganized Moscow Conservatory under Nikolai Miaskovsky. A suite for string orchestra, written in 1949, reveals a vast simplification of idiom. Still thoroughly personal, however, were his polyphonic texture and melodic laconicism.

Galynin's most famous work, and nearly his last, is the *Epic Poem* for orchestra. In 1950, the date of composition, Soviet composers were urgently prodded along certain paths: works tended to be strongly programmatic; harmonic idiom must be made immediately accessible; cantatas, oratorios and other vocal-symphonic genres were emphasized; contemporary, Soviet themes, ideas and images, saturated musical creativity; and the folk idiom must be used, as directly as possible. Galynin had considerably softened his harmonic idiom in the 1949 suite for string orchestra, but otherwise these quasi-directives were

[1] Kabalevsky, 'Tvorchestvo molodykh kompozitorov Moskvy' (Creativity of young Moscow composers), *Sovetskaia Muzyka*, no. 1, 1957, p. 5.

foreign to and extremely difficult for him. They were, in a sense, a negation, if not betrayal, of his training and of his past work. Galynin discarded as impossible the programme for his *Poem*. He likewise ignored contemporary 'Socialist' idioms and any of the vocal forms which abounded in the fifties. He accepted the simpler harmonic idiom and used, for the first time, Russian folk melodies. He was extremely careful in his choice. From two collections made by Balakirev in the nineteenth century, he chose four songs. From *30 Songs of the Russian people* (1900), he selected an intonation to an antique *bylina*, 'Kostriuk', a wedding song, and a religious song, 'Day of Judgment'. From *A collection of Russian folk songs* (1866), he chose the dance song 'Stop, beloved dancers', a *khorovod*.[1] These four themes are used as the expository material of a sonata-allegro form. The development is short, and the principal theme, the *bylina* tune (Example 1), does not figure in it.

Galynin. *Epic Poem.*

Ex.1   *Principal theme (bylina).*

Instead, this theme, and its parts, is developed extensively in the exposition itself. The development actually takes the form of repetition, not unlike the vocal progress of the *bylina*, itself, and is rather disappointingly handled. The possibilities for polyphonic setting are all but ignored, entering tentatively only near the end of that theme's statement (Example 2). The secondary subject is, dramatically, the combination and contrast of the gay wedding song with the religious chant (Example 3a and b). The chant later sounds alone, slower and in the organum style sometimes associated with Russian chant (Example 4). One would ordinarily perceive the fourth tune (round dance) as a codetta of rather large proportions. But its entrance is accompanied by the only significant key change (four flats) of the exposition (Example 5). This area is

---

[1] Khorovod—a ring of dancers, or a ring dance.

Ex. 2 *Polyphonic setting*

Ex.3 *Thematic elements.*

a) *Wedding song*

b) *Russian chant form.*

etc.

x.4 *Chant in organum*

Ex.5 *Round dance*

Ex. 6 *Rhythmic transformation*

Slowly ♩=66

10*

extensive, changes key again (to one flat), and becomes a rare example of light, chamber orchestration. The development leans heavily on the rhythmic implications of the wedding dance and shortly leads to the recapitulation. The energies have accumulated and the principal subject has undergone considerable rhythmic transformation (Example 6). The various orchestral groups are handled independently, giving a poly-rhythmic effect. The wedding song is also transformed—it is now a bit slower and less lusty than previously. The work closes, at a dynamic level of triple piano, with suggestions of the religious chant as background.

Galynin was congratulated on having 'overcome the religiosity of the "Day of Judgment" theme',[1] but this is patently an ideological overdose of protesting. The composer made a minimum of concessions, for 1950, but the work succeeded and was awarded a second degree Stalin Prize in 1951.

By 1951, however, there were indications that Galynin could stomach no more compromise. Late in that year, Galynin's oratorio setting of Gorky's tale on *Death and the Maiden* was published. It was published in piano score only and in a limited edition. Moreover, it seems to have been published in spite of the composer's protests. His ostensible reason for protesting was that he was not yet satisfied with it, and that it needed further revision.[2] Otherwise, Galynin became one of the silent composers of the fifties. A footnote to an article on Galynin by E. Dobrynina reads, in part, 'Because of a serious disease, prohibiting the author from return to work'. In 1957, or late 1956, a work, a violin sonata, was heard on a young composers' forum. Otherwise there seems to be no filling the prolonged gap in Galynin's creative activity. He still lives (1957) in Moscow, apparently with some support of the Union of Soviet Composers.

[1] By B. Shteinpress in 'Epicheskaia Poema', *Sovetskaia Simfonicheskaia Myzyka*, collected articles (Moscow: Muzgiz, 1955), p. 443.
[2] It is not at all unusual in the Soviet Union for composers' works to be published absolutely without their knowledge. The publishing houses (Muzgiz, and the more recent Sovetskii Kompozitor) work, as do all Soviet production facilities, to fulfil and overfulfil quotas. Within each establishment, quotas are redistributed on a competitive, incentive pay basis. There have been numerous occasions of sub-editors approaching teachers for a sheaf of student works. These are duly published, and the composer first becomes aware of it when the publication appears in the network of music stores. Officially, the practice is frowned on.

CHAPTER 24

Otar Taktakishvili

Georgian music, and very likely the whole of Georgian culture, is at a crossroads. It has been mentioned that the path of music could, from this juncture, be absorbed by russification.[1] Or it could, based on a rich and varied folk art, and on an individual tradition, become an independent art, with a certain national integrity. In either case, of course, nationalism results, and one would anticipate a still higher stage of development—that of emergence from the nationalistic nineteenth century into the contemporary world of music. Under the Soviet system of checks, the latter cannot yet be considered. But the present choice of paths will determine whether the move towards maturity will be made as an absorbed part of the colourless Soviet mass, or in parallel, but independent, development with the Great Russian tradition. Otar Taktakishvili's is the generation in whose hands Georgia's musical destiny lies, and Taktakishvili, successful and honoured beyond most of those of his generation, is the most important composer of the group. Taktakishvili's music is not 'contemporary' in any Western sense. The experience of Balanchivadze in the late forties has clearly indicated that the time is not ripe. One seeks, then, for other evidence in the work of Taktakishvili.

Otar Vasil'evich Taktakishvili was born July 27, 1924 in Tiflis. Somewhat unusual is that he remained in Tiflis/Tbilisi: there he came of age, and there he spent his conservatory years. He did not have the Northern (usually Moscow) experience so central in the lives of most of his contemporaries. Georgia, especially in Taktakishvili's early years, was a land of unique political and cultural situation: It was, perhaps, the least resigned member of the Union[2]; its fertility and potential productivity caused it to draw more than its share of central authority; the leader of the Soviet Union was himself a Georgian, and, until the

[1] See Chapters 11 and 21.
[2] A mass, anti-Bolshevik uprising took place in 1924, the year of Takakishvili's birth.

mid-thirties, when he became head of the Soviet secret police, the Caucasus power was Georgian Lavrenty Beria, yet Stalin and Beria were not content with Georgian progress[1]; although Georgian musicians were plentiful, Russian and foreign leaders frequently appeared in key positions in the mid-thirties[2]; and Georgia shared with the other distinct minorities the dilemma of "Soviet nationalism".

This was Taktakishvili's milieu. His only contact with the pre-Soviet past was by hearsay. He was seventeen when the Germans invaded the Soviet Union, and during that conflict he enrolled in the Tbilisi Conservatory. He studied with Sergei Barkhudarian. In 1946 while still a student, he entered a contest to compose a Georgian national anthem. Most of Georgia's leading composers were also entered in the contest—a control factor in the carefully nursed surge of Soviet patriotism after the war. Taktakishvili won the contest, and he was given some measure of publicity—and a condescending pat on the back from his older contemporaries. The course of Georgian, and Soviet, music in 1946 was not toward heroic anthems.

The young composer graduated from the conservatory the following year. His diploma work was a concerto for cello and orchestra—a work of no special merit, apparently, since it is invariably passed over in discussion of the Soviet concerto. A 1947 string trio is unplayed and unpublished. So, in 1948, when the modern idioms and experimentation of the older composers were established as bad manifestations in Soviet music, Taktakishvili's national anthem was again acclaimed. Again, Georgian music was in a unique position. For some reason, the Party had chosen the opera, *The Great Friendship*, by a Georgian, Vano Muradeli, as a departure point for its far-reaching criticism of 1948. They could have chosen any of a hundred works. Muradeli was an untalented, pot-boiling scribbler of vapid, popular tunes; his opera was totally undistinguished, although its libretto inadvertently ignored a current trend in thinking about certain minority groups of the North Caucasus. There was nothing significant about the choice of Muradeli but his nationality: Georgian. This served warning on composers of the peripheral republics, and on Georgian composers in particular. Taktakishvili was safe on two counts: he had not written enough to become any sort of target, and his one successful work was the prize winning anthem. On the strength of that work, in a genre that seemed to satisfy all the

[1] In 1937 Georgian Party leader Budu Mdivani and others were purged. Gregory Ordzhonikidze, apparently because he opposed Mdivani's execution, also died—but with eulogies.
[2] Daniel Sternberg, a Pole with Viennese training (and now the director of a School of Music in Texas) was conductor at the Tbilisi opera in 1937–8.

new creative dicta, Taktakishvili's name was rushed to the top of the list of Soviet Georgian composers. It was a curious position. He was only twenty-four years old, had written very little, and was still a graduate student at the Tbilisi Conservatory under Barkhudarian. Yet, upon his shoulders was thrust much of the responsibility for the future of Georgian music.

Taktakishvili's emergence, then, as a symphonist is important evidence in the search for the path of Georgian musical development. That he should emerge as a symphonist would have been a bad guess as late as 1948. Until then, his only work in the larger form was his diploma work, the 1947 violin concerto. Moreover, Barkhudarian, judging by his own works, was not sympathetic with the symphonic idiom. Finally, that any Soviet composer not already committed should choose a symphony as a point of departure, in 1949, is unusual. That genre had been labelled ineffective in the musical building of socialism in the discussions of 1948 and thereafter. It is not surprising that, save for the choice of genre, Taktakishvili's First Symphony seems to follow most of the creative canons of the late forties. The work is not programmatic, yet the listener can easily discern the heroic, life-asserting imagery. Specifically, the four-movement work opens with a heroic fanfare which is heard throughout the other movements. Its guise is determined by the nature of the movement; thus, in the third movement, the scherzo, it appears as a dance. Its role is especially great in the first movement, where it functions structurally. It is used in the development as contrapuntal material. The main theme of the first movement is also everywhere present. During the last, quiet part of the subordinate theme, its motivic elements supply a constant punctuation. This main theme, in a modal shift to the major, supplies the coda material. The second movement, Andante, is a nocturne-poem. The solo 'cello, on the background of strings *tremolo*, handles an improvisatory melody—a reference to Arob solo technique. In the main section, an oboe solo sounds a folk-like melody which is gradually transformed into a broad, lyrical elegy. Dance motives and rhythms govern the third movement. Here the elegiac melodies of the second movement are further transformed. A conscious attempt is made to duplicate the sound of Georgian folk instruments. This has become a tradition in Georgian symphonic music, especially in Scherzos like this. The finale (rondo-sonata) is short and bright. It functions as a coda to the whole, and the opening fanfare again figures heavily. Taktakishvili does not escape pomposity in the work. This is felt particularly in the first and fourth movements, the latter being a sort of summary of the former. The work was awarded a third-degree Stalin Prize in 1951.

That same year, the composer joined the Party—a rather more usual thing for Transcaucasians than for Russians.

Taktakishvili had begun teaching counterpoint and orchestration at the conservatory while still a student, in 1949. In 1952 he became the artistic director of the Georgian State Chorus, an organization with which he had worked since 1947. Also in 1952, he began a successful conducting career with a programme which included his own works. He had followed his First Symphony with the symphonic poem

Taktakishvili. *Piano Concerto.*

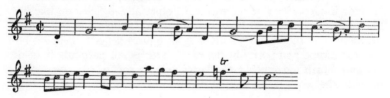

Ex.2 IV *Variation theme.*

Samgori in 1950. Well publicized at the time, it has been well forgotten now. A far more important work is the piano concerto (1951). Here Taktakishvili set about to duplicate his First Symphony. The work is long, in four movements, and the subdued role of the piano suggests a concerto-symphony. The work has no programme, the successive parts contrast severely and naively, and an introductory, fanfare-like melody serves as unifying material throughout the work. These elements have been noted in the First Symphony as well. The two themes of the first movement are pictorially simple (Example 1), causing one to wonder if some programme might not have been in mind. The first of these themes does leitmotiv duty throughout the work, as in the First Symphony. The Scherzo (II) is based on, without quoting, folk song intonations. Here again is the orchestral imitation of a Georgian folk instrument—the *chonguri*. The Andante (III) is song-like and tends toward the Phrygian mode. The finale (Allegro Molto) is a short summation of the work in the form of a variation on another melody of extreme simplicity (Example 2).

Taktakishvili followed the concerto with a *Shutochnaia* (Divertissement) and *Nocturne* for 'cello and piano, and the capriccio *Homeland Tunes* (Rodnye napevy) for orchestra (both 1952). In 1953 he wrote the incidental music to the Georgian play *Steel*, and three miniatures for orchestra, 'Lyric', 'Sachidao', and 'Picture'. These and subsequent works reveal, more than anything else, Taktakishvili's apparent lack of interest in anything resembling innovation. Soviet critics never tire of pointing out Taktakishvili's solid realistic basis, his appreciation for the Russian classics, and his 'rational' harmonies. Some go one plaintive step further:

'Taktakishvili is a stranger to . . . innovation as such. The formative elements in his art are directed toward the truthful depiction of the images of the present day.

However, hasn't the time come for a widening of this circle of images, and also of those genres to which the creative attention of the composer is directed? And, in connection with that, doesn't the necessity arise for a search for new expressive means of enriching (his) musical language[1]

This impressive orthodoxy leads one to the question of folk usage in Taktakishvili's music. City born and city trained, Taktakishvili may be expected to be influenced by the urban folk music heritage—the Cartaline-Kakhetin idiom of Eastern Georgia. This, it may be remembered, tends to modal monophony. Thus, sudden chromatic changes, an

---

[1] A. Tsulukidze, 'The creative path of Otar Taktakishvili', *Soviet Music: articles and materials* (Sovetskii Kompozitor: Moscow, 1956), p. 193.

outgrowth of modal shifts, are quite common in Taktakishvili's music. Moreover, modal alteration and alteration often function for tonal modulation. In the third movement of the First Symphony, for instance, the overall modulatory plan is, roughly, E. Dorian, D. Mixolydian, B. Mixolydian, and B. Aeolian. These are not isolated tonal blocks: cross references in the form of altered notes, especially C-C sharp, G-G sharp, and D-D sharp, often recall the temporarily abandoned modes. It is not to be expected that these tonal-modal qualities will be recognizable by the auditor as Georgian, even, perhaps, by a Georgian. Presumably, however, there is some merit in the fact that they *are* Georgian derived, and not mere copies of what they *do* sound like: the Vienna and St Petersburg schools of the 1880s and 1890s.

Although a Western Georgian musical dialect, the parallelism of the Guri musical idiom is also occasionally found in Taktakishvili's music, as it is, indeed, in the music of most Georgian composers. This powerful, but dangerous element is handled gingerly in Taktakishvili's music, usually amounting to chains of parallel triads, four or five in a sequence. In an idiom otherwise free of parallelism, its appearance must be reserved for moments of special stress or imagery.

The Second Symphony has been heralded as a departure, and it is— for Georgian music. This is Georgia's first lyrico-dramatic symphony. It is not programmatic, but Soviet musical imagery is so stock, and Soviet musical vocabulary is such, that a writer can say of the Second Symphony,

'. . . (it is) a psychological darama (the first in Georgian symphonic music), which reveals the complex inner world of the Soviet man, his struggle for the lofty humanitarian ideal. Boldly delineating the inner contradictions in the figure of our contemporary, the composer at the same time has suffused his hero with active, wilful, and hopeful beginnings, showing him in close inter-relationship with reality.'[1]

It is precisely such statements that bewilder the Western reader and listener, and that show that the moorings of musical vocabulary have been slipped; although which is the pier and which the ship adrift is too early to decide. The music shows that Taktakishvili has moved obliquely from the position of the First Symphony and the piano concerto. This is not a leitmotiv symphony. The contrast of parts is not so slavish. Indeed, it lies more in the opposition of the introductory material to the two main themes rather than between the latter. The incessantly 'noble' character has relaxed markedly. This is what is meant by a

[1] A. Tsulukidze, 'Paths of development of symphonism', *Georgian Musical Culture (GMK)* (Muzgiz: Moscow, 1957), p. 253.

'lyrico-dramatic' symphony. The emotionalism is peculiarly Tschaikovskian (Example 3), especially in melodic handling. The emotional
development seems to culminate in the adagio third movement, after a
second movement scherzo. The finale is a noisy, disappointing after-
thought, which seems to realize the grim, glib promise of the old, 1946
anthem, and nothing more.

Taktakishvili. *2nd Symphony*.

Ex. 3 *I. Main theme.*

Ex. 4 *Mtsyri confined.*

A trumpet concerto (1954) was insignificant but for the choice of
instrument. A Concertino for violin and small orchestra was Taktakishvili's first venture into orchestral economy. As it is, the Concertino
affords a compact view of Taktakishvili's orchestral thinking. The work
is scored for two flutes, oboe, clarinet, strings, and the solo violin. A
harp is used only in the second of three movements.

A further departure for Taktakishvili was the symphonic poem *Mtsyri*.
The poem is based on the Lermontov work and follows the tale of the
hero's monastery confinement, his yearning for freedom, his flight to
that freedom, his reconfinement, and his death. The novelty is that this
is, of course, a programme work. There is, too, a certain breakaway
from Taktakishvili's melodic predictability. The theme depicting
Mtsyri's musings within the atmosphere of his initial confinement has a
halting, though diatonic, effectiveness (Example 4).

If Taktakishvili's productivity has fallen off since the mid-fifties, it is
due in large measure to his joining the privileged ranks of those Soviet
composers who travel, usually in delegations, as representatives of
their country's culture. Taktakishvili is adept at Soviet critical jargon,

although he rattles if off with that special Transcaucasian air of one who is not listening to what he is saying. By his words alone, his judgment would be a severe one.

The musical elements that occur in (one can hardly say 'that distinguish') Taktakishvili's music are the mild modality, the occasional parallelism, and the folk instrument imitation. These are supposedly folk elements, but they are not to the non-Georgian ear. These are, to repeat, easily acceptable as nineteenth-century sounds. Taktakishvili, and Georgian music if Taktakishvili is the weathervane, is at an 1880 stage of development, i.e. twenty to thirty years behind most Russian music. But the position has been assumed here that a value judgment cannot be made on the basis of being either old fashioned or *avant-garde*. The question remains, is it good music; and the answer must be, in Taktakishvili's case, that it is. Moreover, the fact that Georgian music, as represented by Taktakishvili, seems antiquely russified is misleading. Taktakishvili is not russianized. He does not write with the opportunistic cynicism of the Sviridov's and Khrennikov's. He has probably taken a giant step backward, back from the creative impasse of Andrei Balanchivadze, to lay the ground for an advance. Moreover, Georgia has had the experience of such as Balanchivadze. Taktakishvili has made it possible, if the time comes, for another, younger generation to make up the eighty years in their lifetime. After all, Russia herself, between 1834 and 1890, caught up with a Western musical development of over six centuries.

༄༅༅

CHAPTER 25

Kara Karaev

Kara Karaev (Kara Abdul'faz ogly Karaev) is the most critical figure in contemporary Azerbaidzhanian music if not in the music of the peripheral republics of the Soviet Union in general. He represents, as the most talented of his countrymen, the accomplishment of Soviet policy and thinking in the minority republic area. He was well born (the son of an eminent Baku doctor who was struggling at the time of Karaev's birth for an independent Azerbaidzhan), well grounded by L. Rudol'f and Gadzhibekov in Baku, and well trained under Shostakovich in Moscow. Only momentarily sharing the 1948 clouds of suspicion with Shostakovich, he joined the Party in 1949 and returned geographically, spiritually and, as well as he could, musically, to his homeland.

If his fight for a style has resulted in a compromise between rather than a synthesis of his Western training and his national *melos*, one must still admit the popular impact of such works as *Leili and Medzhnun*, *The Seven Beauties*, and some others.

Karaev was born on February 5, 1918, in Baku. His family enjoyed membership in the small, Western-oriented circle of Azerbaidzhan enlightenment. A marked early talent,[1] a strong social friendship with the many-faceted Uzeir Gadzhibekov and a family respect for the craft and profession soon placed Karaev into a programme of musical training. As a class privilege he sat in on courses and lectures at the Baku music school while simultaneously finishing the regular school for one of his station. He improvised 'wildly'[2] at the piano and took more

---

[1] A. Lilienfel'dt in 'Kara Karaev' in the composium *Molodye Mastera Iskusstva* (Moscow-Leningrad, Gosizdat, 1938), p. 255, says, 'Nurtured on European literature and in the European image, Karaev saw the world through a prism of musical images and loved everything that was lacking in the (middle) East.'

[2] Lilienfeldt (*op. cit.*) enlarges on one of Karaev's improvisations: 'This was an unrepeatable improvisation in which a babbling brook in the sandy steppes alternated with victory cries of the Indians taking scalps from the palefaces (and

conservative piano lessons from G. G. Sharaev. In 1935 he entered the Baku Conservatory, studying composition with Rudol'f. The continued contact with Gadzhibekov is not clear until 1938. That year was one of intense musical activity, political activity, and of important decisions for Karaev. The festival of Azerbaidzhanian music was soon to start in Moscow. For it Karaev was preparing a *Poem of Joy*. When Gadzhibekov joined the Party (in 1938 when he became director of the conservatory) Karaev joined the Komsomol. Under the influence of Magomaev's *Nergiz* (1934) and Gadzhibekov's *Ker-Ogly* (1937), and at the urging of Biul'-Biul' (Mamedov), director of the conservatory's folk music workshop, Karaev began to immerse himself in the folk music of Azerbaidzhan.[1] During an expedition in 1938, on which he met the rarely seen Chaban mountain tribesmen, Karaev made further decisions which resulted, on his return home, in reworking the *Poem of Joy*, and in the creation of an extended cantata for chorus, orchestra, and dancers, *Song of the Heart*.[2] The dedication was 'To the great Stalin', and the poetry reflects not only that dedication, but Karaev's thinking at the time. Something of the feverish hat-doffing of Soviet artists in the politically foreboding year of 1938 is also reflected:

We, flowers nurtured by thee (Stalin), bring with us the rapture and happiness of the broad fields of Azerbaidzhan.

Thy name implants in us joy; with gladness the whole world rises, young and old alike saying 'Long live our great leader!'

Thou, thyself, are the happiness of the peoples, the great eye of the people; your name lies on our souls and every word of glory—it is thee.

The work is direct and anthem-like (Example 1). Performances since 1953 have seen certain changes in the words. The cantata ended the Azerbaidzhanian festival in Moscow in a performance at which Stalin was present.

Later in the same year, Karaev was brought to Moscow for further study. On the recommendation of Rudol'f he studied with two Taneev

---

with the) snarls of terrible *bagiry* with the weeping of Iaroslavna; and which finished with powerful bass-note thunder which portrayed the Battle of Borodino.'

[1] It must be remembered that this was no easy task. Sifting out what is Azerbaidzhanian from what is Persian and Turkish never concerned the pioneer —Gadzhibekov, but was now very important to Soviet authority. See p. 73 for an example of the lengths gone to in 'correcting' Gliere's Azerbaidzhanian opera, *Shakh-Senem*.

[2] *Pesnia Serdtsa*. *Sovetskie kompozitory* gives the title *Pesn' Serdets*, i.e. the more formal word for 'song' (as in *Song of Solomon*) and the plural genitive of the second noun.

pupils: composition with Anatolii Aleksandrov, and orchestration with Vasilenko. But the freshness and relative freedom of Shostakovich and the Leningrad school attracted him through the hectic, disjointed, prewar, and early war years. During part of this time, 1941–2, when Moscow was partially evacuated, Karaev directed the fledgling Baku Philharmonic Association. The years 1938–43 were, apparently, not good years for creative activity. The scholarly fugues, unfinished concertos, and free-wheeling piano rhapsodies are none of them published. A string quartet (op. 20) has been lost. An *Azerbaidzhanian Suite* for orchestra (1939) received a performance at the Baku Philharmonic just prior to Karaev's assuming the directorship of that organization.

Karaev. *Pesnia serdtsa.*

Ex. 1 *Theme.*

Karaev. *Veten.*

Ex. 2 *Mardan's aria.*

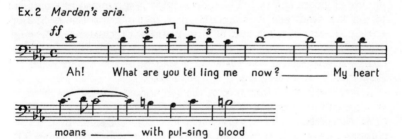

Karaev's outspoken admiration for Shostakovich and the natural, for the time, assumption that Shostakovich was blazing the trail of Soviet music had their logical outcome in 1943 when Shostakovich joined the staff of the Moscow Conservatory and Karaev made the arrangements to study with him. It seems essential in understanding Karaev and his music to appreciate the grip Shostakovich had on him before their association, the classical master-apprentice relationship of their four years together, and the mark left on the younger composer by the older. Shostakovich is, surprisingly, one of the few Soviet composers really to understand classical techniques and teaching as opposed to the usual Soviet romanticism in these areas. Karaev, and many others who made the switch to Shostakovich's tutelage at this time, learned to compose away from the piano. At the same time, the keyboard as teacher of history and theory became important.

One of Karaev's first works exhibiting the Shostakovich influence was his First Symphony in B minor.[1] As Karagicheva points out[2] this two-movement work belongs to those at least partly generated by the commotion surrounding Shostakovich's Seventh Symphony: Khachaturian's Second, Popov's Second, Prokofieff's Fifth, Miaskovsky's Twenty-second, Twenty-third, and Twenty-fourth, and a number of others. The Karaev symphony, though youthful, was, and still is, his most complex, most uncompromising work. The first movement is a stock formal item of two classically contrasting themes. The development is a clever and forceful demonstration of the formidable accomplishments in technique once typical of the 'Shostakovich' school. A sharply dissonant fugato is one of the episodes in this development. The second movement, Lento Moderato, represents a formal departure. The andante, scherzo and finale of conventional four-movement form all seek expression in an extended set of six symphonic variations. Radical changes of tempo, orchestration, and texture, and even harmonic usage, portray what was subsequently criticized as an unrelieved picture of gloom and evil. The movement is programmed as a requiem to the war dead[3] and it is precisely here that one encounters Shostakovich. There is much use of dry, ostinato percussion, of leaping, grotesque melodic imagery, of 'tough' orchestral sounds. Even in the comparatively restful last variation a solo horn and violin pedal 'B' are joined by a tenth-space 'b' in the piccolo.

Before the first performance of the symphony, Karaev was at work, with his countryman and fellow student, Gadzhiev, on the opera *Veten* (The Motherland). This work tends to contradict some of the conclusions one would reach in an analysis of the symphony alone. The story concerns the return, on leave, from the 1943 front of the hero

[1] *Symphony No. 1 in B minor*, subtitled 'In memory of the heroes of the Great Fatherland (Second World) War', was finished in 1943; its first performance was in Tbilisi, December 25, 1944. It has not been published.

[2] Liudmilla Vladimirovna Karagicheva, *Kara Karaev* (Moscow: Sovetskii Kompozitor, 1960, 297 pp., including list of works, bibliography, no index), p. 27.

[3] The epigraph: 'Eternal glory to the heroes fallen in the battles for freedom and independence of our Motherland.'

Aslan to his native Azerbaidzhanian kolkhoz. With his Russian travelling companion, Major Sergeev, he tells of Soviet heroism, whereupon many of the young men and women decide to enlist voluntarily for the front.[1] Among them are Aslan's beloved, Dil'ber, and the extremely reluctant Mardan. The latter is simply not interested in anything outside Azerbaidzhan and is, moreover, jealous of Aslan. At the front, first Dil'ber and Major Sergeev are surrounded. They escape to the partisans, and Mardan is captured. His newly awakened Soviet patriotism helps him resist all efforts by his captors to make him betray the partisans. The partisans and Soviet troops ring the prison compound. The Nazi officer, in desperation, mortally wounds Mardan, but is himself shot by Aslan. Mardan dies with a final call to the incoming Soviet soldiers to fight on to a victorious end for the independence of the Motherland, and they march on, presumably to do so.

Here Karaev, with Gadzhiev, makes an essay into his folk idiom. The essay is unimportant. Neither here nor later does Karaev actually quote folk tunes. Rather, a conscious application, to Romantic Western style, of certain characteristics of the raga-like Azerbaidzhan melodic patterns, in the manner of Asaf'ev, is used. The aria of the co-hero, Mardan, shows characteristics of the Azer *mugami*,[2] *shushter* and *chargakh* (Example 2), although one is also reminded of the conventional Western harmonic minor scale. Moreover, referring to this example, it must be remembered that its 'characteristic' augmented second is more the exception than the rule in the seventy-odd *mugami* recognized by Soviet authorities. The opera, philosophically and historically, is an attempt at synthesis of the Russian and the Azerbaidzhanian. Thus we find the same augmented second colouring the first-act aria of the Russian major Sergeev. The generally positive images of the members of the 'Soviet side', with injections of quasi-national musical specifics, are broadly opposed both in specifics and inception, to the 'Fascist side'. Here is a basic opposition in image type characterized in Russian by the words 'skvoznoe' and 'kontrskvoznoe'.[3]

---

[1] Apparently some Azerbaidzhanian sympathies tended to be pro-German or, at least, anti-Russian. This was not untypical for the Transcaucasus, but the extent of the feeling will probably never be known. By now it is clear that the severe punitive action taken by the central government was grossly inappropriate to the 'crime'. Nikita Krushchev has covered this topic in discussing Stalin's crimes.

[2] A discussion of Azer *mugami* begins in the chapter on Uzeir Gadzhibekov.

[3] 'Skvoznoe'—'kontrskvoznoe', in this case 'open' and 'closed', or 'penetrable' and 'impenetrable': In the present context a distinction between positive and negative portrayal first developed on the Russian stage by Stanislavsky and in music by Asaf'ev. *Skvoznoe* action and imagery is the result of open analysis of

Whereas the musical specifics of Mardan, Aslan, Sergeev, etc., combine in a positive whole, the opposing fascists are seen only through an ominous haze of sound established before the advent of the evil-doers themselves. At least that is the theory. One is reminded, by this formula, as well as by much of *Veten's* music, of the musical formulas for motion pictures of low quality. A Stalin Prize was awarded the work.

In 1946 Karaev finished the conservatory and returned to Baku. His diploma work was the *Second Symphony*.[1] The work, at first hailed as 'an outstanding event in the musical life of Azerbaidzhan',[2] was too close to the 1948 shoals not to be wrecked thereon as 'the fruits of the pernicious influence of formalism'.[3] The work makes self-conscious use of *mugam* types (modified *bayati-shiraz* and *chargakh*), but achieves an idiom thereby closer to the First Symphony than to *Veten*. Although roughly handled in the 1948 discussions[4] and seldom played now, much of the symphony was salvageable and was, indeed, used in the forthcoming ideologically acceptable *Leili and Medzhnun*. The second subject of the second movement is the 'outline' of the second subject of the tone poem, just as a *mugam* is the outline for a melody. The symphony's scherzo is likewise a melodic and rhythmic forerunner of Karaev's mass scenes in *Seven Beauties*.

In the critical years 1947 to 1953, Karaev's most popular and widely played works were written. These are the aforementioned *Leili and Medzhnun* and *Seven Beauties*. He started this period professionally as a teacher at the Baku Conservatory, and creatively with a string quartet (his second) dedicated to Shostakovich. The latter, written in 1947 was dealt a death blow by Zhdanov. In this work the *mugam* usage becomes more direct (Example 3), but Karaev's inclination to the 'minor' (i.e. with augmented second) *mugami* is even more strongly marked. This was also the year of the Song of Happiness, a work for soprano, chorus,

---

characters and their interaction: the sum creates the imagery. *Kontrskvoznoe* action starts with a strong, impersonal, negative image, using that as a source to colour each new 'evil' force as it enters the negative embrace. Thus the negative personality, no matter how noble this entrance, is easily recognizable as the villain; and the positive hero is seen as a generating source for goodness.

[1] Karaev's *Second Symphony* was first performed in 1946 in Baku with L. Ginsburg conducting the Philharmonic. It is unpublished.

[2] Zul'fugar Niazi in *Vyshka*, December 12, 1946.

[3] Iurii Keldysh in 'Porochnye metody raboty Moskovskoi Konservatorii' (The depraved methods of working of the Moscow Conservatory), *Sovetskoe Iskusstvo*, February 28, 1948.

[4] It is well to bear in mind that criticism of Karaev and many of his fellow students was simply another angle of attack at Shostakovich himself. Karaev received personal attention when he returned to Baku.

and orchestra reminiscent of, but 'tougher' than, the 1938 *Song of the Heart*.

Among the many mass works of this period were the *March of Greeting* (1948) dedicated to the thirtieth anniversary of the Red Army, and the *March of the Baku Oilworkers* (1951). Both works are for band. On the occasion of the 800th anniversary of the birth of Nizami

Karaev. *String Quartet.*

Ex. 3 *Mugam usage.*

Giandzhev, the 'Azerbaidzhanian' classical bard,[1] Karaev undertook the composition of the symphonic poem *Leili and Medzhnun*.[2] Though the work is a symphonic poem it is clearly conceived as a ballet suite written to no ballet. The second, *Seven Beauties*, suite was indeed followed by a ballet (1952), and it would be surprising if *Leili and*

[1] Nizami Jamaluddin, or Nizamuddin Abu Mohammed Elyas ibn Yusus (*c.* 1135 to 1203, perhaps 1217) was Persia's leading romantic poet. This is a routine case of Soviet peripheral historical chauvinism. Nizami, though he lived in what is now Kirovabad, was Persian (Iranian) and wrote in Persian. The Azers are, of course, Turkic, and Azerbaidzhani is usually classified as a Turkish regional variant. Both of Karaev's major works (those mentioned) are from Nizami's couplet settings of Persian folk tales.

[2] Usually in English: Leila and Majnun: a famous 'Romeo and Juliet' story in Eastern folklore. It was the subject for Uzeir Gadzhibekov's opera, *Leili and Medzhnun*, considered in the Soviet Union as the first Azerbaidzhanian opera.

Medzhnun were not so treated.[1] In that area of a composer's mental process that cannot be reached through biographies or musical analysis one suspects, in Karaev's case, the ballet is written. The suite is tri-partite, the separate parts being well-worked-out wholes, divided by nadirs of action in the Tschaikovsky manner. The three suite movements also fall roughly into sonata-allegro form; the key plan is classically interesting in this regard:

> Part I   (Introduction)
>   b minor—f minor—b minor
> Part II   (Exposition and recapitulation[2])
>   Subj. A, e minor—g minor
>   Subj. B, C major
>   Subj. A (return) e minor
>   B (return) E major
> Part III (Coda)
>   e minor

Three 'images' provide the musical stock. The first is Fate—evil medieval fate—the bane of young lovers (Example 4). This imagery dominates the first, introductory part. The second part, the longest, shows a musical return to the *'mugam'* style (Example 5). The earlier form of this theme in the Second Symphony has been mentioned. A good number of words have been printed arguing the imagery of this theme: is it Medzhnun's? Is it his expression of love for Leila? If it matters at all, it would seem to be the composer's essay, in music, to accomplish all that the folk tale did when the hero's real name, Gais, is changed to Medzhnun. The latter means 'obsessed by' or 'insane from love'. Perhaps this music and the nature of the conversation about it reveal the gulf growing between Karaev and Shostakovich. The real 'love' image (Example 6) serves as subordinate or coordinate theme to the one just discussed. Beginning brightly, elements of sadness are thematically injected (Example 7), and after the second pause in action the theme of tragedy introduces the third section (Example 8). The introduction serves as a dominant and the subordinate theme (via the C major—a minor analogy) as subdominant, yielding a total scheme: V I IV I. The work was and is frequently played and was awarded a Stalin Prize in 1948.[3]

[1] In 1947, in Stalinabad, Sergei Balasanian's (1902–) ballet, *Leilie Medzhnun*, was premiered. This timing and the sharp, official criticism Balasanian received, may be the reasons for Karaev's postponing further work on the ballet.

[2] A true development is lacking.

[3] The 'degree' of the Prize for *Leili and Medzhnun* is nowhere specified. The previous Prize, shared with Gadzhiev for *Veten*, was of the second degree.

The unqualified success of *Leili and Medzhnun* was undoubtedly the major reason Karaev started immediately on a similar work, the *Seven Beauties*. The starting point was the tale of Nizami from the same cycle as *Leili and Medzhnun*. As a suite it was first performed in Baku on October 13, 1949.[1] It was presented in its final ballet form in Baku on

Karaev. *Leili i Medzhnun*

Ex.4 Fate theme.

Ex.5 *Second theme: related to Medzhnun.*

Allegro

[1] The conductor was Tagi-zade Zyl'fugar ogly Niazi (Zyl'fugar Niazi). The relationship between the conductor and Karaev is much like that between Mravinsky and Shostakovich.

Ex.6 *Love theme.*

Adagio

Ex.7 *Sadness motive.*

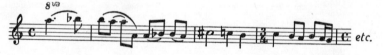

Ex.8 *Tragic theme.*

November 9, 1952, appearing a year later in Leningrad.[1,2] The incredibly bowdlerized libretto bears so little resemblance to the Nizami tale that one reviewer said the ballet should be renamed since the seven beauties figure in the production only as an occasional divertissement.[3] The Nizami story is one of the Thousand and One Nights prototypes or archetypes wherein the Sassanid King, Bahram Gur, is diverted by seven Beautiful princesses, in seven castles of varying colours, telling seven tales.[4] The version adopted by Karaev (read, 'Slonimsky') is complex: The young Shah Bakhram, temporarily lost in the hunt, is shown old portraits of seven foreign beauties by a hermit in a ruined castle. The portraits become alive and collectively beguile the Shah with exotic dances and music until daybreak, when they disappear. Leaving the ruin, the bemused Bakhram comes upon the hut of the strong, simple peasant, Menzner who lives with his equally strong and simple, but beautiful, peasant sister, Aisha. Aisha's music has already anticipated that of the *Seven Beauties* in the introduction (Example 9). In an adagio duet, Bakhram and Aisha establish their monumental love as well as a much-used musical image to represent it (Example 10). The similarities between themes (Examples 9 and 10), ostinato, key, melodic turns, are well noted now. The tyrannical Vizier appears to warn Bakhram of the advancing Khazars. As the Shah, with Menzner, rides off to join the people, the 'ruler-people' musical

[1] Again a fellow Transcaucasian was competing with the same tale. Sul'tan Gadzhibekov's ballet. *Seven Beauties*, partly written before 1948, was killed in infancy.

[2] The ballet was actually finished and in rehearsal in October 1951, but in the communal hearing in the Azerbaidzhainan Union of Soviet Composers in October of that nervous year for the Caucasus, many faults were found in the libretto. It was found to lack proper conflict and social direction, and it failed to delineate the features of the masses—neither fault very serious in a light tale of royal dillydallying with lots of beautiful girls. A comment by critics E. Grosheva and V. Makarov in *Sovetskaia Muzyka*, no. 1, 1952, in an article, 'In the Caucasian Republics', sums it up: 'It will be absolutely necessary in *Seven Beauties* to oppose the court atmosphere with folk reality, mass scenes, and folk dances.' The music was held to be adequate, but the rewriting of the libretto ended Karaev's association (since the early days of *Veten*) with the Azerbaidzhanian stage genius, Idayat-zade. Idayat-zade had suggested much of *Seven Beauties* and had collaborated in the libretto. A specialist was brought in from Leningrad, Iurii Slonimsky. Thus the association between Karaev and the 'slick' Slonimsky started with *Seven Beauties* and continued at least until the ponderous, brutally propagandistic *Path of Thunder* in 1958.

[3] V. Krasovskaia in 'The ballet season in Leningrad', *Zvezda*, no. 9, 1954.

[4] The fourth of these tales found its way through the 'Thousand and One Nights' and became the subject for both Gozzi's and Schiller's dramas, and Puccini's unfinished opera, *Turandot*.

Karaev. *Seven Beauties.*

Ex.9 *Aisha's melody.*

Ex.10 *Aisha-Bakhram, love image.*

Ex.11 *Ruler image.*

image is established (Example 11).[1] The cruel Vizier tightens his grip on the suffering people until Bakhram's return. The latter returns victorious, but confused, (*a*) because Aisha has had second thoughts since she found out he was a Shah and not a simple hunter, and (*b*) because the Vizier consistently befuddles his mind. The evil Vizier is portrayed grotesquely in the *kontrskvoznoe* manner discussed above (Example 12). The Shah drifts further and further from his people, and from reality,

Ex.12 *Vizier theme.*

Ex.13 *Aisha's strength: the people.*

[1] This example is in itself an example of a 'new' Soviet Azerbaidzhan genre: that of the *dzhengi*. The *dzhengi* is defined as a militant dance or march based on folk music of heroic (Soviet) content supposedly created during the days of the revolution when the Azerbaidzhan people were striving to make cause and contact with the Bolshevik forces. However, only Baku could be said to have been even partially in sympathy with the Bolsheviks in 1917-23. The rest of the country was violently against the Bolsheviks and, to the well documented sorrow of the Party; the country folk indeed tried to and succeeded in reaching Bolshevik partisans, in order to annihilate them. The origin, then, of the *dzhengi*, as officially reported, is suspect. Since the *dzhengi* certainly exists, its origins and development are still a matter for scholarly investigation.

and is treated, as is the audience, with a series of harem dancers. As things grow worse, seven workers, representatives of the people, appear to plead with the Shah. They are imprisoned and, finally, the seven beauties reappear to divert the Shah who fails, however, to respond to their individually presented dances and tales. This is Karaev's musical trip around the world: the seven princesses are accompanied by music representing India, Byzantium, Khorezm, Slavo-Russia, Magrib, China, and Persia. In the Nizami telling the Persian princess is 'the very most beautiful of the most beautiful'. But Karaev gets nationalistic mileage (while ignoring ethnic facts) from reposing Aisha, the 100 per cent red-blooded Azerbaidzhanian girl, as fairer still. The seven beauties disappear as illogically and unessentially as they appeared; the people rise against the Vizier; the seven workers are released. Bakhram teeters with indecision but realizes only Aisha's love can save him. The strong-minded girl, however, asks him to abdicate, to become the simple hunter he once was. He reacts adversely, killing her, the only one who can save him. But the people triumph, and Bakhram, morally ruined leaves the country.

The *dénouement*, or part of it, is realized musically. The strongest image, that of the love between Aisha and Bakhram, is re-evaluated as Aisha's (i.e. the peoples') strength and combines with the 'people-leader' image in the finale (Example 13).

Out of Soviet context the ballet is difficult to classify. This would be an important matter if it were not so simple to classify within the Soviet context. In the early fifties the only Soviet ballets firmly on the boards were Gliere's *Red Poppy* and Asaf'ev's *Fountains of Bakhchisarai*.[1] The Karaev *Seven Beauties* is, dramaturgically, nearly identical with the *Fountains* of Asaf'ev. Karaev, nurtured by Shostakovich, impressed by the 1948 Party criticism and strong reverberations thereof through 1953 in Azerbaidzhan, talented and ambitious, had chosen his own path. As in Asaf'ev's opera of 1932, the hero in *Seven Beauties* is kept from happiness by his noble birth which bars him from the folk; he is enamoured of a foreign beauty who for moral reasons makes no return demonstration; she dies and he is morally destroyed. No less striking a similarity is the background of the harem and the frankly erotic dances and costumes which both ballets share. Soviet ballet, without the embarrassing clutter of advertisement, serves many tastes including that of the healthy citizen for a gracefully presented glimpse of flesh.

---

[1] Khachaturian's *Gayaneh* was in eclipse with its composer and was being rewritten. Prokofieff's *Romeo and Juliet* had been removed for revision in 1948: his *Stone Flower* had not yet appeared and would not until a year after the composer's death in 1953.

Musically one finds little difference in 'nationality' between Asaf'ev's leitmotiv for the Tatar Zarema and Zaraev's for Aisha. The Karaev music, in general, is tougher and more instinctively unified. The ballet also falls easily into a second Soviet category. The 1948 Party criticism seemed to point the way to ballet and opera based on contemporary Soviet subjects. But by 1950 it had become clear that, however desirable success, it was impossible to please the authorities. In that year Zhukovsky's *From all one's heart* and Stepaian's *Heroine* were bitterly criticized. This was nearly the last of contemporary themes. The flood of operas and ballets[1] became based on folk tales, glorified history, and the contemporary scene in other lands. Karaev's *Seven Beauties* is one example of the retreat on all creative fronts from contemporary Soviet material.[2]

Karaev's further path reflects a satisfaction with the status of his career. He directed the Baku Conservatory until 1953, stepping down in that year to assume the chairmanship of the Azerbaidzhanian Union of Soviet Composers. There is no indication of the creative struggle, with or without results, so characteristic of Shostakovich. The works after 1952 are of the topical, commissioned sort. Opera 51 through 56, 61 through 63, 66, 67, and 70 are film music and suites or other derivations therefrom. The significant suites are *Tale of the Caspian Tankers*, 1953, and *Vietnam Suite*, 1955, neither of them published. Opus 49 is an Albanian rhapsody; the result of a trip to that country as a delegation member. Aside from these, Karaev, as is the case with many of the peripheral republican artists, has yielded to the central urging to express himself propagandistically to other, less fortunate, minority groups.

Opus 60 is his second ballet, *Tropoiu Groma*.[3] The idea for setting the story of South African passion and racism was not Karaev's but that of Iurii Slonimsky, the Leningrad librettist. Slonimsky encountered the Russian translation of the novel in 1950, began work on a libretto, and had it nearly ready before he met Karaev in early 1952. The Slonimsky 'touch' is unmistakable. The original Abrahams story is 'simplified', re-emphasized, and emotionalized beyond recognition. Abraham's novel tells of the white girl, Sarah, her negro-hating planter father, and her lover, the mulatto, Lenny. Abrahams speaks for

[1] In the period 1948–57 Soviet composers produced 120 operas, fifty-five ballets, and about seventy musical comedies, Boris Iarustovskii reports in *Nekotorye problemy sovetskogo muzykla'nogo teatra*.

[2] *Seven Beauties* is published in piano reduction by Muzfond SSSR, 1954.

[3] *Tropoiu Groma* (The Path of Thunder) is based on the novel of that name by South African Peter Abrahams. The novel was published in New York in 1948.

a mutual solution of the many problems (of which Sarah and Lenny's tragedy is a symptom) by the four elements involved: 'blacks', 'coloureds' (mulattoes), English and, possibly, Boers. Slonimsky reduces this complex relationship, literally, to black and white—natives and colonials. The positive, helpful ideas advanced by the English citizenry by Abrahams are put by Slonimsky in the speeches of Lenny.[1] Slonimsky bases his solution on a speech of the Negro teacher, Mako, after the death of Lenny and Sarah: 'They have killed them . . . you are called to arms! We must act! That is where the path lies!' Slonimsky accepts this as a call for union between bickering blacks and 'coloureds' to throw out all the colonials. This was quite clearly not Abraham's intention.[2] Slonimsky felt that his greatest accomplishment lay in lifting the story out of South African context and making it apply universally in depicting the plight of the colonially oppressed negro. Thus, more than one American has squirmed through a Leningrad performance, indignantly recognizing it as a ballet about the American South.

One avoids a citation of the music in *Path of Thunder* with the easy comment: more of the same. But the question remains, what of the supposedly pervading Shostakovich influence? Karaev is still clearly a Shostakovich pupil. But Shostakovich's expressive vocabulary can become a bag of trite tricks in another's hands. Shostakovich usually goes through the birth pangs: others, among them Karaev, use the fresh life without creating it.

Finally, the question recurs, has Karaev accomplished what he and Soviet theory desire: a creative synthesis of a non-Western musical idiom with Western form, harmony and artist-audience values. The evidence suggests that Karaev has accomplished no such thing. The same evidence suggests that the very idea is a contradiction in terms—for Karaev and many other republican composers.

[1] The ballet includes spoken words. The burden of Slonimsky's libretto cannot be borne without them.

[2] Abrahams' later novel, In *Memory of Udomo* (1956) was published just prior to the ballet's first performance and proved an embarrassment to Slonimsky and Karaev. Abrahams develops here his idea of a South Africa for all, and that of a solution through English philosophy and manipulation of the economy.

꙳꙳

CHAPTER 26

Fikret Amirov

Fikret Amirov (Fikret Meshadi Dzamil ogly Amirov) is the last of a trio of Azerbaidzhan composers considered here,[1] and his inclusion completes, as much as is possible, using three such figures, the picture of Soviet Azerbaidzhanian music. Gadzhibekov had created the naive beginnings of a contemporary 'Azerbaidzhanian' style on Western bases. Karaev has built on that European base and embellished with Azerbaidzhanian sauce. Amirov, on the other hand, has tried to ignore the ubiquitous Europeanisms and concentrates on the folk legacy. If the musical results of both Karaev and Amirov, in spite of their apparently different approaches, sound the same, it is due to the already thorough Europeanization of that legacy mentioned elsewhere.

Amirov was born on November 22, 1922 in Giandzhe.[2] His father was a *tarist*[3] and singer of professional quality. Young Amirov himself studied the *tar* and became a well-known virtuoso thereon. The *tar* being one of the instruments used by the *ashugi* bards, it is reasonable to suppose that the Amirov's had at least a citified knowledge of the *ashug* style. Amirov's prodigious talent grew in an atmosphere of increasing Russification and Westernization in music. It was natural that the young talent was more tractable than that of the conservative, wandering *ashugi*, and equally natural that he should become identified within the ever enlarging sphere of occidental music in Azerbaidzhan. He began to compose for the piano when he was eighteen. Unfortunately these works are not available, but are reported as being strongly influenced by the *tar* idiom.

Amirov was schooled until 1938 in Kirovabad, specializing in the *tar*.

[1] The others: Uzeir Gadzhibekov, p. 132 and Kara Karaev, p. 307.
[2] Giandzhe is now Kirovabad.
[3] For a description of the *tar* see p. 133, n. 1. It seems certain, on the evidence of dates, that the senior Amirov did not use the traditional tuning but the 'correct', tempered tuning introduced by Gadzhibekov.

He went then for a year to a second *uchilishche* in Baku to prepare for conservatory entrance. On the eve of his matriculation into the Baku Conservatory he, with many others, was called into war service. He was badly wounded in the early fighting, returned home, and finally began his studies at the conservatory. His first work for orchestra was a 'Poem' (1941) to which a sequel was written in 1944, 'In memory of the heroes of the Great Fatherland War'. At the conservatory he studied with Boris Zeidman,[1] who gave him the thorough training typical for his generation at the Leningrad Conservatory. The *tar* idiom was replaced, but Amirov still kept his face turned to his own culture. In 1947 he wrote a string symphony, his first, honouring the Persian poet, Nizami. More indicative of his inclinations, but assuming a style too rigid to continue, were his next two symphonic works, both of them 'Symphonic Mugams': *Shur* and *Kiurdi-Ovshari*. These were both composed in 1947–8 and received their first performance in 1948 under Niazi's direction.[2] *Mugams* being what they are, and Western forms being what they are, it was possible to mate each *mugam* and the form but once: a second essay would result in the same music, dissatisfyingly repetitive from both Western and Middle Eastern viewpoint. Amirov was forced to move away from this potential trap. A Stalin Prize, second degree, was awarded the two works.

In 1942–3 Amirov was a director of the Baku Philharmonic and also directed a music *uchilishche*. In 1947, before finishing the conservatory, he became general artistic director of the Philharmonic and remains in that post today. Because of generally poor health brought on by his war wounds he is not as active as some of his colleagues.

He graduated from the conservatory in 1948 and was not untouched by the criticism of that year, although he had joined the Party in 1947. A piano concerto and piano sonata were criticized and discarded as 'formalistic'. Curiously enough, these works were said to have been a calculated return to the *tar*-esque idiom of his early youthful works. An opera, *Ulduz* (1948) is apparently unstaged. Its librettist was the 'formalistic' Idaiat-zade whom Karaev was enjoined to discard in the

---

[1] Boris Zeidman, 1908–, was a Peterburger, who finished the conservatory in 1931 under Shteinberg. He taught at the Leningrad Conservatory until 1939 when he removed to Baku. His advent in Azerbaidzhan was unheralded, and, since he was a Jew, had the flavour of exile. But he changed the structure of musical training and is at least one strong voice in favour of a corrective review of the bowdlerized tradition in folk art. Thus, a Russian Jew is trying to restore what an Azerbaidzhanian, Gadzhibekov, had partially destroyed.

[2] Other Azerbaidzhan composers wrote symphonic *mugams*—among them Tagizade Niazi himself (*Rast*, 1946) and Suleiman Aleskerov (*Baiati-Shiras*, 1952).

midst of the preparation of his *Seven Beauties* in 1951.[1] In early 1949 Amirov prepared an effective *Sonata for Violin and 'Cello,* in unison, to the memory of Uzeir Gadzhibekov who had died in November of the previous year.

Amirov's output, never great, dwindled after 1950. However, a second opera, his most popular, *Sevil',* was performed in Baku in December, 1953. The opera is based on a 1928 drama by Jafar Jabarla and, covering the period 1918–19, with a 1929 fourth act, is concerned with the plight of the Azerbaidzhan Moslem woman and her hopes for better station under Soviet rule. The librettist, Talet Eiubov, added a prologue replete with stereotyped humiliations of pre-Soviet Azerbaid-zhanian womanhood, and introduced a revolutionary, although ficti-tious, demonstration in the second act to tighten up the socio-political direction. The work uses a rude leitmotiv technique: those of the heroine, Sevil', dominate (Example 1).[2] 'Leit-instrumentation' or 'leit-timbres' also stalk the characters through the insipidities of the score. A high point is reached in the chorus scene.[3] The main theme of the heroine intermingles with that of 'the people' (Example 2).[4] The *Varso-vienne* is heard in the altos and basses; *Smelo tovarishch, v nogu!* (Bravely comrade, stay abreast!)[5] is sung by the sopranos and tenors; finally, in the high orchestral voices, the *Internationale* provides a fifth, polito-cophonous part. . . .

Among other successful works composed up to this time, one must include the symphonic suite *Azerbaidzhan,* composed in 1950. It is not the best known of Amirov's orchestral works, but it is one of the few published. Here the experience gained in the two symphonic *mugams* of 1947–8 is further distilled, although the work is clearly not a symphonic *mugam* itself. There is, moreover, compelling argument that it is not a suite either, but a symphony: the first of four movements is a simple sonata-allegro, the second movement is slow, the key relationships of the movements are those of the sonata-at-large, etc., etc. If, on the other hand, the work may not be judged a symphony by reason of a certain programmatic cast[6] or because of the lack of some imaginary depth to

[1] See p. 317.
[2] Example 1a is a harmonized fragment of the *shuster mugam.*
[3] Choruses were only introduced in the second edition (premiered in May 1955). The 'complex' orchestral polyphony was snipped out in 1959.
[4] Example 2 is the *mugam shur.*
[5] 'Smelo tovarishch . . .' is a traditional Russian revolutionary song of 1917–18 derivation, perhaps earlier.
[6] The four movements originally bore subtitles: I, Mingechaur; II, Choban-baiati; III, Holiday on the kolkhoz, and IV, Song of Baku. These subtitles do not appear in the published work (Moscow: Sovetskii Kompozitor, 1957).

which a symphony must probe, then many Soviet 'symphonies' cannot have that name, including a great deal of Miaskovsky and, at least, Shostakovich's Ninth, Eleventh, and Twelfth.[1]

Amirov. *Sevil'*

Ex.1

a)

b) *Sevil''s motive.*

Moi drug   byl   ty   ne   ta - kim
My friend once you   were not thus

Ex.2   *The people.*

Amirov's first-movement primary subject is a virile 6/8 (Example 3) which contrasts classically with a more lyric second subject (Example 4). A review of the form after the brief exposition is unnecessary since it is altogether predictable. Of more interest is Amirov's attention to combinations and sounds: the essentially romantic orchestra includes

---

[1] This is not nit-picking. The symphonic suite, as a form, has in the Soviet Union been called a bastard variant inviting decadent Western tendencies, especially that toward impressionistic sound.

xylophone and vibraphone.[1] The texture of the first subject is heavy and is lightened somewhat with the advent of the second subject in the soft, high piccolo and bassoon. The score frequently calls for horns aloft. The xylophone is used percussively, very much in the style of the Shostakovich orchestral piano. The development involves some melodic fragmentation and the casting of an octave passage in 3/4 time against the 6/8 background. The coda is a short orchestral fanfare in cut time.[2] This is a bravado movement; tuneful, rhythmic, and put together simply with ample display of craft mastery.

The second movement is formally a free variation-rhapsody. Quotations from melodic scaraps (Example 5) reveal 'folk' intervals and melodic turns. Note especially the grace notes, written as such, and similar embellishment in value notes. Finally, the ambiguous shift of 6/8 to 3/4, also obvious in the given examples, is a gradual one. The movement ends in a straightforward 3/4. A similar rhythmic cross-hatching was suggested in the first movement.

If the preceding movement is characterized by melodic excerpts, the third is more a rhythmic ostinato *tour-de-force* (Example 6) with occasional unison, conjunct melodic wails. The movement is dramatically akin to the bombastic sections of the first movement. The last movement announces great things (Example 7), and runs out of breath after the announcement. A more lyric theme, playing subordinate to the opening section, has intonational characteristics linking it to the second movement (Example 8, and cf. Examples 4 and 5). This theme, on the ever more excited background of the heroic opening notes, develops in unison and finally closes the movement and work.

To repeat, this is successful Soviet music. Little has been said about the harmony since there are no unpredictable combinations other than those implied in the melodies quoted. Although written very much under the influence of the 1948 dicta, the suite/symphony saw authoritative republication in 1957 when Julian Krein did the editorial work. It is often played and was heard in the United States in 1959 during the tour of the Moscow Philharmonic Orchestra. With those Western performances embarrassingly in mind, it is difficult to dwell on the work's obvious naiveté, pomposity, triteness, and demonstratively false folk imagery, because the work was received enthusiastically by audiences and some critics in the West. The problem is that the Soviet

---

[1] The vibraphone is most uneconomically included: it appears briefly in the second movement to reinforce some harp passages and nowhere else.

[2] The cut time is unnecessary since the $\frac{6}{8}$ ♫♪ ♫♪ | ♫♪ ♫♪ is simply converted to ♪♪♪♪♪♪♪♪♪♪♪♪, ♩. ♩

Amirov. *Azerbaidzhan* Symphonic suite.

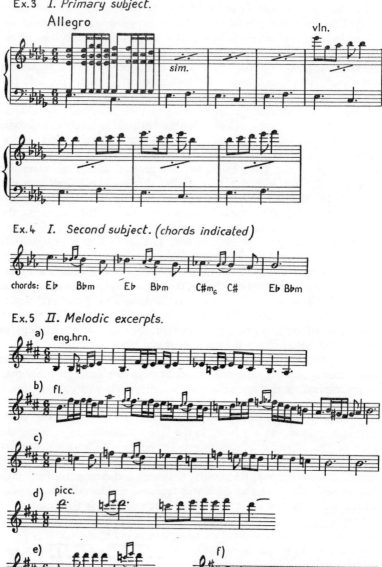

Ex.3 *I. Primary subject.*

Ex.4 *I. Second subject. (chords indicated)*

chords: Eb   Bbm   Eb   Bbm   C#m₆ C#   Eb Bbm

Ex.5 *II. Melodic excerpts.*

a) eng.hrn.

b) fl.

c)

d) picc.

e)

f)

critic and publicist, reasoning from the basis of mass appeal, can make his point much more easily than can the critic seeking values in the music, and not in its reception. The work's chief positive quality is the orchestration, of which Amirov is a master.

Ex.6 *III Rhythmic excerpts.*

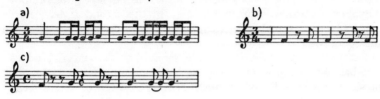

Ex.7 *IV Opening.*

Ex.8 *Lyric motive.*

Other Amirov works include settings of songs by the *ashug* Bairam about Stalin (1950), a two-piano Albanian suite written jointly with Elmira Nazirova[1] (1955) and a piano concerto on Arab themes also jointly with Nazirova (1957) which has not been published.

Amirov received the rank of Peoples' Artist of the Azerbaidzhan Soviet Republic in 1958. He and Gadzhibekov and Karaev represent fairly the accomplishment of Azerbaidzhanian music under Russian and Soviet domination. The Westerner, hard put to find distinguishing

[1] Elmira Mirza Riza kyzy Nazirova was born November 30, 1928, finished the Baku Conservatory in composition under Zeidman in 1954. She is now a teacher of piano at the conservatory.

features among Soviet composers in general, finds it nearly impossible to separate Soviet Azerbaidzhanian composers into stylistic groups. Yet, certain hallmarks not associated with the pseudo-Eastern icing do appear. Two of these are mutually exclusive to the point that they may be defined as style. Where one finds the concentration on the singing melodic line and near-monophony, as in much of Gadzhibekov and some of Amirov, there is an absence of the 'second' style, that of linear, polyphonic settings. Karaev is closer to the second style. Amirov approaches the second style when he consciously purges himself, as in the opera *Sevil'*.

But such differentiation is little more than provincial kindness. Azerbaidzhanian music takes its place with most other minority-republic music as a sub-order of twentieth-century Russian music, whatever that may be. The roots of Soviet Azerbaidzhanian music are identical with those of the Soviet centre, firmly planted in the nationalistic romanticism of the Russo-European nineteenth century, no deeper, no wider.

꒞꒞

CHAPTER 27

Other Young Composers

Ideals, Innovations, and the Seeds of Conclusion

T he face of the younger Soviet generation of composers, as seen from the West, is, understandably, fairly uniform. This chapter continues the consideration of the young generation, briefly mentioning those conventional young men who have achieved some musical stature, at some time, within the Soviet Union. Moreover, a discussion of Soviet ideals for its creative youth; the thinking of the young composer; and the two serious problems for these composers, success, and the notion of contemporary expression; is followed by a brief look at an unconventional composer. In a very real sense, this last part of the last chapter on the youngest generation of Soviet composers is the beginning of the conclusion of this discussion.

ISAAC SCHWARTZ

Isaac Iosifovich Schwartz (Shvartz) was born in 1923 in Romni, Chernigovsk. At the age of eight his family moved to Leningrad where his musical schooling began. He took lessons in the late thirties from Vladimir Fere.[1] Schwartz served in the army and returned to Leningrad, finishing the conservatory under Evlakhov in 1951. Among the usual heroic cantatas and settings of Russian and Soviet poets, his First Symphony stands out, by default, as a major Leningrad contribution. The four-movement work[2] is in the 'heroic' category, the hero in this case being Soviet Youth. Schwartz's ability is greatest in melody, but here the unifying factor of the four movements is not his own

---

[1] Vladimir Georgevich Fere (1902–) was a Miaskovsky student in Moscow and a pianist. From 1936 to 1944 he directed the Philharmonic in Frunze (Kirghizia). In 1945 he joined the Moscow Conservatory staff where he is now a professor. He is active in the affairs of the USC and seems prepared to take over Shaporin's honorary functions.

[2] Schwartz's First Symphony was first performed on November 6, 1954, by the Leningrad Philharmonic under A. Iansons.

melodic invention, but that of Anatolii Novikov's[1] 'Hymn of Democratic Youth'. The image or quotation is well handled, but similar quotations of a folk song on Ermak, and even the *Dies Irae* are contrived and unconvincing.

A later work of Schwartz's, the ballet *On the Eve* (based on the Turgenev novel) was widely advertised, during its creation, as a new, youngblooded work for the Bolshoi Theatre.[2] However, it came to grief when the dancers found it tiresome and refused to co-operate. In any case, Galina Ulanova, the *prima* designate found her part too exhausting.

ANDREI PETROV

Andrei Pavlovich Petrov was born in Leningrad on September 2, 1930. His father is a doctor, but the family is musically oriented. At first, and in spite of some talent, not interested in music, Petrov became serious during the family wartime evacuation in Leninsk-Kuznetskii. In 1944 he studied violin at the Leningrad Pioneer Palace and entered the conservatory *uchilishche* in 1945, continuing into the conservatory under Evlskov in 1949. He graduated in 1954 and continued as a graduate student. He is now working as an editor for Muzgiz, Leningrad.

Petrov is, or was, a prolific composer who received much support in the form of performances in the mid-fifties. He closely approaches the idealized image of the 'Soviet composer', and perhaps the most telling evidence thereof is his utter lack of humour. His works are often topical: *Pioneer Suite* (1951); a symphonic poem *How Steel Was Tempered* (1952); but he is most drawn to ballet. His first, *Cherished Little Apple*, was about young 'Michurinites' (geneticists) and was performed by the children's *samodeiatel'nost'* group at the Gorky Children's Studio in November of 1953. A second ballet, on Pushkin's *Stationmaster* was mounted by the Kirov Theatre ballet school and remained in the repertoire of that school for some time.[3] Petrov's most important work, originally conceived as a ballet on Gorky's *Makar Chudra*, was the symphonic poem *Radda and Loiko*. Here Petrov

[1] Anatolii Novikov (1896–) is important for his mass works. His is perhaps the greatest name among those who operate exclusively with the mass genres—oratorios, cantatas, and songs. He studied at the Moscow Conservatory in 1921–7 under Gliere. His musical life has been long connected with the military. He is a spokesman for orthodoxy and is often a member of foreign delegations.

[2] Word of mouth suggests that the commission was granted at Galina Ulanova's urging. Ulanova and Schwartz had long been close friends.

[3] The two great Soviet ballet schools are associated closely with the Kirov (Mariinsky) and Bolshoi Theatres. The school has the use of the stage for performances several afternoons a year.

reveals his debt to Tschaikovsky. The passion and tragedy of the heroes is reminiscent of the Romeo and Juliet story, and Petrov's music is so similar to Tschaikovsky's setting of the Shakespeare tale as to risk being derivative.

A *Festive Overture* (1955) and a cycle of song settings of the bleak, proletarian poetry of the Italian, Gianni Rodari ('Simple Songs' 1956), reflect further Petrov's posture as an aware, Soviet composer. In 1957 he joined the Communist party.

His later works have included *The Last Night* (1957), a vocal symphonic poem portraying the eve of the storming of the Winter Palace; and *Death of a Pioneer Girl* (1958–9), commemorating the fortieth anniversary of the Komsomol. Finally, he has prepared a third ballet, with a libretto from the sure and experienced hand of Iurii Slonimsky[1] on commission from the Kirov Theatre. This is a tale of a shipwrecked Soviet sailor who finds himself stranded among capitalists. They try to seduce him away from communism with money, girls, etc., etc., for its propaganda value. His resistance is heroic, and so, apparently, is that of the Kirov Theatre dancers: The work seems not to have been staged.

Petrov is active in the USC, delivers many speeches, and is a constant attendant at youth meetings where he has much to say. His musical productivity has declined, due in part, no doubt, to these other activities. His performances in the last three years have been rare.

EINO TAMBERG

Eino Martirovich Tamberg was born May 27, 1930, in Tallin, Estonia. The country was then in its tenth year of independence, a status sought for centuries while under German, Swedish, and Russian (1721–1918) rule. Estonia's folk culture is rich in 'protest' genres, and includes an uncomfortably impressive amount of anti-Russian tales and songs. Estonia's Lutheran choral tradition is still strong, despite the supplantation of the Lutheran service by the Russian Orthodox after 1940, when the country reverted to Bolshevik control.

Tamberg studied at the Tallin Conservatory, finishing in 1953 under Eugene Kapp.[2] He is now a director of music for the Estonian radio.

Tamberg, judging from his, as yet, short lists of works, seeks an

---

[1] See p. 317.
[2] Eugene Arturovich Kapp (1908–) is an Estonian born in Astrakhan. His father, Arther Kapp (1878–1952) was a pupil of Rimsky-Korsakov and Liadov. During the years 1904–20, the elder Kapp was director of the IRMS music school in Astrakhan. Eugene Kapp studied under his father in Tallin and became a professor at the conservatory in 1947, assuming the directorship upon his father's death in 1952. Kapp works mostly in choral and opera idioms.

economy of style not altogether typical of Soviet symphonism. He has not, in fact, ventured into that genre. He is naturally drawn by the high level of vocal (especially choral) art in his country, and that implies in no little measure the *epos* of the Lutheran chorale and other church music. Among his earliest works are the choruses 'Nasha Strana Molodaia' (Our Country is Young, 1949) and three others written in 1953, his graduation year from the conservatory: 'What's the Rush' (Kuda toropish'sia). His graduation work that year was 'Za svobodu naroda' (For the people's freedom), an oratorio. His musical texture is light, and he mounts a certain careful dissonance on the saddles of parallel triads. Two thus enveloped, independent lines create a harmonic tension and relaxation through fleeting moments of bi-tonality on the one hand, and, on the other hand, instances of coincidence, usually in major triads. Orchestrally, he has a tendency to isolate colours by range, a trait shared with a handful of his fellow Soviet composers—notably Shostakovich, whose influence on Tamberg is frequently, although not altogether justifiably, mentioned. He shares with Prokofieff and many Western composers an occasional bent for treating strings percussively, temporarily depriving them of melodic functions.

Perhaps his most significant work to date is his 'Concerto Grosso', a work whose appearance in 1957 raised the asethetic question of whether such an 'ancient' genre had the right to be a part of Soviet music.[1] 'If a composer finds it possible in an ancient genre to embody the images of the contemporary, then (the genre) itself has proved its right to live.' The article continues: Tamberg, in his 'Concerto Grosso' may (have found) his type of the 'light cavalry' of Soviet symphonic music. The work is unified by a consistent harmonic cast (tritone and major seventh) used in the introductory passages of all three movements and referred to thereafter. This work is scored for strings and the flute, clarinet, trumpet, saxophone, bassoon, percussion piano, and harp as solo instruments. In general the three movements amount to an exercise for the alternating solo instruments, with a tendency to use them as a concerted group in the first movement, and to submerge them in a full tutti in the last. The second movement is entirely solo.

Tamberg has written for motion pictures and has a number of songs published.

EDWARD BAL'SIS

Lithuanian music has shared much of its heritage with Poland. Even during Imperial Russian rule, 1795–1918, the Catholic tradition

[1] *Sovetskaia Muzyka*, no. 12 (December 1957, p. 44).

remained strong. Edward (Eduardos) Kosto Bal'sis was born in 1919, the first year of Lithuania's brief (1919, 1939–40) period of independence. He finished the now defunct conservatory in Kaunas with honours in 1950, studying there under Rachiunas.[1]

Bal'sis writes slowly (his list of works is short) and conservatively. He has conscientiously worked with the folk music of his country, and his work reflect that concern. On a rigidly functional, semi-romantic basis, he superimposes the melodic and harmonic fourths and seconds of the Lithuanian *sutartine*.[2] This is reflected harmonically and melodically in his violin concerto (1954). However, Bal'sis's music is far from dominated by the folk idiom. His inclination toward typically thick, Soviet-style orchestration, plus chords with all elements (intervals) present, rather overwhelms the economical pentatonicism of the Lithuanian folk melos. His violin concerto is an essay in this contradiction. The four-movement work uses folk melodies freely, but the principal unifying factor is found in the recitative-like material of the first movement. That movement is titled 'Recitative'; the others: 'Scherzo', 'Improvization', and 'Humouresque'. One might note that these have been described as representing (1) The Lithuanian People, (2) The suffering of the Lithuanian People, (3) The beginnings of social enlightenment, and (4) The happy assumption of Soviet power. The third movement is perhaps the most notable, largely due to its unusually light orchestration. It stands out as a simple, subdued tone poem, and ends with a reiteration of the original recitative, leading directly to the finale. Although the solo violin part is often involved with the injected folk material, it is more aptly characterized by classical (read 'romantic') virtuosity. The solo part is heavily figured and ornamented, leaving the virtuoso violinist with no complaints.

Bal'sis has also written two poems for symphony orchestra, *Vil'nius* (1950) and *Heroic Poem* (1951); some chamber works; and some vocal and vocal-symphonic works.

IDEALS, INNOVATIONS AND THE SEEDS OF CONCLUSION

The techniques and idiom of Soviet music are conservative, or old-fashioned, or restricted, or slick, or chauvinistic, or insular. . . .

[1] Antanas Iono Rachiunas (1905–) studied in Kaunas and, in 1936–9, at the Paris '*Ecole Normal de Musique*. He was already teaching in Kaunas in 1931.

[2] *Sutartine*: a Lithuanian folk music genre, supposedly sung by women at work. It is also used at weddings. The language of the *sutartine* is sometimes used instrumentally to accompany dancing. Characteristic of the *sutartine* are parallel seconds in two-voiced polyphony, invariably with elements of syncopation.

These observations, whatever their source, have been made again and again. But nowhere has it been suggested that these characteristics are the private property of Soviet music. Conservatism, nationalism, insularism, and slick technique are colours in the Western musical kaleidoscope—just as are radicalism, the *avant-garde*, and internationalism. In effect, this robs the Soviet Union of its one basis for a claim to creative uniqueness. To put it another way, Soviet music, in forty years, has added nothing new to the music of the world. There is, of course, no ethical nor creative reason that it should. The factors that *are* unique in Soviet music are that of control, and that of the *preponderance* of the elements mentioned above, to the near exclusion of all else. The latter, encouraged by the former, is what disturbs most Western observers.[1] If it is easily, and often, observed in the West—by writers and by visiting composers—that 'modern' Soviet music is old-fashioned, etc., then it is fatuous to assume that the Soviet musical establishment, too, is not concerned about the notions of modernism, progressiveness, and innovation. After all, the halo and vocabulary, if not the fact, of the revolution, and the new are still about them.

Matters of *novatorstvo* (innovation) and *sovremennost'* ('contemporariness') have received much attention in the last few years: Soviet composers and music publicists are no longer satisfied with the single claim that Soviet music, alone, has continued the great European musical tradition. Indeed, they have complained about re-boiled, nineteenth-century musical soup—at the same time adroitly fending off and reasoning away identical charges of Western origin. It is difficult to say which disturbs the Soviet musician more: his own knowledge of domestic creative stagnation, or foreign suggestions to that effect. One suspects the latter, but there can be no question that established Soviet creative musicians, at least, are greatly concerned about the future of their national art. A hopeful glance is directed at youth.

The young Soviet composers have their own points of view. Any creative fledgling looks for success, security, and individual style. The last is often incompatible with the first two in the Soviet Union. Nevertheless, young Soviet composers, like young composers everywhere, are easily shamed into avoiding what they consider the stereotyped, the old, the well used.

[1] It bears repeating, too, that the other European communist nations, aside from those traditionally dominated by Russia or some non-Western culture, do not exhibit this mono-chromatic musical façade. The composers of Poland, Czechoslovakia, Hungary, and East Germany have styles and approaches as varied as those of their Western European counterparts. Communist leaders of large Parties in Western Europe, most recently Togliatti of Italy, have, without rancour, declared themselves not at all in agreement with Soviet policy in the Arts.

What do they do? And where are they? To answer the questions, two digressions are demanded by way of background.

First: perhaps in any country, certainly in the United States, musical success is often easier gained abroad. Moreover, foreign success is often the entry to success at home. This ancient dynamic has a particularly well defined meaning to young Soviet composers. We have seen how vitally important foreign recognition was to the older and especially the middle generation of Soviet composers. Further, lacking freedom to travel abroad, it has been demonstrated time and again in the Soviet Union that foreign recognition is most easily won by being the centre of a storm at home. The artistic product does not matter. Far more people know about Evgenii Evtushenko's 'rebellion' than have ever read his poetry. If they did read it, his independent, anti-communist glitter would be severely tarnished. Many know about Shostakovich's political troubles who have not heard his music. Millions know the name and fate of Boris Pasternak: considerably fewer have read his novel or his poetry. To the young composer of the Moscow school, these are simple facts, and they act upon them. The names of two students of Khachaturian, himself a master of the 'foreign ploy', have been mentioned at least five times in as many years by returning American composer-tourists as underground writers of *musique concrete*. The two in question are well aware of the shock value of such information. This pair, literally countless times, has intently approached American visitors, be they composers, writers, politicians, or wives of a delegation of American farmers, with the one English sentence they know: 'We are now writing concrete music'. Sometimes notebooks are excitedly pulled out, and names written down. At other times, as with the farmers' wives, great discomfort results. When pressed for examples, two or three pages of nonsense are produced. When pressed insistently for a year, a few promises and a great deal of hedging are added to the nonsense.[1]

The second digression involves a point made in the introduction to Part Four of this paper. The notion that a thriving trade in 'illicit' music—secret concerts, secret composing circles, secret performance organizations—exists, by analogy with the 'underground' school of abstract Soviet painting, is totally false. Mose inter-Art analogies are. The principal reason, that of the relative remoteness of the craft of music, has been mentioned. But even assuming the existence of, say, a 12-tone string quartet, then the idea of locating an auditing area, the

---

[1] The present writer finds curious indeed the report of one returning American who, it seems, spent an evening at the apartment of one of the pair, listening for hours to recordings of his 'concrete music'.

assembling of a (rehearsed) group of musicians, and the gathering of an audience, *all done secretly*, under the conditions of Soviet reality, is unthinkable. A string quartet cannot be nailed on the wall of an apartment.

To return to the question: what does the young composer do who seeks, at least momentarily, to travel paths that are new to him? First, he assembles what guideposts he can. They are few, and their location is such that his search is immediately an overt one. From the beginning, then, he is openly rebelling. Elsewhere in this paper, it has been suggested that the rebel and malcontent is not only accused, but also feels neurotically guilty of being an unproductive, unfair citizen. This generates a loud defensiveness which one would find offensive in any milieu. The typical, Soviet adolescent maverick hates folk music, hates realism, hates classicism, and hates the music of his fellows: This is the Soviet semantics of unorthodoxy. He worships the West, without understanding it, because that, too, is part of the semantics. He is as hidebound, narrow, restricted, and dull as his complete opposite, the idealized, orthodox Soviet man. Thus, one of the fundamental axioms of Soviet control is that not only is orthodoxy closely defined, but so is its lack. So are rebellion, deviation, and any non-Soviet thinking.

What, then, is the solution to the problem besetting Soviet musical thinkers—that of innovation and contemporary expression? The Soviet mind is committed to the ingredients of tradition, contemporary reality, and the future. From an understanding of these should come the new in Art. This is historically sound. But, as we have seen, Soviet tradition is forbiddingly selective, contemporary reality is a word dream, and the future is beautifully predestined—but for that very reason hopeless. Musical technique, desire, and opportunity for young composers are well developed. This constitutes the raw material, and a close parallel is brought to mind: Young Soviet vocalists are now training, in rather large numbers, in Italy. The reasoning is that Russia has the greatest vocal raw material in the world, but that vocal training is deficient in depth. The very serious, post-war crisis in Soviet opera has generated this realistic view. This is necessary, too, for the young, Soviet composer. He needs experience and training abroad, not, necessarily, because it is better, but because it provides depth—it provides another facet against which reasoning about the new can proceed comfortably. The Soviet composers of the old generation who had foreign training are gone now. There are none of significance in the middle generation, and there are none in the younger generation, with one exception.[1]

[1] Since the Baltic states have been part of the Soviet Union only since 1940, nominally, and effectively since 1944, the young Estonian, Latvian, and Lithuanian

ANDREI VOLKONSKY

The sole exception is Andrei Volkonsky. Volkonsky is an able serial composer, perhaps the only one in the Soviet Union. His family background is interesting—he is a prince. The Volkonskys are the 'Bolkonskys' of Tolstoi's *War and Peace*. Andrei's father, Prince Michael Volkonsky, fled revolutionary Russia, as did most of the Russian nobility.

Andrei Volkonsky was born in Geneva, Switzerland, on February 14, 1933. An early display of talent impressed even the French who were tiring of child prodigies between the wars. At the age of eleven, Volkonsky entered the Geneva Conservatory, studying piano there with Dr Auber. Simultaneously he commuted to Paris and began regular lessons with Nadia Boulanger. In 1945 his family quit Geneva for Paris, and Volkonsky continued with Mme Boulanger through 1947. His studies in the West were interrupted by the elder Volkonsky's decision to return to his homeland. A number of such decisions were made after the war. Young Volkonsky was then just fifteen.

Established in the Soviet Union, his training was presently resumed at the Tambov music *uchilishche*. This was not an essential in Volkonsky's training. The family stay at Tambov was clearly to facilitate a difficult adjustment. Volkonsky's study at the *uchilishche* was limited to piano—he took no composition. Nevertheless, the talent and training were not to be denied. In 1950, when Volkonsky was seventeen, he entered the Moscow Conservatory under Iurii Shaporin as a composition student, and the storm began. These were the last years of Stalin's rule. The Komsomol soon found fault with Volkonsky's work. Shaporin had sympathetically given Volkonsky creative room, and, in any case, the young composer was not at all conditioned to creative control. Artistic responsibility was, to him, private property. His response, or lack of it, to the Komsomol and later the Party, was not acceptable. He did not recant, neither did he argue. Somewhat confused, he politely ignored the Party criticism and direction as elements in no way associated

---

composers have, technically, more of a Western European background. This is reflected to some extent in their music, although a musical *avant-garde* had never developed.

Concerning apparent innovation elsewhere: The names of the Estonian composer Piart and the Ukrainian Sil'vestrov were joined with that of Muscovite Volkonsky in an admonitory speech by Tikhon Khrennikov at the Third All-Union Congress of Soviet Composers in the spring of 1962. The speech, appearing in *Sovetskaia Muzyka*, no. 5 (May), 1962, pp. 3–5, took the trio to task for their serial experiments. The music of neither Piart nor Sil'vestrov has been exposed, so far as the present writer knows, to the Western view.

with his Art. His talent, popularity, and polite bearing, plus the presence of Shaporin and others at the conservatory interested in his progress, kept him his conservatory place far longer than one would expect.

Stalin's death seemed to relieve Volkonsky of the pressures he had felt. His music up to this time was vigorous, but lean and spare. His *Concerto for Orchestra* (1953) was played under USC auspices in June of 1954. By now he had frankly settled on a serial technique. Within a week of the performance of the Concerto, his last major, non-serial work, he was expelled from the conservatory. The orthodox outrage of Khrennikov and Kabalevsky had prevailed over the views of Shaporin and Shostakovich.

Volkonsky still had these and other champions. This division of opinion on Volkonsky could be basic evidence of a crack in the monolithic wall of Soviet musical thinking. Over Khrennikov's shrill and repeated objections, the Moscow USC chose further to assist Volkonsky. His relationship with that organization is unique. If he had followed the established pattern of non-conformity—contempt of conservatism, disdain of 'the people' and of folk music, and an uncritical appreciation of anything Western, he would have long since been assigned to piano instruction in a remote *uchilishche*. But he conforms in no way. He is an enthusiastic fan of folk music, but he feels its use in composed music to be an unwarranted violation of a nearly perfect art form. He is not anti-Soviet, nor is he at all pro-Western. He makes his judgments with no reference to politics or nationalism. He is gregarious and fond of people, especially enjoying informal contact with unpretentious people. He does not submit his work for criticism in the USC forums. He is not conscious of that responsibility, and, of course, he knows well what the results would be. No important works, then, are published. His performances are rare—occasionally the pianist Vladimir Ashkenazi, or some other friend, will play a work.

A fairly recent tape of a viola sonata reveals Volkonsky's laconical style. The first of two movements consists of serial utterances in semi-dialogue. These mount in complexity, and experience a lyric metamorphosis in a moment of climax, subsiding quickly into dry statement. Lately, Volkonsky has been drawn to the pointillistic possibilities of various instrumental combinations. His scores have the well-patterned eye appeal of many of his Western contemporaries. Recent plans include an opera. This will use three orchestras: a small chamber group, a jazz band, and an orchestra of Russian folk instruments. The three orchestras sit on stage, surrounding the opera's only prop: a four-floor tower with no windows, no doors, and no passage from one floor to another. In this tower, itself an obvious prison, the lowest floor has been set aside—as a prison. There the hero dwells. On the top floor is the heroine. On the middle floors live contemporary symbols repre- sented by people. The opera deals with the altogether impossible task of uniting the hero and heroine. The chamber orchestra plays only Tschaikovskian music; the Russian folk instrument orchestra, only serial music.

None of these works will be performed in the Soviet Union, and Volkonsky is only perfunctorily interested in their performance there, or in the West. Having been 'discovered' by some misguided foreign visitor, Volkonsky is invariably asked after by foreign music delegations —often to his acute embarrassment. There even seems to be some idea among Western musicians that Volkonsky will continue to function only if they make it clear that they have their eyes on him. Their sense of history is poor. An associated view is equally suspect: that Volkonsky is kept around as a living exhibit of Soviet liberality.

Actually, a large measure of Soviet hope rests on Volkonsky. He walks a tightrope, of course, but he does not follow the conducted pattern of non-orthodoxy which would emphatically end his career. It would seem that Volkonsky feels that something is expected of him. His destiny, and perhaps that of Soviet music, could depend on the flip of a coin.

Conclusion

The first generation of Soviet composers, missing many of their former compatriots, was given an unusual opportunity to regenerate the impetus of the Russian Silver Age in the Arts. That these were, all but to a man, composers of marked conservative tendency, was, at the time, not so important as the fact of their energy and sense of mission. When Miaskovsky lightly dismissed the frantic search for the last creative word as not holding any appeal for him, he had no notion that his personal preference would eventually achieve the stature of a creative imperative. Nor did Gliere carry the idea of conservatism beyond his own work, or, at most, that of his generation. Asaf'ev looked long and searchingly at the history of Russian music, and wrote down his findings in an especially effective language. He had no intention of narrowing the Soviet music historical view to the Russian nineteenth century alone. Prokofieff's occasional return to simplicity was never intended as a model. The older generation witnessed the formation of the machinery of control. They did not recognize it, and they welcomed it in many of its forms. Miaskovsky, Prokofieff, and Vasilenko lived to see it used to criticize them.

Such was the mixed legacy of the older generation.

The middle generation, however, was not the heir. Rather, they were the witnesses if not the creators of another, and different legacy. Theirs was the era of overt control, and, perhaps more importantly, the establishment of proper and acceptable attitudes toward that control. Shostakovich, and his generation, predictably rebelled against the conservatism of the first generation, the more quickly to find their own. They were still European composers. It was Shostakovich, more than any other of his generation, who demonstrated the dangers of reward, and the advantages of punishment. Kabalevsky and Khachaturian, on the other hand, were content with the simpler matter of equating advantage and reward. A further contribution of the middle generation was the placing of a value on cynicism, provided by a small but powerful group of politically successful composers.

The young generation has harvested both crops. With little reference to the West, they have no other traditions. As indicated earlier, the situation of the young Soviet composer is the beginning of the conclusion.

Inherent in the idea of socialist realism is the notion of a chosen people. We have seen that the Soviet mind tends to feel itself in exclusive possession of truth. Yet, the qualities we have observed in Soviet music are not at all unusual in twentieth-century music. Socialist realism is a methodical electicism which is supposedly based on nineteenth-century Russian realism. Yet, we have also seen that the Soviet 'positive hero', art as the handmaiden of social service, righteousness, and healthy optimism were none of them typical of the best in nineteenth-century Russian art.

In a country where every would-be composer studies the same texts in harmony, orchestration, and music history; where the notions of the creatively right and wrong, especially the latter, are closely defined from a single source of unusual authority; where contact with other trends of thinking is restricted; and where deviation from some norm of expression may be punished, it is not unusual that the creative product should be stylistically limited. The element whose lack is most heard in Soviet music is that of open foreign contact.

Russian art has always risen on foreign leaven. This is in no way a value judgment. The foreign element is not present in today's music in the Soviet Union, and its function in Russia's past history is denied. In essence, then, a full circle has been described in the history of Russian music. For the essentially amateur notion of nationalism has returned. There is no reason, other than these, that Soviet music should not play the provocative role in twentieth-century music that Russian music did in the nineteenth century.

One finds similar elements, but in slightly different arrangement on the periphery. Again to generalize: the Russian periphery has traditionally provided the centre with liberalism, hope, idealism, and the movements for reform and change so typical in Russian history. Although the musical product is much the same in the peripheral republics, a fresher, more convincing art results. The composers of Armenia, for example, have not regressed to the ecletic as have their Northern counterparts.

It could be said, however, that no nation which has produced a Prokofieff and Shostakovich has betrayed its role. But, ignoring for the moment the fallacy of a nation producing composers, history may well view these two as the last of mighty Russia's musical tradition.

BIBLIOGRAPHY

a. *Books and monographs*

ABRAHAM, GERALD (Ernest Heal). *On Russian Music.* London: William Reeves, 1939.

AGAIAN, M. *Armianskaia SSR* (in the series 'Musical Culture of the Union Republics'). Moscow: Muzgiz, 1955. 61 pp.

AL'SHVANG, ARNOLD. *Sovetskii Simfonizm* (Soviet Symphonism). Moscow: Gosmuzizdat, 1946. 20 pp.

Antologia Sovetskoi Pesni (Anthology of Soviet Song). Fourth edition, Victor Belyi, *et al.* Moscow: Muzgiz, 1958. 323 pp.

ASAF'EV, BORIS. *Kniga o Stravinskom* (Book on Stravinsky). Leningrad: Triton, 1928. 398 pp.

—— *Muzykal'naia Forma Kak Protsess,* 2 vols. Vol. I, Moscow: Muzsektor, Gosizdat, 1930; vol. II, Moscow: Muzgiz, 1947. 163 pp.

—— 'Muzyka Tret'ego Sosloviia' in *Plam'ia Parizha* (Flames of Paris). Leningrad: GATOB, 1936. 56 pp.

—— *Russkaia Muzyka ot Nachala XIX Stoletiia* (Russian Music from the Beginning of the XIXth Century). Moscow-Leningrad: Akademiia, 1930. 319 pp.

BEGIDZHANOV, ARCHIL. *Dmitrii Arakishvili.* Moscow: Muzgiz, 1953. 175 pp.

BEL'ZA, IGOR. *Kontserty Gliera* (Gliere's Concertos). Moscow: Muzgiz, 1952. 53 pp.

—— editor. *Izabrannye Stat'i Pol'skikh Muzykovedov* (Selected Articles of Polish musicologists). Moscow: Muzgiz, 1959. 140 pp.

BERDYAEV (Berdiaev), NICOLAS. *The Origin of Russian Communism.* Translation from the Russian by R. M. French. London: Bles, 1937. 191 pp.

—— *The Russian Idea.* New York: MacMillan, 1948. 255 pp.

BERNANDT, G. B. (compiler). *Sovetskie Kompozitory-Laureaty Stalinskoi Premii* (Soviet Stalin Prize Winning Composers). Moscow: Gosmuzizdat, 1952. 157 pp.

BOGDANOV-BEREZOVSKII, VALERIAN, and E. F. NIKITINA. *Sovetskie Kompozitory-Laureaty Stalinskikh Premii* (Soviet Composer-Winners of Stalin Prizes). Leningrad: Gosmuzizdat, 1954. 455 pp.

—— and I. GUSIN (editors). *V Pervye Gody Sovetskogo Muzykal'nogo Stroitel'stva* (The First Years of the Building of Soviet Music). Leningrad: Sovetskii Kompozitor, 1959. 285 pp.

Bol'shaia Sovetskaia Entsiklopediia (The Great Soviet Encyclopedia), second edition. 51 vols. Editor in Chief: vols. I–VII, S. I. Vavilov; vols. VIII–LI, B. A. Vvedenskii. Moscow: Gosudarstvennoe Nauchnoe Izdatel'stvo 'Bol'shaia Entsiklopediia', 1949–58.

BOTKIN, GLEB. *The Fire Bird: An Interpretation of Russia.* New York: Revell, 1940. 278 pp.

BROWN, MALCOLM H. *Symphonies of Prokofiev.* MS. 1966.

BUKETOFF, IGOR. 'Russian Chant' in Reese, Gustave. *Music in the Middle Ages.* New York: Norton, 1940. Pp. 95–104.

CALVOCORESSI, MICHAEL D., *A Survey of Russian Music.* Middlesex: Penguin, 1944. 142 pp.

CARD, HENRY, *The History of the Revolutions of Russia to the Accession of Catharine the First* (Including a concise review of the manners and customs of the sixteenth and seventeenth centuries). London: Longman and Rees, 1804. 674 pp.

CARR, EDWARD HALLET. *The Soviet Impact on the Western World.* New York: MacMillan, 1947. 113 pp.

CHICHEROV, V. I. 'Bylina' in *Bol'shaia Sovetskaia Entsiklopediia*, second edition, vol. 6, p. 427. See complete entry under Bol'shaia Sovetskaia Entsiklopediia.

DANILOV, D. KH. *Fikret Amirov.* Moscow: Sovetskii Kompozitor, 1959. 68 pp.

DEINEKO, MIKHAIL. *40 Let Narodnogo Obrazovaniia v SSSR* (Forty Years of Popular Education in the USSR). Moscow: Gosuchpedizdat, 1957. 274 pp.

DEWITT, NICHOLAS. *Soviet Professional Manpower: Its Education, Training and Supply.* Washington, D.C.: National Service Foundation, 1955. 364 pp.

DOVZHENKO, VALERIAN. *Narisi z Istorii Ukrainskoi Radianskoi Muzyki* (Essays on the History of Ukrainian Soviet Music). Kiev: Gosizdat Pictorial Art and Music Literature, 1957. 236 pp.

DRUSKIN, MIKHAIL. *Russkaia Revoliutsionnaia Pesn'ia* (Russian Revolutionary Song). Moscow: Muzgiz, 1954. 162 pp.

DUBOVA-SERGEEVA, UNDINA. *Fortep'iannyi Kollektiv Khudozhestvennoi Samodeiatel'nosti Moskovskogo Universitata* (The Piano Collective of the Moscow University Samodaiatel'nost' [amateur] Art Organization). Moscow: Moscow University Press. 1958. 29 pp.

EASTMAN, MAX. *Artists in Uniform.* New York: Knopf, 1934. 261 pp.

ELAGIN, IURII (Yelagin, Jelagin). *Ukroshchenie Isskusstv.* New York: Chekhov, 1952. 434 pp.

FINDEIZEN, NIKOLAI. *Ocherki po Istorii Muzyki v Rossii s Drevneishikh Vremen do Konsta XVIII Veka* (Essays on the History of Music in Russia From Ancient Times to the Beginning of the XVIIIth Century). 2 vols. Moscow: Gosizdat Muzsektor, 1928. 364, 376 pp.

—— 'Rogovaia Muzyka v Rossii' *Muzykal'naia Starina* (Horn Music in Russia, Musical Antiquity). St Petersburg: Findeizen, 1903. 85 pp.

FITZSIMMONS, THOMAS, PETER MALOF and JOHN FISKE. USSR: *Its People, Its Society, Its Culture.* New Haven: Hraf, 1960. 590 pp.

FREEMAN, JOSEPH, JOSHUAH KUNITZ and LOUIS LOZOWICK. *Voices of October: Art and Literature in Soviet Russia.* New York: Vanguard, 1930. 314 pp.

GALITSKAIA, VERA. See *Muzykal'naia Literatura Zarubeshnikh Stran.*

GARBUZOV, NIKOLAI. *Zonnaia Priroda Dinamicheskogo Slukha* (The Zonal Nature of Dynamic Sound). Moscow: Muzgiz, 1955. 107 pp.

—— *Zonnaia Priroda Tempa i Ritma* (The Zonal Nature of Tempo and Rhythm). Moscow: Academy of Sciences, 1950. 73 pp.

GLEZER, RAISA. *Anatolii Novikov.* Moscow: Soviet Composer, 1957. 50 pp.

GOL'DENSHTEIN, MARIA. *Muzyka v Zhizni Vladimira Il'icha Lenin* (Music in the Life of Vladimir Ilich Lenin). Leningrad: Sovetskii Kompozitor, 1959. 58 p.

GROENFELD, N. and IA VITOLIN. *Latviiskaia SSR* (Latvian SSR)(in the series 'Musical Culture of the Union Republics'). Moscow: Muzgiz, 1948. 45 pp.

GROSHEVA, ELENA. *Dmitrii Kabalevskii.* Moscow: Muzgiz, 1956. 68 pp.

Gruzinskaia Muzykal'naia Kul'tura (see Tsulukidze).

GUERNEY, BERNARD GILBERT. *Anthology of Russian Literature.* New York: Random House, 1960. 452 pp.

GUINS, GEORGE C. *Communism on the Decline.* New York: Philosophical Library, 1956. 287 pp.

HARTOG, HOWARD, editor. *European Music in the Twentieth Century.* New York: Praeger, 1957. 341 pp.

IARUSTOVSKI, BORIS. *Nekotorye Problemy Sovetskogo Muzykal'nogo Teatra* (Some Problems of the Soviet Musical Stage). Moscow: Sovetskii Kompozitor, 1957. 84 pp.

INKELES, ALEX and RAYMOND BAUER. *The Soviet Citizen.* Cambridge: Harvard University Press, 1959. 533 pp.

Istoriia Russkoi Sovetskoi Muzyki (IRSM) (History of Soviet Russian Music). 3 vols. Editorial Committee. Moscow: Muzgiz, 1956–9. 328, 550, 478 pp.

Iz Istorii Russko-Ukrainskikh Muzykal'nykh Sviazei (From the History of Russo-Ukrainian Musical Relations), T. I. Karysheva, editor. Moscow: Muzgiz, 1956.

JELAGIN, YURI. *Taming of the Arts.* Translated by Nicholas Wreden. New York: Dutton, 1951. 333 pp.

KABALEVSKII, DMITRII, editor-in-chief. (See Istoriia Russkoi Sovetskoi Muzyki.)

KALTAK, L. *Tikhon Kikolaevich Khrennikov.* Moscow: Muzgiz, 1946. 45 pp.

KEL'BERG, ANATOLII. *E. G. Brusilovskii.* Moscow: Sovetskii Kompozitor, 1959. 71 pp.

KENIGSBERG, A. *Andrei Petrov.* Moscow: Sovetskii Kompozitor, 1959. 9 pp.

KERR, WILLARD. *Experiments on the Effects of Music On Factory Production*. Stanford: Stanford University Press, 1945. 40 pp.

KHOKHLOV, IURII, editor. *O Kitaiskoi Muzyke* (Chinese Music). Moscow: Muzgiz, 1958. 142 pp.

KHUBOV, GEORGII NIKITICH. *O Muzyke i Muzykantakh* (Of Music and Musicians). Moscow: Sovetskii Kompozitor, 1959. 414 pp.

KREBS, STANLEY. 'Soviet Music Education: Service to the State', *Journal of Research in Music Education*. Vol. IX, no. 2, Fall, 1961. Pp. 83–107.

KREMLEV, IULII. *Esteticheskie Problemy Sovetskoi Muzyki* (Aesthetic Problems of Soviet Music). Moscow: Sovetskii Kompozitor, 1958. 101 pp.

—— *Izbrannye Stat'i i Vystupleniia* (Selected Articles and Speeches). Moscow: Sovetskii Kompozitor, 1959. 304 pp.

—— *Russkaia Mysl' o Muzyke* (Russian Thinking On Music). 2 vols.: I (1825–60) Leningrad: Muzgiz, 1954. 281 pp. II (1861–80) Leningrad: Muzgiz, 1958. 350 pp.

KYRVITIS, KHARRI (Harry). *Eugen Kapp*. Moscow: Sovetskii Kompozitor, 1959. 52 pp.

LAQUEUR, WALTER, and GEORGE LICHTHEIM, editors. *The Soviet Cultural Scene*. New York: Praeger, 1958. 300 pp.

LENIN, VLADIMIR (Ulianov). *On Culture and Art*. Moscow: Izogiz, 1938. 300 pp.

—— *Polnoe Sobranie Sochinenii* (Complete Collected Works). Fifth Edition. 40 vols. Moscow: GosizdatPoliticheskoi Literatury, 1958–63.

LEONARD, RICHARD A. *A History of Russian Music*. New York: MacMillan, 1957. 372 pp.

LOKSHIN, D. *Vydaiushchiesia Russkie Khory i Ikh Dirizhery* (Outstanding Russian Choruses and their Directors). Moscow: Muzgiz, 1953. 131 pp.

LUNACHARSKII, ANATOLII. *V Mire Muzyke: Stat'i i Rechi* (In the World of Music: Articles and Speeches). Collected, annotated, and edited by G. B. Bernandt and I. A. Sats. Moscow: Sovetskii Kompozitor, 1958. 546 pp.

MARTIN, L. JOHN. *International Propaganda: Its Legal and Diplomatic Control*. Minneapolis: University of Minnesota Press, 1958. 284 pp.

MARTYNOV, I. *D. D. Shostakovich*. Moscow: Muzgiz, 1946. 111 pp.

MATHEWSON, RUFUS W. *The Positive Hero in Russian Literature*. New York: Columbia University Press, 1958. 364 pp.

MATSA, I. *Khudozhestvennoe Nasledie i Esteticheskoe Vospitanie* (The Artistic Heritage and Esthetic Training). Moscow: Iskusstvo, 1959, 83 pp.

MEAD, MARGARET. *Soviet Attitudes Toward Authority*. New York: Rand Corporation, 1951. 148 pp.

MILIUKOV, PAUL. *Outlines of Russian Culture: Part II. Literature*, and *Part III. Architecture, Painting, and Music*. Edited by Michael Karpovich and translated by Valentine Ughet and Eleanor Davis. Philadelphia: University of Pennsylvania Press, 1942. 130, 159 pp.

MILOSZ, CZESLAW. *The Captive Mind.* Translated from the Polish by Jane Zielenko. New York: Vintage Books, 1955. 240 pp.

MONTAGU-NATHAN, M. *A History of Russian Music,* Second Edition. London: William Reeves, 1918. 346 pp.

MOOSER, ROBERT ALOYS. *Annales de la Musique et des Musiciens en Russie au XVIIIme Siècle.* 3 vols. Mont Blanc: Mont Blanc, 1948–51. 1460 pp.

MUZALEVSKII, V. I. *Russkaia Fortepiannaia Muzyka* (Russian Piano Music). Leningrad-Moscow: Muzgiz, 1949. 336 pp.

Muzykal'naia Kul'tura Avtonomnikh Respublikh RSFSR (Musical Culture of the Autonomous Republics of the RSFSR), editorial collective. Moscow: Muzgiz, 1957. 407 pp.

Muzykal'noe Vospitanie v Detskom Sadu (Musical Training in Kindergarten). Editor N. A. Vetlugina. Moscow: Uchpedgiz, 1960. 93 pp.

Muzykhovedenie i Muzykal'naia Kritika v Respublikakh Zakavkaziia. Editorial collective. Moscow: Muzgiz, 1956. 510 pp.

NEST'EV, ISRAEL. *Prokofiev.* Translated by Florence Jonas and with a Foreword by Nicolas Slonimsky. Stanford: Stanford University Press, 1960. 528 pp.

—— and G. Ia. Edelman. *Sergei Prokofiev 1953–62: Stat'i i Materialy.* Moscow: Sovetskii Kompozitor, 1962. 2nd ed. 1965.

—— *Russkaia Sovetskaia Pesnia* (Soviet Russian Song). Moscow: Muzgiz, 1951. 34 pp.

NIEMEYER, GERHART, with JOHN S. RESHATAR, Jr. *An Inquiry into Soviet Mentality.* New York: Praeger, 1956. 113 pp.

Ob Ispravlenii Oshibok v Otsenke Oper 'Velikaia Druzhba', 'Bogdan Khmel'nitskii', i 'Ot Vsevo Serdtsa' (On the Correction of Errors in the Evaluation of the Operas 'The Great Friendship', 'Bogdan Khmel'nitskii', and 'From All One's Heart'). Edited by A. Skoblionok. Moscow: Sovetskii Kompozitor, 1958. 62 pp.

OLKHOVSKY, ANDREI. *Music Under the Soviets.* New York: Praeger, 1955. 427 pp.

ORDZHONIKIDZE, GIBI SHIOEVICH. *A. Balanchivadze.* Moscow: Muzgiz, 1959. 176 pp.

ORLOV, GENRICH (Heinrich). *Sovetskii Fortepiannyi Kontsert* (The Soviet Piano Concerto). Leningrad: Muzgiz, 1954. 210 pp.

PARES, BERNARD. *A History of Russia.* Fifth Edition. New York: Knopf, 1949. 547 pp.

—— *A History of Russia.* Sixth Edition. London: Jonathan Cape, 1955.

PEKELIS, MIKHAIL. *Dargomyzhskii i Narodniaia Pesnia* (Dargomyzhskaia and Folk Song). Moscow: Muzgiz, 1951. 210 pp.

—— editor. *Istoriia Russkoi Muzyki* (History of Russian Music). 2 vols. Moscow-Leningrad: Muzgiz, 1940. 883 pp.

PLEKHANOV, GEORGES. *Introduction à l'histoire Sociale de la Russie.* Translated from the Russian by Mme Batault-Plekhanov. Paris: Editions Bossard, 1926. 160 pp.

POLIANOVSKII, GEORGII. *A. V. Aleksandrov.* Moscow: Sovetskii Kompozitor, 1959. 68 pp.

POLUIANOV, P. A. (editor). *Molodye Mastera Iskusstva* (Young Artistic Talents). Moscow-Leningrad: Gosizdat 'Iskusstvo', 1938. 378 pp.

POUGIN, ARTHUR. *A Short History of Russian Music*, Translated by Lawrence Haward. London: Chatto and Windus, 1915. 332 pp.

Programmy muzykal-nikh Kruzhkov: Po obucheniiu Igry na Muzykal'nikh Instrumentakh v Nachal'nykh, Semiletnykh i Srednikh Shkolakh (Music Circle Programmes: For learning to Play Musical Instruments in Primary, Seven-year and High Schools). Moscow: Uchpedgiz, 1959. 192 pp.

Put' Sovetskoi Muzyki—Put' Narodnost' i Realizma (The Path of Soviet Music—The Path of Folk Feeling and Realism). Moscow: Isskusstvo, 1958. An offprint from *Pravda*, June 8, 1959. 20 pp.

RABINOVICH, DAVID. *Shostakovich*. Translated by George Hanna. London. Lawrence and Wishart, 1949. 165 pp.

RAUCH, G. (See Von Rauch.)

REED, JOHN. *Ten Days That Shook the World*. New York: Modern Library, 1935. 371 pp.

RITVO, HERBERT. *The New Soviet Society*. New York: New Leader, 1962. 251 pp.

ROGOZHINA, NINA. *Prokofiev's Cantata 'Alexander Nevsky'*. Moscow: Sovetskii Kompozitor, 1958. 26 pp.

ROMADINOVA, D. *Murad Kazhlaev*. Moscow: Sovetskii Kompozitor, 1959. 11 pp.

ROSTOW, WALTER W. *The Dynamics of Soviet Society*. New York: Mentor, 1954. 264 pp.

RIIMER, M. A. (editor). *Muzykal'noe Vospitanie i Obuchenie v Shkole* (Music Education and Instruction in School). Moscow: Academy of Pedagogical Science, 1955. 102 pp.

RUNOVSKII, S. I. *Programmy Nachal'noi Shkoly* (Primary School Curricula). Moscow: Uchpedgiz, 1958. 167 pp.

RYZHKIN, I. IA. *Russkoe Klassicheskoe Muzykoznanie v Borbe Protiv Formalizma* (Russian Classical Musicology in the Struggle Against Formalism). Moscow: Muzgiz, 1951. 151 pp.

SABININA, MARINA. *Dmitrii Shostakovich*. Moscow: Sovetskii Kompozitor, 1959. 53 pp.

SETON-WATSON, HUGH. *From Lenin to Khrushchev*. New York: Praeger, 1960. 432 pp.

SEZHENSKY, K. *R. M. Glier*. Moscow: Muzgiz, 1940. 24 pp.

—— SCHLIFSTEIN, S. I. (compiler, editor.) *S.S. Prokofiev, Materialy, Dokumenty, Vospominaniia*. Moscow: Muzgiz, 1961.

SHAVERDIAN, ALEKSANDR. *A. A. Spendiarov*. Moscow: Sovetskii Kompozitor, 1957. 66 pp.

—— *Ocherkii po Istori Armianskoi Muzyki XIX-XX Vekov* (Essays on the History of Armenian Music of the XIX and XX Centuries). Moscow: State Music Publishers, 1959. 446 pp.

—— *Bol'shoi Teatr Soiuza SSR* (The Bolshoi Theatre of the USSR). Moscow: Muzgiz, 1952. 228 pp.

SHAVERDIAN, ALEKSANDR. editor. *Puti Razvitiia Sovetskoi Muzyki, Kratkii obzor* (Paths of Development of Soviet Music, a Brief Survey). Moscow-Leningrad: Muzgiz, 1948. 138 pp.

SHNEERSON, GUSTAV. *Aram Khachaturian.* Moscow: Sovetskii Kompozitor, 1958. 76 pp.

SHORE, MAURICE. *Soviet Education: Its Psychology and Philosophy.* New York: Philosophical Library, 1947. 318 pp.

SIMMONS, ERNEST, editor. *Continuity and Change in Russian and Soviet Thought.* Cambridge: Harvard University Press, 1955. 563 pp.

—— *Russian Fiction and Soviet Ideology.* New York: Columbia University Press, 1958. 267 pp.

SKORINO, LIUDMILLA. *A Writer and His Time.* Moscow: Sovetskii Pisatel', 1965.

SLONIMSKY, NICOLAS. 'Development of Soviet Music', *Research Bulletin on the Soviet Union,* vol. II, no. 4, April 30, 1937. New York: American Russian Institute for Cultural Relations with the Soviet Union.

—— *Music Since 1900.* Third Edition. New York: Coleman Ross, 1949.

—— 'Soviet Music and Musicians', offprint from *The Slavonic and East European Review,* vol. 22, no. 61, December 1944.

SLUSSER, ROBERT M. 'Soviet Music Since the Death of Stalin', in *The Annals of the American Academy of Political and Social Science,* vol. 303 ('Russia Since Stalin'). Philadelphia: 1956. 10 pp.

SOKHOR, ARNOL'D. *Aleksandr Petrovich Borodin.* Moscow: Sovetskii Kompozitor, 1959. 53 pp.

—— *Russkaia Sovetskaia Pesnia* (Soviet Russian Song). Leningrad: Sovetskii Kompozitor, 1959. 507 pp.

—— *V. P. Solov'ev-Sedoi.* Moscow: Sovetskii Kompozitor, 1959. 45 pp.

—— *V. P. Solov'ev-Sedoi: Vokal'nye Sochineniie* (Vocal Works). Leningrad: Muzgiz, 1952. 175 pp.

SOKOLOV, IURII. 'Byliny' in *Bol'shaia Sovetskaia Entsiklopediia.* First Edition. Vol. 8, p. 323. Moscow, 1927.

Sovetskaia Muzyka: Stat'i i Materialy (Soviet Music: Articles and Materials). Moscow: Sovetskii Kompozitor, 1956. 324 pp.

Sovetskaia Muzyka: Teoreticheskie i Kriticheskie Stat'i (Soviet Music: Theoretical and Critical Articles). Editorial Collective. Moscow: Muzgiz, 1954. 670 pp.

Sovetskaia Simfonicheskaia Muzyka: Sbornik Statei (Soviet Symphonic Music: A Collection of Articles). Various authors. Moscow: Muzgiz, 1955. 537 pp.

SPECTOR, IVAR. *An Introduction to Russian History and Culture.* New York: Van Norstrand, 1954. 477 pp. Second edition.

TOMASIC, DINKO. *The Impact of Russian Culture on Soviet Communism.* Glencoe, Illinois: Free Press, 1953. 287 pp.

TOMKINS, STUART. *The Russian Intelligentsia: Makers of the Revolutionary State.* Norman: University of Oklahoma Press, 1957. 282 pp.

TREADGOLD, DONALD. *Twentieth Century Russia.* Chicago: Rand McNally, 1959. 550 pp.

TROTSKY, LEON. *Literature and Revolution.* New York: Russell and Russell, 1957. 256 pp.

TRUMNEVA, M. P. *Planirovanie Uchebnogo Materiala v Shkolakh Sel'skoi Molodezhi* (Planning Study Material in Schools for Farm Youth). Moscow: Uchpedgiz, 1959. 32 pp.

TSULUKIDZE, A. (editor). *Gruzinskaia Muzykal'naia Kul'tura* (Georgian Musical Culture). Moscow: Muzgiz, 1957. 444 pp.

VASILENKO, SERGEI. *Stranitsy Vospominaniia* (Pages of Recollections). Moscow: Muzgiz, 1948. 103(?) pp.

VASINA-GROSSMAN, VALENTINA. *Iurii A. Shaporin.* Moscow: Muzgiz, 1946. 42 pp.

VETLUGINA, VATAL'IA. *Razvitie Muzykal'nykh Sposobnostei Doshkol'nikov* (The development of Musical Potential in Pre-Schoolers). Moscow: Uchpedgiz RSFSR, 1958. 246 pp.

V Gody Velikoi Otechestvennoi Voiny (In the Years of the Great Fatherland [Second World] War). Editorial collective. Leningrad: Sovetskii Kompozitor, 1957.

VODARSKY-SHIRAEFF, ALEXANDRIA (compiler). *Russian Composers and Musicians: A Biographical Dictionary.* New York: H. W. Wilson, 1940. 158 pp.

VON RAUCH, GEORG. *A History of Soviet Russia.* Translated from the German by Peter and Annette Jacobsohn. New York: Frederick Praeger, 1957. 493 pp.

WILLIAMS, ALBERT RHYS. *The Russian Land.* New York: New Republic, 1927. 294 pp.

WILSON, EDMUND. *The Triple Thinkers.* New York: Oxford University Press, 1948. 270 pp.

ZAVALISHIN, VYACHESLAV. *Early Soviet Writers.* New York: Praeger, 1958. 394 pp.

ZENKOVSKY, VASILII. *A History of Russian Philosophy.* New York: Columbia University Press, 1953. Translated by George L. Kline.

b. *Periodicals*

De Musica. Asaf'ev. Leningrad, 1925, 1926, 1927 (three issues). Non-affiliated, identified with Leningrad Association of Contemporary Musicians. Not the same series as Asaf'ev. *De Musica* (1923), a single volume.

Iuzhnii Muzykal'nyi Vestnik (Southern Musical Herald). Martsenko. Odessa, 1915–18. Non-affiliated.

Khorovoe i Regentskoe Delo (Choral and Conducting Matters). Moscow (?), (?)—1917. Conservative.

K Novym Beregam (Towards New Shores). Beliaev and Derzhanovsky. Moscow: 1923 (three monthly issues). Unofficial organ of ACM.

Lad (Harmony). Asaf'ev and Loure. Petrograd: Muzo Narkompros, 1918 (one issue). Publishes ACM platform. Apparently a continuation of the defunct *Melos*.

Melos. Asaf'ev and Suvchinskii. Petrograd, December 1917, January 1918 (two issues). Non-affiliated; militantly apolitical.

Muzyka (Music). Derzhanovskii. St Petersburg/Petrograd, 1910–16. Avant-garde, spokesman for *Mir Iskusstva* (The world of Art). Revolutionary, but non-party.

Muzyka. (Music). VL. Messman. Leningrad-Moscow (?), 1922. Nominally Marxist; identified with *Proletkul't.*

Muzyka i Byt (Music and Living). Braudo. Leningrad, 1927. Popular journal reflecting ACM views.

Muzyka i Oktiabr' (Music and October). Editorial collective. Moscow, 1926. Workers' magazine published by the Russian Association of Proletarian Musicians.

Muzyka i Penie (Music and Singing). Seliverstov and Privalov. St Petersburg, 1894–1909 (?). Church music.

Muzyka i Teatr (Music and Theatre). Bernshtein. Moscow: State Institute of Music Education, 1922–4. Oriented toward proletarian groups.

Muzykal'naia Kul'tura (Musical Culture). Roslavets. Moscow: Muzgiz, 1924 (three issues). Established by ACM.

Muzykal'naia Letopis' (Musical Chronicle). A. N. Rimsky-Korsakov, with Braudo and Asaf'ev. Leningrad, 1922–6. Non-affiliated.

Muzykal'naia Nov' (Musical Virgin Soil). Sergeev, Chemodanov, Chernomordikov. Moscow: RAPM, 1923–4.

Muzykal'nyi Sovremmenik (Musical Contemporary). A. N. Rimsky-Korsakov. Petrograd, 1915–17. With accompanying *Chronicle.* Non-affiliated.

Muzykal'noe Obrazovanie (Musical Education). Konstantinov and Pshibyshevsky. Moscow, 1926–30. Mostly non-affiliated, but occasionally reflecting Moscow Conservatory RAPM. Title changed to *Art Education,* 1928.

Novaia Muzyka (New Music). Asaf'ev, Ginzburg. Leningrad: Triton. 1927–8. Oriented toward ACM.

Orfei (Orpheus). Asaf'ev. Leningrad, 1922 (one issue). ACM oriented.

Proletarskii Muzykant (Proletarian Musician). Moscow, 1929–32. Official organ of RAPM.

Russkaia Muzykal'naia Gazeta (Russian Musical Magazine). Findeizen. St Petersburg/Petrograd, 1894–1918. Non-affiliated.

Sovetskaia Muzyka (Soviet Music). Various editors. Moscow: Muzgiz, 1933. Irregular in thirties. Yearly issue during war, otherwise monthly. Official organ of the Union of Soviet Composers and the Ministry of Culture. Replaced all journals in 1933.

Sovremenaia Muzyka (Contemporary Music). Beliaev, Derzhanovsky, Sabaneev. Moscow: Academy of Art Sciences, 1924–9. An unofficial ACM journal.

Bibliography 353

c. *Musical Compositions*

AMIROV, FIKRET
Azerbaidzhan (Symphonic Suite). Moscow: Sovetskii Kompozitor, 1957.
Sevil' (Opera in four acts, 1953). Baku: Azmuzgiz, 1957. With libretto
 by T. Eiubov on poem of Jabbarli. Piano score.
Kiurd(i)-Ovshari (Symphonic Mugam, 1948). Baku: Azmuzgiz, 1959.
Shur (Symphonic Mugam, 1948). Baku: Azmuzgiz, 1958.
ARAKISHVILI, DMITRII
Skazanie o Shota Rustaveli (Tale of Shota Rustaveli: opera in three
 acts, 1910–14). Libretto by Khakhanashvili, with A. Shanshiashvili,
 and I. Mchedlishvili. Selections published.
ASAF'EV, BORIS
Bakhchisaraiskii Fontan (The Fountain of Bakhchisarai: ballet, 1934).
 Moscow: Muzgiz, 1939 (piano score).
Kavkazskii Plennik (The Caucasian Prisoner: ballet, 1936–7). Unpublished. Excerpts.
Plamia Parizha (Flames of Paris: ballet, 1932). Unpublished. Excerpts.
BALANCHIVADZE, ANDREI
Concerto No. 3 for Piano and String Orchestra (1952). Tbilisi: Muzfond
 SSSR, 1958.
Symphony No. 2 (1957?). Moscow: Sovetskii Kompozitor, 1961.
BAL'SIS EDVARDAS
Concerto No. 1 for Violin and Orchestra (1954). Moscow: Sovetskii
 Kompozitor, 1958.
GADZHIBEKOV, UZEIR
Ker-Ogly (opera: 1932–6). Unpublished. Excerpts.
Leili i Medzhnun (opera in four acts, six scenes: 1907). On poem of
 Fizuli. Baku: Azmuzgiz, 1959.
GALYNIN, GERMAN
Epicheskaia Poema (Epic Poem: 1950). Moscow: Muzgiz, 1954.
Quartet No. 1 (1947). Moscow: Sovetskii Kompozitor, 1958.
Suite for String Orchestra. Moscow: Sovetskii Kompozitor, 1957.
GLIERE, REINHOLD
Concerto for Cello and Orchestra (op. 87, 1947). Moscow: Muzgiz, 1948.
Concerto for Coloratura Soprano with Orchestra (op. 82, 1943). Moscow:
 Muzgiz, 1959.
Concerto for Harp and Orchestra (op. 74, 1939). Moscow: Muzgiz,
 1948.
Concerto for Horn and Orchestra (op. 91, 1951). Moscow: Muzgiz, 1952.
Krasnyi Mak (The Red Poppy, ballet in three acts: 1926–7; new
 edition, 1949). Moscow: Muzgiz, (?). New edition unpublished.
Mednyi Vsadnik (The Bronze Horseman, ballet: 1948–9). Unpublished.
 Excerpts.
Shakh Senem (opera in four acts: 1923–5). Unpublished. Overture
 published: Moscow: Muzgiz, 1934.

2

KABALEVSKY, DMITRII

Concerto for Violin and Orchestra (op. 48, 1948). Moscow: Muzgiz, 1949; in pocket edition, 1959.

Kola Briun'on (Colas Breugnon, op. 24, 1937, opera in three acts). Libretto by V. Bragin on Romain Rolland. Selected excerpts for chorus and piano published: Moscow: Muzgiz, 1938. Overture (op. 24 *bis*) published: Moscow: Muzgiz, 1956.

Lenintsy (Lenin Lads and Lassies, cantata for children's, youth, and mixed choirs, op. 63). On words by E. Dolmatovsky. Moscow: Muzgiz, 1960.

Nikita Vershinin (opera, op. 53, 1954). Libretto by S. Tsenin on Vs. Ivanov's play 'Armoured Train 14–69'. Piano score Moscow: Muzfond, SSSR, 1955.

Sem'ia Tarasa (The Taras Family, opera in four acts, op. 47, 1947). Libretto by S. Tsenin on B. Gorbatov's 'The Unsubdued'. Moscow: Muzgiz, 1955.

Sonatina for Piano No. 1 (op. 13, 1930). Moscow: Muzgiz, 1931.

Symphony No. 1 (C-sharp minor, op. 18, 1932). Moscow: Muzgiz, 1934.

Symphony No. 2 (C minor, op. 19, 1934). Moscow: Muzgiz, 1937.

Symphony No. 3 '*Requiem*' (B minor, op. 22, 1932). With chorus, words by N. Aseev. Moscow: Muzgiz, 1935.

Twenty-Four Preludes for Piano (op. 38, 1943). Moscow: Muzgiz, 1945 and 1959.

KARAEV, KARA

Leili i Medzhnun (Orchestral suite, 1947). Second edition: Baku: Azmuzgiz, 1958.

Sem'Krasavits (Suite 1949, and ballet 1952). With libretto by I. Idaiat Zade and Iu. Slonimsky. Ballet unpublished. Suite: Baku: Azmuzgiz, 1960.

Tropoiu Groma (Paths of Thunder, ballet, 1958 (?)). Ballet unpublished. Suite No. 1: Moscow: Sovetskii Kompozitor, 1960. Suite No. 2: Moscow-Leningrad: Sovetskii Kompozitor, 1960.

Veten (Homeland, with D. Gadzhiev, 1945). Opera, unpublished. Excerpts.

KHACHATURIAN, ARAM

Concerto for Piano and Orchestra (1936). Moscow: Muzgiz, 1956 (pocket score).

Concerto for Violin (1940). Moscow: Muzgiz, 1941.

Gaiane (ballet in three acts, seven scenes: 1942, new edition 1952). Piano score: Moscow: Sovetskii Kompozitor, 1962. Suite No, 1: Moscow: Muzgiz, 1959 (pocket score). See also *Schast'e*.

Schast'e (ballet, 1939). Original form of *Gaiane*. Suites.

Spartak (ballet in four acts, nine scenes). Libretto by N. Volkov on Spartacus story. Piano score: Muzgiz, 1960. Symphonic Scenes from: Moscow: Sovetskii Kompozitor, 1960. Suites (3): Moscow: Muzgiz, 1960.

Symphony No. 1 (1934–5). Moscow: Sovetskii Kompozitor, 1960.
Traurnaia Oda Pamiati Vladimir Il'ich Lenin (Funeral Ode to Lenin, 1948). From motion picture 'Vladimir Il'ich Lenin' (1948). Moscow: Muzgiz, 1948.

KHRENNIKOV, TIKHON
Mat' (Mother, opera in four acts, eight scenes: op. 13, 1956). Libretto by Faiko on Gorky. Piano score: Moscow: Muzfond SSSR, 1956.
V Bur'iu (In the Storm, opera in four acts, six scenes; 1936–9). Libretto by A. Faiko and N. Virta, on story by latter. Moscow: Muzgiz, 1958.

MIASKOVSKY, NIKOLAI
Symphony No. 1 (C minor, op. 3, 1908). Moscow: Muzsektor Gosizdat, 1929.
Symphony No. 5 (D major, op. 18, 1918). Moscow: Muzsektor Gosizdat, 1923; and Moscow: Union of Soviet Composers, 1948.
Symphony No. 16 (F major, op. 39, 1935–6). Moscow: Iskusstvo, 1939; and Moscow: Muzgiz, 1947.
Symphony No. 21 (F-sharp minor, op. 51, 1940). Moscow: Muzfond SSSR, 1941.
Symphony No. 27 (C minor, op. 85, 1949). Moscow: Muzgiz, 1951.

PETROV, ANDREI
Radda and Loiko (Symphonic poem, 1954). On Gorky. Moscow-Leningrad: Muzgiz, 1955.
Bereg Nadezhdy (ballet, 1958–60). Unpublished. Suite: Leningrad: Sovetskii Kompozitor, 1960.

SHAPORIN, IURII
Dalekaia Iunost' (Song cycle). On Blok. Moscow: Muzgiz, 1940.
Dekabristy (The Decembrists, opera in four acts, nine scenes, op. 25 (?), 1953). Libretto by Rozdestvensky on A. Tolstoi. Piano score: Muzfond SSSR, 1954.
K Chaadaevu (To Chaadeev, cantata, op. 22 (?), 1949). On Pushkin. Moscow: Muzgiz, 1950.
Na Pole Kulikovym (On the Kulikov Field, symphony-cantata for soloists, mixed choir, and orchestra, op. 14, 1937). On Blok. Piano score: Moscow: Muzgiz, 1941; Full score: Moscow: Muzgiz, 1946.
Skazanie o Bitve za Russkuiu Zemliu (The Tale of the Struggle for the Russian Land, oratorio for soloists, mixed choir and orchestra, op. 17, 1942–4). Piano score: Moscow: Muzgiz, 1950.

SHCHEDRIN, RODION
Concerto for Piano with Orchestra (1954). Moscow: Sovetskii Kompozitor, 1959.
Konek-Gorbunok (ballet, 1955, revised 1958). Unpublished. Suite: Moscow: Sovetskii Kompozitor, 1958.
Ne Tol'ko Liubov' (opera, 1960–1). Unpublished.
Symphonie No. 1 (1958). Moscow: Sovetskii Kompozitor, 1959.

12*

SHEBALIN, VISSARION
  Overture on Mari Themes (op. 25, 1941). Moscow: Union of Soviet Composers, 1941; and Moscow: Muzgiz, 1958.
  Symphony No. 1 (F minor, op. 6, 1925). Moscow: Muzgiz, 1932.
  Ukroshchenie Stroptivoi (The Taming of the Shrew, opera in four acts, five scenes, 1955). Libretto by Gosenpud on Shakespeare. Piano score Moscow: Muzfond SSSR, 1956; and Moscow: Sovetskii Kompozitor, 1958.
SHOSTAKOVICH, DMITRII
  Aphorisms (for piano, op. 13, 1927). Leningrad: Triton, 1927.
  Concerto for Cello and Orchestra (op. 107, 1959). Moscow: Muzgiz, 1961; also in pocket score, 1961.
  Concerto for Violin and Orchestra (op. 78, 1947-8). Moscow: Muzgiz, 1957.
  Iz Evreiskoi Narodnoi Poezii (From Jewish Folk Poetry, song cycle for soprano, contralto, and tenor with piano, op. 79, 1948). Moscow: Sovetskii Kompozitor, 1961.
  Ledi Makbet Mtsenskogo Uezda (Lady Macbeth of Mtsensk, or Ekaterina Izmailova, opera in four acts, op. 29, 1930-1). Moscow: Muzgiz, 1935.
  Nos (The Nose, opera in three acts, op. 15, 1927-8). Libretto by Price on Gogol. Unpublished. Orchestral excerpts.
  Quartet No. 1 (op. 49, 1938). Moscow: Muzgiz, 1940.
  Quartet No. 3 (op. 73, 1946). Moscow: Muzgiz, 1960.
  Quartet No. 6 (op. 101, 1957). Moscow: Sovetskii Kompozitor, 1957.
  Quintet (op. 57, 1940). Moscow: Muzgiz, 1941.
  Song of the Forests (oratorio for tenor and bass solo, children's and mixed choruses, with orchestra, op. 81, 1949). Words by E. Dolmatovsky. Moscow: Muzgiz, 1962.
  Symphony No. 1 (op. 10, 1924-5). Moscow: Muzgiz, 1926; pocket score: Moscow: Muzgiz, 1957.
  Symphony No. 4 (op. 43, 1935-6). Moscow: Muzgiz, 1963, and Moscow: Sovetskii Kompozitor, 1962.
  Symphony No. 5 (op. 47, 1937). Moscow: Muzgiz, 1939, and Moscow: Muzgiz, 1956.
  Symphony No. 7 (op. 60, 1941). Moscow: Muzgiz, 1942 and 1958.
  Symphony No. 8 (op. 65, 1943). Moscow: Muzgiz, 1947.
  Symphony No. 9 (op. 70, 1945). Moscow: Sovetskii Kompozitor, 1961.
  Symphony No. 10 (op. 93, 1953). Moscow: Muzgiz, 1960 (pocket score).
  Twenty-Four Preludes and Fugues (1950-1). Moscow: Muzgiz, 1952.
SHWARTZ, ISAAC
  Symphony (1954). Leningrad: Sovetskii Kompozitor, 1958.
SVIRIDOV, GEORGII
  Paticheskaia Oratoria (Overture 'Pathetique', 1959). On Maiakovsky. Moscow: Muzgiz, 1961.

Poem in Memory of Sergei Esenin (oratorio-cantata for tenor, bass, chorus and orchestra). Piano score: Sovetskii Kompozitor, 1958.

TAKTAKISHVILI, OTAR
Concerto for piano with orchestral accompaniment (1951). Moscow: Muzgiz, 1953, and Tbilisi: Muzfond SSSR, 1958.
Concertino for Violin and Small Orchestra (1955). Moscow: Sovetskii Kompozitor, 1957.
Mtsyri (Symphonic poem, 1957). On Lermontov. Moscow: Muzgiz and Sovetskii Kompozitor, 1958.
Symphony No. 2 (1953). Tbilisi: Muzfond SSSR, 1958.

TAMBERG, EINO
Concerto for Orchestra (Concerto grosso, 1957). Moscow: Sovetskii Kompozitor, 1958.

BIOGRAPHICAL INDEX OF COMPOSERS